I shall pass through this life but once.
Any good, therefore, that I can do
Or any kindness I can show to any fellow creature,
Let me do it now.
Let me not deter or neglect it,
For I shall not pass this way again.

—Etienne de Grellet

THE
HEART of
GOODNESS

A RADIANT PATH TO A
RICHER, FULLER LIFE

JO ANN LARSEN

Jo Ann Larsen

Shadow Mountain • Salt Lake City, Utah

To my parents—Ivin and Alice Jackson—
whose lives exemplify the heart of goodness

© 1999 Jo Ann Larsen

All rights reserved. No part of this book may be reproduced in any form or by any means without permission in writing from the publisher, Shadow Mountain, P. O. Box 30178, Salt Lake City, Utah 84130.

Shadow Mountain is a registered trademark of Deseret Book Company.

Library of Congress Cataloging-in-Publication Data

Larsen, Jo Ann.
    The heart of goodness : a radiant path to a richer, fuller life / Jo Ann Larsen.
        p.   cm.
    Includes bibliographical references and index.
    ISBN 1-57345-226-2 (hb)
    1. Altruism.   I. Title.
BJ1474.L37   1999
177'.7—dc21   98-8495
                                                                             CIP

Printed in the United States of America   72082-6222

10   9   8   7   6   5   4   3   2   1

THE
HEART of
GOODNESS

Contents

Originating and flowing from God's own perfect essence, goodness is its own reward, endowing us all with comfort, peace, love, and security while simultaneously bettering our world. Further, through goodness we experience the wondrous rapture of being alive and ultimately discover the path to happiness and inspired meaning in our lives. Thus, for goodness' sake, John Wesley advises, "Do all the good you can, in all the ways you can, to all the souls you can, in every place you can, at all the times you can, and with all the zeal you can, as long as ever you can."

In briefly describing my own richly rewarding exploration of such goodness, the words of Tillotson are germane: "The short sayings of wise and good men are of great value, like the dust of gold and the sparks of diamonds."

It is of such mettle that this book is composed. As I researched deeply into potential content, it seemed I was mining brilliant gold nuggets and glittering white diamonds from a depthless repository of human knowledge regarding goodness. And as I encountered these preserved treasures, I often paused to savor and revere their wisdom.

My appreciation of the depth and beauty of thought that exist regarding goodness greatly intensified as I comprehended a simple truth: In speaking of goodness, thousands of accumulated voices—many from the grave and across the ages—proffered messages inherently embodied in simple but profound writings of the Bible. Beheld in their spiritual light, thus for me biblical scriptures regarding goodness took on consummate brilliance.

Over a period of several years, what first began as a simple project inevitably evolved into one of considerable depth and breadth. As I explored intricate dimensions of goodness and discovered gems of great value, I felt compelled to carefully place each into small patterns that ultimately constituted the whole of a comprehensive mosaic. There, each gem hopefully reflects upon others, with the entirety of the mosaic vividly illuminating the very heart of goodness.

Throughout my writing sojourn, I tacitly and doggedly addressed an adult audience. At project's end, however, I was just short of stunned to find that *The Heart of Goodness* spoke to yet another audience—that of children. As an educator and mother of five, I realized almost every page contained a story or concept through which an adult could teach children about goodness. In an age of starkly declining values, with the world's future depending on the relative goodness of next generations, I felt a certain joy in receiving what seemed an unexpected bonus.

Writing this foreword constituted the last act of this book's creation. Reason suggests that my own relief at completion was rivaled by that of my editor, Linda Gundry. I thank you, Linda, for your generosity of spirit, your patience, your skill, and lastly your indispensable and timely sense of humor. Your own well-endowed heart of goodness prevailed in times of trial as the book painstakingly took definitive form.

As well, I thank you, Patty Parkinson, as the oft-pressed typographer of the book, for your skill in creating the manuscript's published form and for your patience and good-heartedness in making what must have seemed innumerable (but to me, very vital) improvements. And I thank you, Ron Stucki, as the book's designer, for your elegant presentation of *The Heart of Goodness* to its audience.

I also thank you, Shelly, as my oldest daughter, for your ingenious and creative research skill, making possible the well-rounded umpteen dozen footnotes at book's end. And I thank you, Rani and Erin, my other two daughters, for being foot runners and procurers of widely scattered books.

Finally, I thank you, Ron Millett and Sheri Dew of Deseret Book Company, for envisioning the possibilities of and supporting this intensive project. Across the years, to your hearts of goodness I owe much.

How delightful is the company of generous people, who overlook trifles and keep their minds instinctively fixed on whatever is good and positive in the world about them."[1]

Thus says Van Wyck Brooks of the people who nurture their fellow beings and thus reveal hearts of goodness. People who keep a promise or a secret, who share a dream, who return a smile, who listen to a child, or who go the second mile—these are but a few of the kinds of people who lead with a good heart. Acts of the heart are everywhere, simply waiting for recognition. All around us are people who give quietly to charities, who volunteer to feed the homeless, or who truly do look after their neighbor. Or, further, those people who stop to help a stranger, forgive when they have been wronged, or respond with generosity even when they have little to give.

The natural response to do good comes from deep within an intangible soul, for goodness is inherent in the very spiritual material of which the soul is constructed. The soul, then, endowed at birth with an innate "goodness response," intuitively wants to emanate warmth and goodwill. But sadly, sometimes ill treatment, abuse, poor modeling, debilitating mood disorders, or other maladies exact a toll on a person's physical or mental well-being. Thus, the innate goodness of a person's soul so affected cannot rise to the surface or make its promising mark in the world.

Instead, a person's soul is captive to a hard shell, not easily penetrated, that protects that person from outsiders and impairs sensitivity to others. In such instances, one's soul instinctively knows today what one's mind may only understand tomorrow, or may never even know—that there is no happiness in life unless the soul is free to do its work. For the soul was meant to adjoin with other souls and, hand in hand, to conquer the travails of life. The soul is substantially sustained and revitalized through its virtuous works and the force of goodness that flows between itself and other souls.

Alluding to such soul sustenance is Albert Schweitzer. Once asked why a man of his genius would forfeit a civilized life among his intellectual peers to reside among the savages of Africa "on the edge of the primeval forest," Schweitzer replied, "I have had the pleasure of doing good. That is privilege enough for any man."[2] In so saying, Schweitzer indirectly refers to being "soul fed" as a result of intensely pursuing his native inclination to increase the world's goodness.

All men require certain tangible and intangible conditions in order to exist. Without ample food, warmth, safety, and shelter, the soul cannot assert itself or perhaps even survive or reside within its physical body. By the same token, without ample spiritual nourishment, the soul cannot thrive or rise to its God-endowed potential within the body. Primary among the soul's intangible needed nutrients are the powerful emotions of *love* and *compassion* and their cousins, the acts of *kindness, giving*, and *caring*. These five qualities—the focus of this book—are the positive forces that bond human beings together and sustain and comfort their souls.

Love, the first dimension of human bonding, is the climate in which all living creatures flourish. People of all ages and stages of maturity and all levels of success need love and recognition to thrive. Thus, in loving, we often need to extend ourselves repeatedly to establish ties with others, for, as Cathy Morancy conveys, "Love is not measured by how many times you touch each other but by how many times you reach others."[3] It is, in fact, a law of life that the human soul can flourish only when it loves another or when it basks in love from that other's soul. And when one is loving and loved at the same time, the best of worlds exists.

Love itself has many nuances, existing on a continuum, with more faint or muted feelings at one end and those of profound intensity at the other. Moving toward the continuum's deeper end, such feelings shade into consummate love, affection, and devotion. Here, at the soul level, when two people experience overflowing love, they can reach an exalted state—a state of overpowering human joy and completion that exceeds even that of sexual intimacy. Capturing such consummate love is Indian philosopher Rabindranath Tagore, who wrote to a beloved friend, "After you had taken your leave, I found God's footprints on my floor."[4]

Compassion is the second dimension of human bonding. Related ever so closely to love, compassion is a full-bodied, stirring arousal in our hearts and souls of the desire to aid others. Such keen desire is prompted by the distress we recognize in others and by our wish to comfort or rescue them, sometimes at the expense of our own lives. In a desperate, mechanical world in which we encounter many strangers and must daily overcome the differences between ourselves and others, particularly differences of race, religion, and nationality, it is compassion that becomes our salvation. It is through compassion that we can contribute significant goodness to a world where people need, as they have never needed before, the gift of understanding and empathy.

The other three dimensions of human bonding—kindness, giving, caring—are often instantaneous and spontaneous responses that come not necessarily from our attachment to a particular person. Rather, they spawn from our profound commitment to, and investment in, the welfare of those who share our same life journey—or sometimes our stormy path. Of this path, Powell Davies writes, "We are all lonely under the stars. All strangers are sojourners here on earth."[5] If, then, each of us can create for the other a refuge of warmth and comfort, we may be of eminent aid to each other in negotiating the travails of life.

As we ponder the actions of loving and extending compassion and those of rendering service through kindness, giving, and caring, we realize the vital role we can play in acting not as destroyers but as builders and preservers of relationships. And in interweaving our own lives with others, we can enrich and fortify each other. To this point, while taking a tour of California's giant sequoia, Lewis Timberlake recalls the tour guide pointing out that sequoia trees have shallow roots resting barely below the surface.

Having grown up in a rural area, Timberlake knew that if tree roots did not grow deep into the earth, strong winds would level the trees. He thus challenged the guide's statement. Responding, the guide pointed out that sequoia trees, unlike other trees, grow only in groves, intertwining their roots under the earth's surface. Therefore, when storms occur, the trees sustain each other and keep each other upright.

Reflecting upon this insight, Timberlake compares the root structure of sequoia trees to the root structure required of strong relationships. "There's a lesson here," he notes. "In a sense, people are like the giant sequoias. Family, friends, neighbors, the church body and other grounds should be havens so that when the strong winds of life blow, these people can serve as reinforcement and can strive together to hold each other up."[6]

Almost all people hunger for significant relationships with others, but, even more importantly, they yearn for at least several deeply rooted love relationships upon which, occasionally, they may lean and, in turn, be leaned upon. These significant relationships are vital, sometimes even to our survival, as they ultimately bring purpose and meaning to our lives. Capturing the essence of such relationships is Vii Putman, who observes, "The entire sum of existence is the magic of being needed by just one person."[7]

Whether we receive or extend to others love, compassion, or other forms of service, we benefit greatly in an age Neil Millar has characterized as "contorted by violence." Regarding this age, Millar observes, "I have no doubt whatever that people are born to kindness as a wind is born to movement. After all, if tenderness were rare instead of normal, wouldn't the newspapers give it headlines? *MOTHER CHERISHES FAMILY—BLIND PERSON HELPED ACROSS STREET—PRISONERS VISITED—DESTITUTE PEOPLE CARED FOR—BOY SHARES HIS LUNCH WITH PUPPY—BUSY SCHOOLGIRL TAKES TIME OFF TO TEACH FATHER HOPSCOTCH*—and on and on. But such events are not news; they are as common and as beautiful as dandelions."[8]

Thus, in an age contorted by violence, goodness still abounds among us—a goodness shrouded at times by noise, by fanfare, by bright lights, by vulgarity, or by the shock of evil across the TV screen or in the newspaper headlines—but nevertheless goodness worth finding and celebrating. There is, after all, a common soul in man that reaches toward the common good, toward the alleviation of pain, and toward the buoying of the human spirit. And that goodness, well worth perpetuating, benefits ourselves as well as others, for, as Henry David Thoreau reflected, "Goodness is the only investment that never fails."[9]

If we but focus on man's basic and inherent God-given nature, rather than on his superficial and artificial creations, we find no limit to the goodness abounding there. We discover goodness in truth, honesty, courage, worship, appreciation, effective habits, family and friends, neighbors and brotherhood, and a host of other areas. And if we discover and incorporate such goodness in our lives, this goodness will salve and expand our souls, for there is a heartfelt cry from each soul for more depth and purpose in everyday life.

In particular, we can create goodness by what we do for others, often in small, unobtrusive gestures and actions—an encouraging word, a thoughtful gift, a gentle touch, perhaps a few minutes of patient listening. It is to our advantage to create and to add to goodness wherever we go, to step out of our normal arena and to follow our hearts into the realm of the extraordinary and exquisite, where man meets man, soul to soul.

When we contribute to goodness, we create a better world, for it is as Phillips Brooks has said: "No man or woman of the humblest sort can really be strong, gentle, pure and good without the world being better for it, without somebody being helped and comforted by the existence of that goodness."[10] We may also greatly improve the beauty of our inner spiritual landscape and move into the rich interior landscapes of others by responding to what our human souls invite us to do.

We literally have within us the capacity to set our souls "free to give for the sheer, beautiful sake of true giving," writes Daphne Rose Kingma. "In giving freely, purely, for no reason and every reason, you move into another person's emotional landscape—not because you must, not because you have no choice, but because in your heart . . . you have felt the spiritual necessity of acting out your love."[11]

Cellist Pablo Casals adds to Kingma's reflections: "Each man has inside him a basic decency and goodness. If he listens to it and acts on it, he is giving a great deal of what it is the world needs most. It is not complicated but it takes courage. It takes courage for a man to listen to his own goodness and act on it. . . .

"Do we dare to be ourselves?" asks Casals. "This is the question that counts."[12]

Even if we do dare to be ourselves, we may underestimate our ability to enrich lives. "The majority of us lead quiet, unheralded lives as we pass through this world," observes Leo Buscaglia. "There will most likely be no ticker-tape parades for us, no monuments created in our honor. But that does not lessen our possible impact, for there are scores of people waiting for someone just like us to come along; people who will appreciate our compassion, our encouragement, who will need our unique talents. Someone who will live a happier life merely because we took the time to share what we had to give.

"Too often," he concludes, "we underestimate the power of a touch, a smile, a kind word, a listening ear, an honest compliment, or the smallest act of caring, all of which have the potential to turn a life around. It's overwhelming to consider the continuous opportunities there are to make our love felt."[13]

Thus, from a larger perspective, by quantitatively dispersing love, we fortify the condition of goodness, increasing in the world the relative proportion of goodness to evil. Goodness itself is integral to a greater universal order, a point Harry Emerson Fosdick makes: "Goodness is not an accident but . . . a disclosure of something everlasting, light from a central sun, living water from an eternal fountain. As the New Testament puts it: 'He who does good is of God.'"[14]

In this respect, M. Scott Peck makes a sober observation regarding the potential impact upon the world-at-large of even a single person's good or evil intent. Says Peck, "The whole course of human history may depend on a change of heart in one solitary and even humble individual—for it is in the solitary mind and soul of the individual that the battle between good and evil is waged and ultimately won or lost."[15]

Appending Peck's perspective, John Steinbeck adds, "I believe that there is one story in the world, and only one, that has frightened and inspired us. . . . Humans are caught—in their lives, in their thoughts, in their hungers and ambitions, in their avarice and cruelty, and in their kindness and generosity too—in a net of good and evil. I think this is the only story we have and that it occurs on all levels of feeling and intelligence. Virtue and vice were warp and woof of our first consciousness, and they will be the fabric of our last, and this despite any changes we may impose on field and river and mountain, on economy and manners. There is no other story. A man, after he has brushed off the dust and chips of his life, will have left only the hard, clean questions: Was it good or was it evil? Have I done well—or ill?"[16]

From another perspective, to embrace and perpetuate goodness is to meet a moral obligation to our fellow men. Reflecting on this obligation is Albert Schweitzer, who says, "I have always held firmly to the thought that each of us can do a little to bring some portion of misery to an end."[17]

Obviously, our daily impact upon others is far from neutral. In instances that matter, we either help or harm people. We either extend a hand to others who desperately need that hand or we don't. We either choose the right or we don't. In essence, we either add to the goodness of this world or create a void of such goodness. In the space we occupy on this earth, we may even create a black hole that drains goodness. Germane to this discussion, Paul Lowney reflects, "No one owns his own life. Everyone—no matter how insignificant—has an effect on someone else, just as a stone sends out ripples when cast into still water. A person whose life doesn't touch another's is a person without a shadow."[18]

In this vein, as human beings, we may live for ourselves and believe that we're accountable only to ourselves. Or we may adopt a position that requires a quantitative shift in perspective—that we are in a universe that places us in everyone else's universe as well. As such, who we are and what we do affects others, and others must absorb, good or bad, the consequences of our actions. Thus, it is often our nobility in discharging obligations and our adherence to an inalterable standard of ethics that elevates us—above circumstances or whim—to put others' good before our own.

Goodness, it appears, is our soul's calling on this earth. And it is our charge, without expectation or exception, to emanate love and acceptance to all we encounter. For many reasons, we must extend our best selves to those who need us, count on us, and love us. Essentially, for our own sake and for that of mankind, our challenge is always to perpetuate and embrace good. In today's age, when we do good, we support a compelling movement embraced by many others—a movement to make the earth a better place for everyone.

In the interest of perpetuating good, we must also give "directed attention" to the cause of daily making goodness the center of our awareness. As we allow ourselves to openheartedly pursue channels through which unconditional love may flow, such emphasis, figuratively speaking, may change for the better the cultural DNA of our physical bodies as well as the intangible DNA of our hearts and souls.

To embrace and perpetuate goodness leads us, in fact, to perhaps the most heady of human experiences—the binding of hearts and souls—our own to those of others. Through all of recorded history, evidence exists that goodness unlocks the doors to human potential and human happiness. Goodness is God's success formula—and He invites all of us to experience its amazing results.

I

. . . .

ON LOVE

At the heart of all goodness is *love*, the bonding emotion of
human beings. Love explains the goodness that occurred
when a five-year-old boy was asked by his Sunday School
teacher to bring "something green that you love" to class for St.
Patrick's Day. The next Sunday, as all the children trooped in
with various green items of clothing and other articles, this boy
proudly brought—dressed in green—his four-year-old sister.[1]

As human beings, we ache for the clear assurance that we are
of value to other people. And when we take the initiative to
softly shower others with love, we connect with these people,
warming their hearts and our own. Through reaching out with
love, we remind ourselves we are not alone; that love thrives
under conditions of warmth, tenderness, and gentleness; and that
through combining these gestures with patience, we offer gifts
of self that allow us to grow closer to, and to form lasting bonds
with, one another.

To move toward love is to open our soul to another human
being and, at the soul level, to unabashedly expend energy from
our deep interior to meet the needs of or to enrich the life of
another. It is, in fact, through the flow of pure love from one
soul to another that two people can come to feel profoundly

connected to each other and experience a dual ascension of their souls.

To love is to give without thought of receiving; it is to consider the safety, growth, and happiness of another to be as significant as that of our own; and it is to offer quiet understanding, loyalty, and forgiveness. To love is also to extend the readiness to be inconvenienced and to unselfishly dedicate time to—and to share resources with—another. And further, to love is to courageously share the hidden parts of ourselves, complete with our fears and follies, and to unconditionally accept the complexities and irrationalities of another.

Moreover, to love is to provide another with a sense of complete security and absolute trust, for as Maxim Gorky has suggested, "When one loves somebody, everything is clear—where to go, what to do—it all takes care of itself and one doesn't have to ask anybody about anything."[2] Of such security and trust Ardis Whitman adds, "It is not surprising that heaven comes down to touch us when we find ourselves safe in the heart of another person. Human love is like the shine of gold in the prospector's pan—so different from its surroundings that it seems we must have found it in a better world."[3]

And, finally, to love is to affirm others, accepting them for who they are—not for who we wish them to be. But in affirming others, we must extend ourselves even further than we might assume. Reflects Alain, a French philosopher and essayist, "It is a small thing to *accept* people for what they are: if we really love them we must *want* them to be what they are."[4] Such absolute affirming allows others to relate to us freely, and without risk, at the soul level.

We experience a rapturous freedom in total loving and in totally being loved. Loving enables us to be open, and, through concentrating on other people, to forget ourselves and our own failings and adversities. Conversely, being loved enables us to experience through others the deepest form of acceptance, freeing us from the tyranny of being judged by our own imperfections. Finally, to simultaneously love and be loved causes us to feel warmth deep within our souls or, as David Viscott so aptly observes, "to feel the sun from both sides."[5]

Thus, to exchange love is to reap love's precious rewards, for love kindles joy in the human heart, greatly enriching both giver and receiver. Love is the only thing in the world of which anyone cannot give or get too much. And love is something we all yearn for—for love is vital.

❤ ❤ ❤ ❤ ❤ ❤ ❤ ❤

LOVE IS VITAL

The need to love and to be loved is paramount. It is the magic of love that keeps our spirits alive and sustains our hearts and souls. And as "the heartbeat of the universe,"[6] love is the single most important force shaping our physical, emotional, and spiritual lives. To this point, a man recalls what a seasoned physician once said to him: "I have been practicing medicine for thirty years, and I have prescribed many things. But in the long run I have learned that for most of what ails the human creature the best medicine is love."

"What if it doesn't work?" the man asked, to which inquiry the physician replied, "Double the dose."

In this vein, Ardis Whitman notes, "Love is the most important thing in our lives. It is the mortar that holds people together in marriages, the hearthstone around which a family grows. It is the saving grace that dissolves our mistakes in human relationships; it is the greatest joy of our lives."[7]

The joy that generates from a loving relationship is illustrated in a story Joan Benny tells about her father, Jack Benny. Describing Sunday mornings as a special time she and her father spent together, Joan writes that her father would wake her up for traditional Sunday breakfast and afterwards the two would take a drive. But invariably, when the pair got into the car and her father turned the ignition key, the car wouldn't start. Describing her father's subsequent actions, Joan says, "He would then push and pull every button on the dashboard, twist all the knobs and pump the accelerator, but the motor still wouldn't budge. At length he would sigh and say to me, 'Honey, the car just won't start until you give me a kiss.'

"So I did, and it did—and off we went. For a long time I believed there was some kind of scientific connection between kissing and car-starting."[8]

Through devoting to his daughter a structured and predictable portion of his time and attention, Jack Benny gave her a gift—a bouquet of memories—that she would treasure for a lifetime. Applicable to his actions is an observation of Stephanie Mallarme, who notes, "Every soul is a melody which needs renewing."[9]

Just as in the preceding instance, we all need renewing and we all ache for—and starve without—ongoing validation that we are loved. Figuratively, at least, our souls wither and die without love. And with love, our souls flourish. When love is active, healthy, and shows itself often, it is as though it flows from a wellspring deep inside a person, having no end. In a full, loving relationship, each person's spring of love feeds the other.

Ample studies have demonstrated the relationship between loving touch and the health or even survival of babies in hospital wards. A similar relationship has been demonstrated between the well-being and longevity of seniors in nursing homes and having access to pets they can love and be loved by. From such studies, one might speculate that love, as an intangible force, offers life-sustaining sustenance to an intangible soul.

❤ ❤ ❤ ❤ ❤ ❤ ❤ ❤

LOVE IS HEALTHY

Living and *loving* are two sides of a coin, the bonding of which is indispensable to man's emotional well-being. In fact, says Howie Schneider, "The most important thing in life is to love someone. The second most important thing in life is to have someone love you. The third most important thing is to have the first two happen at the same time."[10]

To love, and thus to achieve emotional health, we must become, and remain, vulnerable, allowing ourselves to feel emotions and to risk pain—a condition that is not without its hazards, for as C. S. Lewis observes, to love anything is to risk having your heart wrung and broken. But if you don't take the risk, the alternative is worse, for people who hoard love shrivel and die on the inside.[11]

Alternatively, to embrace love is to preserve the health of the soul. In *The Art of Loving*, Erich Fromm emphasizes that love allows man to overcome his separateness and to leave the prison of his aloneness. Love thus addresses the deepest need of man, which is to transcend the emotional, physical, and spiritual gaps between himself and others.[12] Speaking of the affinity that binds souls when genuine love surpasses the space between two people, St. Bernard of Clairvaux reflects, "We find rest in those we love, and we provide a resting place in ourselves for those who love us."[13]

To exercise such eclipsing love is an act of faith. Fromm writes, "Whoever is of little faith is also of little love. . . . 'Having faith' in another person means to be certain of the unchangeability of his fundamental attitudes—of his love. Only the person who has faith in himself is able to be faithful to others."[14]

Both giving and receiving love generate awesome people power. *Giving love* flows from personal inner resources, and in that sense, Anne Morrow Lindbergh defines love as a motivating force that allows us to offer strength, power, freedom, or peace to another person. Love, she says, isn't a result, such as bestowing someone with a bouquet of flowers. Rather, love is the energy or power within one's self that propels the giving of the flowers.[15]

Receiving love also has a powerful effect on people, for when they are loved, they love themselves more. In fact, nothing enhances a person's self-esteem more than being loved by another, as Robert Conklin emphasizes: "When the words 'I love you' are expressed to you for the first time, your world blossoms; your heart glows with inspiration, confidence and thoughts of the mountains you can move. It's more than an emotional kick; suddenly you like yourself more than you ever have before."[16]

Capturing the ecstasy of receiving such exquisite love, Charles Morgan observes, "There is no surprise more magical than the surprise of being loved. It is God's finger on man's shoulder."[17]

It was in a Texas nursing home that two beings from two very different circumstances felt "God's finger" on their shoulders as they met and began sharing love. A retired engineer in his late eighties, for two years Jim Newton daily came to a nursing home to visit his comatose wife, at whose bedside he patiently sat until she died. It was during these visits that Jim and five-year-old Michael Harris, a mentally handicapped boy with cerebral palsy, developed a growing relationship.

Jim and Michael's story is one of devotion of an elder to a small child desperately in need of such commitment. It is also the story of the devotion of a child to the elder who needed to be needed. As well, their story is one of rich and enduring love that has spanned more than a generation.

Since they first met, Jim and Michael, a ward of the state, have been together—even after Michael, in 1987, was moved to a children's facility over three hundred miles away. Unable to bear the thought of Michael's being alone, within three days of Michael's move Jim had packed his belongings and moved to be close to Michael's facility. There, Jim has continued making daily visits to Michael, who is always overjoyed to see Jim when he arrives.

Jim describes similar joy. And when, at the end of the day, he tucks Michael into bed, he kisses him good-night and tells Michael he'll be back tomorrow. In the process, says Jim, "I tell him that I love him, and that God loves him too."[18]

♥ ♥ ♥ ♥ ♥ ♥ ♥ ♥ ♥

LOVE REQUIRES TIME

"What the world really needs is more love and less paper work," quips Pearl Bailey.[19] Although speaking tongue-in-cheek, Bailey focuses on an issue greatly pertinent to loving—that of diverting time from worldly pressures to make time for love.

A key mistake we may make in today's harried, fast-paced world is relegating the people we love most to the backdrops of our mind, instead focusing on routines and schedules and pursuits of other investments. But in such rushing, Ardis Whitman stresses, we pay an exorbitant price: "In these scrambling, scrabbling, striving days, most of us are clock-watchers trying, in a frantic minute, to solve not only our everyday problems but the profound ones that need mellowing. Our rushing is understandable but too costly."[20]

Often, we sense we're giving our loved ones short shrift but feel frustrated that "there's never enough time." Addressing this time dilemma in *First Things First*, Stephen Covey writes, "We're constantly making choices about the way we spend our time, from the major seasons to the individual moments of our lives . . . and also living with the consequences of those choices. And many of us don't like those consequences—especially when we feel there's a gap between how we're spending our time and what we feel is deeply important to us."

Covey then distinguishes between what he calls "the clock" and "the compass." The clock represents our commitments, appointments, schedules, goals, activities, what we do with and how we *manage* our time. Conversely, the compass represents our vision, values, principles, mission, conscience, direction—what is important to us and how we *lead* our lives. Most of us run by the clock—driving ourselves according to what time it is and where we're supposed to be—rather than by the compass—setting our direction for *true north* (our dearest priorities) and committing our time in a manner that takes us to our destination (a life of enduring meaning).

To conduct our lives by the compass, we must distinguish between the *urgent* and the *important* things in our lives, and to this end Covey gives help: When most people talk about urgency, he explains, they typically use key phrases such as "stressed out," "used up," "unfulfilled" and "worn out." But when they talk about importance, they use phrases like "confident," "fulfilled," "on track," "meaningful," and "peaceful." Covey also notes that "urgency itself is not the problem. The problem is that when urgency is the dominant factor in our lives, importance isn't." By contrast, when "importance" is a predominates, we opt foremost for choices that give our lives meaning.[21]

Illustrating the concept of importance and putting "first things first" is an incident Edward R. Murrow tells involving

Ralph Bunche, a 1950 Nobel Peace Prize winner. Asked by Murrow if he had a special place of honor for his prize, Bunche replied that the prize was around the house somewhere.

"You mean it's not framed and hanging on the wall?" Murrow wanted to know.

"No," responded Bunche, noting that the only trophy on the wall was a small note his son had scribbled the day his Nobel Prize was announced. When he arrived home from the United Nations, on the table he had discovered this lasting treasure. The note read, "Dear Daddy. I am happy that you got your Nobel Prize. Love Ralph."[22]

Still another instance of "first things first" is related by Gary Burghoff, who played Radar in the TV series M*A*S*H. A guest star appeared with Mike Farrell, who played BJ Honeycutt, and the guest star saw that Farrell had brought his two young children to the set of the show. Noting that Farrell was obviously baby-sitting, the guest star concluded that Farrell had drawn for the day the unlucky job of tending the couple's children. In effect, he suggested, Farrell had "lost the toss."

Replying with a laser-sharp rebuttal, Farrell said of the figurative toss, "Nope! Won it."[23]

♥ ♥ ♥ ♥ ♥ ♥ ♥ ♥

LOVE NEEDS UPKEEP

Love needs upkeep and time to flourish; otherwise it may die on the vine. "Love never dies of a natural death," stresses Anais Nin. "It dies because we don't know how to replenish its source, it dies of blindness and errors and betrayals. It dies of illness and wounds, it dies of weariness, of withering, of tarnishings."[24]

What does it mean to kill love? Shanti Niliya explains: "Yesterday I killed . . . my son's joy . . . in the victory of his team.

I complained about his dirty clothes . . . torn at the seam. The day before I killed my daughter's pride in the dress she made. . . . I pointed out its faults, then added faint words of praise. . . . One day I killed friendship, . . . turned affection into hate. I misunderstood, that's all . . . but it was too late."

Niliya continues, "I killed my spouse's love . . . not with a mighty blow. . . . It died bit by bit, year by year . . . so slowly. . . . Tonight I saw the light of love die slowly in her look when she reached toward me with her hand . . . and I picked up a book."[25]

Just as, over time, love flourishes and deepens with an abundance of loving behaviors, so love slowly fades in exposure to the same abundance of abrasive behaviors. Chronic negative responses such as criticism, sarcasm, labeling, name calling, or put-downs wear deeply at love's roots. And, not unexpectedly, neglecting to carefully oversee, refurbish, and reenergize vital relationships is the "root of innumerable tragedies." Thus cautions Paul Johannes Oskar Tillich, who further warns that any vital relationship "requires watchfulness and nourishment; otherwise, it is taken from us. And we cannot recapture it."[26]

When times are rough and feelings are strained, it is easy to undervalue, and even to abandon, relationships potentially capable of providing essential love and support. Among those relationships so often lost are marital ones, which, in today's disposable world, slip so easily from our grasp. A case in point is a husband who was considering divorce. After attending therapy for a time, he began to increasingly value his marriage. One day he shared the following reflection with his therapist:

"In our backyard there are some wooden barrels—cut in half—the kind you make flower pots out of," he relates. "They've been empty and bone dry. One day, I looked in one of the barrels and found a hearty green plant with beautiful red flowers. The plant had come up with all the rain we had lately in what had once been barren soil. That flower represented to me our marriage—we're making something out of nothing. The flower is magnificent—and there are no thorns or stickers. I've committed to water that flower from now on and to keep it healthy and strong."[27]

This observation came from the lips of a man who came within months of abandoning a relationship of some years' duration, but who fortunately returned to invest one last time. He found that his relationship—like the near-hidden plant that blossomed in the barrel—was also capable of flowering into something of ultimate worth. He simply needed to dedicate concentrated effort to bring the relationship to full bloom.

Most marriages—as well as other love relationships—are capable of blossoming if we are willing to cultivate their embryonic possibilities. So that our relationships don't wither or wane, we need to act as their gardeners, over time giving them the necessary nutrients and minerals necessary to develop strong roots. If we are willing to systematically water, weed, and cultivate our relationships, ultimately we too can have flowers.

Sometimes parent-child relationships are the ones needing nourishment and repair, as in the instance of Brent West, who discovered that he could "have flowers" in his relationship with his father. West relates his story: "A dozen years ago, someone asked me if I was close to my father. Because I had lost my mother when I was young, I guess that person thought it would be natural for me to be very close to a remaining parent. Unfortunately, the answer was no. And I wasn't very proud of that answer.

"Actually, I didn't feel totally responsible for the lack of closeness myself. And this wasn't the first time I'd been asked that question. But for some reason the question hit me harder this particular time. Maybe it was because I didn't feel, deep down, that it was right for a son not to be close to his father. Maybe I finally came to the conclusion that it wasn't just my father's responsibility to assure we were close; or maybe, even, this time it seemed more urgent—after all, Dad wasn't getting any younger. So, I resolved to become closer to my father and I formulated a plan I thought might work."

Since his father's birthday was close at hand, and since his father had been trying to keep his weight under control, West arranged for his father to obtain a health spa membership. West hoped that through sharing fitness activities, he and his father could draw nearer, a plan that worked.

"For over ten years, except when I was out of town, Dad and I were together three days a week," West relates. "We exercised, we talked, we grew very, very close. Last year, Dad suddenly died. He was in excellent health, so it was a shock, altogether unexpected. Even though I miss him dearly—even more so because we had grown so very close—I feel a profound peace, knowing I didn't procrastinate regarding an important resolution. 'First things first.'"[28]

♥ ♥ ♥ ♥ ♥ ♥ ♥ ♥

LOVE EQUALS ACCEPTANCE

Genuine love is always affirming. Nothing else can expand the human soul more than experiencing love given fully and freely—without conditions, expectations, or hidden agendas. Such redeeming love sparks the soul to grow, to reach for its potential, and to spring exquisitely into full bloom.

Elizabeth Byrd alludes to her own "soul growth"—a growth stimulated by her mother when Byrd was young and vulnerable. Byrd credits her mother with conferring upon her, through many affirming acts, the precious gift of self-esteem.

Illustrating, Byrd describes an incident when she was seven years old and her mother was planning a formal tea. Eager to help, Elizabeth brought her mother a bouquet of dandelions. "Many a mother would have thanked me and plumped the ragged weeds into a milk bottle in the kitchen," Byrd observes. "But my mother arranged them in her loveliest vase on the piano between tall candelabra. And she made no simpering explanation to her guests about 'little Betty's flowers.'"

And what was the effect of her mother's affirming actions? "Now," says Byrd, "whenever I see flowers at a party, I remember the pride I felt that my dandelions, treasured above roses, had the place of honor."[29]

In reminiscing, Byrd has a "forever" memory of an experience that inalterably affirmed her mother's unfailing and nonnegotiable love. In essence, Byrd experienced unconditional love, which—according to one source—is the superior of three categories of love. The first category of love is the "if" kind—a love given to us *if* we meet specified requirements: "If you do this, then I will love you." "If" love is conditional, a love with strings attached, a love offered in exchange for something another person wants. Motivated by self-centeredness, the purpose of "if" love is to gain something in exchange for what it gives.

A second category of love is the "because" kind: "I love you because of (something you are) (something you do) (something you have)." Essentially, one person's attribute makes that person attractive to another person, who deems that the first person, by virtue of this attribute, is worthy of love. "Because" love is conditional; thus the "loved one," fearing loss of love, may feel the need to hide mistakes or to mask the "shadow side" of his or her personality. The "loved one" may also fear that, in the future, he or she might lose admired attributes, and thus lose the one who finds the attributes attractive. Or, similarly, that the other person might become attracted to someone possessing another, more attractive quality and thus absent the relationship.

The third category of love is "in spite of" love. This love has no strings attached and expects nothing in return. A person is loved not because of what that person has or what that person can do but because he or she exists. With "in spite of" love, people do not have to deserve such love, nor must they earn it. Instead, they are loved as they are—in their entirety and in their essence—in spite of faults or bad habits. With such love, there is no impermanence. Human hearts are desperately hungry for this love because it is unconditional. We are loved because of our infinite worth—for the very fact we are on the planet.[30]

Victor Hugo underscores the importance of our experiencing such unconditional love: "The supreme happiness of life is the conviction of being loved for yourself, or more correctly, being loved in spite of yourself."[31] And Walker Percy sums up with a bit of homespun wisdom: "We love those who know the worst of us and don't turn their faces away."[32]

Philosopher Eric Hoffer experienced childhood trials that ultimately taught him the meaning of unconditional love and the equation that love equals acceptance. Hoffer's mother died when he was seven, and later the same year, he suddenly went blind. Until he regained his eyesight at fifteen, he was cared for by a Bavarian peasant woman named Martha. Of her he writes, "This woman must have really loved me, because those years are in my mind as a happy time. I must have talked a great deal, because Martha used to say again and again, 'You said this . . . you said that.' As a result, all my life I have had the feeling that what I think and what I say are worth remembering. She gave me that."[33]

Obviously, Martha's intense love and total investment in Hoffer's welfare, and her all-embracing daily commitment to his well-being, strengthened and filled out Hoffer's soul. Martha's avid attention to what Hoffer said also provided liberal re-inforcement—not only of what he thought—but of *who* he was. Feeling so completely valued, Hoffer most likely returned Martha's love, completing the circle, and he thus undoubtedly increased Martha's sense of worth and life purpose. Without expectation, Martha may have thus garnered "soul returns," for when we love another wholly, and when each loving act we extend finds its home, our own soul also flourishes.

♥ ♥ ♥ ♥ ♥ ♥ ♥ ♥ ♥

LOVE HAS A VOICE

Love likes to hear itself. Love recognizes when genuine feelings flow from the heart, and sometimes when the words of love come, they help someone cope with deep despair or extend to that someone a moment of joy. To hear words of love is to feel hope for a brighter day. It is to feel intrinsically valuable—perhaps even accepted with delight—despite faults and frail-ties. And it is to experience the miracle of a profound emotional linkage that transcends even barriers of race to unite us with our fellow men.

Feeling the potency of love's voice is Eda LeShan, a well-known writer, who speaks of a pending crisis due to acute "writer's cramp": "All I was doing, sitting at my desk, was push-ing papers around—getting more and more anxious about the article and two book outlines that were past due," she reveals. "I felt tired and frustrated, and on top of everything else, it was a gorgeous day and I wanted to go out for a walk."

After crumpling and throwing away page after page, LeShan suddenly recalled another incident, years before, and another writing crisis. Interrupting her then was a phone call from Fred

Rogers, who "was out of his 'Neighborhood' en route to a vacation." To the inevitable question, "How are you?" LeShan told Rogers *exactly* how she was: "I moaned and cried and said I was desperate, and I'd never finish the book," she admits. In return, Rogers soothingly and lovingly responded, "Oh Eda, you are such a beautiful person, and we need you and love you."

"After about twenty minutes of tenderness," LeShan recalls, she hung up and began writing in earnest. As she worked, she confesses to becoming a bit chagrined: "Why, that son of a gun was treating me like a fourteen-year-old," she thought. Nevertheless, the "treatment" worked. And just as Rogers's caring words had earlier proved pivotal, similarly the memory of his words had an impact in her later crisis. LeShan says that recalling those words left her feeling "refreshed, invigorated—*young*—" and confident she could produce.[34]

Love's voice prevailed in yet another poignant instance related by Ruth Ryan. Speaking of her husband, Nolan Ryan, a legendary baseball pitcher whose career spanned twenty-six years, Ruth tells of a moment that imprinted a memory and established an affirming pattern that was to continue for years. She relates, "It probably happened the first time on the high-school baseball diamond in Alvin, Texas, in the mid-1960s." After that, similar moments happened repeatedly for nearly three decades. Inevitably, "sometime during the game, Nolan would pop out of the dugout and quickly scan the stands behind home plate . . . looking for me. I'd raise my hand in a quick wave and flash him a smile. *I'm here for you. Good luck!*

"He would find my face and grin back at me, maybe snapping his head up in a quick nod as if to say, *There you are; I'm glad.* Then he'd duck under the roof and turn back to the game."

Says Ruth of her still-vivid image: "It was a simple moment, never noted in record books or career summaries. But of all the moments in all the games, it was the one most important to me."[35]

Unlike Nolan Ryan, too often we love but don't say so. And sometimes time runs out before the true significance of a particular relationship dawns on us, preventing us from expressing our ever-abiding, deepest feelings of love to that person. Sadly, sometimes it is only catastrophe or crisis that awakens us to such feelings of love. Poignantly expressing this thought, G. K. Chesterton observes, "The way to love anything is to realize that it might be lost."[36] Supplementing, Christopher Morley observes that if people discovered they had only five minutes left in this world, they would occupy every public telephone (and probably use every cellular phone), calling others to stammer out their feelings of love.[37]

Faith Baldwin tells of a woman who was deeply grateful that her husband had expressed his feelings of love to her—in time. After having left his home on a dismal, rainy morning, her husband inexplicably returned, sat with her at the breakfast table, and the two chatted together companionably. In particular, the husband spoke of his love for his wife and children and the happiness they had brought him. As he arose from the table and turned to go, he told his wife not to worry—that he would drive carefully—and, as he left, he kissed her good-bye. Says Baldwin, "He never came back."[38]

At times, we may have deep regrets for not having expressed love in time. Rabbi Harold S. Kushner tells a story of a friend—another rabbi—who officiated at the interment of a woman. At the end of the ceremony, the woman's husband refused to leave her graveside. Resisting the rabbi's promptings to retire with the other mourners, the husband lamented, "'But rabbi, you don't understand. I loved her.' 'Yes, yes, I understand,' the rabbi replied.

'I appreciate the fact that you loved her, but you ought to go back to your car now—there are people waiting.'

"'No, you don't understand,' the man said, 'I loved her. And once I almost told her so.'"[39]

In a world that desperately needs love, if you do love—say it now. It takes but a moment to say "I love you," "I appreciate you," "I'm glad you're home"—to acknowledge love and to keep it alive. We face the choice of expressing our love every day. We can speak out or say nothing. But love locked in our hearts cannot reach others or have an opportunity to come to fruition. "Love doesn't just sit there like a stone," emphasizes Ursula K. LeGuin. "It has to be made, like bread, remade all the time, made new."[40]

Yet, in a world focused on clock watching and getting ahead, we often experience having "no time" for the remaking of love. Indeed, in our fast-paced, superficial world, we often confuse coldness with maturity and choke down what is warmest and best in us. Elaborating, Ardis Whitman notes, "Who does not remember moments when warm and loving words struggled for utterance and were caught back and replaced by something meaningless? We think we are sophisticated when we are casual and unsentimental, but the truth is that trying to get along without sentiment is like trying to live in a world without flowers or music or the warmth of a fire."

We often hide our tenderness under a cloak of sophistication, afraid that people will think us "soft," Whitman continues: "We say 'Thanks,' when we mean, 'God bless you,' and 'So long,' when we mean, 'I'll be lonely without you.' Too many of us condemn true sentiment along with sentimentality, and so live on the surface of things when we really want to speak and act from the heart."[41]

And yet, who is there who is so wise, so strong that he or she does not need to express and experience words of love?

Not he, relates Jamie Buckingham, who tells of growing up in a family in which members were never demonstrative. In particular, Buckingham speaks of his father, who, in Buckingham's earlier years, never expressed love to his family. But, Buckingham relates, as his father grew older, he also grew far less inhibited, to the point that he was no longer ashamed or embarrassed to cry or to kiss his wife in front of his children and grandchildren. As he observed his father "moving rapidly toward eternity—becom[ing] free," Buckingham reveals, "I realized how stiff and unyielding I remained in many areas of my own life."

Buckingham's love for his father expanded as he observed his remarkable changes; and he recognized—but felt paralyzed to act upon—his growing longing to express to his father his full affection. When saying good-bye, for instance, instead of kissing his father, he still extended his hand. Relates Buckingham: "Even the words, 'I love you,' stuck in my throat. . . . It was something I wanted to do but was afraid to try."

Finally Buckingham could stand the growing inside pressure no longer. And so, one Saturday morning—his "sophisticated and twisted concepts of masculinity" still churning—Buckingham took the thirty-five-mile drive to his father's home. Once there, he found his father in his study, sitting in his wheelchair; but in contemplating his intended announcement, he suddenly felt embarrassed. However, he stresses, this untoward feeling was not to deter him: "I was forty-six years old—[my father] was eighty-six. But I had come this far and was not going to back out."

Choking up, Buckingham leaned over his father and said simply, "I love you." And then he bent down and kissed his father, first on one cheek, and then the other, and, finally, on the top of his bald forehead.

In response, Buckingham's father gently reached up, put his strong hands around his son, and gently pulled him down so he could put his arms around his son's neck. For a long time, the two remained embraced in this awkward position. When finally they released, with a quiver in his voice, Buckingham's teary-eyed father said to him, "I know you love me. But I hope you keep right on telling me—until the day I die."

Buckingham himself felt emotionally buoyed and released by his actions, and he reports, "Something broke loose in me that Saturday afternoon. Something that had been knotted up for years." As he drove home, Buckingham felt his spirits soar. At last, he, too, was free.[42]

Buckingham speaks of love—of love priceless but undervalued—of love needing to be expressed, encouraged, treasured, and fully acknowledged. Something deep within his soul was permanently "reformatted" when Buckingham fully acknowledged his love for, and his need to express that love to, his father—a transforming experience anyone can opt for who undervalues or sells short truly precious relationships.

♥ ♥ ♥ ♥ ♥ ♥ ♥ ♥

LOVE IS ACTIVE

In *My Fair Lady*, Eliza Doolittle interrupts her ardent suitor in the midst of his passionate profession of love by exclaiming, "Words, words, words, I'm so sick of words. . . . If you're in love, show me."

Just as love needs to be heard, love also needs to be felt through actions. "Love talked about can be easily turned aside, but love demonstrated is irresistible," stresses W. Stanley Mooneyham.[43] Ralph Fiennes, the Oscar-winning actor in *The English Patient*, captures the essence of "love demonstrated," equating its expression to life success. Possession of money or a prosperous business does not equate to being a truly successful human being, emphasizes Fiennes. Rather, true success comes when, "as human beings, [people] have a fully developed sense of being alive and [are] engaged in a lifetime task of collaboration with other human beings—their mothers and fathers, their family, their friends, their loved ones, the friends who are dying, the friends who are being born."

The bottom line of success, finishes Fiennes, "is all about being able to extend love to people. . . . Not in a big, capital-letter sense but in the everyday. Little by little, task by task, gesture by gesture, word by word."[44]

Consistent with Fiennes's definition of "love demonstrated," when love is active, it doesn't just perform in the easy times, or when it is convenient, or when it isn't tired. Instead, love performs steadily, even under difficult circumstances, anytime it knows a loving response is needed. Consider the instance of a single mother roused from sleep at midnight by a phone call from her daughter requesting a pick-up from a friend's home, where she was spending the night. In response to her daughter's explanation that she "just wanted to come home," the mother reluctantly agreed to give her a ride. During the ten-minute drive to the friend's house, the mother, sleepy and frustrated, reviewed her initial emotional response. Suddenly, the thought occurred to her: "Where would my life be without my daughter?"

Relates the mother, "When I arrived, my daughter climbed into the car and, as she had earlier sensed my frustration, she began to apologize. Interrupting her, I said gently with conviction, 'Don't worry about it. *You're worth it.*'"

"Leaning over, she gave me a hug and, with substantial relief in her voice, said softly, 'Thank you, Mom.'"

In this instance, the mother discovered not only that her

daughter was "worth it"—but that her choice to respond benignly and with encompassing love was also worth it. The mother's understanding response touched her daughter deeply, who, in turn, reciprocated with a loving response; and the actions of each served to strengthen the bond between the two.

Love remains active when one leads from the heart, as Eleanor Roosevelt did in an instance she later described. Troubled, she asked a friend for advice regarding a problem, remarking, "My mind tells me to do this, but my heart tells me not to."

Responding, her friend counseled, "When in doubt, follow your heart and not your mind. When you make a mistake of the heart, you don't feel so bad."[45]

To keep love active, one must commit not only time but also one's heart to this cause. An open Christmas letter in the form of a newspaper column written by this author serves to illustrate:

"Funny, isn't it, that in our busyness we forget what our busyness is all about. If we look far enough below the surface, we find that our activity is inextricably linked to the welfare of those we love.

"We are running, working, organizing, scheduling and performing because all this activity will somehow benefit people who, ironically, need us—our love, time and attention—much more than anything else we can provide.

"And we may be startled to realize that our busyness means nothing if the people we love are no longer there.

"So, at Christmas, a time that symbolizes the deep and abiding love of God for mankind, I write to you, loved ones, to tell you of gifts I want to give you this year—gifts of love—gifts of myself.

"I want to keep foremost in my mind that human life is tenuous and precious, and that I am extremely fortunate to be here and to have you with me each hour of each day. I want to remember your profound value each time our lives touch.

"I want you to know daily of my love for you. I want you to hear it in my voice, see it in my eyes, feel it in my touch. I want you to experience the bonding that exists between us and I want you to feel cherished. I want you to hear my words: 'I'm proud of you.' 'I've missed you.' 'I'm so lucky to have you.' 'No wonder I love you so much.'

"I want to be there when you need me. I want to see your world through your eyes, and I want you to feel free to share your heart and your soul without feeling judged. I want you to feel our relationship is a safe place and a retreat from the world.

"I want my actions to convey to you that you need not be perfect—that your imperfections are essential to the process of growing. I am reminded of the little boy who asked his teacher before giving a talk, 'Teacher, is it okay if I do the very best I can?' That is all any of us can hope for, to do the very best we can.

"As you make your mistakes, I want you to see mine. We are fellow travelers—perhaps at different stages or learning points— who are making this lifetime journey together. Let us hold hands and walk together in our growth.

"I will work at always recognizing, as one poet put it, 'the subtle difference between holding a hand and chaining a soul.' I want my love to encourage you to be all you wish and all that you can be. I want you to travel in directions you have not yet pursued—with or without me. You are free and I wish always to honor that freedom. I cherish your being in my space but I do not need you for my own use.

"I want to give you my time—to share it freely and without reservation—whenever you need it.

"I want you to count on my commitment and loyalty to you.

I have created boundaries around our relationship that protect your confidences and vulnerabilities.

"I want to love you for those same vulnerabilities and to respect you for your strengths.

"I want to express my appreciation frequently to you for just being you—for filling a vital space in my life—and for giving me so many personal gifts of love. When, in my fallible state, I wound a fragile part of you, I want to make amends and have you hear the words: 'Forgive me,' 'I was wrong,' 'I'm sorry.'

"Love is not a single act but a climate—a work in progress—in which we can grow and discover and learn together. I want to cultivate that climate and celebrate our love all year long."[46]

❤ ❤ ❤ ❤ ❤ ❤ ❤ ❤

LOVE HAS A SOFT TOUCH

Love responds to the admonition that "feelings are everywhere—be gentle."[47]

Love has a soft touch and a quiet voice. It expresses itself through smiles, through tender words, through friendly eyes, and through warmth that radiates from the soul. The sounds of love have the same gentle resonance as the sounds of children expressing their feelings, the coupling of which Edward L. Flom came to equate.

Irritated at his two-year-old daughter, Julie, Flom decided on an old Army routine to punish her. He recalls, "When she spoke to me, I required that every sentence begin and end with the word *sir.* 'Sir, may I go out and play, sir?' 'Sir, the boys are picking on me, sir!'

"Later I had to go to the drugstore and invited Julie to accompany me (provided, of course, that she sit in the backseat of the car). About halfway to [our destination], I felt a little hand on the back of my neck and heard this statement: 'Sir, I love you, sir.' That did it! I quickly changed routines and learned yet another lesson."[48]

In this instance, Flom was pulled up short by the contrast between his own insensitivity and abrasiveness and his daughter's soft touch and tenderness toward him. In experiencing her love at a deeply penetrating "soul level," Flom learned a life lesson regarding love—a lesson perhaps otherwise impossible to convey.

Also caught short were the parents of a child who picked a flower from a neighbor's garden. In her nineties, P. L. Travers— who was this small child and who, much later, wrote the book *Mary Poppins*—tells of this incident. Passing, on her way home from kindergarten, a garden containing a marvelous sunflower, Travers became enthralled with it. The sunflower had a "great golden face"—and it was a sunflower so marvelous, she recalls, "that it looked at me as though it were a miracle. . . . I thought, 'It's God.'"

Young Travers plucked the flower and took it home, but the garden's indignant owner subsequently reported the "theft" to her parents. Admonished by her parents that she shouldn't take other people's flowers, Travers replied, "But it's God." For her parents, Travers's words abruptly altered the whole equation. Recognizing the tenderness and preciousness of her feelings, they "didn't at all vilify me," she reports. "They just advised me tenderly not to do it again."[49]

Possessing a soft touch, Travers's parents were easily swayed toward tenderness by the poignancy of a child's innocent, but inherently accurate, perception of a miracle in her world.

Love can be communicated through literal, as well as figurative, touch. In the instance of the birth of premature twin girls, it was literal touch that snatched one twin from death. The larger of the sisters, at birth weighing slightly over two pounds, quickly began gaining weight and thriving; her lighter and weaker twin did not.

At one month, the condition of the more fragile twin suddenly became critical. Despite intensive medical interventions to alleviate her breathing difficulties and to stabilize her heart rate, this twin's condition continued to deteriorate. As a nurse on duty contemplated the crisis, she remembered a strikingly simple procedure—common in Europe—that involved double-bedding of multiple-birth babies, especially those born prematurely. Desperate for a solution, the nurse elected to place the weaker twin in her sister's incubator.

No sooner had she done so than did the weaker twin snuggle up to her lost sister. Astonished medical personnel watched as, within minutes, the weaker twin became calm and her blood-oxygen readings improved. They were further astonished to observe—as the weaker twin slept—that her stronger sister wrapped her tiny arm around her. Soon thriving, the weaker twin accompanied her sister home, where, the parents thereafter reported, they were still sleeping and snuggling together.[50]

Of the power of literal, heartfelt touching, Smiley Blanton reflects, "I have always had a warm feeling for the father of the prodigal son in the Bible parable. He had every reason to be hurt and humiliated by his child's conduct. But when the prodigal finally came home, the father did not wait in the door with a prim word of welcome and a reluctant handshake. . . . He 'ran, and fell on his neck, and kissed him.'"[51]

This biblical father instinctively knew that touch can create an atmosphere of affection, of understanding, and even of forgiveness that permeates a soul. We all have woven into the fabric of our beings a profound yearning for the softest and most loving of touches, for our souls have a need for validation, for completion, and for the healing that emanates from such touch.

Whether it be a light touch to the shoulder, the delicate ruffling of someone's hair, or an engaging hug, touching—gently and tenderly—is soul food. Touching nourishes in human beings the vital sense of being alive and desired. And when touching communicates deep caring or concern for another, in possibility, an actual transfer or flow of energy may occur between souls.

The power of touch is something to which concert pianist Marta Korwin-Rhodes can attest. When Warsaw was besieged by the Nazis during World War II, Korwin-Rhodes was a volunteer in a hospital, caring for the wounded. Walking through a ward late one night, she heard the sobbing and moaning of a soldier, who, in his agony, had buried his face in his pillow to avoid disturbing anyone.

Korwin-Rhodes wondered how she could possibly help. Then, with sudden inspiration, she looked at her hands and thought, If I could transmit vibrations in harmony through the piano, why could I not transmit harmony directly without an instrument? Reaching out, she gently took the soldier's head in her hands. In turn—with sudden force—he tightly gripped her hands with his own. In a moment of reverence, as Korwin-Rhodes continued to tenderly cradle the soldier's head, she prayed that his pain might abate. As she did so, the soldier's sobs gradually quieted. Then, slowly releasing her hands, he drifted off to sleep.[52]

Korwin-Rhodes's touch greatly comforted and eased the soldier's pain. Even though the soldier was a stranger, she was, through touch, able to communicate with him at a much deeper level than words can reach—the level of the soul.

Although touch may not always produce such dramatic

results, its impact is still often powerful. Awareness of touch, and its power, can bring a new vibrancy to even the most common-place of experiences, as illustrated in a diary entry Helen Keller wrote as a youth:

"I have just touched my dog. He was rolling on the grass with pleasure in every muscle and limb. I wanted to catch a pic-ture of him in my fingers, and I touched him lightly as I would cobwebs. But lo, his body revolved, stiffened and solidified into an upright position, and his tongue gave my hand a lick. He pressed close to me as if he were fain to crowd himself into my hand. He loved it with his tail, with his paw, with his tongue. If he could speak I believe he would say to me that paradise is attained by touch."[53]

As Keller's poignant description illustrates, sometimes even a single touch can evoke the ambiance of love. It is, indeed, the capacity to project passionate concern and devotion through touch and other loving avenues that lies at the heart of all deeply rooted and lasting human relationships. The universal language of touch, however, is the most incontestable and trusted means of conveying love, for loving touch does not lie. And it is some-times due to the surprise element of being touched—and to the emotion the touch subsequently evokes—that even very small gestures can precipitate major changes in relationships and feelings.

Touching transcends the space between self and another person when words are hard to find; when words aren't enough; when there are no words; or when someone wants to share joy, show support, or communicate understanding and empathy. Touching is an embrace from the heart, creating warmth and support, and—at times—a feeling of comfort, security, and safety. As well, touch and closeness quietly equal each other.

But touch must be respectful. Although touching is of

extraordinary value, at times because of substantial life trauma, serious depression, or particular cultural conditioning, people may experience touch as distressing, or touch may cause feelings of fear or even acute anxiety. Illustrative is an instance of a surgeon, formerly uncomfortable with human touch, who discovered, on the night of his own surgery and in the early morning hours of pain and fear that followed, touch's significant meaning.

To that point, the surgeon's touch with patients had always been always impersonal, professional, brief, and to the point. Nevertheless, he had no problem touching unconscious bodies on the operating table, for there, focusing on the task at hand, his thoughts were preoccupied with the body—rather than the soul—of a human being.

It was a nurse who taught the surgeon his profound lesson regarding touch. One night, as he lay gravely ill and filled with agony and despair, a nurse entered his hospital room. After going through her routine and paces, she turned back after heading toward the door, spontaneously stepped to the sink, moistened a clean washcloth, and silently wiped the surgeon's unshaven face. Her only words? "This must be hard for you."

Stunned, the surgeon felt his eyes filling with tears. A stranger had taken time—through words and precious touch—to acknowledge his humanity. "For a moment," he says, "she became God's hands."

As a consequence of the nurse's actions, which prompted in the surgeon a total transformation regarding the meaning of touch, this surgeon resolved never again to touch just a physical body. Rather, he says, forevermore, "I will touch a human being."[54]

❤ ❤ ❤ ❤ ❤ ❤ ❤ ❤ ❤

LOVE IS A LEARNING EXPERIENCE

A provocative thinker, Eleanor Roosevelt once observed, "The giving of love is an education in itself."[55]

As a form of education, our giving of love requires that we stretch our emotional and spiritual selves to comprehend the feelings of those who are significantly different from ourselves. Establishing the relationship between perception and love, David Grayson observes, "How it improves people for us when we begin to love them."[56] Ironically, as Grayson suggests, when we begin to love others more, they become more appealing to us. And conversely, as our attitudes improve, we also are likely to become more appealing to those we are beginning to love.

Enlarging our capacity to feel for, and to love deeply, our fellow men includes acquiring the imagination to see people in the context of their perplexities and needs. We must also perceive accurately how to expend ourselves effectively in their behalf. Stretching our souls to love more often, and more substantially, can be painful and demanding, for such growth requires vulnerability, commitment, and constant vigilance. But change has precious, inherent rewards, for deep-felt adjustments allow us to interlace hearts and intertwine souls. And as we mature, there appears no end to the love we can ultimately experience, for, as Zelda Fitzgerald reflects, "Nobody has ever measured, even the poets, how much a heart can hold."[57]

Relating an experience that broadened her ability to understand other people, and thus love them more sensitively, is Jo Ann Able, who relates, "Having grandparents who emigrated from Bosnia-Hercegovina, I have watched with both interest and despair the events of the recent past in that area of former

Yugoslavia. When an opportunity unexpectedly presented itself to help a Bosnian refugee family resettle in the United States, I quickly and almost unthinkingly jumped in. My desire initially was to love and to help, but I acquired a valuable lesson in the process.

"This family, while not wealthy before the war, had lived comfortably—a middle-class home with stylish furnishings, adequate transportation, and friends and family nearby. They arrived in the U.S. with the clothes on their backs and two pieces of carry-on luggage among the five of them."

In her zeal to provide for their needs—or her perception of their needs—Able overwhelmed the family, she reveals: "I visited them frequently, the car always full of clothing, toys, food, furniture, or other household items. I decided the first hide-a-bed was too shabby and they needed another one. I was certain the mother, a seamstress, shouldn't be without a sewing machine, notions, and fabric. My 'goodwill' went on and on. While, yes, the family needed provisions, what they needed more was breathing space, time to wonder at the miracle of being together (the father had been imprisoned for sixteen months), and enjoyment of the newly found freedom of again making plans as a family. Once I realized this and understood the perplexity of their needs, I became more effective at giving love. I could be a friend, a listener, an advocate, and a facilitator. They now could be their own providers and, in fact, help provide for others with the abundance that my friends and family had heaped upon them.

"I deeply love this family, but now I also understand them. Love became an exercise in learning."[58]

♥ ♥ ♥ ♥ ♥ ♥ ♥ ♥ ♥

LOVE GRACES GOD'S CREATURES

One early morning, a mother cat entered a blazing building five times to rescue, one by one, her offspring. And then—with paws burned and eyes blistered shut—she began moving the kittens across the street.

Discovering the badly burned mother cat and her litter, a fireman took them to a shelter for medical treatment. Sometime after her painful and remarkable recovery, the mother cat and three surviving offspring were adopted. Of Scarlet, the mother cat, so named because of red patches visible through her singed fur, the shelter's manager observed, "She's a wonderful, gentle animal who did a courageous thing. It shows with all creatures, animals or people, there's no way of measuring a mother's love."[59]

Also, in love's name, two dogs risked their lives to save their owner, Jim Gilchrist, of Innisfil, Ontario. On February 24, 1995, in thirty-five-below-zero weather, Gilchrist left his lakeside cottage for a daily walk with Tara, a rottweiler, and Tiree, a golden retriever. As the weather began to worsen, Jim lost direction, wandering out onto the iced-over lake. Suddenly, he crashed through the ice, followed by Tara, who, hearing Jim's cries, had raced to him. As the two thrashed about, Tiree appeared.

As Jim helplessly struggled, Tiree inexplicably dropped to her stomach, slowly crawling across the ice to him. Fortuitously, at the same time, Tara mounted Jim's back and climbed onto the solid ice. With both dogs free, Jim thought that perhaps by grasping their collars he could pull himself to safety. The dogs, however, had something else in mind. Standing up as the two-hundred-pound Gilchrist hung on to them, the dogs intently clawed backward, pulling him onto solid ice.[60]

In the 1930s, an instance of enduring parent-child love

prevailed in Burma. On this occasion, Ma Shwe, a work elephant, and her three-month-old calf became trapped in the rising flood-waters of the Upper Taungdwin River. Elephant handlers standing above the elephants on twelve- to fifteen-foot-high riverbanks could not retrieve the screaming calf and her mother.

Still keeping her footing, Ma Shwe used her trunk to continually pull back the drifting calf. When the calf washed away, Ma Shwe plunged fifty yards downstream to retrieve her. Then, gaining position by pinning the calf against the bank, Ma Shwe lifted the calf with her trunk. Rearing up, she placed her on a rocky ledge five feet above water. Falling back into the torrent, she subsequently disappeared downstream.

Having witnessed this scene, perplexed elephant handlers focused on the shivering calf eight feet below them, precariously balanced on a narrow ledge. Unable to initiate a rescue, a camp manager was tremendously relieved in hearing, as he tells, "the grandest sounds of a mother's love I can remember." Having crossed the river and climbed the bank, Ma Shwe was rushing to her calf, "calling the whole time—a defiant roar, but to her calf it was music. The two little ears, like little maps of India, were cocked forward listening to the only sounds that mattered, the call of her mother."

Seeing that her calf was still safe on the ledge across the river, Ma Shwe changed her call to a rumble signifying pleasure. Then left alone, mother and calf spent the night, each where they were. In the morning, Ma Shwe crossed the receding flood waters and rescued her calf from the ledge.[61]

Love also graced a pair of canaries, which, once adopted, seemed blissfully happy together. In due time, they were provided a nest area and ample nesting material. Apparently happy with the new possibilities, Snowball, the female, supervised—designing and decorating the nest—while Sunshine, the male, followed her construction orders. Soon an egg appeared, and then a tiny chick hatched, and, if reflected in their continuous bursts of song, the happiness of the two parents seemed boundless.

The chick, named Punkinhead because of his orange color, grew to a fledgling and soon, tottering out of the nest, graduated to a perch. Then one day, after suddenly plunging head-on from the perch to the cage floor, he died. Although both parents grieved, Snowball was inconsolable, refusing to let her owners or Sunshine near her adored baby's body. Now, with broken heart, her bursts of song reduced to cries and moans. Seeking to redeem the situation, a puzzled Sunshine repeatedly tried to maneuver Snowball away from the baby. Thwarting his efforts, she repeatedly tried to revive her baby.

Apparently settling on a plan, Sunshine himself stood guard over Punkinhead for a time, encouraging Snowball to fly to the seed cup and eat. Each time she left, he placed one piece of nesting straw over Punkinhead, and in this way he gradually completely covered the baby bird's body. When his task was completed Snowball did not try to undo Sunshine's efforts but instead flew to her perch, where she continued in mourning. Thereafter, Sunshine continued consoling Snowball until one day she finally started singing again.

Of the couple, storyteller and owner Bonnie Compton Hanson remarks that Snowball may never have understood Sunshine's "quiet labor of love and healing." But, she says, the pair "remained joyously devoted for as long as they both lived. Love does that, you know."[62]

Love also magnificently prevailed in a story Loren Eiseley tells of two mated sparrow hawks. In this story, Eiseley recounts how his experience created a lifetime abhorrence to seeing any bird imprisoned.

In the 1950s Eiseley, assigned to restock a zoo, traveled to an abandoned mountain cabin intent on capturing birds. Knowing that a deteriorating cabin always draws birds, Eiseley slowly and quietly entered the pitch-dark cabin, holding a spotlight to blind any roosting birds, thus preventing their escape. Placing a short ladder against the far wall, he climbed to a high shelf, expecting the shelf to yield his first birds.

As Eiseley snapped on the flashlight, great wings began beating and feathers flew. As he grasped the bird nearest him, her mate, with a sharp cry, attacked Eiseley, digging his claws and beak into Eiseley's hand. When the flashlight went askew during the struggle, the bird's mate—now able to see—whisked neatly through a hole in the roof.

Despite the young male hawk's ferocious resistence, Eiseley ultimately won. Now the bird who had saved his mate by diverting Eiseley made no outcry. Resting hopelessly in Eiseley's hands, the hawk peered at him with a fierce, almost indifferent glance, apparently neither giving nor expecting mercy.

In the morning Eiseley, carrying the hawk in a small box, moved him from the cabin to outside grass. Soon, arriving trucks would take him to a city zoo, there to spend the rest of his life. *And a good thing, too*, thought Eiseley, painfully aware of his aching hand. Yet something ethereal, perhaps even sacred, had struck Eiseley regarding this hawk. Realizing that the magnificent creature was born free and God-ordained to fly the high heavens with his lifetime mate, Eiseley felt compelled to free the bird.

Now in Eiseley's hands, the hawk—with wings folded properly to still movement—lay limp and hopeless. As the bird gazed beyond Eiseley for a last glimpse of his mate, the man gently laid the hawk on the grass. For a long moment the bird lay still, perhaps not sensing his freedom. Then, in a flash he shot straight up, hurtling skyward toward his mate. Silence prevailed momentarily. And, then, from far up somewhere, a cry came ringing down.

Relates Eiseley, "I was young then and had seen little of the world, but when I heard that cry my heart turned over." Then came a return cry "of such unutterable and ecstatic joy that it sounds down across the years and tingles among the cups on my quiet breakfast table."

Shifting his position, Eiseley could now see the hawk's mate farther up; she had probably soared restlessly above them for untold hours. With the male hawk rising fast, Eiseley witnessed the pair meeting "in a great soaring gyre that turned to a whirling circle and a dance of wings. Once more, just once, their two voices joined in a harsh wild medley of questions and response, struck and echoed against the pinnacles of the valley. Then they were gone forever, into those upper regions beyond the eyes of men."[63]

❤ ❤ ❤ ❤ ❤ ❤ ❤ ❤ ❤

LOVE BESTOWS GIFTS

In this life you've had wonderful experiences before when you've given or have gotten healthy doses of love. These gifts of love involve bestowing a gift of self—sometimes just when that gift is needed the very most.

As you remember the special gifts of love you've had, you may even choke up or go teary-eyed. Some of these gifts may be among your most priceless memories. Speaking of a particular memorable gift, one person says, "Probably the nicest gift I can ever recall was when our grown daughter sent her father and me roses on her birthday and thanked us for the gift of life."

Says another person, "One very touching gift was when I was experiencing extreme stress in my life. My wife and family pre-arranged to sweep me away from my office and take me on a pic-nic. I was overwhelmed by the investment of time and concern they showed—as busy as they were, they still extended themselves for me."

Even another person relates, "A gift I'll never forget was when my mother-in-law took me and my sisters-in-law to lunch and gave us each an envelope with one hundred dollars in it. Then she took us to a mall and told us we had to spend that money on ourselves in the next two hours or give the money back."

At times, we all have also mused regarding what we might like to give a loved one, whether, in actuality, bestowing such a gift is even possible. Several people—who earlier spoke of their wishes—responded:

"I would love to give my friend an 'exotic bloom' in winter—one in her favorite color—with a note expressing an unexplored or never-divulged feeling."

"I would like to keep my friend home to be with his family on Christmas. He leaves for Kuwait on Monday."

"The greatest gift I could give to the world would be to introduce my mother and my wonderful wife to more people."

"It's my wish that all the lonely people in the world could have someone."

"If I could give a gift of love, it would be World Peace, that *all* would be blessed with health and joy, and those who are homeless would be no longer."

"If I could give a gift of love, it would be to give my dad a week of perfect health. . . . He has a rare and painful form of arthritis in his spine."

"If I could give a gift, it would be to reunite my mother and grandmother for a day. My grandmother passed away ten years ago."

Truly *possible* gifts of love come in assorted forms and shapes and are personalized to the receiver's needs. "My sixty-year-old grandmother just got an associate degree in psychology so I'm giving her a subscription to *Psychology Today*," reports one woman. Reports another: "My husband loves Albert Einstein and I finally found a big poster of Albert for him."

Gifts of love often take time: "My children get out of school early on Friday afternoons, so we call Friday our family day," says a mother. "After school we just go 'park-hopping'—we drive from one park to another and the kids have ten minutes to play on the equipment. Or we'll go to a museum, the library, or the pet store for a fish or two for our aquarium."

Gifts of love can also come at times of quiet desperation or of terrible trauma: "I was so sick and lonely on my birthday and I just couldn't tell anyone," says one woman. "And then several friends dropped by and I was moved to tears when they just took over for an hour. One made a pot of soup and others straightened the house and changed the bed."

Another woman relates, "My world turned upside down when my son-in-law was killed and my daughter was hospitalized for three weeks. I didn't realize until weeks after the funeral that several neighbors had canned the basket of pears sitting in my kitchen."

People who give gifts of love emphasize different aspects of gift giving. Some say, for example: "I love giving bold gifts, like when I know a friend is having a bad time, I'll announce, 'I'm coming over and taking you to lunch. I know you need a break.'"

"I love to give books because they continue to influence a person's life long after you've given the gift."

"I like to do things for people who really need nurturing. I learned there are people out there who really respond to a hug or an encouraging word."

"I like to give gifts I make—that involves a special part of me."

And what about kids? Adults delight in giving gifts of love to them, and kids delight in receiving. Kids like surprises such as good back rubs, little notes on their beds, a "you can choose" evening, a trip out to a movie or ice cream store, or having a special story read out loud.

Gifts of time seem to be among those kids and adults crave. But no matter what gift of love people give or receive, it seems that personal attention matters the most. One teen sums it all up: "What I really like is 'the thought that counts' part of a gift, favor, or action."

As a holiday, Christmas is a time of gift giving and Sigrid Undset, a Nobel prize winner, reminds us to remember our God-given gifts. Undset says, "And when we give each other Christmas presents in His name, let us remember that He has given us the sun and the moon and the stars, the earth with its forests and mountains and oceans—and all that lives and moves upon them. He has given us all green things and everything that blossoms and bears fruit—and all that we quarrel about and all that we have misused—and to save us from our foolishness, from our sins, He came down to earth and gave us Himself."[64]

Too often, at Christmas our own shortsighted giving is limited to material ones, when gifts of love and of self could add much more, and be much more consistent with the true spirit of Christmas.

Thus, next Christmas, you might bestow such intrinsic gifts as the gift of respect, of patience, of expressing love openly, of tolerance of differences, of time and focus, of gentleness, of accentuating positives, of forgiveness, of humor, of courtesy, of appreciation, of opportunity, of believing in another, of affection, of encouraging, or of cherishing.

And, when Christmas is gone, Howard Thurman encourages, consider that the passing of that holiday is just a beginning of the year's gift giving:

When the song of the angels is stilled,
When the star of the sky is gone,
When the kings and princes are home,
When the shepherds are back with their flock,
The work of Christmas begins:
To find the lost,
To heal the broken,
To feed the hungry,
To release the prisoner,
To rebuild the nations,
To bring peace among brothers,
To make music in the heart.[65]

❤ ❤ ❤ ❤ ❤ ❤ ❤ ❤ ❤

LOVE HAS INTEGRITY

Love knows the difference between *loving* and *liking* somebody or something. Love thus keeps its integrity by expressing itself only when intense positive emotions are felt. To love is to experience such powerful feelings as passion, devotion, or tenderness. To like is to enjoy or to have a fondness for, or to find something pleasing or agreeable or attractive. The difference lies in the strength of the emotions: *love* deepens as it seasons over time, but *like* does not.

When love appears, its expression can have deep meaning and dramatically increase the bonding between people, but the word *love* itself is sometimes used thoughtlessly or carelessly, thereby losing its power and meaning. In one instance, the action of cartoonist Charles Schulz showed that he instinctively realized the difference between *love* and *like*. Dining at a friend's home, Schulz wore an elegant Nehru jacket, which his friend wanted to complement with a heavy chain, complete with a medallion upon which, in large entwined letters, the word *LOVE* was boldly engraved.

Taking the medallion, Schulz held it for a few minutes but then handed it back. Overwhelmed with the intensity of the medallion's message, Schulz explained, "It's just a little too much for me." He then asked his friend, "Do you have one that says *LIKE?*"[66]

Schulz's reaction to the medallion's overstatement is not unlike that of Jo Coudert, who notes that frivolous use of the word *love* trivializes its meaning. She particularly objects to advertisers frequently tossing around the word *love* in commercials designed to sell products, as in "We love our customers." Such promotions are transparent, she says, and, as customers, "we know perfectly well they love us for our money or vote, not ourselves."

"Love is a private emotion," she concludes. "It is a deep and strong feeling. To bandy it about lightly with this sort of shallow sentimentality is about as convincing as asserting that paper napkins can make it through the wash."[67]

Goodman Ace also emphasizes that people too often use the word *love* rather than *like:* "There is too much love in the world and not enough like," he asserts. People love cheeseburgers, a woman's hat, a sunset, a movie, a pair of Bermuda shorts, an ocean voyage, or a broiled lobster.

Thus, "love trips lightly upon the tongues of the emotional where a little like would make for an endearment more enduring. People are always falling out of love. No one ever falls out of like. Where love is too often demanding, like is most often understanding."[68]

Love thus preserves its integrity when used sparingly and with forethought, particularly when romancing. In such instances— when the word *love* is used carelessly—persons may innocently believe they are loved when they are only liked. Such misuse of the word *love* puts people in emotional jeopardy, with the likelihood they will ultimately incur pain and disappointment.

To love is to also commit—an issue to be contemplated before one chooses between the words *love* and *like.* Commitment implies dedication of substantial time, energy, and resources to a relationship; and love is created through the deepening of feelings within that context. Thus, expecting commitment—in instances when the word *love* has been misused or abused—also puts people at risk.

Also disconcerted with the loose use of the word *love* is Nathaniel Branden, who observes that at no time in history has the word *love* been used so promiscuously as at present. As we bandy the word around freely, we compromise it, he emphasizes: "Just as a currency, in the process of becoming more and more inflated, has less and less purchasing power, so words, through an analogous process of inflation, through being used less and less discriminately, are progressively emptied of meaning.

"It is possible," Branden finishes, "to feel benevolence and goodwill toward human beings one does not know or does not know very well. It is not possible to feel love. . . . Love by its very nature entails a process of selection, of discrimination. Love is our response to what represents our highest values. Love is a response to distinctive characteristics possessed by some beings but not by all. Otherwise, what would be the tribute of love?"[69]

♥ ♥ ♥ ♥ ♥ ♥ ♥ ♥ ♥

LOVE BESTOWS AFFECTION

After dropping his granddaughter off at school, a grandfather returned fifteen minutes later, appeared at the classroom door, and asked for his granddaughter. When she appeared, he informed a surprised and very pleased child, "You forgot to kiss me good-bye."

Certainly this child's heart must have been warmed by the affection she felt emanating from her grandfather. In turn, she must have reciprocated such feeling. In fact, of all people, children most openly and sincerely extend affection to others, as emphasized by Holman F. Day, who reflects, "The purest affection the heart can hold is the honest love of a nine-year-old."[70]

Affection is that soft, warm side of love often expressed in the form of devotion, fondness, tenderness, or endearment. Juddu Krishnamuri refers to the joy of such soft feelings when he reflects, "To love is to have this extraordinary feeling of affection without asking anything in return."[71]

Affection is perhaps best recognized in the feelings one has in holding a baby. "What feeling is so nice as a child's hand in yours?" asks Marjorie Holmes. "So small, so soft and warm, like a kitten huddling in the shelter of your clasp. A child's hand in yours—what tenderness it arouses, what power it conjures up. You are instantly the very touchstone of wisdom and strength."[72]

As such, affection warms our souls, representing the benefit and possible outcome of a maturing relationship. C. S. Lewis's classical statement regarding affection captures this element as "the humblest love." Affection, he notes, "gives itself no airs . . . and almost slinks or seeps through our lives. It lives with humble . . . private things; soft slippers, old clothes, old jokes, the thump of a sleepy dog's tail on the kitchen floor." Moreover, affection, as "the least discriminating of loves," flourishes without expecting much of those it unites or demanding in them sterling qualities. Instead, affection "turns a blind eye to faults" and "revives easily after quarrels."

Further, elaborates Lewis, "the especial glory of Affection is that it can unite those . . . people who, if they had not found themselves put down by fate in the same household or community, would have nothing to do with each other." Thus affection creates for us a wider circle of relationships than would otherwise be so. And, he adds, affection broadens our minds, "teaching us first to notice, then to endure, then to smile at, then to enjoy, and finally to appreciate, the people who 'happen to be there.'"[73]

Complementing Lewis's observations is Iris Origo, who remarks she has had a varied and interesting life; has lived in beautiful places; and has met remarkable people. But now that she is older, the people she recalls are those to whom she has "been bound by affection." She vividly remembers these people, whom she credits with teaching her about life. Of her memories, she writes that—of those she has retained—all have "passed through the filter, not of my mind, but of my affections."[74]

At times, affection may be felt from afar—from a longtime admiration and study of another, as illustrated in an instance involving Helen Keller. Accompanied by a companion, Keller was browsing in a department store when a clerk—who knew of her triumphant struggle with lifelong blindness and deafness—recognized her. As he stood some distance from Keller, the clerk watched her with the deep-felt affection and respect he had long held for her and her achievements. Suddenly, Keller began to energetically communicate with her companion, who, after listening to her words, turned to the young man. Keller, she relayed, had just told her someone standing behind her was emanating a feeling of deep affection. Then said the companion, "She would like to meet you."[75]

Affection can also be communicated across cultural barriers. British novelist William Golding tells of an incident occurring in 1931 while he was attending his first year of Oxford. Having walked to a nearby park, Golding was standing on a small bridge overlooking a stream when he saw a mustached figure approaching. As the man walked over and stood by his side, a shocked Golding recognized that the man was Albert Einstein, then a visiting professor at Oxford.

At the time, Einstein, who was German, knew no English, and Golding knew only two words of German. Despite the language barrier, Golding tells of beaming at Einstein, trying wordlessly to convey by his bearing all the affection and respect the English felt for him. For perhaps five minutes the two stood silently together on the bridge. And then, tells Golding, "With true greatness, Professor Einstein realized that any contact was better than none. He pointed to a trout wavering in midstream. He spoke, '*Fisch*.'"

Golding's brain reeled as he recognized he was "mingling with the great," and yet he was helpless to respond. He relates, "Desperately I sought for some sign by which I might convey that I, too, revered pure reason. I nodded vehemently. In a brilliant flash I used up half my German vocabulary: '*Fisch. Ja. Ja.*'

"For perhaps another five minutes we stood side by side. Then Professor Einstein, his whole figure still conveying goodwill and amiability, drifted away out of sight."[76]

Affection plays a particularly vital role in buoying the spirits of the disheartened, as in the case of Hubert Humphrey, who, shortly before his death from cancer, observed, "The greatest gift that has come to me is the affection of so many—far more important than people feeling sorry for me. In fact, feeling sorry for someone is simply to give him a little pain reliever. Love is a healing force."

Affection is also often subtle, shy, and private, just as it sometimes exhibits a maturity acquired only with the seasoning of love. Jo Ann Able illustrates with a story concerning her in-laws. Throughout her ten or twelve years of marriage, Able conveys, she had rarely seen outward displays of affection between her mother- and father-in-law, who didn't hold hands, readily give compliments, or use terms of endearment so familiar to her own earlier family experience.

However, one day when she was visiting alone with her in-laws, she did see an unusual display of affection. On this occasion, as the three looked through a high school yearbook, her father-in-law pointed out his wife's picture and asked, "What do you think of my little dark-haired beauty?" Before Able had time to mentally compare the gray-haired woman in front of her with the lively-looking, dark-haired seventeen-year-old in the photo, her father-in-law approached his wife from behind and encircled her waist with his muscular arms. Joyfully he picked her up, swung her around, and whispered, "Pretty special, huh?"

It was not until her mother-in-law's funeral, a number of years later, that Able realized the full significance of this event. Her insight occurred when a cousin of her mother-in-law's laughingly remarked how she and her sister used to spy on Able's in-laws while they were courting, describing the couple as being quite affectionate and hugging and kissing each other unreservedly.

With regard to what she learned that day about affection, Able gives this perspective: "Many times affection is present but has been buried deeply under the heavy layers of life. With my parents-in-law, some of their layers included beginning their marriage and family in the early years of the Great Depression, moving from place to place in search of employment, finally building a home from used or scrap lumber, and losing a young son to a medical condition that should have been diagnosed by a doctor."

Able concludes, "Although affection does at times get buried by the burdens of everyday life, the wonderful part about it is that, in spite of its softness, it can work its way up through dense layers and most unexpectedly, almost proudly, announce itself."[77]

• • • • • • • •

LOVE RESPECTS FREEDOM

Love—real love—does not pressure or insist on time, attention, or affection from another. Love allows another the freedom to *choose* his or her response: "My love must be willing to let you grow in directions I haven't traveled," reflects Clint Weyand. "If I don't give you this freedom, my love is only a thinly disguised method of controlling you."[78]

Love realizes that others must be free, for human freedom is a precious thing and the human spirit vigorously reacts against those who would restrict, or take away, that freedom. To truly love another is thus to allow complete autonomy and freedom of movement so that, as M. Scott Peck has said, "the distinction between oneself and the other is always maintained and preserved."[79]

Of such distinctions in marriages, Anne Morrow Lindbergh reflects, "Ideally, both members of a couple in love free each other to new and different worlds."[80] Rainer Maria Rilke adds, "A good marriage is that in which each appoints the other guardian of his solitude. Once the realization is accepted that even between the closest human beings infinite distances continue to exist, a wonderful living side by side . . . makes it possible for each to see the other whole against a wide sky!"[81]

Further referring to such distinction, Kahlil Gibran, an early twentieth century Arabian poet and philosopher, offers a classic statement regarding marriages. Known as "the Prophet" for his writings that reflect "an expression of the deepest impulses of man's heart and mind," Gibran reflects:

Love one another, but make not a bond of love:
Let it rather be a moving sea between the shores of your
    souls.
Fill each other's cup but drink not from one cup.
Give one another of your bread but eat not from the same
    loaf.
Sing and dance together and be joyous, but let each one of
    you be alone,
Even as the strings of a lute are alone though they quiver
    with the same music.
Give your hearts, but not into each other's keeping.
For only the hand of Life can contain your hearts.
And stand together yet not too near together;
For the pillars of the temple stand apart,
And the oak tree and the cypress grow not in each other's
    shadow.

As elegantly as Gibran writes of marriage, he writes of par-
enting and of the distinction between self and other required
there:

Your children are not your children.
They are the sons and daughters of Life's longing for itself.
They come through you but not from you,
And though they are with you yet they belong not to you.
You may give them your love but not your thoughts,
For they have their own thoughts.
You may house their bodies but not their souls,
For their souls dwell in the house of tomorrow, which you
    cannot visit, not even in your dreams.
You may strive to be like them, but seek not to make them
    like you.
For life goes not backward nor tarries with yesterday.[82]

If the distinction between self and others does not exist—as
Gibran's eloquent writings suggest it must—love itself does not
exist. As Ann Oakley exhorts: "If love . . . means that one person

absorbs the other, then no real relationship exists any more. Love evaporates; there is nothing left to love. The integrity of self is gone."[83]

The ability to fully love, and yet to live distinctly separate from another person, is inextricably linked by gradation to level of maturity. Indeed, divulges Karl Stern, "The evolution of human growth is an evolution from an absolute need to be loved toward a full readiness to give love."[84] Thus, the less mature people are, the less capacity they have to operate autonomously in a relationship; and the more likely they are to use a relationship exclusively for their own selfish ends. Their souls undeveloped and needy, such persons operate from positions of control and domination, rather than love, in relating to a partner.

Psychiatrist Smiley Blanton emphasizes that in its configuration, sometimes "love" is not love at all. Instead, masquerading as genuine love is possessiveness. Blanton describes listening often to patients who, in order to secure personal value, attach themselves to another person, in the process stifling and crushing that person.

Inasmuch as humans are born completely dependent on others, their challenge is to mature to the extent that they don't use others to fill emotional vacuums in themselves. Unchecked self-centeredness and possessiveness, if not conquered through maturity and healthy progression to adulthood, may destroy any relationship.

Conversely, genuine love gives others the room to *be*. Genuine love is liberating, not confining, and releasing, not clutching. Those who truly love "know that the closer the relationship, the more essential it is to create and preserve little areas of separateness, little oases of isolation where the soul can renew itself." Such persons also know "you can never put your brand on another human soul" without the risk of destroying that soul.[85]

People often usurp others' freedom and autonomy by imposing their own "shoulds," or will, upon them. We all have internal
measuring standards by which we assess the behavior and attitudes of others. Yet, too often, we don't recognize that our own
measuring standards are idiosyncratic. Our standards do not
measure what is real; they reflect what we know, what we have
experienced, and that with which we are comfortable. And when
others don't fit our subjective measurements, we tend to deem
them flawed.

Within reason, and certainly when other people are not
harming themselves or others, they must be free to respond as
they choose. Our bottom line is to release others from having to
be like us and, whenever possible, to celebrate differences rather
than viewing them as threatening. Germane to this challenge are
the sage words of Ralph Waldo Emerson: "Never try to make
anyone like yourself—you know, and God knows, that one of
you is sufficient."[86]

But what if we want a behavior change in someone we love?
Then we must *invite*—not demand—what we want. Such responses as "Would you be willing . . ." or "I would appreciate . . ."
need to replace "You have to . . ." or "If you don't, then . . ." To
demand may be to get not what we want but what we deserve.

With real love, there is no room for ownership of one person by the other; rather, there is only stewardship of this
moment's experiences.[87] In fact, Jess Lair advises, "If you want
something very, very badly, let it go free. If it comes back to you,
it's yours forever. If it doesn't, it was never yours to begin with."[88]

Thus, sometimes—with no absolute life guarantees of "forever love"—a person must let go, often with great pain, realizing that a loved one wants to be elsewhere. "In a deteriorating
love affair, you may be deeply torn between the choice of holding on or letting go," advises Paul B. Lowney. "If you remain

indecisive, the internal conflict can depress you and even make you ill. You should make a quick determination whether to hold on by fighting or let go by retreating.

"Holding on unsuccessfully is like clenching your fist tighter and tighter until you knuckles turn white. Letting go is like opening your fist. It feels better, but your hand is empty."[89]

In one sense, letting go can be an unselfish act, a realization that "letting go" may be equivalent to "loving," for when one truly loves, one does not cling to another but gives room for that person to choose his or her own life circumstances. Letting go, then, sometimes represents a formidable test of genuine love.

Freedom and love are also inextricably linked in regard to the care of, and respect for, animals. Trappist Monk Thomas Merton once wrote in his journal, "A very small gold-winged moth came and settled on the back of my hand and sat there, so light I could not feel it. I wondered at the beauty and delicacy of this being— so perfectly made. I wondered if there is a name for it, as I had never seen such a thing before. It would not go away, until, needing my hand, I blew it lightly into the woods."[90]

Inherent in Merton's writings is a reverence for both the moth and its absolute freedom. If human beings truly love animals, they will honor animals' right to freedom and—to the extent feasible—provide such freedom.

Jeffrey Moussaieff Masson and Susan McCarthy, authors of *When Elephants Weep*, affirm animals' need for freedom. They provide examples of creatures who, when given freedom, appear to "revel in life." Illustrating, they cite an instance of a two-year-old panda at a Chinese breeding center who was allowed a rare foray into an outdoor enclosure. Bursting from its "darkened cage . . . the panda . . . trotted up a hill with a high-stepping gait, and somersaulted down. Again and again it raced up the hill and rolled back down." George Schaller, who wrote of the panda, tells, "It exploded with joy." Indeed, Masson and McCarthy conclude that for nearly all creatures, "freedom gives joy."[91]

♥ ♥ ♥ ♥ ♥ ♥ ♥ ♥ ♥

LOVE MUST MATURE

"Love is what you've been through with somebody," reflects James Thurber.[92] Inherent in Thurber's observation is the realization that love—real love—is not an event but a process entailing the deepening, over time, of caring feelings. As with a seedling that becomes a tree, capable in its maturity of coming to full bloom and yielding favorable fruit, love requires seasoning and the test of time to bring forth its yield. Also, as with the tree, love's full-bodied expression has form and structure that bespeaks its dependability and capacity to weather storms. And, just as the tree's "growth rings" reflect the history and weathering of the tree, love's indelible memories reflect both the tribulations and victories of a seasoned relationship.

When it comes to romance and "falling in love," love must necessarily involve the element of time. "Perhaps people can fall in love in a moment, but mature love is like a tree, moving slowly from the seed in the ground to the sheltering splendor of its prime," Ardis Whitman notes.[93]

And Mary-Lou Weisman adds, "The possibility for real love begins after the fall. . . . While falling in love is an accident that can happen to two ill-suited strangers who won't even like each other in a few days, staying in love is a sustained act of will between two respectful and self-respecting individuals. Falling in love is a free ride; staying in love is work."[94]

Shifting from a perceptual set of "being in love" to one of "loving" is key to a relationship's maturation. Thomas Szasz writes: "When men and women are in love, they share the mistaken belief that they live in the same world; when they 'love' one another, they acknowledge that they live in different worlds, but are prepared once in a while to cross the chasm between them."[95]

Speaking to the principle that a relationship needs sufficient time to mature, Whitman says of love's growth, "Love is always a work in progress. Loving people need time to deepen their affection, to appreciate each other's differences, and to share each other's joys and griefs. So it is sad when divorces come with small provocations, when parents and children give up on each other, when friendships falter at the first injury; for thus we forfeit a great work of art—the long love."[96]

Speaking of one such "long love," Eda LeShan tells of sharing the hospital visiting room with an elderly couple while she was visiting a friend. The couple sat close to each other, the husband consigned to a wheelchair, and the two—oblivious of anything else—radiated deeply felt love and a total communion of spirit.

Of her experience, LeShan says, "For the half hour that I watched they never exchanged a word, just held hands and looked at each other, and once or twice the man patted his wife's face. The feeling of love was so thick in that room that I felt I was sharing in their communion and was shaken all day by their pain, their love, and something sad and also joyful: the fullness of a human relationship."[97]

In another instance, a couple absorbed a vital blow that, except for their deep and enduring love, might have permanently strained or even destroyed their marriage. This true story is captured by Pamela Johnson in a work entitled "Henry's Healing":

"'Are you Henry and Laurel Deane?'

"My wife and I nodded slowly as the policeman stood in our

front room and looked gravely at each of us and our two boys. . . .
'I have some bad news.'

" 'Is it about my son David William?' I asked, adding proudly,
impulsively, 'He's training at Lake Powell to be a scuba diver.' I'd
had an ominous feeling all day. I would soon know why.

" 'Yes,' the policeman cleared his throat.

" 'There's been an accident. For some reason his oxygen tank
malfunctioned and he didn't come up in time. I'm sorry.'

"My mind reeled back to a few days before when David
begged me, 'Dad, please talk Mom into letting me go to Lake
Powell.'

" 'You've let your school grades slip badly,' I had tried to
sound stern with my almost-sixteen-year-old.

" 'I got my Eagle. Aren't you proud of me for that?' he said
innocently. 'I'll do better in school, I promise. I'll do anything to
go, Dad, please.' Of course my heart melted to this fun-loving
boy, the fourth of six children, and I let him go.

"At this moment, I hated the principle called 'free agency.' I
was jarred out of my deep thoughts as my family's sobs brought
me back to reality, the present; my boy was dead. The policeman had left and we all clung to each other.

" 'Laurel Deane, it's all my fault, I—if I hadn't let him go.'

" 'Henry,' I felt her arms tighten around me, 'I don't want to
ever hear you say that again. We both made the decision and it's
hurting us both to the core, but self-blame will not get us
through this.'

"She hadn't said to me, 'I told you so. I didn't want him to go
in the first place.' Her forgiving me helped me through the next
painful days.

"As I hovered over David's casket, I noticed the hurt look that
seemed to be in his facial expression. I squeezed his hand:
'David, I know you can hear me. You must have suffered a lot—

those last few minutes. Son, I'm sorry for both of our hurts, but there are no regrets between us. We were about as close as a father and son could have been. The thing that's hard about losing you—is that I love you so much—and I'll miss you more.'

"Laurel Deane and I had our own ways of coming to terms with David's death. Laurel believes it must have been his time to go according to the Lord's will and ways. She has great faith. I reason that if a law of nature is broken, God doesn't often intervene. We both clung to our belief that heaven is a happy, peaceful place, and that we would see David again.

"It had been weeks since David's death. One of my other sons approached me tentatively. 'Dad, why haven't we been taking our brand new boat out this summer?'

"I hesitated before answering. I hadn't shared my fear with anyone. 'I haven't dared take it out on the water—because of what happened to David.'

"Laurel Deane spoke up firmly, 'David would have wanted it that way, for us to be out as a family on the water in the boat he loved.'

"I would have to overcome my fear by trying out the boat again, for David.

"A friend who saw David just before he drowned said, 'David never looked happier.' We took the boat out that weekend, and for the first time since David's passing, we looked beyond the sorrow to the joy of David's memory and life with us."[98]

The long love is a soul love—a love ultimately permanently unscathed by any extraneous or circumstantial event. Such was the love of the couple in the hospital and that between Henry and Laurel Deane. In the first instance, the elderly couple experienced a spiritual bonding, intensified in its physical presence, perhaps by the knowledge of death's near and eminent claim on one of them. In the case of Henry and Laurel Deane, their enduring love was fortified, rather than shaken, in the wake of their beloved son's death. In the instance of both couples, "a great work of art—the long love" magnificently prevailed.

❧ ❧ ❧ ❧ ❧ ❧ ❧ ❧ ❧

LOVE GOES THE DISTANCE

At times, under unexpected circumstances, love asks that we give intensively to another person for an extended time period, or even over the course of a lifetime. Spouses may care for their mates through terminal bouts of cancer or other illnesses; families for a disabled member; adult children for a waning elder; or parents for children who become injured, who are retarded, or who have other birth defects. Often, then, love unequivocally dedicates itself to sustaining and to assuring the quality of that person's life.

In this regard, Ben's mother is a prime example of such dedication. Years ago, when Ben lost his eyesight in his late teens, his mother reacted with fierceness, determined that Ben ultimately achieve complete independence. Her dedication is reflected in an incident that occurred as Ben—with his parents—crossed a busy street. Ben recalls overhearing his father say, "Mother, take hold of Ben's hand." He also overheard his mother's response: "Father, Ben must learn to walk across the road alone. There will be many busy roads in his life, and he won't always have us to take his hand."

In all areas of his life, Ben's mother encouraged him to reach not just for independence but for excellence. Determined that her son succeed, and in an era with few resources for the blind, Ben's mother spent many hours in Ben's last years of high school aiding him to master essential concepts and subjects. Due to his mother's tutoring and to his own mother-instilled absolute dedication to becoming independent, Ben obtained a high school diploma. And then the time for college arrived.

But Ben's state university turned down his application—there was no room for the blind. Ben's mother, however, would not be deterred. Making an appointment with the dean of the university, she discussed Ben's situation with him. Apologizing for not accepting Ben's application, the dean explained that no tutors were available and that most textbooks were not published in Braille. Nor did the university have teaching aids for the blind. To that, Ben's mother responded, "I will be Ben's eyes. I will read his books to him. I will go with him to every class. I will take his notes for him, and together we'll work on his assignments."

And so it was that, four years later, Ben graduated with honors from the university. And, as a result of his mother's enduring love and dedication, Ben succeeded in the profession of his choice—the insurance business—where he performed for more than fifty years. As an agent rated in the top performance ranks, Ben became a longtime member of the Million Dollar Roundtable and a legend in the insurance industry.

Ben's mother's consummate investment in Ben's welfare was reflected in his proactive attitude toward his blindness. He was often to remark that, to him, blindness was not a handicap—just an inconvenience.[99]

As in the case of Ben, sometimes loving actually takes the form of courage that is quiet and long-suffering—hard, even, to identify without a study of circumstances over time. In such cases, people carry on, enduring with supreme dignity and without complaint.

Examples of such long-term courage, says June Callwood, "involve the steadfastness of ordinary people in monotonous jobs, in parents who matter-of-factly raise handicapped children, in those who live in never-ending pain without hating the world, in adults who, stalwartly giving up malice and suspicion, teach themselves to relax and trust."

Such quiet but stubborn courage or bravery, reminds Callwood, is seldom recognized by the people who bear the arduous burdens.[100] Thus was most likely the case of the parents of Olympic runner Glenn Cunningham, who—with great love—went the distance with him.

At age seven, Glenn Cunningham incurred severe damage to both legs in a freak accident when a can of gasoline ignited a smoldering fire in a potbellied stove and the worst happened. Told that he would be an invalid for the rest of his life, Glenn insisted, "I *will* walk! I will! I will!"

He did walk. And he even ran. Glenn Cunningham was later to set world running records, becoming the outstanding miler of his age and an Olympic medal racer. His courage, quiet and enduring, was present as he overcame obstacle after obstacle; and so was the steadfast courage of his parents, who supported Glenn in every way.

It was Glenn's mother who reached out and brushed back the hair from Glenn's forehead when he shouted his intent to walk again, replying, "Yes, Glenn, you will walk again." It was Glenn's mother who, when Glenn's legs weren't healing in the months to follow, applied a sweet-smelling salve to them every day and patiently kneaded his limp leg muscles. And it was Glenn's mother, ever by his side, who rushed to catch him as he took his first faltering steps.

It was also Glenn's father who unknowingly prepared Glenn for his trial to come. Before the accident, Glenn's father, who could run like a deer, had often told Glenn that he was a "natural" for running. He had taught Glenn how to pump his arms to get more speed, and how to pace himself for a long run. And it was his words—words of advice always given to his children—

that kept Glenn going the day he stumbled home after the accident: *Never quit. Run on. Work your problems out.*

It was Glenn's father, too, who continued to give him hope.
One day, at a time when Glenn could muster little more than a
hippity-hop gait, Glenn's father took Glenn with him to hunt
rabbits on the prairie. And the next time father and son went out,
Glenn's father unhitched a horse from the wagon and thrust the
animal's black tail into Glenn's hands, admonishing: "Hang on to
that. Let's go."

As the horse surged forward, Glenn gritted his teeth. After
he had taken but a dozen floundering steps, his father stopped
the horse and, with a pleased expression on his face, turned and
said to Glenn: "You *run*, boy! Don't complain. Just keep trying."

It was after miles and miles of walking and determined,
relentless exercise over several years that Glenn, without telling
his parents, impulsively entered his first race at the school track
meet. It was also without proper shoes and clothes, facing com-
petitors all bigger than he, and without knowledge of the rules
of the run that Glenn ran the race.

Remembering his father's advice, Glenn held back at first,
then put on a little speed, finally catching up with, and passing,
the front runners. The next thing Glenn knew, he was coming
up to a string stretched across the track. Ducking so it didn't
catch his head, he suddenly saw the crowd waving excitedly for
him to go back. "You have to *break* the string to win!" one man
roared. Glenn frantically ran back and snapped the string. He
had won.

It was his father's words, as he walked home after winning,
that Glenn heard ringing in his ears: "Run on—never quit."[101]

In Glenn's case, there were three quiet heroes—he and his
mother and father. When life's race seemed lost, when the odds
appeared unbeatable, when the pain was too much, they, as well

as he, had endured and passed the test. As a result, Glenn gave back much to the world, establishing, at the end of his track career, a youth ranch that helped more than nine thousand troubled youth.

♥ ♥ ♥ ♥ ♥ ♥ ♥ ♥ ♥

LOVE EXTENDS ITSELF

Love extends itself on a daily basis—sometimes in the form of sacrifice—as an adult daughter relates: "It was dreadfully difficult to get my carpenter father to dress up. But when my mother died, Pop bought a handsome suit and went heart-brokenly to her funeral dressed to the teeth.

"A year or so later," she says, "I saw a similar suit in that store and remarked to the clerk about Pop's dislike for sprucing up. The elderly clerk said to me, 'My dear child, your father came here often to admire the fine clothes we carry, but he always said his kids needed things more than he needed clothes.' My eyes filled with tears as the old fellow went on: 'Your father told me that, anyway, he felt dressed up inside himself, and I believed him. He smiled so much, he just had to be wearing a darn nice suit around his heart.'"[102]

In this instance, the daughter, brought to an abrupt halt by the clerk's words, suddenly realized and was overcome by her father's immeasurable commitment to his family. Over the years, through quiet and unassuming actions, her father had made many sacrifices and forfeited much for his family.

Such also was the case of cellist Pablo Casals's mother. His father had agreed to stay in Brussels while his mother, Pablo, and his two younger brothers went to Paris in pursuit of Casals's career. Recognizing her son's remarkable talent, Casals's mother intended to promote, at any cost, his future as a musician. Her husband unable to send funds, the wife had to support the family. Finding living quarters "in what was little more than a hovel," she left home every day in search of subsistence. Casals recalls there "was barely enough for the little ones to eat."

At seventeen, Casals himself finally found a job as a second cellist at a music hall. However, the hall was far away, and without money for train fare, he walked to work and back carrying his cello.

During a bitterly cold winter, the situation finally became desperate. "At last the strain of the work and the lack of food proved too much," Casals recalls. "I became very ill and had to stay home. My mother worked harder than ever, to feed us and buy the medicines I needed. She sewed late into the nights. She was always cheerful and did everything to keep up my spirits."

One day, ill in bed when his mother came home, Casals— with astonishment and dismay—realized she no longer had her beautiful, long, black hair. Remembers Casals, "Her hair was now ragged and short. She had sold her hair to get a few extra francs for us."

Of his mother's reaction, Casals says, "She laughed about it. 'Never mind,' she said. 'Don't think about it. It is only hair, and hair grows back.'"

It was Casals's pleasure, later in life, to provide for his family. Even early on, as he gained some earning power, Casals writes, "Nothing gave me greater joy than being able to provide some comforts for my mother and two younger brothers or to help my father get better care for his dreadful asthma." Thus, in a loop, love extended itself, returning to increase the well-being of those who had sacrificed so much.

In extending itself, love also takes no time off. Love is a sentinel, ever watching over those in its care, as in the instance of Norman Lobsenz. Once, a number of years ago, his young wife became desperately ill. After many exhausting weeks of aiding her, he worried whether he could sustain such intensive care. One evening—drained of all strength and endurance—he remembered a long-forgotten incident:

"I was about ten years old at the time, and my mother was seriously ill. I had gotten up in the middle of the night to get a drink of water. As I passed my parents' bedroom, I saw the light on. I looked inside. My father was sitting in a chair in his bathrobe next to Mother's bed, doing nothing. She was asleep. I rushed into the room.

"'What's wrong?' I cried. 'Why aren't you asleep?'

"Dad soothed me. 'Nothing's wrong. I'm just watching over her.'"

Of his vivid experience, Lobsenz further relates, "The remembered light and warmth from my parents' room were curiously powerful, and my father's words haunted me. 'I'm just watching over her.' The role I now assumed seemed somehow more bearable, as if a resource had been called from the past, or from within."[103]

Through his father's own earlier example, Lobsenz learned an invaluable lesson—one of patience and commitment to a loved one. In turn, from the imprinted image of his dad watching over his mother, Lobsenz drew the vitality necessary to address his own adversity. As a legacy, the modeling of love thus is often perpetuated throughout generations, affecting many more than those people in a present relationship.

In extending itself, love is also thoughtful, noting events important to loved ones and remembering to give congratulations, to celebrate happy occasions, or to comfort and to extend condolences. And love always looks after its own—offering support and encouragement whenever such gestures are vital to the well-being of loved ones. A letter of support from an adult daughter to a mother illustrates the gift of reassurance that love can offer when shadows cross a loved one's path:

The letter reads: "Mom: It'll be okay. You can handle this. You're the strongest person I know and I've always, and still do, look up to you.

"I'm as proud as a daughter could be that you're my mom. I admire your courage and conviction to do the things you know in your heart are right.

"I know you don't feel very strong right now but I promise you—you'll pull through. You have the talents and the skills and you are a survivor. You always have been.

"If there is one thing you have taught me, it is that adversity is there for a reason—whether it is to make us stronger or to test our resolve, or both. This will pass. Granted, this is a big, ugly, scary adversity—but it is still smaller than you. You're bigger and stronger than this monster—and you can take him. God won't give you anything you can't handle.

"This may be the fight of your life, or perhaps just one of them, but this monster can't take you if you don't let him. I know you feel as if you have to wait—and that you can't do anything about this looming problem—but you can train yourself and prepare yourself for the fight. You can make sure that you're a prize-fighter in top condition when you go into the ring.

"I love you and I will always be here for you. I'm rooting for you and I know you'll win. Now, go get him, tiger. Love, your daughter."

In this instance, the unequivocal love the mother extended to her daughter over the years returned itself, substantially buoying the mother's spirits. Conversely, her daughter, given the opportunity to reciprocate, offered unerring support to her own mother in ways she, herself, had before experienced.

❤ ❤ ❤ ❤ ❤ ❤ ❤ ❤

LOVE GIVES ITS ALL

Love is clear about its allegiance and freely gives its time, energy and resources, whether to friends or family. In all ways, love nurtures and enhances relationships, and love will fight, even to the death, to protect a loved one. Illustrating the bonding of love and commitment is a World War I story of a badly injured soldier who could not get back to the safety of his lines. Against an officer's orders, the soldier's friend went out to rescue him. This friend returned mortally wounded, and the soldier he carried back was dead.

Angry at the second soldier, the officer reprimanded him for disobeying orders: "Now I've lost both of you. Giving your life for your friend wasn't worth it. He was going to die anyway."

"But it was, sir," replied the dying man, "because when I got to him, he said, 'Jim, I *knew you'd come.'"[104]

In this instance, love put itself on the line without any thought for itself. The loyalty one soldier felt for another—and the compelling need to express that loyalty under the most dangerous of circumstances—took precedence over life itself.

Also illustrating how willingly love puts its life on the line is author William Manchester, who tells of his experience in revisiting Sugar Loaf Hill in Okinawa, where, thirty-five years earlier, he had fought as a marine. It was when he revisited Okinawa that he understood, at last, why he "jumped hospital" three decades earlier and, "in violation of orders, returned to the front and almost certain death.

"It was an act of love," he reveals. "Those men on the line were my family, my home. They were closer to me than I can say, closer than any friends had been or ever would be. They had never let me down, and I couldn't do it to them. I had to be with them, rather than let them die and me live with the knowledge that I might have saved them. Men, I now knew, do not fight for flag and country, for the Marine Corps or glory or any other abstraction. They fight for one another."[105]

In yet another instance, a bombardier in World War II made a profound sacrifice to save others of the bomber's crew during a mission. On this particular trip, a searing hot bomb aborted, ejecting into the plane. Everyone on board knew that if the bomb detonated, they would all die.

So, one bombardier chose to pick up the bomb. The bomb weighed so much that he had to put his arms around it, hug it to his body, and hold it to his neck and down his chest and legs. The bomb—pressed against the man's chest and legs—burned not just the man's skin, but also his internal organs. In unspeakable pain, and knowing the profound consequences should he drop the bomb, the bombardier, praying and gritting his teeth, continued pulling the bomb toward the door. Aghast at his plight, others moved toward the bombardier to help but were adamantly refused, as he knew they would also be horribly disfigured. Finally, the man reached the door and by himself ejected the bomb.

As a result of his sacrifice and terrible injury, the bombardier was permanently disabled and unable to work. As well, throughout the rest of his life, he experienced intense, chronic pain. The men who flew the mission with this bombardier loved him immensely because of his sacrifice for them and never forgot his noble deed. Thus did they meet regularly with the bombardier and his family to convey their love. And, every year, the men faithfully gave him a percentage of their income to help him monetarily with his family expenses and medical bills, sharing with him the rewards that life had given to each of them.[106]

A final poignant story, written by Afton Grant Affleck and

entitled *Greater Love Hath No Man*, illustrates the selfless depths at which love gives its all: "The rubber raft was sailing down the glassy river as smoothly as a huge duck," Affleck relates. "The sky was overcast. A cool, brisk wind was blowing from the northeast. Nine-year-old Ryan sighed contentedly as he turned over on his stomach to ease his sunburned back. He'd never been so utterly, ecstatically happy. He thought of his dad who had consented to let him run the river with him and with Travis, his older brother. 'Dad's my very best friend,' he thought. Then, he dozed.

"The next thing he knew he was struggling for breath. Water was forming a whirlpool around him. He could hear someone screaming his name, but the current kept sucking his body down and down. There was a gurgling in his lungs; he thought his lungs would burst. He kept losing consciousness. Every time he came to the edge of giving up, someone called his name, and he would madly struggle upward.

"Sixteen-year-old Travis made it to the river bank and pulled himself up over the sharp rocks. His right leg was bleeding, and he was sure his shoulder was broken. His eyes scanned the boiling river for his dad and for his little brother. He couldn't see either one of them.

"It was all so sudden. Travis didn't know what had caused the raft to overturn. He was choking on regurgitated filth. He saw two men diving into the water. Then he saw Ryan, head and shoulders above the water. He looked as if he was just standing there. Travis struggled to scream his brother's name; no sound came. Just as he saw a man reach out to rescue Ryan, he fainted.

"Travis and Ryan were taken to a small hospital and placed in beds, side by side. Ryan, who was in shock, had not wept or uttered a word. Travis felt as though his heart would break. He tried but he could not penetrate Ryan's consciousness.

"After an hour's silence, he said: 'Ryan, did you see Dad after the boat overturned?'

"Ryan began sobbing—great wracking sobs.

"'Ryan, Ryan,' Travis cried.

"Finally Ryan quieted. 'Travis,' he said, 'I was standing on Dad's shoulders.'

"After the water receded, the body of Ryan and Travis's father was found, his right foot wedged between two boulders."[107]

For Ryan's father to give his life was to offer his love to his son in fullness and purity, following Christ's admonition, "Greater love hath no man that this, that a man lay down his life for his friends" (John 15:13).

* * * * * * * *

LOVE CHERISHES

She, who has been married to him for nearly sixty years, gets misty-eyed when he brings out a harmonica, long-ago retired, and plays a familiar tune.

He gently teases her about the bargain he got for two dollars—the cost of a marriage license over a half century ago. And then she softly reminds him, "But look at all the upkeep."

Of their relationship, he says she makes him feel important. She insists he have the best chair, the biggest piece of cake, even the best plate (not, he reassures, that he wants it!). But, he adds, she'll make it an issue if he doesn't have the best.

She says she's always felt secure with him, has always known he was loyal, moral, kind, and good. And, oh, yes, though they've been married almost sixty years, he still treats her with the same impeccable courtesy as when they were courting. He makes her happy with his enduring sense of humor, and he is always gentle. As well, he's always made even intimate moments a deeply felt expression of love.

He says she always calls him dear and that every day of living with her is still an adventure. She's always at his side, consistently reassuring him his mistakes aren't important—that anyone could have likewise easily erred. She's his sweet, his darling, the "peg of his heart." He loves her with all his heart and will cherish her throughout the eternities.

They are an adoring couple—an intimate couple—a couple who have spent a lifetime revering, respecting, and investing in their relationship. And the payoff? After sixty years, they are still in love—and they cherish each other.

Of such exquisite relationships, Sir Hugh Walpole reflects, "The most wonderful of all things in life, I believe, is the discovery of another human being with whom one's relationship has a glowing, depth, beauty and joy as the years increase."[108] And, applicable to the purity and God-endowed nature of such love, William Lyon Phelps reflects, "Two persons who love each other are in a place more holy than the interior of a church."[109]

Also exquisitely descriptive of such relationships is the ancient Brahman adage, "When the one man loves the one woman and the one woman loves the one man, the very angels leave heaven and come and sit in that house and sing for joy."[110]

When a relationship has evolved to a mode of consummate depth and beauty, of purity, of reverence, and of elegance, the two intertwining people have achieved the ennobled and exalted plane of cherishing each other. The perfect symmetry of such cherishing involves a continuity between two souls who have wedded—and explored their reciprocal relationship—in the realm of the spirit. Illustrative of cherishing's potential spiritual essence is a previous work by this author, inspired by the all-encompassing, exultant love between her own parents—the previously mentioned couple. This work reads:

In contemplation, *cherishing* is a word that even has the sound of tenderness, of holding dear, of warmth toward another coming from the soul. Cherishing is the ultimate expression of love held ever precious throughout the years. Although time is a critical element, cherishing may uncommonly evolve rapidly as two people—consistently connecting at the soul level—ever so quietly touch each other at their innermost cores.

Cherishing is first of all love, but one can love without cherishing. Cherishing is an exalted form of love, the highest, noblest, strongest feeling one person can have for another. Such love has come to maturity and fruition—a bonding of the physical, emotional, intellectual, and spiritual dimensions shared in common.

Cherishing requires the sharing of time and space together and a mature seasoning of the relationship as it is cultivated, renewed, and celebrated daily. Cherishing can evolve—in addition to couples' relationships—in others as well.

One who cherishes regards another not as an extension of self but as a unique, forever becoming, beautiful person. That person also envelops the other with a cloak of dignity and respect, refraining from condemnation and rejection. Too, he or she creates an environment so safe the other can share innermost feelings, dreams, failures or successes without fear of recrimination.

His or her love is not demanding, nor does it depend on merit or worthiness. Neither does it keep score.

Further, there is room for mistakes without penalty, even big ones, for mistakes are regarded as essential to the process of becoming. And there is always forgiveness.

The one who cherishes also sees in the other a reflection of his or her own humanness and the miracle of life. That person treats the other with the same tenderness, devotion, and awe he or she would extend to a newborn child.

The one who cherishes desires to connect to the other, to experience that person's deepest inner self and to share, in return, his or her own. Experiencing bursts of love coming from deep within, that person expresses love through acts of tenderness, appreciation, and devotion and ever affirms the other's presence and worth. His or her consistent affection and affirmation endows the cherished one with a calmness and contentment emanating from often being quietly assured of the other's love.

For most couples, cherishing is a quest—a condition unattained but not unattainable. For couples to fully cherish requires total commitment to the relationship and to progressively becoming more deeply involved, more vulnerable, more responsive, more sharing, and more intimate.

Finally, cherishing involves commitment of time.

Nathaniel Branden tells of lecturing on the importance of devoting time to a relationship. After his presentation, a young couple approached him, both partners expressing how happily in love they were. "But one thing troubles me," the husband said. "How do you find time for intimacy?"

In response, Branden inquired as to what the man did for a living and was told he was a lawyer. Given this information, Branden then said, "There's one thing that troubles *me*. Given how much you love your wife, how do you find time to attend to your law practice?"

Responding to the disoriented look on the man's face, Branden next said, "The answer seems obvious, right? I mean you *have* to attend to your law practice, don't you?"

Slowly Branden's point began to dawn on the young man as Branden continued: "When and if you decide that love means as much to you as your work does, when success in your relationship seems as important to you as success in your career, you won't ask, 'How does one find time?' You'll know."[111]

Couples who cherish each other, of course, understand this perfectly.

❤ ❤ ❤ ❤ ❤ ❤ ❤ ❤

LOVE IS ABSOLUTE

Absolute love doesn't abandon others under harsh conditions or upon shattering changes in circumstances. Rather, absolute love conveys to another person—unequivocally—"I'll always be there for you." One person who conveyed the message of absolutely "being there" was Elizabeth, the Queen Mother of England. Martha Dunagin Saunders tells the queen's story, which took place during the Blitz on London in 1940. When the queen was asked whether she intended to send her children, Elizabeth and Margaret Rose, from England for their own safety, she responded, "The children will not leave unless I do. I shall not leave unless their father does, and the king will not leave the country in any circumstances whatever."[112] To her country, Queen Elizabeth's message was clear: "I'll be there."

In another moving instance, Mother Teresa describes a father's absolute love for a child adopted by the sisters in the Children's Home, the Shishu Bhavan, in Calcutta. Mother Teresa recalls, "One of the abandoned children we had in our Shishu Bhavan I gave to a very high-class and rich family. After a few months I heard that the child had become very sick and completely disabled. So I went to that family and said, 'Give me back the child and I will give you a healthy child.'

"The father looked at me and said, 'Take my life first, then take the child.' He loved the child from his heart."[113]

This father's absolute love is consistent with that of Rabindranath Tagore, who speaks of his own child. Reflects Tagore, "I do not love him because he is good, but because he is my little child."[114]

In yet another instance, Christopher Reeve—famous for his movie role as Superman—was the recipient of absolute love when his wife, Dana, was "there" for him. After a 1995 riding accident left him paralyzed, at the critical moment he first became conscious, Christopher awoke to find Dana at his bedside. As she lovingly touched his head, Dana said softly, *"This* is who you are, not your body."[115]

Still another instance of absolute love—this related by Ivan Turgenev—involves that of a sparrow. Turgenev tells of returning from hunting, walking along the avenue of the garden, with his dog Tresor running ahead. Suddenly Tresor, taking shorter steps, began to steal along as though tracking game.

Looking along the avenue, Turgenev saw a young sparrow— yellow about its beak and down its head—on the ground. With a wind that day violently shaking the birch trees, the bird had fallen out of the nest. Helplessly flapping its half-grown wings and unable to move, the sparrow was proving vulnerable to any predator.

As Tresor approached, Turgenev relates, a startling event occurred: "Suddenly darting down from a tree close by, an old dark-throated sparrow fell like a stone right before his nose, and all ruffled up, terrified, with despairing and pitiful cheeps, it flung itself twice toward the open jaws of shining teeth."

Amazingly, notes Turgenev, the sparrow "sprang to save; it cast itself before its nestling. . . . All its tiny body was shaking with terror; its note was harsh and strange. Swooning with fear, it offered itself up!

"What a huge monster must the dog have seemed to it! and

yet it could not stay on its high branch out of danger. . . . A force stronger than its will flung it down.

"My dog Tresor stood still, drew back. . . . Clearly he too recognized this force." Hastening to call off the disconcerted dog, Turgenev felt some reverence as he went away.

"'Yes,' he says, 'do not laugh. I felt reverence for that tiny heroic bird, for its impulse of love.'

"Love, I thought, is stronger than death or the fear of death. Only by it, by love, life holds together and advances."[116]

Finally, absolute love also manifested its brilliance in the instance of Robert B. Powers. As a child, and in a strange city, Powers once became extremely worried his father might abandon him. Relating this fear to his father, his father responded, "That's impossible because of love. I couldn't leave you, Rob, if I wanted to. Love is stronger than the trace chains on a twenty-mule-team wagon."

Of the exalted and absolute love of an omnipresent Father in Heaven, Powers adds, "Man today is like the child of fifty years ago. He is terrified that God may abandon him. But if mere man's love is as strong as steel trace chains, then God's love is unbreakable. So man—and mankind—are safe!"[117]

♥ ♥ ♥ ♥ ♥ ♥ ♥ ♥ ♥

LOVE BINDS FRIENDS

In a small chapel at Northwestern University is a statue of two hands raised in prayer. The story that inspired the statue goes back to the year 1490.

Though the statue is simple, it represents the friendship between two young apprentices in France who had often confided in each other their desire to study painting. But each of the friends, Hans and Albrecht, were too poor, and such study would take money. Finally, however, the pair settled on a solution. One of the boys would work and earn money while the other studied. Then, when the lucky one became rich and famous, in turn he would aid the other in his studies. They tossed a coin and Albrecht won the chance to study first.

So, while Albrecht went to Venice, Hans worked as a blacksmith. As quickly as he received his wages, Hans forwarded them to his friend. The months stretched into years, and at last Albrecht returned to his native land, an independent master. Now it was his turn to help.

The two men met in joyous reunion, but when Albrecht looked at his friend's hands, tears welled up in his eyes. Only then did he discover the extent of Hans's sacrifice. Hans's gnarled fingers could never handle a painter's brush. And so it was, in humble gratitude, that the great artist, Albrecht Durer painted a portrait of the work-ridden hands that had labored so that he might develop his talent—a portrait he presented to his devoted friend.

That is why, as a symbol of friendship and sacrifice, the masterpiece was reproduced in the chapel at Northwestern University.[118]

Because of Hans's permanent sacrifice, Albrecht was privileged to become a master. He, in turn, in the deepest parts of his soul, understood his friend's sacrifice and felt a love for Hans beyond comprehension. The permanent bond of friendship between Hans and Albrecht is aptly depicted in Frances Farmer's observation: "To have a good friend is the purest of all God's gifts, for it is a love that has no exchange of payment. It is not inherited, as with a family. It is not compelling, as with a child. And it has no means of physical pleasure, as with a mate. It is, therefore, an indescribable bond that brings with it a far deeper devotion than all the others."[119]

To illustrate the surprising conditions under which friendships may develop, Marguerite Yourcenar refers to a passage in a book that tells of a small girl who had not yet given her cat a name. Surprised at this, someone asked, "But how do you call him?" To this question, the girl replied, "I don't call him. He comes when he wants."

Says Yourcenar of this passage, "So, too, do friends often come to us through the most improbable of chances."[120]

It was through the most improbable of chances that two of America's greatest writers became friends. James Barrie, a young student hurrying along the streets of Edinburgh toward the University, bumped into a tall, slight person. Recovering his balance, the stranger—Robert Louis Stevenson—turned toward Barrie, protesting, "After all, God made me."

"Maybe, but He is growing rather careless," responded Barrie, relieved he hadn't been whacked by the stranger's cane.

At this, Stevenson, with irresistible charm, asked, "Do I know you?"

"No," answered Barrie, "but I wish you did."

"Let's pretend I do," said Stevenson, suggesting that the two head for the nearest tavern. Talking for hours, they began what was to become a lifelong friendship.[121]

Speaking of types of friendship, Jane Howard writes that we may have "friends of the road, ascribed by chance, or friends of the heart, achieved by choice. Friends of the road are those we happen to go to school with, work with, or live near. They know where we went last weekend and whether we still have a cold. Just being around gives them provisional importance in our lives, and us in theirs."

By contrast, "a friend of the heart is one who perceives me as one of the better versions of myself," informs Howard. "We make good music, this friend and I, and we make good silences, too.

As for politeness, we don't confuse it with generosity. . . . At times we argue. . . . We travel together. . . . When cash and time are short, a trip across town will do. Anywhere, just so we can gather, hone and compare our reactions. And, coming and going, we absorb each other's histories."[122]

Particularly with friends of the heart, people can reveal their innermost core at no personal expense or risk. Miraculous energy flows between two people who risk enough to get below the surface, to become totally open with each other, and to respond with a whole heart. When trust is complete, friends often feel as if they have found, in the words of Isabel Norton, "a second self."[123]

Such close friends are also intuitive. "The best friends are those who know how to keep the same silences," reflects Fulton J. Sheen.[124] Elaborating, Henry J. Nouwen notes, "The friend who can be silent with us in a moment of despair or confusion, who can stay with us in an hour of grief and bereavement, who can tolerate not knowing, not curing, not healing, and face us with the reality of our powerlessness, that is the friend who cares."[125]

Of the total confidence that two people may share in each other, Ralph Waldo Emerson also adds, "The glory of friendship is not the outstretched hand, nor the kindly smile nor the joy of companionship; it is the spiritual inspiration that comes to one when he discovers that someone else believes in him and is willing to trust him."[126] Friends of this nature, according to Ed Cunningham, are also "those rare people who ask how we are and then wait to hear the answer."[127]

For numerous reasons, friendships are sacred and miraculous, enabling us to relate soulfully to others. We all need at least one trusted friend, and our lives are enriched when we have many. Friendships provide essential support, offering us a haven in a storm and a place of light and joy when rainbows appear. They also are mainstays in our lives, offering us the security of knowing we are loved and needed—both essentials to our soul.

Of the vital impact of friends, Merle Shain reflects, "The people in one's life are like the pillars on one's porch. . . . Sometimes they hold you up [and] . . . sometimes they lean on you, and sometimes it is just enough to know they're standing by."[128]

❤ ❤ ❤ ❤ ❤ ❤ ❤ ❤

LOVE IS HOMEMADE

"Even if I dropped one hundred balls and missed every block, my family and friends back home would say, 'Good game,'" reflects Joe Senser, Minnesota Vikings football player.[129]

Aside from the abiding support of good friends, Senser speaks of the deep and inherent affirmation one craves coming from one's roots—the family. Reinforcing the importance of such roots is Margaret Mead, who observes, "One of the oldest of human needs is having someone to wonder where you are when you don't come home at night."[130] And, adds Joyce Brothers, "When you look at your life, the greatest happinesses are family happinesses."[131] Such is the nature and function of one's family.

"A man's family sets him apart from all other living creatures," reflects Robert Nathan. "Who else has children he can call his own for longer than it takes to set them on their feet or on their way? The most loving animals, the vixen, the bear, the lioness, teach their cubs to make their own world, and to forget them; after the eagle has taught her eaglet to fly, she will see him no more. . . . Calf, colt, grasshopper, dragonfly, all go their separate ways as soon as they can; only man stands with his children from first to last, from birth to death, and to the grave."[132]

Nathan speaks of the profound meaning of family to those members who constitute it. His observations are particularly pertinent in a disposable era in which so many things are "throwaway" and we cannot unequivocally count on the support of surrounding people and organizations.

Among the vital functions of the family is that of providing nurturing, as in the instance of a young boy whose even younger brother, in the dead of night, began slipping into the older boy's twin bed. When asked why he let his brother share his little bed, the older boy explained that when his younger brother slept in his own bed, he had nightmares. When he slept with his older brother, he had cartoons.

Another of a family's functions is that of providing safety and security to its members. Sharon Whitley knows just what this means. A news reporter, Whitley tells of a time when, just out of college and living on her own, she began to teach special education in a town several hundred miles from home. Her father, who had always attentively listened anytime Whitley needed him, was especially concerned about her safety away from home. "Not to worry," Whitley confidently told her father during a weekend visit. She would be fine.

It was several evenings later that Whitley worked late in her classroom and realized, upon exiting the school, that the grounds were dark and deserted. Not only that, all the school gates were locked. After some searching, Whitley found just enough room to squeeze under a gate at the rear of the school. Pushing her purse through first and lying on her back, she laboriously edged through the escape route.

Uneasy at her circumstances, Whitley walked hastily toward her car in the parking lot. Suddenly she heard voices and, turning around, she saw a large group of teenage boys approaching from perhaps a half a block away. Immediately recognizing that the boys were wearing gang insignia, Whitley picked up her pace; so did the boys. They had begun taunting her, and it was evident they meant her harm.

As she ran across the grass, Whitley frantically searched her purse for her key ring, but it was nowhere to be found. Suddenly, as she neared her car, her fingers wrapped around a loose key in her purse. Clutching the key, she tried it on the car door and, miraculously, the door opened. Sliding onto the seat, she locked the door just before the boys surrounded the car. Just as they began kicking the car's sides and banging on the roof, she drove away to safety.

The next morning, assisted by school staff, Whitley located her key ring at the spot she had squeezed through the school gate. Where, then, had the loose key come from? Whitley could not solve the puzzle. When she arrived back at her apartment, the phone was ringing—it was her father. Preoccupied with her ordeal, it was a moment or two before Whitley attuned to what he was saying. He had forgotten to tell her he had had an extra car key made and had slipped it into her purse—just in case she ever needed it![133]

In Whitley's case, her father provided nurturing and safety at a personal level. Within a larger scope, families also provide such elements. Speaking to this point is Kendall Hailey, who observes, "The great gift of family life is to be intimately acquainted with people you might never even introduce yourself to, had life not done it for you."[134]

And, adds William Raspberry, "One of the remarkable if seldom remarked benefits of marriage is that it makes kinsmen out of strangers. It unites kingdoms, settles wars, links cultures [and forges bonds that otherwise] are all but impossible."

He continues, "When I think of the diverse individuals who have become special to me because they married a relative of

mine, our educational and cultural differences shrink to insignificance. They have a call on my resources, and I on theirs, not
because of any special deservedness, but because they are family."[135]

Speaking of yet another indispensable family role—that of
providing shelter and transition for generation upon generation—is Jane W. Lund. On an excursion, Lund tells of passing a
fallen tree, "a giant of the forest," in obvious decay. Many years
later, when she, with her grandchildren, once again visited that
memorable niche, the area where the tree had fallen was over-
grown with new life.

Parting the thick undergrowth in search of the massive
stump, Lund "expected that it, too, had decomposed and
returned to the earth." But, she notes, "to my surprise, it was still
there, its tenacious roots still clinging to the same earth they had
first invaded. Inside its circular structure, much of the wood had
rotted away; but, from its center, a young pine grew . . . nourished and protected by the roots of another generation!"

Continues Lund, "I contemplated the profound, wordless
message. I remembered my nurturant others . . . those who had
lent me their roots . . . who had protected and nourished me
until I became strong.

"I looked at my grandchildren, dwarfed in the splendor of
that mountain retreat, and felt a renewed commitment to be
there . . . to steady . . . to enlarge and nourish each of them.

"'Look,' I said, 'see that little tree growing from the center of
the old stump?'

"'Is that old stump its father?' one of them asked.

"I could not say," finishes Lund, "but whatever else it may
have been . . . , it surely was an 'evidence of hope.'"[136]

In this life—for good or for bad—family is foremost in
meaning to us. As Anthony Brandt has observed, "Other things

may change us, but we start and end with family."[137] And we are imprinted forever by our childhood experiences, as in the instance of singer Linda Ronstadt, who recalls that songs in her childhood were part of her family's everyday activities. "You sang when your hands were in the dishwater," she relates. "You sang while bringing in the firewood. You sang sometimes spontaneously at the dinner table. It never occurred to me that other families didn't do this."[138]

A repository of positive memories, in fact, is the choicest treasure a family can extend to its members. Reflects Og Mandino: "The greatest legacy we can leave our children is happy memories: those precious moments so much like pebbles on the beach that are plucked from the white sand and placed in tiny boxes that lie undisturbed on tall shelves until one day they spill out and time repeats itself, with joy and sweet sadness, in the child now an adult. . . . Memories. Love's best preservative."[139]

Sometimes the absolute meaning of family does not have full impact on family members until one member is in jeopardy or is dead, as in the case of a husband who, watching helplessly as his wife and son died in a freak accident, could only choke out the words: "They're gone. I wish I had spent more time with them." Likewise, another person—the wife of a deceased police officer—speaks of the tenuousness of life and the swiftness with which a loved one can be lost. "One day you're talking happily at the dinner table," she says. "The next, you're picking out a gravestone."

Reminiscences of Jimmy Stewart—whose son Ronald was killed in action at Da Nang in 1970—also enhance understanding of the emptiness one feels in losing a family member. Stewart, himself a former World War II bomber pilot decorated for valor, reflects, "We lost our oldest boy in Vietnam. . . . I was in on the Vietnam memorial from the very start of it, and every time I go to Washington I go there. There are fifty-eight thousand names, but I can pick out my son's name almost with my eyes closed."[140]

Recognizing, from hindsight, the vital importance of the family is Harold Kushner, who emphasizes, "Sooner or later, we all learn that our immortality is rooted not in our professional involvements and achievements, but in our families. In time, all of our wins and losses in the workplace will be forgotten. If our memories endure, it will be because of the people we have known and touched."

He continues, "There is a verse in the Biblical Song of Solomon that reminds me of the mistakes of my younger days when I was away every evening, giving other people advice about their family problems. 'They set me as a keeper of the vineyards, but my own vineyard I did not keep.'"[141]

Finalizing thoughts on the family is Admiral Richard E. Byrd, who, in 1934, spent five solitary and thought-provoking months on an Antarctic expedition. In his isolation, with a blizzard raging and himself very ill, for weeks Byrd expected to die in his lonely outpost. Facing his own mortality, Byrd pondered life's meaning, comprehending now that the simple unpretentious things were most important. Much preoccupied in thoughts of those at home, in his diary he wrote of the family, reflecting, "In the end, only two things really matter to a man, . . . the affection and understanding of his family. . . . The family is an everlasting anchorage, a quiet harbor where a man's ships can be left to swing in the moorings of pride and loyalty."[142]

♥ ♥ ♥ ♥ ♥ ♥ ♥ ♥

LOVE EMBRACES ITSELF

"If an individual is able to love productively, he loves himself, too; if he can love *only* others, he cannot love at all," reflects

Erich Fromm.[143] Thus, fully loving oneself precedes being able to fully love others. Such loving, further, is a precondition for being able to extend goodness—as a way of life—to others, for as Anne Morrow Lindbergh observes, "If one is out of touch with oneself, then one cannot touch others."[144]

Fully loving ourselves entails foremost recognizing that we, as all other earthly beings, are invaluable simply because we are—a concept embodied in the Talmud, which teaches that "every man has the right to feel that 'because of me was the world created.'"[145]

Fully loving ourselves also entails recognizing that we, as ever-differentiating human beings, have a right, and a responsibility, to nurture ourselves and to perpetuate our growth. Distilling our own obligation to ourselves, Immanuel Kant writes, "The greatest human quest is to know what one must do in order to become a human being."

We are all in the endless quest of becoming—of creating, with our own chisel, our own masterpiece—that of ourselves, asserts Bernie Siegel. Biologically it is our destiny to be similar to every other human being in our basic physical composition; yet, our DNA—that blueprint, or set of instructions, with which we arrived on this earth—makes us as unique as our fingerprints.

"We're all given an assignment in life to discover the ways in which we're exceptional, and then to live a joyful life," Siegel continues. And from his unique perspective, he also observes, "God gave us all certain gifts, but it is up to us to decide how to use them in such a way that even the Being who gave them to us will look down one day in admiration and say, 'Hmmm, I never thought of that way before.'"[146]

And Bruce Barton adds, "If you have anything valuable to contribute to the world, it will come through the expression of your own personality—that single spark of divinity that sets you off and makes you different from any other living creature."[147]

Viewing ourselves as having a "single spark of divinity" implies the vital need to take care of ourselves—physically, emotionally, intellectually, and spiritually. It is to consider ourselves forever-growing human beings worthy of investing in our own well-being, for our own sakes. It is to remember that in our later years, we are or will be the reapers of any harvests we sow for ourselves; that however short we will eventually be on youth, we can be long on maturity; and that as long as we live, we can continue to make of ourselves all that we can.

When we view ourselves as "masters" chipping away each day at our own masterpieces, others—as well as ourselves—are beneficiaries, for we can give back amply to the world and to add to its goodness. "The most consummately beautiful thing in the universe is the rightly fashioned life of a good person," observes George Palmer.[148] And, adds Rufus M. Jones, "That kind of life is not an accident. It is a highly creative work of art. Plato, who opened up almost every major problem of life, always insisted that a person's life must, first of all, be a beautiful creation."[149]

Perhaps life's greatest challenge is to continually refine ourselves so finally at last we *do* know how to fully live. Speaking of the concerted effort involved in such refining, Harry Emerson Fosdick says, "No horse gets anywhere until he is harnessed. No stream or gas ever drives anything until it is confined. No Niagara is ever turned into light and power until it is channeled. No life ever grows great until it is focused, dedicated, disciplined."[150]

As human beings, we are unique and unrepeatable events in the universe. Refining thus becomes a challenge of accepting ourselves as the treasures we are. We may not—in the world's eyes or our own—come into life supposedly as adorned as others. Nor must we. *To be ourselves, to fully develop our own attributes, and to give all that we might, is to stand unadorned—in and of ourselves—as perfect products of nature ever in the process of becoming.*

To this point, Frank Norris tells of buying a silver soup ladle. The wide selection ultimately included one "that was plain and unadorned as the unclouded sky—and about as beautiful. But the price!" It was nearly double the cost of the rest, Norris emphatically told the salesman. In turn, the salesman explained that in highly ornamental ware, flaws are not visible. Rather, defects are often touched up with wreaths and beading. Thus, the plain one must be superior because any defect would be immediately apparent.

"There, if you please," concludes Norris, "is a final basis of comparison of all things . . . the bare dignity of the unadorned that may stand before the world all unashamed . . . in the consciousness of perfection."[151]

Alan Loy McGinnis, a psychologist, also adds enlightenment to the process of self-acceptance so key to acknowledging and celebrating our own heavenly-endowed and invaluable worth. Says McGinnis: "Good psychotherapists are like astronomers who spend their lives studying the stars, trying to determine why certain stellar systems behave as they do and why black holes exist. At the end, they are in awe of the grandeur of it all."

He continues: "There is vast mystery and beauty surrounding the human soul. It would be [as] presumptuous of me to attempt to overhaul that system as for an astronomer to remake the solar system. If I can help patients understand who God made them to be and then help them to *be* those men and women, it is quite enough."[152]

We can infer from McGinnis's words, then, that refining involves challenging ourselves to discover and capitalize on our capabilities. "We don't know who we are until we see what we

can do," emphasizes Martha Grimes.[153] And, augments Clifton
Fadiman: "It is a great pleasure to do something you are good at.
It is a small but unarguable one to do something you are bad at.
Last summer I cleaned an outdoor catch basin, removing from it
the conglomerate evidence of a violent winter and spring. I did it
awkwardly, slowly, doubtless stupidly, but with a peculiar satisfaction, richer in certain ways than the satisfaction I get in
writing, . . . which is a job I know I can handle with passable
competence."[154]

Refining further consists of extracting amusement from our
own plights and predicaments and, in so doing, creating a silent
source of strength within ourselves. In this regard, Winston
Churchill makes a subtle but compelling observation: "We are all
worms, but I do believe that I am a glowworm."[155]

The late Israeli Prime Minister Golda Meir speaks of her own
quest to develop strengths. "I was never a beauty," she says.
"There was a time when I was sorry about that, when I was old
enough to understand the importance of it and, looking in any
mirror, realized it was something I was never going to have.
Then I found what I wanted to do in life and being called pretty
no longer had any importance.

Only later in life did Meir realize that *not* being beautiful was
an asset, one that definitely forced her to develop her inner
resources. She writes, "I came to understand that women who
cannot lean on their beauty and need to make something on
their own have the advantage. I cannot think of anything more
terrible than looking back at the end and feeling that you have
not written well in the Book of Life."[156]

Finally, refining entails simply persevering. Helen Hayes says
of her earlier years that a producer "told me that, were I four
inches taller, I could become one of the greatest actresses of my
time." So, says Hayes, "I decided to lick my size.

"A string of teachers pulled and stretched till I felt I was in a medieval torture chamber," she relates. "I gained nary an inch—but my posture became military. I became the tallest five-foot woman in the world. And my refusal to be limited by my limitations enabled me to play Mary of Scotland, one of the tallest queens in history."[157]

♥ ♥ ♥ ♥ ♥ ♥ ♥ ♥ ♥

LOVE INTERTWINES SOULS

Love exists when two souls reach each other through feelings, words, or touch. It is only at the soul level, in fact, that people experience the positive emotions that bind two persons together. Describing an experience with his three-year-old daughter that makes this point evident is Dennis Larsen. One night, as he was tucking his daughter into bed, Larsen had what he calls "an experience that gave me as great a joy as I will ever know."

After he had pulled the covers up and placed her doll snugly by her side, he kissed his daughter good night. He remembers starting to go, but the look in his daughter's eyes seemed to be saying, "Please stay." So, he says, "I remained quietly by her side. We began looking tenderly into each other's eyes. We looked at each other for quite a long time, neither of us moving, neither of us talking, just looking and saying with our eyes things only eyes can say. It was a Divine moment."

He continues, "Finally, I broke the silence and said, with all the Divinity of my soul: 'Jennifer, I love you.' The room filled with a Divine Essence and she began to cry. I softly asked her if she loved me. She raised her head and began to hug me tight. I could feel her tears against my cheek as she nodded 'yes.'

"Never in my life have I experienced a more beautiful

moment. Soul had touched soul in a spirit of Divine love, and neither of us will ever be the same again."[158]

In actuality, Larsen speaks of a spiritual communion between himelf and his daughter, bringing with it confirmation that, as beloved children of a beloved Father in Heaven, they were divinely bonded through something greater than themselves. Further, Larsen must have felt a stirring within himself affirming that he and his daughter were a part of a larger whole in which they had a divine role of immense, yet incomprehensible, proportions.

Speaking similarly of an incomprehensible exultation, Ardis Whitman describes flying at a high altitude and seeing a continent of shining clouds spread beneath her. Recalling the scene as being "haunted by a strange joy so penetrating that the place seemed not to be there," Whitman says this of her ethereal experience, "I thought of myself as living and walking in a land like this, and I, who am the more gregarious of humans, knew in a flash of deep illumination that there was in the universe a light, a stuff, a tissue, a substance in company with which one would never be lonely. The experience left the compelling certainty that we dwell safely in a universe far more personal, far more human, far more tender than we are."[159]

Both Larsen and Whitman figuratively encountered a sliver of eternity—a wondrous, inspiring moment in which they felt at one with the heart of the universe. Of such transcendent happenings, Whitman notes that they occur when people feel "transported to the very presence of God . . . [and] are made aware of a joy surpassing all else in life and an order that underlies this troubled world."[160]

Also emphasizing that we are one with the universe, J. Allen Boone observes, "We are members of a vast cosmic orchestra in which each living instrument is essential to the complementary and harmonious playing of the whole."[161] And Paul Davies adds, "We really do seem to play a fundamental role in the working of nature. So in some sense we're not just a trivial add-on into the universe, not like extras that have stumbled onto the great cosmic set just by accident. We're truly written into the script, we're truly meant to be here."[162]

Echoing these sentiments is Brian Swimm, who reflects, "Our own deep experiences, the realm of the psyche, the soul, the feelings of the human, this too is as much a part of the universe as the stars of the gravitational interaction. It is a primary illustration of the underlying order of the universe."[163]

In *The Quiet Voice of Soul*, Tian Dayton asserts that we can learn to see the workings of the soul in the wonders of day-to-day living. "Soul seems mysterious because we cannot see it," he remarks. "Often we seek knowledge and experience of the soul in the extraordinary. But I believe that soul is fundamentally *ordinary*, available to us all the time. . . . The soul is constant. It is we who waver from it."

Becoming better acquainted with our souls takes a simple shift in awareness. We don't have to search outside of ourselves to find soul—rather, we have only to remove the emotional, psychological, and intellectual barriers that block our soul's expression, Dayton emphasizes. And few situations in life are as conducive to soul making as committed relationships, for they force us to resolve issues that allow us to "continue our life process of finishing our unfinished selves."

Through loving others, we participate, with those others, in a joint process of soul discovery and stretching, and the more issues we resolve, individually and interactively, the deeper we are able to love, singularly and collectively.

As we truly love, we experience our mind, body, and soul—which are ever-present—as coming together as an integral whole. Such mind-body-soul integration takes place in the context of everyday life as we progressively learn the value and lessons of give and take; of discipline and sacrifice; and of loyalty and commitment.

Thus, in our quest to love more fully, we evolve to higher levels of maturity and soul development. And, observes Dayton, "When we learn to use everyday life as our personal journey toward self and soul, we grow gradually toward a higher state of consciousness and a more meaningful existence. . . . It was John Keates who said, 'Call the world, if you please, the vale of soulmaking.'"[164]

❤ ❤ ❤ ❤ ❤ ❤ ❤ ❤ ❤

LOVE GARNERS SOULMATES

In a 1919 love letter penned to her future husband, American novelist F. Scott Fitzgerald, Zelda Sayre wrote, "Scott—there's nothing in all the world I want but you—and your precious love—All the material things are nothing. . . . I'd do anything—anything—to keep your heart my own—I don't want to live—I want to love first, and live incidentally. . . . Don't you think I was made for you? I feel like you had me ordered—and I was delivered to you."[165]

Here, Zelda alludes to her conclusion that she and her husband are soulmates, customized for each other; and if she were alive for us to ask, she would probably say they were destined to be with each other forever.

Some intimate pairs who regard themselves as soulmates simply deem they were enough alike, and that they invested heavily enough in their relationship, to achieve a strong spiritual union. Conversely, other intimate pairs who believe they are soulmates also believe they had a spiritual commitment to each other in a premortal existence. In such instances, couples also believe they came to this earth in search of, and were divinely designated for, each other. A piece by Erin Larsen serves to illustrate such belief:

> Though they are caged
> Our souls have touched
> And when they parted
> They took a part of the other with them.
>
> Say no farewells
> We will always be together
> And do not fear as you go into battle
> I will go with you;
>
> Your sorrow
> Will be my sorrow
> Your pain will be my pain
> I will feel it with you.
>
> If you should fall
> And death claim your life
> I too will fall
> And death will visit me.
>
> Somewhere in the night sky
> Our souls will meet once again
> Together, they will dance
> Among the stars.[166]

Baal Shem Tov speaks of the spiritual entwining and connection of spiritual soulmates, reflecting, "For every human being there rises a light that reaches straight to heaven, and when two souls that are destined to be together find each other, the streams of light flow together and a single brighter light goes forth from that united being."[167]

Baal Shem Tov speaks of a union of souls that is transcendent, superseding this earthly experience, and of a divine union that is so pure and filled with light that two souls become one. Whether he uses "union" in this sense to describe becoming one in form or one in spirit, we cannot infer. But we can infer he is speaking about a love between two souls having fathomless depth.

Regardless, the incomprehensible "oneness" of the deeply soulful relationship is a union that we must honor and respect, for we will never know all the complexities, dimensions, and inner landscape of such divine relationships, the soul moments of which give us glimpses of the flash points of eternity.

Such soul relationships have myriad characteristics, including the following:

• a reverence for the gift of the relationship.

• a depth of feeling that is mutual.

• a propensity to perceive and articulate the highest and finest in each other.

• an unwavering commitment to each other's growth.

• a sharing of a rich inner life with each other.

• a commitment to self-discovery.

• an alikeness in sensitivity, in appreciation of beauty, and in acceptance of differences in the other.

• a drawing together, through love and mutual assistance, to bring about necessary relationship changes.

• an exhibiting of persistence as well as strength of will and fortitude in the face of adversity.

• a faith in the goodness that abounds in the world and the wish to perpetuate it together.

• a presence of spiritual emotions that cannot be expressed through ordinary words.

• a growing consciousness of each other's souls and a likewise expanding sense of closeness to God.

• a growing consciousness of the divinely approved and ordained role of one's paired spiritual existence in the hereafter.

For most of us, a vital question is how we can reach for, or achieve, such a transcendent spiritual state with another, particularly if our relationship has been beset with conflict or problems. Although there are no specific answers, in his book *Soulmates,* Thomas Moore provides general insights. Such insights lend hope that two souls can inch closer and closer toward a oneness in spirit and eloquence.

Creating a soulful relationship, says Moore, "offers two difficult challenges: one, to come to know oneself . . . and two, to get to know the deep, often subtle richness in the soul of the other. Giving attention to one side usually helps the other. As you get to know the other deeply, you will discover much about yourself . . . and you can be more accepting and understanding of the other's depth of soul."

For a relationship to enter the realm of soul, a foremost challenge is to view that relationship as having at its core two people whose souls are in the process of unfolding and weaving together a tapestry of many different strands of themselves. When we marry, in addition to linking our lives to another individual, we are also offering to each other "the opportunity to enter, explore, and fulfill essential notions of who we are and who we can be. In this sense marriage is not fundamentally a relationship between two persons, but rather an entry into destiny, an opening to the potential life that lies hidden from view until evoked by particular thoughts and feelings of marriage."

Further, we discover in marriage that a coupleship is not designed to offer unadulterated happiness; rather, it is another of life's initiations, and in its fullness, marriage is a soul institution. "At one level marriage is about relationship, but at another it is the creation of a vessel in which soul-making can be accomplished," observes Moore. While marriage may look like an arrangement of persons, in actuality—at its deepest level—marriage is "a profound stirring of souls. Like all initiations, it marks a fundamental shift in perceptions of oneself and one's world."

To care for the soul, and thus the soul of the marriage, couples must use means in a marriage that match the soul's sacred dimensions, laying at the foundation of the relationship genuine spirituality as a bedrock ingredient in their love. Referring to Jung's concept of the "sacred marriage"—which Jung defined as a union at a far deeper or higher level than personalities and lives—Moore reflects that such a union remains sacred "not only because it is a precious and revered way of forming human lives, but also because it is a . . . special way in which spirituality pours into life."[168]

❤ ❤ ❤ ❤ ❤ ❤ ❤ ❤ ❤

LOVE GROWS WITH ADVERSITY

"Love can achieve unexpected majesty in the rocky soil of misfortune," reflects Tony Snow.[169] And thus it was with Russian dissidents Natan Sharansky and his wife, Avital, who were separated in 1974, the day after their wedding. Having been granted an exit visa that expired that day, Avital immigrated to Israel, this event coinciding with authorities denying Natan permission to leave Russia. These key events were to mark the beginning of Natan's grueling, public battle with Soviet authorities to allow him to join Avital in the West.

In his book *Fear No Evil*, Natan speaks of his long-awaited reunion in 1986 with Avital in a Frankfurt airport, where they were left alone in a room for ten minutes and, in awe, could only sit and gaze at each other. On the day the couple were separated, Natan's last words to Avital were, "I'll follow you soon." Nearly thirteen years later, with simple eloquence, Natan would say to Avital, "Sorry I'm late."[170]

Love also achieved "unexpected majesty" in the case of Victor Frankl. In his classic, *Man's Search For Happiness*, Frankl recalls that it was during a forced march from a concentration camp to a faraway work site that he, then a Nazi prisoner of war, learned a depthless lesson of life relating to love and soul.

During this march, Frankl, along with his fellow prisoners, stumbled for miles in the darkness and icy wind, over big stones and through large puddles, along the one road leading from camp. They were goaded by accompanying guards, who shouted at the prisoners and drove them with the butts of their rifles. Slipping on icy spots, Frankl and the other prisoners supported each other time and time again, dragging one another up and onward. No one spoke, but Frankl's mind was preoccupied.

"My mind clung to my wife's image, imagining it with an uncanny acuteness," he remembers. "I heard her answering me, saw her smile, her frank and encouraging look. Real or not, her look was then more luminous than the sun which was beginning to rise.

"A thought transfixed me," he writes. "For the first time in my life I saw the truth as it is set into the song by so many poets, proclaimed as the ultimate wisdom by so many thinkers. The truth—that love is the ultimate and the highest goal to which man can aspire. Then I grasped the meaning of the greatest secret that human poetry and human thought and belief have to impart: *The salvation of man is through love and in love.* I understood how a man who has nothing left in this world still may know bliss, be it only for a brief moment, in the contemplation of his beloved.

"In front of me a man stumbled and those following him fell on top of him," Frankl continues. "The guard rushed over and used his whip on them all. Thus my thoughts were interrupted for a few minutes. But soon my soul found its way back from the prisoner's existence to another world, and I resumed talk with my loved one: I asked her questions, and she answered; she questioned me in return, and I answered."

Throughout his terrible adversity, while enduring the inhumane treatment of the guards, Frankl continued to cling to the image of his wife. "A thought crossed my mind," he recounts. "I didn't even know if she were still alive. I knew only one thing—which I have learned well by now: Love goes very far beyond the physical person of the beloved. It finds its deepest meaning in his spiritual being, his inner self. Whether or not he is actually present, whether or not he is still alive at all, ceases somehow to be of importance. . . . There was no need for me to know [whether my wife was alive]; nothing could touch the strength of my love, my thoughts, and the image of my beloved."[171]

Within his experiencing, Frankl's mind was seared with a profound lesson—that in loving another from the deepest reaches of the soul, one can absent momentarily from the ravages of even the most horrific of experiences. For Frankl, life's existence funneled down to its most meaningful and most precious commodity, deeply loving and being deeply loved by another. Death itself was not to fear; it was no issue. The spiritual experience of loving transcended life itself.

Only rarely may we find ourselves in circumstances similar to Frankl's in which, literally facing our own deaths, we contemplate the precious value of a relationship. For that reason, the quiet voice of the soulful relationship—subordinate to the intense daily stresses—often remains unnoticed and unheard. Yet this soulful realm is where we find the true meaning, not only of our relationships, but of our lives.

Also in the context of terrible adversity was another couple's love born. It was 1949 when Paul Ignotus, a one-time Hungarian Press attaché to Britain, returned to Budapest to see his ailing father, only to be promptly arrested by the AVO security police. Thereafter, Ignotus spent the next seven years in Communist prisons, the first eighteen months of which he was repeatedly tortured. Subsequently, he was forced in a secret trial to "confess" he had willingly assisted "Western imperialists and capitalists."

About the same time Ignotus was facing his secret court, Florence Hatay—a young adult and daughter of an English mother—left her office to visit a hairdresser. Arrested by the AVO "while [her] hair was still dripping wet" and accused of being a spy, Hatay spent months in a prison dormitory. In this terribly confined space, "thirty-nine women slept in fourteen bunks . . . [breathing] air that came through a tiny window blocked by an iron plate. The stench was terrible. For fourteen months not a drop of hot water to wash with."

In 1953, with a change in the country's presidency, conditions improved; and the following year Florence was moved to a special section of the prison and given a bed of her own. Says she, "Compared to what I had been through, it was paradise."

When, in her cell, Florence heard a tap-tap-tap, muffled, irregular, but methodical, she realized that someone was sending a message. Having read Arthur Koestler's *Darkness at Noon*, Florence remembered the alphabet in Koestler's book: one tap for A, two for B, and the like, with taps combined in various systematic intervals to allow word formation. Listening for a long time, however, she could make no sense out of what she heard— until she realized the language was English. Joining in the conversation, she discovered that the man in the cell below hers was an old friend of her father's. In the cell next to his was Paul Ignotus, with whom Florence began a relationship.

The conversations relayed between Paul and Florence were slow and ceased altogether when guards were near. When Florence discovered Ignotus could hear her footsteps, the couple adopted a new system of slow and heavy pacing. Throughout the next year, in arduous and painstaking conversations, the pacing pair carried out one of history's most remarkable courtships. Says Florence, "I never walked so much in my life."

The couple explored their favorite authors, their health, their childhood, and then, trudging back and forth to convey meaning, they discussed marriage, a honeymoon, children.

One morning in the spring of 1955, Florence received no answer from Paul, and later that year—for no given reason—she was released from prison. Months afterward she received a covert message: Paul "had been taken to another prison and had no hope of freedom. But then, as he had reached 'the limit of human endurance,' the incredible happened. Russia's Bulganin and Khrushchev, planning to visit Britain and not wishing to be embarrassed by British labor leaders' demands for the release of a long list of jailed Social Democrats, ordered Ignotus, among others, set free."

It was then that Paul and Florence met for the first time— "she, at thirty-two, still somewhat recovering from her prison experience; he, at fifty-six . . . hollow-cheeked and scraggy-necked, with bowed shoulders, but with a jutting chin and a strong, level gaze." A few weeks later—their love forged and made complete through their shared adversity—the couple married.

As a member of a group that helped spark the Hungarian revolution, thereafter Paul Ignotus fought for Hungary's freedom. But when the Soviet army tanks moved in, and then the Russians kidnapped the Premier, Ignotus knew no hope was left. Subsequently, "Paul and Florence walked all night through the marshy swamps and minefields to freedom across the Austrian border."[172]

❤　❤　❤　❤　❤　❤　❤　❤

LOVE ENFOLDS BROTHERS

"I think it is humanity's function to cherish all its people as dearly as loyal members of a nuclear family cherish one another," Neil Millar writes.[173] Within this context, which Millar terms "the wide embrace," if we love, we have a choice—to love only those to whom we are the closest or to love all others simply because they *are,* and simply because they are—as human beings—*of our own kind.* We can also extend that choice to all God's creatures. As an unknown author observes, "I have found . . . that those who love a deer, a dog, a bird, and flowers . . . are usually thoughtful of the larger needs that may be ours. . . . Who for God's creatures will plan . . . will seldom wrong his fellow man."[174]

Love—that essence which gives us worth and our lives meaning—*is* readily attainable. Usually, simply loving another person is enough for that love to return to us. Thus, our challenge is to offer love rather than wait for love to be bestowed. To wait may be to wait forever, for others' choices are beyond our control. But to love is a choice we may make momentarily. We have but to bestow love—or to reach for it—for love, reflects Mother Teresa, "is a fruit in season at all times, and within the reach of every hand."[175]

To extend love to another is to experience incomprehensible growth as a human being, emphasizes Daphne Rose Kingma: "In choosing to love . . . those whose names, faces and true circumstances you will never really know, you will be moved palpably, inescapably, into understanding that loving and being loved is one true human vocation."

Your perception of yourself will also improve. "You will see yourself as an offering, generous, bountiful soul, as well as a needing human being," Kingma further observes. "You will feel connected, centered, received—deeply bonded to the human stream. In giving love, you yourself will understand that we are held in the web of life—and delivered to our divine humanity—by . . . the love . . . that we give and receive."[176]

Erich Fromm defines love as an attitude determining a person's relationship to the world in general, not just toward one person: If you truly love one person you love all persons, you love the world, you love life; and in this context, you are experiencing brotherly love, which underlies all other types of love.[177]

As human beings, we may extend to others consummate brotherly love—a love that manifests goodwill toward all men and seeks nothing in return. Such redemptive love "is the love of God operating in the human heart," wrote Martin Luther King. "You love all men not because you like them, not because their ways appeal to you, but you love them because God loves them."[178]

Pure brotherly love is the universal spiritual bonding glue of mankind, one person to another. There is no other bonding material. Relates Pierre Teilhard de Chardin, "Love alone is capable of uniting living beings . . . to complete and fulfill them, for it alone takes them and joins them by what is deepest in themselves."[179]

The choice to extend brotherly love is portrayed in *The Hiding Place*—a book describing the extraordinary World War II experiences of Corrie and Betsie ten Boom, two Dutch sisters interned in a concentration camp because they had aided Jews. Early on, as the Gestapo hunt for Jews became more fervent, the hiding places more scarce, and the danger more eminent, ten Boom's father, a watchmaker, was an eminent model of such love:

One night, at the ten Boom home, a young hospital intern surreptitiously knocked at the door. To Betsie and Corrie, who both answered the knock, came the intern's desperate plea: "Would you take a Jewish mother and her baby into your home?" Glancing behind the intern, the sisters saw a terrified young mother, anxiously cradling a bundle. Instantaneously, Betsie reached for the baby and the intern hastily left. Knowing the baby needed safe harbor where its cries would not endanger others, Corries and Betsie agonized over a solution.

The next morning, a clergyman from a small nearby town—with a house set back from the street in a wooded park—stopped by the ten Boom shop searching for a scarce part for his watch. Realizing the location's potential, Corrie approached the clergyman regarding hiding the mother and baby. "They will most certainly be arrested otherwise," she pleaded.

Relates Corrie, "Color drained from the man's face. He took a step back from me. 'Miss ten Boom! I do hope you're not involved in any of this illegal concealment. . . . It's just not safe! Think of your father! And your sister. She's never been strong.'"

Bringing the baby to the clergyman, Corrie writes, "I pulled the coverlet back from the baby's face. The man bent forward, his hand in spite of himself reaching for the tiny fist curled round the blanket. For a moment I saw compassion and fear struggle in his face. Then he straightened. 'No. Definitely not. We could lose our lives for that Jewish child!'

"Unseen by either of us, Father had appeared in the doorway. 'Give the child to me, Corrie,' he said.

"Father held the baby close, his white beard brushing its cheek, looking into the little face with eyes as blue and innocent as the baby's. . . . 'You say we could lose our lives for this child. I would consider that the greatest honor that could come to my family.'"

In a later instance, both sisters stood naked, "watching a concentration camp matron beating a prisoner. 'Oh, the poor woman,' Corrie cried. 'Yes, may God forgive her,' Betsie replied. And . . . Corrie realized that it was for the souls of the brutal Nazi guards that her sister prayed." Of their travel by train to the concentration camp, Corrie writes, "As usual, Betsie had given to others everything she had. The Bible that Nollie had smuggled to her she had torn up and passed around, book by book."

Quietly, it seemed, as Betsie continued to unconditionally love, another elusive love—His love—seemed to hover over the sisters. In the camp, for example, although extremely ill herself, Betsie insisted on sharing her small bottle of liquid vitamins with others. Strangely, the bottle continued "to produce drops," recalls Corrie. "It scarcely seemed possible, so small a bottle, so many doses a day." In administering to the growing number of sick women, each time she "tilted the little bottle, a drop appeared at the tip of the glass stopper."

Viewing His strength as sustaining them through times of profound horror, a dying Betsie—ever concerned about others— told Corrie we "must tell people what we have learned here. We must tell them that there is no pit so deep that He is not deeper still."

Staring at her sister's wasted form, Corrie exclaimed, "But when will all this happen, Betsie!"

"Now. Right away. Oh, very soon! By the first of the year, Corrie, we will be out of prison!"

Betsie's prophecy came true. Betsie, dying soon after, was thereby released. Corrie, in viewing Betsie shortly after her death, remembers that "the care lines, the grief lines, the deep hollows of hunger and disease were simply gone. . . . Happy and at peace. Stronger! Freer! This was the Betsie of heaven, bursting with joy and health. Even her hair was graciously in place as if an angel had ministered to her."

By the first of the year, Corrie was also released, only later to learn that her "release had been the result of a clerical 'error,' one week later all women her age were taken to the gas chambers."[180]

♥ ♥ ♥ ♥ ♥ ♥ ♥ ♥ ♥

LOVE SURPASSES THE GRAVE

Love can surpass the grave in both directions—through simple remembrances of the living for the dead or through spiritual influence of the dead upon the living. It was an incident of love demonstrated through the living that tugged at the heartstrings of a woman who, many years ago, was waiting for a train in a small town. Wandering into a florist's shop, she noticed a ragged little boy—the shop's only customer—who, with great care, was selecting six beautiful red roses.

Leaning down, the salesperson asked the boy what name he wanted on the card and to whom the roses should be delivered. Answering, the boy indicated he would take the roses with him but asked the clerk to write on the card, "Happy Birthday, Mother."

As the boy left the shop, the clerk and the observing woman exchanged glances, each noticing that the other was overtly touched by the boy's actions. A short while later, as the woman looked out the train window while the train pulled slowly away from the station, she saw the same small boy—still carrying his bouquet of roses—going through the gate of a small country cemetery.[181]

Love also ultimately surpassed the grave when Jack Benny, in preparation for his death, took prior action to comfort Mary, his wife of forty-eight years. In December 1974, on the day after Benny's death, Mary received a single long-stemmed red rose. Day after day, a similar flower continued to arrive.

Finally, a puzzled Mary called the florist for an explanation.

Some time before her husband died, she was informed, Benny had stopped at the florist's shop to send Mary a bouquet of roses. As he was leaving the shop, he suddenly turned back to request that the florist—upon his death—send his wife a single rose every day. As Mary was to later learn, her husband had actually included a provision in his will specifying she was to receive one elegant red rose each day for the remainder of her life.[182]

In facing his own mortality, Benny wanted Mary—if she survived his death—to know of his consummate love for her. Although he gave Mary the gift of a daily rose, Benny's greater gift to her was the reminder of his ever-abiding love, the rose perpetuating that remembrance each day. In offering such a gift to Mary, in essence, Benny communicated his love beyond the grave.

In another instance, love spoke from the grave in the form of an inexplicable event occurring after the death of Marjorie Holmes's mother. Experiencing an extended illness, and sensing she might not live much longer, Holmes's mother had devoted herself to putting her affairs in order. Among her preparations, she had left handwritten instructions in a small Bible, where her children knew they were.

But, despite her preparations, Holmes's mother could not accomplish in her lifetime one vastly important thing to her— the healing of wounds existing between two grown children who, for years, had been in constant conflict. Despite, even, her prayers and tears, no progress had been made. And now, after her death, as her children worked together to dispose of and to distribute her belongings, tensions mounted and tempers flared. Even in death's face, hostilities refused to vanish.

It was the second night when the children saw their mother's Bible on a table by the bookcase—not the little Bible she often used, but a heavy old family Bible, stuffed full of family records, that had long been relegated to the top shelf of that same book-case. The children were stunned. None of them recalled having placed the Bible on the table, and they could think of no logical explanation for the Bible's sudden appearance in a place that had several times been cleared and dusted.

As the siblings realized the significance of the Bible's presence, they all sat down together. One sister opened the Bible to its marker and began to read aloud from the thirteenth chapter of John. Of the several scriptures read, none was more piercing to all than the scripture "A new commandment I give unto you, That ye love one another; as I have loved you, that ye also love one another" (John 13:34).

Tears welling in her eyes and her voice choked with emotion, the sister who was reading could go no further. Says Holmes of subsequent events, "The two who had been so tragically separated groped out for each other's hands. Then they embraced, holding one to the other as if never to let go.

"The peace they made that night was to last. The bridge of death had become the bridge of love."[183]

Final powerful instances of love surpassing the grave spring from the solemn activities surrounding the Vietnam Veterans Memorial in Washington, D.C. In a *U.S. News & World Report* article entitled "A Sacred Place on the Potomac," Stewart Powell speaks of this galvanizing and moving memorial: "'The Wall,'" he observes, "has become more than just an astonishing powerful remembrance of the 58,132 who fell in a bitterly divisive war. Indeed, many of the fifteen million people who have descended the gently sloping path along the V-shaped granite Wall have come not merely as visitors but as pilgrims."[184]

In a companion piece, "The Wall That Heals," William Broyles Jr. writes of repeatedly visiting the wall since its 1982 dedication. Broyles, a former Marine who served as an infantry lieutenant in Vietnam, observes he was never alone. "At all hours of the day and night, in snow, rain and fog," no matter how atypical the conditions, he always encountered other visitors.

"And that is how it should be," Broyles accentuates, "for this monument to the dead exerts a magic power on the living. Those who come to the Wall become part of it. They touch it, rub it, sing to it, pray against it, stare at it—and they talk to it. The Wall is like a character in a play whose silence makes all the other characters speak.

"There are as many reasons to come to the Wall as there are visitors," he continues. "Some come to remember, some to mourn, some come to bear witness, some simply to feel the emotion of the place. Others come to give gifts and messages to the dead . . . military medals, flowers, candles, stuffed animals, toys, combat boots, needlepoint, jiggers of whiskey, records, C rations, statues of saints, rosaries, . . . unit patches and insignia, dog tags, American flags. . . . There are photographs of loved ones, children grown to adults while the dead slept, photos of the dead themselves—in a new military uniform or smiling with their buddies, frozen innocently in time, ignorant of fate.

"And there are messages—letters, poems, essays, notes, as if the dead could read: 'Dear Michael: Your name is here but you are not. I made a rubbing of it, thinking that if I rubbed hard enough I would rub your name off the Wall and you would come back to me. I miss you so.'

"And: 'My dear friends, it is good to touch your names, your memories, and to visit with you. I've struggled in your absence. . . . I've looked for you for so long. . . . I've wished so hard I could have saved you.'

"And: 'Here I am again, with empty arms and memories. But as my tears fall, I am thankful to God for having had you for twenty-one years and for all the remembered love and happiness we shared. I will hold you in my memories and wait for another night when I dream of you again. Mom.'

"And: 'Cary, I'll always love you. Linda.'"

Broyles, who notes he has yet to walk from one end of the Wall to the other without tears, believes that Wall now represents more than a memorial to the tragic Vietnam War. The Wall "is like some sacred place where this world meets the next, where the living meet the dead. Its intersecting slabs of black granite lead down into the earth. It puts us in touch with that journey we must all make from life to death. . . . [The Wall] is a window, a passage, a reminder . . . that there are mysteries beyond any of us. The long rows of names—so many names—are so specific that the effect is overwhelming. As you gaze into the Wall, looking for some clue, you always see your own reflection."[185]

❤ ❤ ❤ ❤ ❤ ❤ ❤ ❤

LOVE IS FOREVER

"Love," says Helen Hayes, "is perhaps the only glimpse we are permitted of eternity.[186]

When we soulfully love—whether as a parent or child, as a partner in marriage, or as a friend—our greatest wish is that love will live on forever. In a 1944 letter to her husband, poet Laurence Whistler, from whom she was separated during much of World War II, British actress Jill Furse expresses her hope of forever-love.

When she was small, she was full of joy, Furse writes, "but it has taken me nearly all the years in between to recover it, because no one allowed me to believe it until you gave it back to me. . . . I need all eternity to love you. It's when I think of that—often here alone by the bedside candle—that I find all this separation hard to bear. . . . Beloved—the days go on. I do not miss you, for you have given me so much I still feel I am with you."[187]

Furse speaks fervently of wanting to love her husband throughout all eternity, inherently expressing her belief that this will be so. So throughout history have others held beliefs that they, upon departing this earth, would return to loved ones, a point aptly conveyed by Ralph Waldo Emerson, who says of man's belief in immortality, "Here is this wonderful thought; wherever man ripens, this audacious belief presently appears. As soon as thought is exercised this belief is inevitable."[188]

Norman Vincent Peale reinforces such belief, observing, "I firmly believe in the continuation of life after what we call death takes place. I believe there are two sides to the phenomenon known as death—this side, where we now live, and the other side where we shall continue to live. Eternity does not start with death. We are in eternity now. . . . We merely change the form of the experience called life."[189] Mirroring Peale's certainty that earth life is but a punctuation in eternity is Victor Hugo, who, at age eighty-three and approaching the end of his life, reflected: "When I go down into my grave I can say like many others, I have finished my day's work, but I cannot say I have finished my life. My day's work will begin again the next morning. Death is not a blind alley, it is a thoroughfare; it closes upon the twilight. It opens upon the dawn."[190]

Also conveying belief that men—on their way through eternity—but momentarily pause on earth is an unknown author, whose passage regarding death is considered a classic. Muses this author:

"I am standing upon the seashore; a ship at my side spreads her white sails to the morning breeze and starts for the blue ocean.

"She is an object of beauty and strength, and I stand and

watch her until—at length—she hangs like a speck of white cloud just where the sea and sky come down to mingle with each other.

"Then someone at my side says, 'There! She's gone.' Gone where? Gone from my sight—that is all.

"She is just as large in mast and hull and spar as she was when she left my side and just as able to bear her load of living freight to the place of destination.

"Her diminished size is in me, not in her; and just at the moment when someone by my side says, 'There! She's gone,' there are other eyes watching her coming and other voices already to take up the glad shout, 'There she comes.'

"And that is dying."[191]

Inherent in the concept of immortality is that loved ones will meet once again after departing, a point Peter Marshall emphasized often from his pulpit. Marshall, who, years ago, was the chaplain of the United States Senate, reflected, "Death has no scissors with which to cut the cords of love." After Marshall died a premature death in January 1949, his wife Catherine speaks of her travails in becoming a widow and hearing the term "the late Peter Marshall." And it was not until spring melted into summer that year that Catherine's heart finally found a new peace.

Marshall tells of her ensuing transformation from grief to faith when, one evening, she experienced "a tempest of emotion" related to Peter's death. In her grief, she tells, suddenly "there was wrung from me an unspoken prayer, 'O God, I want to believe that Peter is alive somewhere. But all I can feel is a great aching voice, a gigantic emptiness.'"

There was no answer then, but sometime during the night Marshall awakened. "The confusion in my mind was gone," she says. "Clear, rounded thoughts were waiting there, as if they had been dropped into my consciousness during sleep. 'Simply have

faith that he is with you whenever you need him. Assume it—
and the feelings and the proof will come later. Accept this on
faith . . . though you have no idea how it can come about.'

"That was all," Marshall said.

But then as she lay awake in the night, she remembered an
incident occurring a week before her husband's death. Visiting
friends in a nearby city, she and Peter were sleeping in twin beds
when a surprising thing happened. Sometime after the lights
were out and the house was quiet, "suddenly I had put one hand
toward the other bed, and had found Peter's hand stretched out
in the darkness waiting for mine. He had asked, 'How did you
know that my hand was there?'

"And I had answered, 'I don't know. *I just knew.*'

"Now the space between us was wider, much wider—greater
than the distance between any twin beds," Marshall observes. "It
stretched across the eternities that divide the world of the seen
from the world of the unseen. Somewhere out in that emptiness,
an outstretched hand was waiting for me."

As with Marshall, other broken-hearted have the challenge
of coming to terms with the death of loved ones and living on
with faith that they will see those loved ones again. And when
taking steps to heal, the living often find it difficult to let go, to
take new steps and to achieve new maturity; for, as Marshall
observes, "When a deep injury to the spirit has been sustained,
the tendency is to shut the heart to others, lest hurt be heaped
upon hurt."[192]

Reinforcing Marshall's words regarding the difficulty of letting go is a poignant story attributed to Strickland Gillilan: "A
man had a little daughter—an only and much-beloved child. He
lived for her—she was his life. So when she became ill and her
illness resisted the efforts of the best obtainable physicians, he

became like a man possessed, moving heaven and earth to bring about her restoration to health.

"The father's best efforts proved unavailing and the child died. The father was then totally irreconcilable. He became a bitter recluse, shutting himself away from his many friends and refusing every activity that might restore his poise and bring him back to his normal self.

"But one night he had a dream. He was in Heaven, and was witnessing a grand pageant of all the little child angels. They were marching in an apparently endless line past the Great White Throne. Every white-robed angelic tot carried a candle. He noticed that one child's candle was not lighted. Then he saw that the child with the dark candle was his own little girl. Rushing to her, while the pageant faltered, he seized her in his arms, caressed her tenderly, and then asked:

"'How is it, darling, that your candle alone is unlighted?'

"'Father, they often relight it, but your tears always put it out.'

"Just then the father awoke from his dream. The lesson was crystal clear, and its effects were immediate. From that hour on he was not a recluse, but mingled freely and cheerfully with his former friends and associates. No longer would his little darling's candle be extinguished by his useless tears."[193]

As loved ones attend to the dying, they are assured of immortality through, and can find comfort in, Bible scriptures. "The question of every grief-stricken heart is met by the words of Jesus," writes D. H. Martin. "'Because I live, ye shall live also.' . . . The grave is but a hyphen between two worlds" (see John 14:19).[194] Peale also stresses: "The New Testament teaches the indestructibility of life. It describes Jesus after His crucifixion in a series of disappearances and reappearances. This indicates He is trying to tell us that when we do not see Him it does not mean He is not there. Out of sight does not mean out of life."[195]

Drawing from inalterable convictions of the greatness and goodness of Christ, Ralph W. Sockman also adds his unwavering belief in immortality: "I should hold the hope of immortality had Christ never risen. But as I catch the spirit of Christ's integrity, I feel convinced that I can trust Him when he says about the hope of a life beyond: 'If it were not so, would I have told you that I go to prepare a place for you?'"[196]

❤ ❤ ❤ ❤ ❤ ❤ ❤ ❤ ❤

LOVE FLOWS FROM GOD

"One night I dreamed I was walking along the beach with the Lord," read the lines of an anonymous writing. "In many scenes I noticed footprints in the sand. Sometimes there were two sets of footprints, other times, there was only one.

"This bothered me because I noted that during the low periods of my life, when I was suffering from anguish, sorrow or defeat, I could see only one set of footprints, so I said to the Lord, 'You promised me, Lord, that if I followed, you would walk with me always. But I notice that during the most trying periods of my life there has been only one set of footprints in the sand. Why, when I have needed you most, have you not been there for me?

"And the Lord replied, 'The times when you have seen only one set of footprints, my child, are the times when I carried you.'"

Inherent in this poignant story is the message that our Father in Heaven is ever with us—we are the only ones who falter, who question His being, His presence, or maybe even His interest. We are the ones lacking faith in His love, the strength and intensity of which is documented repeatedly in the New Testament, many of those times in the writings of the apostle John. John, for example, records, "God is love" (1 John 4:16), suggesting that Deity's love is so transcendent and consummate that we, as mortals, cannot possibly comprehend its profound and glorious nature.

These words attest to our Father in Heaven's love for us. Just as with any loving parent, our Parent has given us, through scripture, repeated messages of love that meet our universal psychological and spiritual need to be loved. Love is as essential to our souls as the air we breathe is to our bodies. And to feel absolutely whole in mind, body, and spirit, we, as God's children, must know that we are loved—not only by our fellow beings but by our heavenly Parent, from whom all love ultimately originates and emanates. Boldly underscoring this point is Sri Chinmay, who advises, "You can forget everything if you want to. But don't forget one thing: You are God's child, God's very, very own."[197]

At times, our Father in Heaven brings about miracles in our lives without our asking; but perhaps as many times, those miracles occur in answer to prayer. "Prayer is not asking. It is longing of the soul," Mohandas Gandhi said.[198] And when we need the strength and support of a heavenly Parent, through prayer we can share the "longing of our soul" with Him. He, in turn—in His wisdom—responds to those longings.

It is through praying that "we link ourselves with the inexhaustible power that spins the universe," Alexis Carrel advises.[199] Abraham Lincoln was one who believed unequivocally in that universal "inexhaustible power" and the literal power of prayer. Lincoln, who beseeched God earnestly concerning the Battle of Gettysburg, describes an answer to his prayers: "I went into my room one day and locked the door and got down upon my knees before Almighty God and prayed to Him mightily for victory at Gettysburg. I told Him that this war was His, and our cause His cause, that we could not stand another Fredericksburg or Chancellorsville.

"Then and there I made a solemn vow to Almighty God that if He would stand by our boys at Gettysburg, I would stand by Him, and He did stand by you boys and I will stand by Him. And after that, I don't know how it was, and I cannot explain it, soon a sweet comfort crept into my soul. The feeling came that God had taken the whole business into His own hands, and things would go right at Gettysburg, and that was why I had no fears about you."[200]

On another occasion, Abraham Lincoln said of the guidance he had often felt from God: "I have had so many evidences of His direction, so many instances when I have been controlled by some other power than my own will, that I cannot doubt that this power comes from above. I frequently see my way clear to a decision when I am conscious that I have not sufficient facts upon which to found it. . . . I am satisfied that when the Almighty wants me to do, or not to do, a particular thing He finds a way of letting me know."[201]

In one instance, prayer played a pivotal role for an entire nation in the outcome of a life-saving event. In October 1942, the world's attention turned to Captain Eddie Rickenbacker and his men, who were reported lost at sea. On a mission to deliver a vital message to General Douglas MacArthur, then headquartered in New Guinea, the men were forced to ditch their B-17 Flying Fortress in the ocean somewhere over the South Pacific.

For nearly a month Captain Rickenbacker and his companions drifted in their three rafts, fighting the water, the weather, and the scorching sun, recoiling as giant sharks rammed their rafts.

But starvation proved to be their most formidable enemy; it

would take a miracle to sustain them. And a miracle occurred, as the world was to note.

In his own words, Rickenbacker tells of this miracle: "That afternoon we finished the service with a prayer for deliverance and a hymn of praise. Talk tapered off in the oppressive heat. With my hat pulled down to keep out the glare, I dozed off. Then something landed on my head. I knew that it was a sea gull. Peering out from under my hat brim without moving, I could see everyone staring at that gull. It meant food—if I could catch it."[202]

Rickenbacker did catch the gull. The men in the rafts ate the flesh of the gull and used the intestines for bait to catch fish. Playing a key role in saving the lives of Rickenbacker and his men, this gull, hundreds of miles from land, appeared and served to sustain and renew the hope of the survivors.

When the men were finally rescued, each had a story, several of which Margaret Lee Runbeck tells in a newspaper article entitled "We Were on That Raft—A Hundred Million of Us." Says Runbeck of the experience of one man, "When Colonel Hans Christian Adamson was rescued, he wrote to his wife: 'I have found a nearness to our Creator which I have never known before, and I am certain that this new feeling is going to affect both our lives in the future. While the drifting was a horrible experience, something wonderful has come of it.'"

And, reported Corporal John F. Barteck: "I'm glad that plane fell. It took a lot of nonsense out of my life. I shall like the things I liked before, but there is something now inside me that won't permit me to forget that God stayed right by us out there."

In her article, Runbeck describes how the world's attention was intensely riveted both on the disappearance and the subsequent rescue of the captain and his men. Why it was, she does not know, but when the men were reported missing, the world didn't give up on them. Somehow we knew that Rickenbacker would be back, she relays. "Something will take care of him. You wait and see," seemed to be the public's general attitude. People began to pray for the men, and New York's Mayor La Guardia requested the entire city to join in praying. And, says Runbeck: "I don't doubt that thousands of them did. Even the ones who didn't know how to pray had a kind of faith about them.

"Well, anyway he came back," Runbeck continues. And people eagerly read of the rescue in the newspaper, the accounting of which contained something unusual. Four paragraphs down, the word *God* appeared. It gave Runbeck a funny feeling, she says. "And more than that. A strange excited feeling, as if . . . we had somehow been amplified by Rickenbacker and that gull, and those verses from Matthew read in the bobbing yellow rafts."

And then there were the stirring words of Rickenbacker in the newspaper that people read carefully: "And this part I would hesitate to tell, except that there were six witnesses who saw it with me. A gull came out of nowhere, and lighted upon my head—I reached up my hand very gently—I killed him and then we divided him equally among us. We ate every bit, even the little bones. Never did anything taste so good."

Says Runbeck of Rickenbacker's report: "There was something so moving in those simple words—a sort of Biblical excitement about them." And when Rickenbacker and his men shamelessly admitted they had prayed on those rafts, another unusual thing happened: Others came out to tell their stories. Suddenly, prayer was in fashion. "Some people began praying, experimentally, for the first time in their lives. Others came out into the light and admitted they always *had* prayed. And, what's more, that God had heard them praying."

And, so it was that a hundred million people shared the

adventure with Rickenbacker and the gull, says Runbeck. And the lives of many were changed, and people began to believe, just as Colonel Barteck had expressed, that "God stays right out there with us."[203]

❤ ❤ ❤ ❤ ❤ ❤ ❤ ❤ ❤

LOVE RETURNS TO GOD

"We love him, because he first loved us," wrote the apostle John (1 John 4:19). Thus, existing in possibility is a two-way flow of spiritual love from God to man and, in return, from man to God. God's love is consistent and eternal, and ever available; and we have only to tap into His spiritual love to complete the circle. Those who focus exclusively upon goodness, and upon serving their fellow men, draw close to God and His love; and, in turn, in feeling God's love, they emanate love that returns to Him.

People who radiate love toward God often have a calm and peaceful countenance, a sense of confidence that they know the Master, that they are in His hands, and that He is with them, watching over them, as would any loving parent. For some, it is as though a profound physical and "soulful" transformation has occurred; and a definitive warmth and illumination accompany their demeanor from experiencing—and returning—God's pure love.

An example of such spiritual glow is portrayed in the following elegant story. Placed in an earlier era, the story concerns a prominent actor in New York City who, through well-perfected oratorical skills, could completely captivate any audience. One night after his recitation, the actor received tremendous applause, and, as he reappeared on stage to take his bows, a woman in the crowd called for him to recite the twenty-third Psalm.

The woman's request startled the actor, but being familiar with the scriptural passage, he consented to her wish. As he delivered the recitation, he endeavored to mold and beautify it with all the color, emotion, and personality he could call forth. His delivery was exact, and his memory of the psalm perfect; and as he concluded his oration, the crowd burst into a thunderous applause, acknowledging his superb recitation.

But as the applause subsided, the actor called an elderly man from the front row to the stage and asked him also to recite the psalm. Although appearing nervous, the man consented and, turning to the crowd, closed his eyes and bowed his head. Then, softly and with reverence, he spoke these words:

> The Lord is my shepherd; I shall not want.
> He maketh me to lie down in green pastures: he leadeth me beside the still waters.
> He restoreth my soul: he leadeth me in the paths of righteousness for his name's sake.
> Yea, though I walk through the valley of the shadow of death, I will fear no evil: for thou art with me; thy rod and thy staff they comfort me.
> Thou preparest a table before me in the presence of mine enemies: thou anointest my head with oil; my cup runneth over.
> Surely goodness and mercy shall follow me all the days of my life: and I will dwell in the house of the Lord for ever.

When the elderly man concluded by saying "Amen," there was no thunderous applause, nor cries of praise—but neither was there a dry eye in the crowd.

Pausing in silence for a moment, the prominent young actor then faced the audience and said: "Ladies and gentlemen, I know the words to the twenty-third Psalm, but this man knows the Shepherd."[204] The humble man who "knew the Shepherd" followed God's first and greatest commandment: "Thou shalt love the Lord thy God with all thy heart, and with all thy soul, and with all thy mind" (Matthew 22:37). This man also most likely tended to the Shepherd's other sheep, following Christ's admonition to "love one another as I have loved you" (John 15:12).

The one who "knew the Shepherd" also most likely knew that men cannot possibly love God in a vacuum. Rather, he knew that loving others teaches us how to love God. This man's exquisite humility and compelling depth of soul came from participating in a never-ending circle of love encompassing both the Shepherd and himself. Eligibility to participate in this divine circle required also that he be a man who loved the Shepherd's other sheep.

❤ ❤ ❤ ❤ ❤ ❤ ❤ ❤ ❤

LOVE HAS HANDS

Shortly after the culmination of the Second World War, the population of a devastated European city began their heartbreaking and wearying work of restoration. In the old city square had stood a large statue of Jesus Christ, with hands outspread in an attitude of invitation, and on the pedestal were carved the words, "Come unto me."

As the restoration progressed, master artists and sculptors eventually reassembled the figure, with the exception of the hands, of which no fragments were found in the surrounding rubble. It was suggested—since the hands could not be found—that artisans fashion new ones.

Later came a public protest: "No, leave the statue without hands." So, today, in the public square of that city, the restored statue of Christ stands without hands, and on its base are carved the words, "Christ has no hands but ours!"[205]

Elaborating through poetry the need for men to "use their

own hands" and their total selves to serve others, Annie Johnson Flint writes:

> Christ has no hands but our hands
> To do His work today.
> He has no feet but our feet
> To lead men in His way.
> He has no tongue but our tongue
> To tell men how He died:
> He has no help but our help
> To bring all to His side.[206]

It is often through our hands that God works his miracles, as in the instance of Elzeard Bouffier, a French folk hero who quietly went about his life's work. Newspaper columnist Jerry Johnston tells his story: "Elzeard Bouffier was a shepherd who lived in a parched, unpleasant French town," he relates. "His wife and son had died, so to keep his spirits up he went into the wilds every day and planted acorns. In time, an entire forest grew around him. The lush landscape brightened the attitude of the townfolk. Hope returned. Farms began to flourish. But Elzeard Bouffier was never detected. The authorities saw the incredible *natural* forest as a miracle from God.

"It was—a miracle worked through Elzeard Bouffier."[207]

In using our hands to serve others, we serve God, for, as Matthew recorded, Christ said, "Inasmuch as ye have done it unto one of the least of these my brethren, ye have done it unto me" (Matthew 25:40).

General Booth, the founder of the Salvation Army, is a significant example of a man who "used his hands" to serve others. When Booth became blind, his son Bramwell broke the news to him.

"You mean I am blind?" asked the general. "I shall never see your face again?"

"No," said his son, "probably not in this world."

Moving his hand across the counterpane until he could grasp his son's, Booth observed: "I have done what I could for God and for the people with my eyes. Now I shall do what I can for God and for the people without my eyes."[208]

As well, Mother Teresa used her hands in the service of God's children. After her 1997 death at eighty-seven years of age, *Time* wrote of Mother Teresa, "She was not some saintly relic but a willing servant of her God." On on occasion, she is quoted as saying, "Let every action of mine be something beautiful of God."[209] And on another, "The other day I dreamed that I was at the gates of heaven. And St. Peter said, 'Go back to Earth, there are no slums up here.'"[210]

In their commitment to God and man, both Booth and Mother Teresa followed the Master. During his ministry, Christ provided the supreme model of service, administering to the sick, raising the dead, restoring sight to the blind and hearing to the deaf, blessing little children, and healing those afflicted with leprosy. And with his pure love and compassion, he spiritually lifted all to whom he administered or taught.

In his teachings, Christ commanded men to "love one another" (John 13:34)—in essence, charging the care for his children to their fellow beings. And, although in his absence, God performs wonders and miracles from above and from behind the scenes, he asks us to serve our fellow man without reservation. And there is much to do.

"There are so many out there whose burden you can lift," points out Gordon B. Hinckley, prophet and president of the Mormon church. "There are the homeless, there are the hungry, there are the destitute all around us. There are the aged who are alone in rest homes. There are the handicapped children and youth on drugs and the sick and the homebound who cry out for a kind word. If you do not do it, who will?"[211]

Also illuminating the vital need for men to serve one another is Lillian Katz, a world-renowned educator: "Each of us must come to care for everyone else's children," she teaches. "We must recognize that the lives of our children and grandchildren are intimately linked to the lives of everyone else's children. After all, when one of our children or grandchildren needs life-saving surgery, someone else's child will perform the operation; when one of our children is a victim of violence, someone else's child will perform the criminal act. So the 'good life' is possible for our children—only if the good life is available to *all* other people's children."[212]

II

♥ ♥ ♥ ♥ ♥ ♥ ♥

ON COMPASSION

"Could a greater miracle take place than for us to look through each other's eyes for an instant?" asks Henry David Thoreau.[1] As one person sees through the eyes of another, that person experiences *compassion*, which, as with love, rests at the heart of goodness. It is compassion—the yearning of the heart to merge with others and to alleviate their suffering—that, together with love, binds us together as human beings.

♥ ♥ ♥ ♥ ♥ ♥ ♥ ♥ ♥

COMPASSION BINDS SOULS

Compassion speaks to man's soul. Indeed, compassion may be viewed as God-given, an attribute of mankind accompanying the human condition, deliberately designed to allow emotional and spiritual connections, or bonding, between loved ones or even complete strangers. Compassion knows we are all in the same strait, that "but for the grace of God there go I."

In addressing our common humanity, compassion also recognizes that, as Philip Johnston notes, "there isn't much difference between the one asking and the one being asked. It bridges the gap between us and them; it inspires us to respond to a stranger's grief as if it were our own."[2]

As a soul-binding ingredient, compassion further "hurries us without reflection to the relief of those who are in distress," says philosopher Jean-Jacques Rousseau;[3] and compassion thus represents a remedy to one of the world's greatest ills—man's inattention to his fellow men. The words of Mother Teresa, an eminent model of compassion, bring focus to the urgent need in the world for this quality: "The biggest disease today is not leprosy or tuberculosis, but rather the feeling of being unwanted, uncared for, and deserted."[4]

It is to this appalling loneliness of human beings that compassion addresses itself, ever seeking to feed starved souls of lost and broken people and to salve their gaping wounds.

To feel compassion is to be quickened to our own spirituality and to the quivering of our own heart—a heart potentially made pure by its keen sensitivity to life's suffering. In so feeling, we explore the deepest aspects of ourselves and each other. In this state there potentially exists in each of us an ever-growing consciousness and awakening to the preciousness of life, living, and love that perhaps brings us closer, conjointly with others, to a divine connection with God. Such is the essence of a story set in the late forties and related by A. J. Cronin. In this instance, compassion bound together the souls of a great crowd.

Cronin tells of an explosion in South Wales that entombed fourteen miners. For five days the men remained buried and the villagers prayed as rescuers frantically tried to reach them. Then, as the rescuers were digging underground, they heard faintly from deep within the mine's collapsed structures the strains of the hymn, "O God, Our Help in Ages Past."

As the miners, weak but unharmed, were brought out of the mine, the hymn they had sung to keep their courage intact was taken up by the huge crowd gathered in the pit yard. Reverberating as it was sung by a thousand voices, the hymn echoed with great fervor and joy throughout the narrow valley. Cronin, who, as a physician, had gone into the depths of the earth with the rescuers, says of this event: "As I came to the surface with the liberated men, this great volume of sound caught me like a tidal wave—as a demonstration of human faith . . . moving beyond words."[5] In his humility, Cronin thus recognized that this miraculous occurrence had swept the crowd into the realm of the spirit where all had experienced an incomprehensible melding of souls.

Another instance of compassion binding souls is embodied in a letter a young Mormon missionary wrote to his family, which reads:

"Dear family: Yesterday my companion and I were going down a hill, 'el cerro,' one of the poorer sections of Soledad [Venezuela]. As we were walking, I heard a whimper and looked over. In front of a locked-up house there were two little boys covered with mud and ants and more. One was mumbling incoherently, the other, the smallest, was asleep in the dirt. As I witnessed the scene, I've never felt before how I felt at that moment . . . but the story of the 'Little Match Girl' came to mind.

"My companion and I called a neighbor over. She said the children's mother always neglects the children—at least that's what my companion later said she said. I wasn't listening to her. My attention was riveted on the boy in the sand. I went over and picked up and held him and just started crying . . . like I'm crying now as I write to you. I gave the neighbor money for some food for the children. She said she'd bathe the child I held. I handed the little boy to her and cried all the way down the hill.

"There are so many 'little match people' out there. Let's try to pick up and hold the 'little match people' in our lives—like Jesus did. I had a great feeling of consolation because I knew that my family, as always, are holding the 'little match people' . . . 'for behold, are we not all beggars?'

"Love Always, Your Son, Brother and Servant, Elder Turner"[6]

In yet a third instance of compassion binding souls, in World War II a seriously wounded English soldier received aid from a German soldier. Relates the wounded British soldier of his "enemy": "He carried me for seventy yards to the beach, then looked down at me, smiled, put a cigarette in my mouth, lit it, and put his lighter in my pocket. Then he took off his white shirt, tore it into shreds and dressed my wounds. Having done this, he kissed me, with tears in his eyes, and then walked away to attend to other wounded."[7]

Perhaps it was because of similar full-bodied compassion that, in this same World War, the lives of two stretcher-bearers were spared. Carrying a casualty as they were returning to their lines, the bearers heard a rustling in the bushes and the click of a rifle-bolt. Out into their path stepped a menacing Japanese soldier with a cocked rifle pointed directly at them. Looking at the two men, and then at the third man they carried on the stretcher, without a word or gesture, the Japanese soldier dropped the muzzle of his rifle and faded back into the jungle.[8]

Thus it is that, through compassion, members of two opposing or even warring sides may experience the common human bond inherently existing between themselves and those they are resisting or harboring hatred for. Compassion is thus God's leveler—an additive to the human race to aid people in overcoming the animosity that inevitably occurs when they encounter stark differences between themselves and others.

♥ ♥ ♥ ♥ ♥ ♥ ♥ ♥ ♥

COMPASSION HAS SOUL

Centuries ago, compassion emanated soul when Pythagoras, a Greek philosopher born in 580 B.C., allayed a brother's pain. Witnessing one day a puppy being beaten, Pythagoras took pity, ordering the beating to stop, and imploring, "Stop, do not beat it; it is the soul of a friend which I recognized when I heard it crying out."[9]

Recognizing a sacred kinship, Pythagoras felt the puppy's cries within his own soul. Such consummate compassion moves us to the far inner reaches of our divinity, for as Jeremy Taylor reflects, "It is not the eye that sees the beauty of heaven, nor the ear that hears the sweetness of music, but the soul."[10]

Yet, because we emanate from the same divine source, we have divine core likenesses to others, including that of "heart": "There is no feeling in a human heart which is exists in that heart alone—which is not, in some form, in some degree, in every heart," apprises George Macdonald.[11] Consistent with such musing, compassion knows that in each being beats a universal heart—a heart that speaks similarly to strings of goodness and to pangs of sorrow and suffering. And it is thus to the heart, the passageway to the soul, that compassion speaks.

It was to such common heart Jesus responded when he saw the multitude "and was moved with compassion toward them" (Mark 6:34). Jesus not only had compassion on the multitude— he fed them. Instead of turning his back on those who had followed him for three days in the wilderness, as his disciples had urged, he looked into their tired faces and hungry souls. He must have thought of their strong loyalty and love for him, of their burdens, their enduring patience, their childlike faith, and for them felt divine compassion.

For us, Jesus provides a model of consummate compassion—
unerring lifetime acts of accompanying others "to the place
where they [were] weak, vulnerable, lonely, and broken."[12] Says
Henry J. M. Nouwen of our own like journey: For many of us,
"this is not our spontaneous response to suffering. What we
desire most is to do away with suffering by fleeing from it or
finding a quick cure for it."[13] Thus, being compassionate often
does not come easy. To be consummately compassionate, we
must search the hearts and touch the souls of others. And for
that, our own soul must be open and inviting.

Speaking to the incongruency between an intellectual wish
to be compassionate and actual inaction in heart-rending situations is Sue Monk Kidd. "Compassion often eludes me," she
relates. "I remember the time I wept before a television image of
a homeless man lying in an American gutter. Three weeks later I
stepped over a homeless man on a sidewalk in New York without looking back. . . . But as I strode away, I had the odd feeling
that somewhere Someone was looking at me, waiting for an
explanation, a reason."[14]

In choosing a response to suffering, our pristine challenge
from that Someone is contained in Luke 6:36: "Be compassionate as your Father is compassionate." Providing an eminent
model of such compassion was the Good Samaritan—a man
who had "soul." In this biblical story, Jesus relates:

"A certain man went down from Jerusalem to Jericho, and fell
among thieves, which stripped him of his raiment, and wounded
him, and departed, leaving him half dead." By chance, a certain
priest appeared, but passed by on the other side, as later did a
Levite. Finally, a Samaritan, an outcast with whom Jews had no
dealing, appeared. "When he saw the wounded man, he was
moved with compassion," and he succored and bound his

wounds, "set him on his own beast, and brought him to an inn, and took care of him."

There, the Samaritan left money at the inn for the man's care, and told the innkeeper, "Whatsoever thou spendest more, when I come again, I will repay thee" (Luke 10:30–35).

The wounded man represents all creatures who suffer, and our global human challenge is to not "pass on the other side" but, instead, whenever possible to render unfettered compassion. In so doing, we expand our ability to render compassion and to enlarge our souls.

Richard Kirkland, a confederate soldier during the Civil War, was a man who did both with a "courage which transcend[ed] mere bravery." Writing Kirkland's story is Octavus Roy Cohen, who describes him as "one of the greatest and least-known heroes of American history."

As a nineteen-year-old sergeant in Company E of the Second South Carolina regiment, Kirkland participated in a December 13, 1862, Fredericksburg battle staged by the Union "in the face of hopeless odds." Of this battle, Cohen writes, "Students of the War between the States have declared that the tactical errors of the Federal generals were beyond counting and that the heroism of the attacking Union troops defied description."

For probably the only time in the war, in every manner the Confederates had advantage: in numbers, in a magnificent defensive position, and in an unassailable offensive position. Nevertheless, under orders, the Union attacked repeatedly, each time rebuffed, their "dogged, desperate courage . . . epic." Relates Cohen, "Eventually, the series of assaults ended. The ground in front of the sunken road was a solid blanket of blue: the uniforms of dead and dying men. That was the price they had paid for their gallantry. Historians have estimated that five thousand

Union troops were killed or wounded in that three hours of bitter fighting.

"And, as darkness fell over the field, a ghastly sound arose; the cries of the wounded and dying. They called for help, for water. They tried to drag themselves back toward their lines. Never before had so gory a carpet been stretched over so small an area." That night, Richard Kirkland was among the Confederate soldiers listening to the unending eerie and agonizing sounds of men suffering and dying. Kirkland had seen ghastly sights and sounds in battle, but nothing in his past experience prepared him for this. As Kirkland paced back and forth that night, the knowledge that "no man dared emerge into that no man's land between armies . . . tore at his nerves as combat never could."

The men out there were no longer Kirkland's enemies—they were terribly suffering fellow beings who needed aid. "And all night long they lay out there suffering and dying, denied a few precious drops of water, denied help, denied any alleviation of their pain." At daylight, with a great personal struggle resolved in his heart, Kirkland sought the company officer. His face pale and voice trembling, he asked for permission to assist the wounded. Countering with protestations was an officer who pointed out to Kirkland he would vainly sacrifice his life. However, Kirkland persisted and prevailed, the officer finally declaring he had "no right to refuse so noble a request." Imploring that God would protect Kirkland, the officer relinquished him to his mission.

Hurrying back to his own company, Kirkland obtained two canteens full of fresh water, and holding the canteens, he vaulted over the stone wall and faced the Union lines. A dozen trained Union sharpshooters raised their rifles as "Kirkland stood motionless, erect, and unafraid," but no shots were fired. Slowly, he walked straight toward the Union position and, reaching the first wounded man, knelt by his side and gave him water, placing a knapsack under his head as a pillow and an overcoat over him. Calmly he moved to the next man, and then the next, each time repeating the same nurturing gestures.

"By this time, Kirkland's purpose was apparent to the troops of both armies. He didn't hurry. If he was aware of his danger, he gave no sign," reports Cohen. Each time he ran out of water, he retreated to his own line, each time again reappearing with more water, and once more vaulting the wall. As he worked, "a vast silence hung over the field," all watching Kirkland "doing all that one man could do; doing more than any other man dared to do." All that day, Sergeant Richard Kirkland crossed and recrossed the field, succoring the wounded men and saving many lives. Only when darkness enshrouded the field did he return to his own lines.

There, no one praised him—for there were no words, even moving words to describe his actions, only understanding and deeply heart-felt commendation on each side. "But," ends Cohen, "many of the men, Gray and Blue, who had watched Kirkland perform his valorous deed must have realized that, despite the carnage, here was living proof that this indeed was destined to be again a nation, one and indivisible."[15]

Richard Kirkland emulated pure compassion, the God-given compassion of soul, deeply touching all other witnessing souls. As was the case with Kirkland, to become consummately compassionate—bringing a brilliance of soul to the fore—is to spiritually unite and integrate God, self, and brother. Germane are words of an unknown author: "I sought my soul but my soul I could not see. I sought my God but God eluded me. I sought my brother—and I found all three."[16]

♥ ♥ ♥ ♥ ♥ ♥ ♥ ♥ ♥

COMPASSION RECOGNIZES OUR ONENESS

Compassion recognizes we are all "one in the universe," that we originate from the same God-given source, and that we share the same spiritual and earthly journey through life. The following story, anonymously told, illustrates:

"One cold winter day, a ragged little urchin stood on a street corner of a large city, selling newspapers. His feet were bare and he had no coat. As he stood there shivering, a woman walking past noticed the child. She approached him and said, 'Come with me, Dear. I want to buy you a coat and some shoes.'

"A smile lighted the boy's cold little face as he took the woman's hand. Leading the boy to a large, warm department store, the woman completely outfitted him from head to toe in warm clothes.

"As the boy was putting on the last of his new clothing, the woman paid the bill and slipped quietly out the door. When he finished dressing, the boy looked for the woman to thank her, but was told by the clerk that she had gone.

"Running from the store, the boy frantically looked up and down the street until he found the woman. Rushing to her, he took her hand and said, 'Lady, why did you go? I wanted to thank you.'

"'You're most welcome, Dear,' she said, smiling.

"The little boy then looked up into her face and said solemnly, 'Lady, who are you? Are you God's wife?'

"'No,' she softly replied. 'I'm just one of His children.'

"'Oh, I knew it!' he said, smiling through his tears. 'I just knew you were some relation!'"[17]

If, at that moment, this woman had consciously recognized the "oneness factor"—that we are all "one with God"—she might well have also told the boy that, inasmuch as we are all God's children, he, too, was a relation to God, and thus, even to her.

Capturing the sense that we, as fellow beings taking our sojourn on earth, are all related, Bruce Bawer observes, "The higher you climb in your family tree, the more you'll realize that the tree's not really a tree. For as its branches divide again and again, more and more of them reconnect with one another, as well as with the branches of family trees of everyone else on earth."

Also using the analogy of trees is Pablo Casals, who reflects, "We ought to think that we are one of the leaves of a tree, and the tree is all humanity. We cannot live without the others, without the tree."[18]

Nor can we escape that we are touched, in some form, by almost everyone that we meet. "There is no such thing as a 'self-made' man," says George Matthew Adams. "We are made up of thousands of others. Everyone who has ever done a kind deed for us or spoken one word of encouragement to us has entered into the make-up of our character and of our thoughts, as well as our success."[19] And John McDonald appends, "A piece of us is in every person we can ever meet."[20]

Further illuminating is Albert Schweitzer, who accredits much of who he was and what he became to others who often imperceptibly influenced him. "In significant moments of our lives," he asserts, ". . . much of what has become our own in gentleness, kindness, ability to forgive, truthfulness, faithfulness, submission in suffering, we owe to people in whom we experienced these qualities." And if significant others knew how they have blessed our lives, they would be amazed to learn what we had acquired from them.[21]

From a grander, panoramic perspective, an unknown author adds, "Our personalities weave a colorful life's tapestry. The intense personality colors often clash when viewed microscopically, but form a beautiful display when viewed from God's perspective." God himself is actually the Creator who puts together these magnificent tapestries, reflects newspaper columnist Jerry Johnston. Expanding, Johnston writes of our oneness—as fellow beings—with God and the universe: "The Creator is not a magician who pulls creation out of thin air. He's a master quilter. He doesn't make things from whole cloth; he stitches bits and pieces together."

As an artist, a creator "specializes in 'collages'—works of art assembled from fragments," Johnston continues. He takes a seashell, a key, a photograph, a feather, then arranges them into striking designs.

"God creates by arranging pieces of the world into stunning new patterns.

"I saw that in church on Sunday. There we sang a hymn written by a Methodist minister, read a scripture translated by an Anglican scholar and studied the life of an ancient Jewish prophet.

"Yet everything was stitched together in one seamless act of worship.

"I see God's 'quilting' in the Bible itself—in all those voices and personalities expressing themselves in poetry, short story and essay.

"Yet it all blends into one inspired text.

"And I see the quilt of God in my own inner life, in this internal hodgepodge of British church music, Mexican mysticism and Yankee gumption that—in moments of truth—feel so unified to me.

"In fact," Johnston ends, "If I were a theologian, I'd even toss out the notion that God created the world that way—as a collage. He composed it from a million fragments."[22]

Within this context, the intricate interwovenness, or the "oneness" of people, is captured by Jane W. Lund in a piece called "Patchwork." In her poem, Lund inherently likens the permanently imprinted interrelating of people to the forming of a quilt:

It rests at the foot of my bed,
Well stricken by years of using.
Each splash of color,
Each random design
Adds a touch of joyfulness and nostalgia—
A bit of Tommy's shirt,
A scrap of Jenny's dress—
Pieces rescued from the rag bags
of our worlds.
Made into something wonderful!

Ours was a labor of love.
Shoulders ached;
Fingers bled;
And at day's end,
Change seemed small.
Today, I cannot remember how or by whom
It was designed, or cut, or sewn;
But in its tiny stitches
I see pieces of the quilters—

Ethel's wisdom;
Carolyn's faith;
Raelene's commitment;
Julie's loyalty;
Bev's generosity.
I remember our struggles and heartaches;
Hopes and dreams;
Love, and Faith.

Is it any wonder
We have chosen

To call quilts
"Comforters"?[23]

Interrelating to others may emerge in surprising ways and at surprising times, as in an instance described by Ardis Whitman. As Whitman tells, on a spring afternoon long ago in Paris, she was greatly saddened and preoccupied by what she considered the betrayal of a trusted friend. As she approached the towers of Notre Dame, and since the cathedral's darkness seemed to match her mood, she decided to tour the building. Once inside, a guide, "a tiptoeing old man, round as an apricot, and bursting with knowledge," assumed the role of her tour guide.

Whitman tried to listen to the guide but she was increasingly overtaken and overwhelmed by her sorrow. And, then, to her horror, she began to cry. Taken aback by her emotion, the guide increased the eloquence of his lecture but, when the tears seemed endless, he suddenly stopped in a dimly lit aisle and turned to Whitman. Reaching for her hand, "in his quaint English, [he said softly,] 'Hold to me. Hold to me. I am here.'

Says Whitman, "We stood so in the pouring light and for that instant sorrow gave way to understanding. In a rush of joy and tenderness I saw and felt the love in the world, the goodness of human beings, the reach of hands to each other; saw it and felt as though it were a palpable presence flooding the ancient church."[24]

❤ ❤ ❤ ❤ ❤ ❤ ❤ ❤ ❤

COMPASSION IS CHILDLIKE

"Cosmic upheaval is not so moving as a little child's pondering the death of a sparrow in the corner of a barn," reflects Thomas Savage.[25]

Compassion is not sullied by life experiences but flows pure and gentle from the wellspring of the soul, as flawless and guileless as the tender emotions of any child. An enlightened observation made by a small girl and related by her father, Arthur Gordon, gives life to this concept:

"Once at sunset my small daughter and I sat watching the tide come in. It was a quiet evening, calm and opalescent. The waves sent thin sheets of molten gold across the dry sand, closer and closer. Finally, almost like a caress, an arm of the sea curled around the base of the dune. And my daughter said, dreamily, 'Isn't it wonderful how much the sea cares about the land?'

"She was right, with the infallible instinct of childhood: It *was* a kind of caring. The land was merely passive—and so it waited. But the sea cared—and so it came. The lesson was all there in that lovely symbol: the willingness to act, to approach, to be absorbed, and in the absorption to be fulfilled."[26]

The childlike nature of compassion is further illustrated in a story by Pamela Johnson entitled "No Room in the Inn."

"'What part are we going to give Ryan?' a teacher asks as the members of the Sunday school staff of the Congregational church plan their annual Christmas pageant.

"We all consider. Finally, the director of the play suggests, 'How about one of the innkeepers? This would make him feel important. Yet it's a small enough part that he won't forget his line.' We agree.

"We all want Ryan to feel included. He is the blonde-headed boy in special education whose eyes are blue like the sky. I know he is special because he always seems happy.

"The night of the performance, there is standing room only. Ryan's eyes shine and his face beams. He has practiced his line until he knows it perfectly.

"As the play progresses, Ryan stands proudly before the audience and clearly tells Mary and Joseph, 'We have no room in this inn.'

"'Where can we go? There is no room anywhere and my wife is ready to have her baby,' Joseph protests.

"'There's no room in this inn,' Ryan the innkeeper says again. The couple slowly walk away. Ryan pauses as if he has forgotten his line. Someone behind the curtain prompts him. 'There is no room in this inn.'

"Ryan hesitates only a moment, then blurts out, 'Wait, Joseph and Mary. Come back. You can have my room.'

"There isn't a dry eye in the place at this spontaneous selfless answer. Ryan's response and ensuing smile warms each heart with the true meaning of Christmas."[27]

In a final instance, the childlike nature of compassion—as well as love personified—is embodied in a note written by a seven-year-old to her grandparents, who, as out-of-town guests, were expected to stay in her bedroom. This note illustrates the purity of motive and emotions that accompany consummate compassion:

> Dear grandparents if you
> come to my house before I get
> home this note is for you
> the flashlight is for a night
> light if you need it on
> my dresser between my doll in
> the blue dress and radio with
> all the animals and other things
> on it. there is a bag there is
> pastiachos in side you may eat
> some if you want My desk with
> doll on it has pencils, pen, Magic
> Markers, paper and other things you
> mite want to use in the Book

shelf there might be a
book you might want to read you
are welcome to my room
and ever thing in it Even
My tape recorder, radio, am fm
you can also play
tapes and listen to TV on it
your welcome hope
you have a nice trip here
Love Julie your granddaughter

Written by a loving child, this note constituted an entirely innocent and open welcome to her grandparents and was intended to ensure their complete comfort. The exquisite feelings she expressed came from deep within her soul.

Sadly, as we progress toward adulthood, our souls often become shrouded by progressive layers of cultural programming. Thus, we lose the childlike compassion we so flawlessly and purely radiated when younger. To the extent we seek to intensify our understanding of others and their pain, we regain access to our souls and our ability to experience compassion. To boldly fill our souls with such emotion creates positive energy that enhances these souls and adds to the world's goodness.

❤ ❤ ❤ ❤ ❤ ❤ ❤ ❤

COMPASSION EMBODIES EMPATHY

"To understand any living thing, you must, so to say, creep within and feel the beating of the heart," W. MacNeil Dixon observes.[28] Within this context, consider the empathic response of one American woman, Leslie Laurence, toward newly captured POWs in the 1991 Persian Gulf War.

"Like many Americans, I'll always be haunted by images of

the first POWs taken in the Persian Gulf," she relates. "Watching them paraded on Iraqi TV—their faces bruised and vacant, their voices feeble and halting—I wept to think what they and their families were going through. Although I'd never experienced anything remotely similar, I felt their pain."[29]

From Laurence's compassionate description, it is possible to recognize the agonizing plight of these POWs and to imagine— albeit incompletely—the abject fear and agony they must have felt. Defining such empathy, Jess Lair says simply, "Empathy is your pain in my heart."[30]

Lair's definition of empathy is vividly illustrated by a husband who, through inordinate tenderness, conveyed to his wife that her pain was his pain. Sue Monk Kidd, who was that wife, speaks of her husband's evident anguish for her: "Once when I was going through a difficult time, my husband touched his finger to the tears winding down my face, then touched his wet finger to his own cheek. His gesture spoke volumes to me. It said: 'Your tears run down *my* face, too. Your suffering aches inside *my* heart as well. I share your wounded place.'"[31]

Also germane are the moving feelings of Jeff Wheelwright, a part-time volunteer serving meals to the homeless of New York City. Wheelwright describes the "pain in his heart" he experiences in working with these suffering people. Of significance is that he personalizes the plight of the homeless, singling out among them *individuals* who suffer:

"In the morning, coming back into Grand Central Terminal on my way to work, I watch my people moving aimlessly among the streams of commuters. I pick out the familiar faces, the lost expressions.

"You know, you could do that too—pick out a familiar face . . . make a one-way connection to a fellow human," Wheelwright advises. "It's simple. . . . Just break stride long enough to identify a homeless person. . . . You don't *have* to address the one you choose, or hand him money. But remember him. Will he be in the same spot the next morning? Look around for him. If you miss him for a day or two, you'll wonder whether he's all right. When you see him again, be glad. Think kindly; say a prayer for him. Give him a window into your heart."[32]

In personalizing the near-hopeless plight of a homeless person, Wheelwright's discerning insights stretch far beyond appearances. And for good reason: Looks are deceptive. In fact, observes Helen Hudson, they are so deceptive that "people should be done up like food packages with the ingredients clearly labeled."[33] And Neil Millar appends, "This is an age in which much is packaged and thus hidden—from water to wisdom, pickles to politicians. People, however, can't be safely packaged and labeled. Each of us is an infinite symphony of facts, enormous chords, shimmering, dissolving, resolving. To judge a citizen of eternity by any human epithet is like judging an orchestra by one trill on the flute."[34] In keeping with this perspective, to be empathic then is to blot out how a person "looks" and to consider how he or she is similar to us and what feelings and emotions we would experience under similar circumstances.

How would we feel, for example, if we were homeless? Without shelter, without emotional support, without knowing where our next meal was coming from, and without any of the material goods that give us comfort and security? How would we feel without the routine and the sense of well-being that accompanies going to work every day; retrieving the newspaper in the same spot every evening; going to the same church on Sunday; or, even being able to whimsically plunk down money for a luxury item? The answers to such questions help us look through another's eyes. It may be, though, that our "seeing" will occur in our hearts, for that is where we register our empathy and compassion for another. "We may not always see eye to eye, but we can try to see heart to heart," reflects Sam Levenson.[35]

To develop more empathy for others, look for their *inner child*. Several authors have made reference to the "child in man," including Friedrich Nietzsche, who observes, "In every real man a child is hidden who wants to play."[36] Woody Harrelson also adds, "A grownup is a child with layers on."[37] Inside most people is a vulnerable child, a child who is unsure of himself, who experiences fear and hurt, and who easily feels slighted or unimportant. In many there is a child inside who is disillusioned by painful life experiences or who has been cheated out of positive ones—maybe even a child-adult who never had the opportunity to mature. Franz Kafka captures the sense of the assailable "child in man," noting, "A man's embittered features are often only the petrified bewilderment of a boy."[38]

Though we try, it is sometimes difficult to experience empathy for those who differ from ourselves. Offering a pertinent perspective, Karl Menninger uses an analogy related to fishing:

"When a trout rising to a fly gets hooked and finds himself unable to swim about freely, he begins a fight which results in struggles and splashes and sometimes an escape. . . . In the same way, the human being struggles . . . with the hooks that catch him. Sometimes he masters his difficulties; sometimes they are too much for him. His struggles are all that the world sees, and it usually misunderstands them. It is hard for a free fish to understand what is happening to a hooked one."[39]

There is wisdom in seeking to understand others—for their sake and for ours. When we truly empathize with another human being, in the process we become better acquainted with our own inner selves, a necessity for deeper empathic responding. As Justin O'Brien has stressed, "Each of us really understands in others only those feelings he is capable of producing himself."

♥ ♥ ♥ ♥ ♥ ♥ ♥ ♥ ♥

COMPASSION REVERES ALL LIFE

Inherent in compassion is reverence for life, a recognition that all life is God-given, that it is precious and irreplaceable, and that all men have God-given souls. In experiencing such reverence, one sorrows not just for the suffering of one person but for all mankind. Illustrating are the poignant emotions of a senior citizen, one of forty from Ohio touring Washington, who visited the Vietnam Veterans Memorial. Informed that the long walk to the memorial would be too difficult in the rain, the senior still made the trek.

After a walk that seemed to take forever, the senior finally reached the wall. Noticing his tears, a young man passing by asked: "One of yours, sir?"

"'Not *one* of them, son,' he replied. 'All of them.'"[40]

Through his anguished tears, this senior expressed profound sorrow for the loss of invaluable life and for the untold and incomprehensible human cost of war. In so doing, he demonstrated his hallowed reverence for humanity. Similarly, Nicholas Berdyaev says, "In a certain sense, every single human soul has more meaning and value than the whole of history with its empires, its wars and revolutions, its blossoming and fading civilizations."[41]

Of the preciousness of the human soul, Sam Levenson declares, "I believe that each new newborn child arrives on earth with a message to deliver to mankind. Clenched in his little fist is some particle of yet unrevealed truth, some missing clue, which may solve the enigma of man's destiny. He has a limited amount of time to fulfill his mission and he will never get a second chance—nor will we. He may be our last hope. He must be treated as top-sacred."[42]

Leon Bloy adds, "Human personality and individuality written and signed by God on each human countenance is something altogether sacred, something for the Resurrection, for eternal Life. . . . Every human face is a very special door to Paradise, which cannot possibly be confused with any other, and through which there will never enter but one soul."[43]

In his 1971 book *Something Beautiful for God*, Malcolm Muggeridge first introduced Mother Teresa's compassionate work to the world. Therein, he wrote of her profound reverence for life—a reverence initially incomprehensible to him. Yet, in the late sixties, what initiated as a brief life trek with Mother Teresa when interviewing her for a later televised broadcast was to profoundly shift that less-than-soulful perspective.

Initially, Muggeridge admits to distastefully distancing himself from Mother Teresa and her "derelicts," as reflected in the desultory interview questions he posed. Why, he asked, would she, under such appalling conditions, work in the slums, "with the poorest of the poor," when her lot could surely be more comfortable? Why would she seek to save children in a country where some deemed there were too many children? Why, with such meager resources, would she and her sisters perpetuate charitable activity that could make so little difference in the lives of teeming millions? And why would she endanger young sisters by engaging them in working with the dying and derelict?

Muggeridge's attitude, he confesses, further surfaced in a Bengal hospital in viewing "a scene of inconceivable confusion and horror, with patients stretched out on the floor, in the corridors, everywhere." There, Muggeridge saw a man, just brought in, whose throat had been cut from ear to ear. "It was too much," he relates. "I made off, back to my comfortable flat and a stiff whisky and soda, to expatiate through the years to come on Bengal's wretched social conditions, and what a scandal it was, and how it was greatly to be hoped that the competent authorities would . . . and so on."

Brooding over the hospital incident, Muggeridge contrasts his behavior to that of Mother Teresa: "I ran away and stayed away. Mother Teresa moved in and stayed in." She *chose* to tarry "amidst all the dirt and disease and misery," signifying, he reverently acknowledges, "a spirit so indomitable, a faith so intractable, a love so abounding, that I felt abashed."

Muggeridge was particularly struck with Mother Teresa's sense of the perfect equality of all persons—regardless of status or attributes. Of this universal truth, he subsequently wrote that the God-endowed equality of men "is the only quality there is on earth." Such equality cannot be destroyed by the men's attitudes or deeds, but "like the rain from heaven, falls on the just and the unjust, on rich and poor alike."

Muggeridge describes Mother Teresa's cradling, in her hands, a tiny baby girl, "so minute that her very existence seemed like a miracle." With an exalted tone and a face "glowing and triumphant," she proclaimed of the child, "See, there's life in her!" Of this scene, Muggeridge writes, "This life in us, in the world, in the universe, . . . however low it flickers or fiercely burns, is still a divine flame which no man dare presume to put out, be his motives ever so humane and enlightened."

In contemplating universal equality, Muggeridge concludes, "To suppose otherwise is to countenance a death-wish. Either life is always and in all circumstances sacred, or intrinsically of no account; it is inconceivable that it should be in some cases the one, and in some the other. The God Mother Teresa worships cannot, we are told, see a sparrow fall to the ground without concern."

As Muggeridge filmed, he ascended in capacity to feel compassion. In visiting the Home for the Dying, and in mingling with lepers and unwanted children, he experienced three piercing phases: "The first was horror mixed with pity, the second compassion pure and simple, and the third, reading far beyond compassion, something I had never experienced before—an awareness that these dying and derelict men and women, these lepers with stumps instead of hands, these unwanted children, were not pitiable, repulsive or forlorn, but rather dear and delightful; as it might be, friends of long standing, brothers and sisters."[44]

Compassion, which recognizes that all living creatures are unprecedented events in the universe, also rightly extends from ultimate revere for man to ultimate revere for all other living things. And compassion comprehends and respects that many creatures in the world, in similar circumstances, experience shades of the same emotions that we humans do, including fear, anxiety, sadness, compassion, and joy.

Penetrating concern for life's creatures is inherent in the instance of an elderly man walking the beach at dawn. Ahead, the elder saw a young man picking up starfish and flinging them into the sea. Finally catching up with the youth, the elder asked the youth why he was returning the starfish to the sea. The answer? The stranded starfish would die if left until the morning sun.

"But the beach goes on for miles and there are millions of starfish," the man countered. "How can your effort make any difference?"

"The young man looked at the starfish in his hand and then threw it to safety in the waves. 'It makes a difference to this one,' he said."[45]

Victor Gollancz, author of *Man and God*, speaks of the "ethic of reverence" for all life. From his perspective, "a man is truly ethical only when he obeys the compulsion to help all life which he is able to assist, and shrinks from injuring anything that lives.

"Whenever I injure life of any sort," he observes, "I must be quite clear whether it is necessary. . . . People must first have considered in each individual case whether there is a real necessity to force upon any animal the sacrifice of death for the sake of mankind, and they must take the most careful pains to ensure that the pain inflicted is made as small as possible.

"Whenever an animal is in any way forced into the service of man, every one of us must be concerned with the suffering which it has thereby to undergo. . . . The ethic of respect for life . . . makes us keep on the look-out together for opportunities of bringing some sort of help to animals . . . to make up for the great misery which men inflict on them."[46]

St. Isaak of Syria views those who have compassion for life's creatures as having a "charitable heart." Explaining, he says, "It is the heart of him who burns with pity for all creation—for every human being, every bird, every animal.

"He looks at the creatures or remembers them, and his eyes are filled with tears. His heart also is filled with deep compassion and unlimited patience; it overflows with tenderness, and cannot bear to see or hear any evil or the least grief endured by the creature.

"Therefore he offers his prayers constantly for the dumb creatures and for the enemies of truth and for those who do him harm, that they may be preserved and pardoned. And for the reptiles also he prays with great compassion, which rises without measure from the depths of his heart till he shines again and is glorious like God."[47] Meister Eckhart also reflects, "Every creature is full of God and is a book about God."[48] Eckhart's inference is that animals are among God's creatures and—as do men—animals have a divine and sacred nature.

Supporting Eckhart's supposition are writings drawn from the Kabbalah: "God nourishes everything, from the horned buffalo to nits, disdaining no creature—for if he disdained creatures due to their insignificance, they could not endure for even a moment. Rather he gazes and emanates compassion upon them all. So should you be good to all creatures, disdaining none."[49]

Illustrating such reverence and compassion for life's creatures is the mother of essayist Scott Russell Sanders, who tells of her, "Once again this spring, the seventy-seventh of her life, my mother put out lint from her clothes dryer for the birds to use in building their nests. 'I know how hard it is to make a home from scratch,' she said. 'I've done it often enough myself.'"[50]

Albert Schweitzer, who also revered earth's creatures, said of an early life experience, "As a small child, I could not understand why I should pray for human beings only. When my mother first had kissed me good night, I used to add a silent prayer that I had composed for all creatures."[51]

Albert Schweitzer tells of the moment his reverence for life's creatures came within full consciousness. As a boy, Schweitzer was with friends who proposed that they go up into the hills and kill birds. Reluctant, but afraid of being scorned, he accompanied the group. Arriving at a tree in which a flock of birds was singing, the boys prepared for the kill by putting stones in their catapults. But then Schweitzer heard the church bells begin to ring—mingling music with birdsong—and to him, the music represented a voice from heaven. Shooing the birds away, he went home, his priorities clear: reverence for life was more important to him than any fear of being taunted or laughed at by his peers.[52] Notes Schweitzer, as the bells rang, he remembers how deeply moved and grateful he was that, on that day, "they rang into my heart the commandments 'Thou shalt not kill.'"

Noteworthy is that Albert Schweitzer also furnished

mankind with a crowning model for revering life—and thus passageway to deeply bonding to the human stream. Indeed, his consummate reverence for life undergirded his remarkable rendering of service to all creatures. To us, the beneficiaries of his legacy, he endows a prophetic caution: Man's very existence and survival rest upon fervent revering of life; and, only through such revering, can man "build a new humanity." Such revering, he advises, "comprises the whole ethic of love in its deepest and highest sense [and] is the source of constant renewal for the individual and for mankind."[53]

❤ ❤ ❤ ❤ ❤ ❤ ❤ ❤ ❤

COMPASSION MOVES GOD'S CREATURES

Jeffrey Moussaieff Masson—author of *Dogs Never Lie about Love*—writes of a hippopotamus compassionately aiding an antelope. Of this heroic wild animal rescue, he tells, "In some extraordinary wildlife footage I was privileged to watch, a small impala antelope in Africa races away from a pack of wild dogs into a river where she is immediately seized by a large crocodile. Suddenly a hippopotamus rushes to the rescue of the dazed antelope.

"The crocodile releases his prey and the hippo then nudges the small animal up the bank of the river and follows her for a few feet until she drops from exhaustion. Instead of leaving, the hippo then helps the little creature to her feet and, opening his mouth as wide as possible, breathes warm air onto the stunned antelope. The hippo does this five times before returning to the forest.

"There is no possible explanation for this remarkable behavior except compassion," Masson concludes.[54]

Consistent with growing assertions that many animals feel compassion, consider an array of surprising and often gripping deeds performed by creatures, great and small:

"A mysterious, sad-eyed dog" was rumored to attend local funerals, there to comfort grieving families. At the hospital, Debbie Sorenson had heard such rumors. Nevertheless, when a funeral procession passed by her house, she was shocked to see her own Basset, Barney, slip his collar to join the procession. She was also shocked to see the procession immediately opening to provide him a place. After proceeding with the hearse to the cemetery, and after sitting with the family throughout the service, Barney returned home.[55]

A seven-year-old female gorilla named Binti—carrying her own baby on her back—rescued a toddler who fell eighteen feet into the gorilla exhibit. Cradling the child in her arms, Binti placed him near a door where zookeepers could retrieve him. During this period, another female gorilla also made gestures that appeared protective of the boy.[56]

A woman, wading waist-deep off the Florida coast when an undertow pulled her down, said of her experience, "I felt something give me a terrific shove up onto the beach. When I got to my feet no one was near, but in the water about eighteen feet out a dolphin was leaping about. A man standing nearby said that the dolphin had shoved me ashore."[57]

Running for her life, a badly frightened doe attempted to elude coyotes closing in on her. Penetrating a small group of range cows and calves grazing up a wash, the totally exhausted and terrified doe sprawled out among them. Coming to the rescue, one cow made a rush at the approaching coyotes and the other cows closed ranks around the downed deer and calves. After circling the group several times, the exasperated coyotes left, the cows started grazing again, and the relieved doe—still panting—got up and slowly walked away.[58]

In a similar rescue, wild dogs chased a zebra herd until they successfully separated a mare, foal, and yearling. As the remaining zebras vanished over the hill, the pack surrounded their victims. As the mother and yearling desperately tried to protect the foal, suddenly ten zebras thundered toward the scene. Galloping up and engulfing within their ranks the three embattled zebras, the herd galloped away again. Within minutes, the wild dogs lost their enthusiasm for the chase.[59]

During freezing weather, several pilots dropped hay to a seriously traumatized and weak caribou herd who, caught in deep snow, could find no forage. After the hay drop, the pilots several times flew over the herd to observe the results. Astonished, they watched stronger herd members gathering hay in their mouths and delivering the hay to weaker animals who could not reach it. This the stronger animals did before feeding themselves.[60]

A group of blackbirds—seemingly in mourning—perched in a large pine tree, emitting a chorus of sounds as, on the ground, they observed a fallen comrade. One by one, many flew from their perches to the downed bird's side. When at last sure their friend was dead, and finished with their mourning ritual, in unison the birds flew away.[61]

Tessa, a German Shepherd, moved to rescue Percy, the family parakeet, in a story Sharon Meininger tells: As a fierce storm raged, Percy escaped from his cage and flew into the pouring rain, the hard wind tossing him to and fro as he disappeared. Immediately Mike, a teenager, accompanied by the dog Tessa, initiated action to retrieve him. Soon dissuaded by the raging storm, Mike returned to the garage. Despite Mike's repeated calls, however, Tessa did not return. Eventually the dog came back, holding in her huge mouth the trembling little bird. Tessa gently deposited him into Mike's hand. Although wet and shaking, and minus a tail, Percy was otherwise intact.[62]

A wildlife biologist saw two jaybirds lighting on the same tree branch, one jay offering a morsel of food held in its beak to the other. Lifting its crested head, the second jay hungrily accepted the gift poked down its throat. Viewing this atypical behavior, the astonished biologist raised his binoculars for further study. Soon the reason became clear: the first jay was feeding the second because he could not feed himself—the second jay's beak was broken off nearly at the base.[63]

Animals, it seems—in addition to rendering compassion—can actually appeal to men for such aid. Recently, for instance, a "wildly quacking mallard" begged for help by continually placing herself in the path of a moving police car. Tells the Associated Press article of this incident, "After the patrol car pulled over, the mamma mallard led the officers to a storm drain where nine baby ducks were trapped.

"'I had never seen anything like it,' said officer Christopher McMullin.

"The duck confronted McMullin's cruiser Sunday on a quiet access road near the Bensalem Police Department. The officer tried to drive around the bird, but it kept walking around in circles to block the vehicle.

"So McMullin got out of the car.

"'I heard this cheeping of baby ducks over to my left,' McMullin recalled. 'And now I know why this duck's going crazy.'

"With the mother duck quacking in the background, McMullin and two other officers pried off the storm grate and reunited the family."[64]

❤ ❤ ❤ ❤ ❤ ❤ ❤ ❤

COMPASSION UNDERSTANDS DISABILITY

Compassion knows that no matter how much a human body, or even mind, is twisted or racked with pain, within each person rests a precious soul. A mother, in fact, tells of one day envisioning the great and noble soul of her severely handicapped baby. For her, the experience contained a profound spiritual message, delivered through a higher power, to comfort and assure her that a day would come—although not on this earth—in which her child would be restored to full function.

In a story of an outgoing and high-achieving young Indian student, Rajendra K. Saboo captures the "sense of soul" so key to understanding the heart-rending position of the disabled. This young man, who always walked with crutches, was approached one day by a classmate who asked about the cause of his problem. When the youth answered "infantile paralysis," his classmate questioned him further regarding his misfortune, asking him how he could possibly face the world. "'Oh,' the boy replied with a smile, 'the disease never touched my heart.'"[65]

This young man, whose answer surprised his questioner, inherently realized that only his body—not his soul—had been afflicted with a debilitating earthly condition.

We all know people with disabilities—and we ourselves may even be among this population. If not, we never know when we might join the ranks of the disabled, by accident or by suddenly becoming struck with blindness, deafness, cerebral palsy, Hodgkin's disease, or another physical malady. Such an incidental change in fortune is demonstrated in an accident incurred by movie star Christopher Reeve, who, thrown from a horse, is now paralyzed. To his everlasting credit, Reeve has become a high-profile advocate for other people who, through accident or illness, are paralyzed.

Instead of reaching out to those with disabilities, many people are quick to dismiss or to overlook such persons, considering them, by nature or accident, as inferior or flawed. They forget that perhaps it is only by a stroke of luck or genetics that they are not one of those they have branded as being less fortunate, or of less worth, than themselves.

Speaking of the luck of the draw as it pertains to life, John Cowper Powys reflects that "in our world, we should feel nothing but plain, simple, humble reverence for the mystery of misfortune."[66]

Realizing that we all have "soul"—and that no absolute measuring standard at the soul level categorizes us according to relative value—is enough to promote our extending a compassionate hand to our fellow man. We are of the same ilk. We have all descended, as spirit children, from the same Father in Heaven—a Father who makes no distinctions with regard to worth. We are, as it were, brothers and sisters, traveling the same perilous journey, taking the same steep, mountainous route. And, looking back as we make our climb, we can grasp the hand of someone behind, pulling that person up to our own position in our mutual ascent.

With respect to disabilities, most of those so afflicted face them with a bravery that many of us, prone to often complain about life's little annoyances, cannot imagine. Representative of such courageous demeanor is Itzhak Perlman, a violinist whose legs were paralyzed by polio at age five. Perlman, who urges people not to judge the disabled by their outward appearances, emphasizes that most people adapt well to their disabilities and they simply want others to respond likewise:

"Ask many of us who are disabled what we would like most in life and we will say, 'To be a better father' or 'To be promoted in my job.' You would be surprised how few would say, 'Not to be disabled.' We accept our limitations. It is others who have problems understanding that and accepting us."[67]

In extending understanding and compassion to the disabled, Beverly Sills, a renowned opera singer, lends an admirable model.

When her first child was nearly two, Sills was informed her daughter was almost totally deaf. Ironically, she would never hear her mother sing. Coincidental in timing to this tragedy, Sills also bore a mentally retarded son.

Sills, who stayed home with her children when they were young, reveals that, at first, she kept asking a self-pitying question, "Why me?" Only when she began asking the more looming question, *"Why them?"* did she start to effectively cope. Her larger perspective garnered her strength, she notes, creating in her a subsequent lifetime focus on volunteering her talents to alleviate the challenges connected with birth defects.[68]

Expanding on Sills's perspective is Hubert Humphrey, who, before his death, spoke of his first grandchild, a mongoloid child. "We couldn't understand why," he observes. "But out of that experience came a whole new sense of values for our family. This little girl taught us more love than all the Sunday school teaching I've had. I began to really understand what it means to love and be loved."[69]

In their observations, Sills and Humphrey capture the profound nature and core of compassion—a completely selfless attitude toward those afflicted and an enlightened view of disability through the lenses of the soul.

The following poem teaches much relative to being at ease with, and communicating support for, those with disabilities. This piece, penned by an unknown author, represents the soul needs of such persons:

> Blessed are you who take the time to listen to difficult
>   speech,
> For you help me to know that if I persevere, I can be under-
>   stood.
> Blessed are you who never bid me to "hurry up"
> Or take my tasks from me . . .
> For I often need time rather than help.

Blessed are you who stand beside me as I enter new and
  untried ventures,
For my failures will be outweighed by the times I surprise
  myself and you.
Blessed are you who asked for my help
For my greatest need is to be needed.
Blessed are you who understand that it is difficult for me to
  put my thoughts into words.
Blessed are you who, with a smile, encourage me to try once
  more.
Blessed are you who never remind me that today I asked the
  same question twice.
Blessed are you who respect me and love me just as I am.

♥ ♥ ♥ ♥ ♥ ♥ ♥ ♥ ♥

COMPASSION RECOGNIZES POTENTIAL

Charles Osgood says of babies, who epitomize the very nature
of potential, "Babies are pure potential. You pick up a little baby
and you're amazed by how light it is, but you feel also that you're
holding the future, the earth and the sky, the sun and the moon,
and all of it, everything, is brand new."[70]

Compassion recognizes in every human being the same pure
potential of which Osgood speaks—a divine potential generated
and radiating foremost from the soul. Compassion also realizes
that any human being may experience untoward circumstances
that can leave his or her potential untapped, battered or bruised,
or crushed—as it were—under a heel. Compassion thus strives,
in each person it meets, to honor that person's potential and to
invite that potential to find form or to surface. Such is the case
in the following story in which compassion steadied a frightened
young man and his faith in himself.

That young man was John Carmichael, a Scottish minister in

his first church position, who always dreaded Sundays and the thought of a potentially disastrous lecture. Overall, Carmichael judged his ability to perform as inferior and worried that, in his present ministry, he was doing poorly and that his congregation viewed him with pity and contempt. And then one day, to his terror, his worst fears were realized. The stern elders of his Scottish kirk filed solemnly into the vestry.

Carmichael waited tensely, braced for what he thought was to come—a recital of those very "faults" he had seen in himself and was now absolutely sure others had also observed. But this was not to be. Rather than intending to reprove the young minister, the elders had come to tell him not to be afraid. "Next Sabbath before you begin to speak," was their message, "we ask you to say to yourself, 'They're all loving me.' And it will be true. From the oldest to the youngest, we will all be loving you very much."[71]

In this case, the elders recognized Carmichael's potential and, through their actions, bolstered his self-esteem and elevated his self-confidence. They did so by saying, in a word, "It won't matter if you make a mistake. You don't have to be worried. We all love you and we all have faith that, with our complete support, you will grow and mature into your present calling." Through their magnanimous, and unanimous, gesture, the elders assured the young minister of their love and of his position. Their intent is consistent with a lesson inherent in an anonymous piece called "The Parable of the Rose."

In this parable, a certain man planted a rose and watered it faithfully, and before it blossomed he examined it. He saw the bud that would soon blossom—and also the sharp thorns. And he thought, "How can any beautiful flower come from a plant burdened with so many thorns?" Saddened by this thought, he neglected to water the rose, and, before it could bloom, it died.

So it is with people. Within every eternal soul there is a rose—the Godlike qualities planted with us at birth, growing amid the thorns of our earthly defects or lacks. Yet, tragically, there are often souls among us whose roses are not apparent to many observers; and these observers stand back so as not to be pricked by the perceived thorns, or flaws, of those considered wanting. Thus, no one "waters the roses" within these souls, and the roses therefore wither or never bud.

Often it takes a deeply compassionate person to show wanting souls the roses within themselves—to point out their divine potential, or what Christ called "the kingdom of heaven within them" (Luke 17:21)—and to help them recognize their nobility. And it often takes a compassionate person to extend to these wanting souls the vital watering and nutrients they need so desperately and to help them to extract the thorns so that all might recognize the blossoming roses.

Echoing these sentiments is Tian Dayton, who observes that in this life "we need a guide to show the way and to help anchor the way as we seek ourselves, someone who is willing to walk with us as we keep ourselves on our path. As C. S. Lewis has said, 'It takes two to see one.'"[72]

Through other lenses, compassion may recognize potential in someone who has been beaten and abused, physically and emotionally, to the point of partial or complete dysfunction; in someone with pronounced disability; or in someone who is aging and who, by virtue of that aging, in the world's view has lost value. In *Evidence of Hope*, Jane W. Lund speaks through analogy of such vulnerable people:

"I have two chairs that are each over 100 years old," tells Lund. "One occupies a coveted corner of my living room. Its rockers are worn. Scratches and nicks testify to the fact that it has been well used.

"I regard the chair for its age, the quality of its material, and for its superb craftsmanship. It is fashioned from solid oak. The hand-carved back is high. Ten ornate dowels extend downward to the seat. Each piece of the old rocker has been hand-turned and precisely fit by the caring hands of a master craftsman. Working parts have been skillfully replaced with new materials carefully selected so as to embellish its integrity and beauty. As I sit and rock, the chair sings and sobs its history. . . . In my mind's eye, I can envision generations of others whose loving use and care have elevated the old rocker to the status of a 'treasured antique.'

"Another old chair stands in the corner of my garage," she continues. "It is broken . . . perhaps beyond repair. It was rescued from the top of a trash heap. Like my fine old rocker it, too, is solid oak, and beautifully designed. But weather has separated the grain of its fine wood and it is twisted and warped. Missing rungs have been replaced by cross-wires. Its once lovely leather seat is marked with the residue of paint cans left by careless workmen.

"I, too, am acquiring the marks of age. When anyone will listen, I sing and sob the details of my history. My worn parts are systematically replaced with 'new technology' to restore and embellish my fading beauty. I hope, because of my age, the workmanship of my life, and the quality of my experience, that I will become someone's cared for, and appreciated 'antique.'

"I wish that everyone born could be valued as a fine collectable, but they are not. The wreckage of the undervalued and abused is found everywhere. It is not because they were made of inferior material or flawed by shoddy workmanship. It is simply because no one recognized or appreciated their potential to be beautiful, useful, and unique."[73]

Addressing, also through analogy, the "wreckage of the

undervalued and abused" is an unknown author who tells this story: "Once there was a mosaic artist who, with minute care, chipped each piece of colored tile or glass until it was exactly the right size and shape for his purpose. One morning when arriving at the studio earlier than usual he discovered his young assistant privately completing a mosaic of his own.

'The master looked at the mosaic and saw that it was good. 'My boy,' he said, 'Where did you get the pieces for this?'

"'They are the little broken pieces that I swept up from the floor, master,' replied the lad.

"'Nay, not I, but you are the master,' the artist pronounced, 'for I have a plenitude of material for my mosaics, but you have created a wonderful mosaic with the pieces I threw away.'"[74]

Kurt Klein was a man compelled to work with the "pieces" at a time when Gerda, his wife-to-be, was "broken," a story news reporter Karen Boren tells. "It was June 1942 when Gerda watched her parents disappear in the long lines of Auschwitz," tells Boren. As a fifteen-year-old, Gerda "was sold into slave labor for ten German Reichmarks. As she was toiling under inhumane conditions, her husband-to-be was in America desperately trying to get his parents out of Germany before it was too late. . . . Tragically, his efforts would be in vain: Kurt Klein's parents perished at Auschwitz, unable to join the children they had sent to safety in 1937.

"By the time Kurt's Fifth U. S. Infantry Division of Patton's Third Army arrived in Volary, Czechoslovakia, Gerda was one of one hundred twenty young girls left of four thousand who had been force-marched one thousand miles to Volary, where they were locked in an abandoned factory. A torrential rain had doused the bomb meant to obliterate the evidence of the Third Reich's cruelty."

It was then that Gerda saw a jeep approach, "on its hood, no longer the swastika, but the white star of the American Army." And it was also then that a handsome young lieutenant approached her. Kurt, that young soldier, remembers, "I saw these emaciated figures walking across the yard—it was a totally devastating experience. . . . I was taken aback by these dying young women."

Boren describes what happened next: "In a habit born of some six years of Nazi occupation and degradation, Gerda automatically 'warned' this soldier that she was a Jew. 'So am I,' was his firm reply.

"'This was the greatest moment of my life,' says Gerda." And when Kurt held the door of the factory for Gerda, this simple symbolic gesture endeared him to her, restoring her faith in humanity.

"Kurt remembers that as she walked with him through the deserted factory where her friends were slowly dying, Gerda quoted the great German poet Goethe, saying, 'Noble be man, merciful and good.' Said Kurt, 'Nothing could have better expressed the grim irony of the situation.'

"Surely Kurt was looking into the beauty of Gerda's soul because at liberation she weighed only sixty-eight pounds and her hair had turned white," notes Boren. "She was rushed to a field hospital, where between typhus and pneumonia she was unconscious for a week. The nurses said in astonishment that they could circle her thigh with their fingers.

"When her soldier visited her at the hospital, he brought her a prized piece of chocolate. Then he came back with *Life* magazines. Pointing to the large letters L-I-F-E, he asked her, 'Do you know what it means? It is a fine word for you to learn.' Say it, he said. 'That's right,' he told her as she repeated the word and smiled, 'that's what I wanted to see.'

"As her strength returned and her hair became black again,

Gerda smiled more and more often. Kurt brought her flowers and continued to teach her English. They married in Paris a year later and immigrated to Buffalo, New York.

"It didn't take so long, really, until Gerda could quit going to the grocery store every day to be sure the shelves were still stocked and she wouldn't be hungry again," Boren relates. "And there was only one time, after a friend had loudly disparaged Roosevelt in a restaurant, when Gerda made Kurt call the man to be sure he hadn't been arrested in the dark of the night.

"Two daughters and a son have now made Kurt and Gerda grandparents," Boren finishes. "The grandchildren can hardly understand what their beloved grandmother endured. One asked, 'Grandma, why were you hungry? Why didn't you use your credit card?'" And another grandson had to this to say about the Holocaust: "Why didn't you write to your congressman about that guy Hitler?"[75]

❤ ❤ ❤ ❤ ❤ ❤ ❤ ❤

COMPASSION STIRS THE SOUL

"Do not the most moving moments of our lives find us all without words?" asks Marcel Marceau.[76]

It is often compassion speaking to our souls that creates such moments, as in the instance of a nearly-blind mother and her young daughter, Robin. Related by Pamela Johnson, the story opens as Robin enters the house—door banging behind her—to call her mother to come chase butterflies with her.

Says Robin's mother: "I groaned and picked up another potato. 'I'd love to, Robin, if I ever get this done.'

"'Then you'll have something else to do,' she complained.

"I paused, peeler in mid-air. Potatoes would wait but time with my daughter wouldn't always be there.

"'You're right,' I smiled. 'It's too nice outside to stay in a stuffy house. Let's go.'

"Robin hesitated. 'Mom, aren't butterflies too small for you to see?'

"Robin had always been unusually perceptive about my near blindness. 'It'll be okay.' I patted her shoulder. 'I can view one through your eyes.'

"Out in the warm sunshine, it didn't take Robin long to find a Monarch butterfly we could follow. 'He's real colorful, Mom, with brown and yellow wings. I wish you could see him.'

"'I'm afraid your butterfly moves too fast for that,' I chuckled. 'I have an idea, though. You tell me when he is by the big things I can see. Then at least I'll know where he's at.'

"The two of us chased the butterfly around the yard, and I felt like a kid again. The soft grass tickled my hot toes, and the slight breeze refreshed the humid day. Meanwhile, Robin explained, 'The butterfly is by a tree and going toward the sky. Now he's near the hedge but is headed for the garbage cans.'

"Soon Robin told me, 'I've lost him.'

"I suggested we take a rest so we flopped down under our old sycamore tree.

"After a minute Robin said, 'Maybe I can think of a way for you to see a butterfly.'

"I squeezed her hand. 'I'd love to watch one, Robin.' I shrugged. 'But I don't know how I can.'

"'A butterfly is one of God's prettiest creations,' Robin reflected. 'He and I will just have to find a way for you to look at one. I'll be back.'

"She scurried away, and I marveled at her simple faith. While I waited for her, I looked around at the majestic purple mountains, the green in the tree and the yellow ball of sun. Even though I missed most of the details in my surroundings, I was grateful. What if my world remained in total darkness?

"I must have dozed because the next sound I heard was Robin's eager voice as she shook me awake. 'Mom, I have something to show you.'

"She thrust a bottle into my hands.

"I moved it next to my face and squinted until my eyes focused on a brown and yellow something that darted inside the jar.

"'A butterfly!' My voice was filled with the awe I felt.

"'I captured him just for you.'

"'He's beautiful.' My throat tightened, and I could hardly go on. 'He's so near. I can watch him with my own eyes while he spreads his tiny wings.' I held the bottle away and hugged her. 'Thank you, Robin. Thank you, God,' I whispered.

"'You can keep him,' Robin offered.

"'I'd like to, honey, except no one, especially a butterfly, wants to be cooped up in a bottle.'

"'Oh! Mom, if you let him go, you won't be able to see a butterfly anymore.'

"'No, but I'll always remember.'

"Once more I stared at what I could glimpse of his tiny wings. For a trembling moment my eyes lingered. I was not quite ready to let this moment of seeing go. I longed to engrave his colors in my mind. I peered at him until my eyes blurred. Then I gave the jar back to Robin. I had viewed a butterfly. It was enough.

"'Mom, do you ever feel like you're in a bottle?'

"'What do you mean?'

"'Well, if I was a butterfly in a bottle, I don't think I'd see much around me. That must be how it is for you.'

"I was touched by her insight. 'Yes, I guess that's how it is

unless I have someone like you to show me things like butterflies.'

"'I'll go dig up a worm for you to look at.'

"'Oh, no,' I laughed as I turned up my nose. 'I think we can
pass on that one.'

"We walked back to the house embracing a new kind of
closeness.

"Someday, when Robin soars away to find her own life, she
and I will have forgotten that the potatoes were left unpeeled.
Yet, we will treasure the memory of our butterfly and afternoon
spent together."[77]

The story of Robin and her mother exemplifies an instance
of compassion stirring the heart. Robin's mother's heart was
stirred, first, by viewing the butterfly, but in addition, by her
daughter's deeply compassionate gesture. And through that gesture, mother and daughter lived out a few moments they would
forever treasure.

♥ ♥ ♥ ♥ ♥ ♥ ♥ ♥ ♥

COMPASSION CHALLENGES OUR SENSITIVITY

"An old rabbi once asked his pupils how they could tell when the
night had ended and the day had begun," an old Hasidic tale
begins.

"'Could it be,' asked a student, 'when you can see an animal
in the distance and tell whether it's a sheep or a dog?'

"'No,' replied the rabbi, to which the pupils demanded, 'Then
when is it?'

"'It is when you can look on the face of any man or woman
and see that it is your sister or brother. Because if you cannot see
this, it is still night.'"[78]

This Hasidic tale bespeaks the foundation upon which com-

passion rests—that is, the necessity of "seeing" others prelimi-
nary to any response to their suffering. We are ever in close
physical proximity to others. Yet, daily—because we pass
through so many lives while usually preoccupied with our own—
we often fail to notice others' suffering.

Erma Bombeck speaks to the challenge of sensing heartaches
within others despite our own preoccupations. Her sensitivity to
this lack was heightened on a day she had scheduled air travel.
At that time, Bombeck felt so bombarded and harried that she
fancifully envisioned getting her own unlisted apartment. Thus,
she eagerly anticipated having thirty minutes of quiet time while
she awaited departure from the airport. But once there, and in
process of becoming situated, Bombeck incurred an unwelcome
interruption. Beside her, an elderly woman remarked that the
weather was cold in Chicago.

Bombeck's response was cool and sharp, but the woman
remained undeterred and began speaking of her trip. Eyes fixated
on her book, Bombeck's responses remained flat—until the
woman said her husband's body was on the plane. She'd been
married for fifty-three years, she mentioned, and was alone at the
hospital when her husband died. Though she wasn't even
Catholic, a nun had taken her home because she didn't drive.
And the funeral director had kindly let her ride with him to the
airport.

In finally perceiving the woman's hidden torment and
tragedy, Bombeck was shocked. Never more than then had she
detested herself, she reflects. At her side was an intensely dis-
tressed human being beseeching aid, who, in desperation, had
appealed to a stranger. Yet she—the stranger—had been utterly
uninterested and unhearing of her fellow traveler's pleas.

Then Bombeck did what hopefully anyone would do.
Closing her book, she listened intently as the woman spoke

numbly and unabatedly until the boarding call. As Bombeck settled into her seat on the plane, from elsewhere came again a familiar voice: The weather was cold in Chicago. Burdened by her own initial chilliness, Bombeck recalls thinking of the woman's seating companion and praying, "Please God, help her listen."[79]

Tacitly Bombeck implores us all to be more sensitive to others' human dramas. And here, Ashleigh Brilliant's words aptly apply: "If we could all hear one another's prayers, God might be relieved of some of his burden."[80]

❤ ❤ ❤ ❤ ❤ ❤ ❤ ❤ ❤

COMPASSION IS CREATIVE

At times, compassion must be creative, as the fellow beings it aches to assist must save face. Or they may not believe or understand how assistance might relieve their pain or fulfill their needs.

On one occasion, such compassion prevailed creatively—and with inordinate sensitivity—when a volunteer brought to a cancer ward several zoo animals, anticipating that patients might gain comfort from holding and petting them.

As the volunteer made her rounds, one patient refused to leave his room. "He was bitter and angry," she relates. "Shame was with him." But recognizing he was somewhat curious about the animals, she extended a pet and asked, "Would you like to touch?"

"Oh, sure, sure," retorted the man. "With these hands?"

Thrusting his fingerless hands into the volunteer's face, the mortified patient gazed at the floor. Recognizing his extreme pain, she gently suggested, "Here, then—with your palms." At that, the patient eased his hostility. "With each animal he became softer," she recalls. "For once there was something besides his illness. He began to cry. 'This is so beautiful,' he said. 'I will never forget this.'"[81]

In the preceding incident, this volunteer reached the soul of a deeply wounded human being—this because of her sensitive and creative response to his intense shame and deep feelings of inadequacy.

In an earlier era, compassion responded creatively for another reason—in this instance, accepting help equated to loss of self-sufficiency. Robert W. Youngs tells of an elderly widow, a neighbor, in desperate need of medical care. Knowing she would resist direct aid, Youngs imaginatively secured a pill box from his druggist, filled it with gold coins, and wrote on the box, "One to be taken when required." After wrapping the box, he left it at her door.[82]

In a final instance, compassion was creative in the case of Abraham Lincoln, who—possessing penetrating understanding of human nature—ever sought to protect people's feelings. Because Lincoln's White House doors were always open to the public, goes the story, the ease with which others could approach him "vastly increased his labor. It also led to many scenes at the White House that were strangely amusing and sometimes dramatic."

Early in 1865, certain influential citizens of Missouri, then in Washington, formed a committee to secure executive intervention in behalf of oppressed fellow-citizens. Having been appointed to approach the president, with trepidation several committee members one day entered the White House. With Grant on the march to Richmond and Sherman's army sweeping down to the sea, they envisioned a preoccupied president intensely pondering the momentous events then developing. They were thus greatly surprised when they were cordially received and invited to enter the president's office.

In behalf of oppressed Missourians, one committee member—
the ex-governor—took the floor: "With the most solemn delib-
eration he began: 'Mr. President, I want to call your attention to
the case of Betsy Ann Doughterty,—a good woman. She lived
in ———— County, and did my washing for a long time. Her husband went off and joined the rebel army, and I wish you would
give her a protection paper.' The solemnity of this appeal struck
Mr. Lincoln as uncommonly ridiculous.

"The two men looked at each other,—the governor desperately in earnest, and the President masking his humor behind the
gravest exterior. At last Mr. Lincoln asked with inimitable gravity,
'Was Betsy Ann a good washerwoman?'

"'Oh, yes, sir; she was indeed.'

"'Was your Betsy Ann an obliging woman?'

"'Yes, she was certainly very kind,' responded the governor
soberly.

"'Could she do other things than wash?' continued Mr.
Lincoln, with the same portentous gravity.

"'Oh, yes; she was very kind—very.'

"'Where is Betsy Ann?'

"'She is now in New York, and wants to come back to
Missouri, but she is afraid of banishment.'

"'Is anybody meddling with her?'

"'No; but she is afraid to come back unless you will give her
a protection paper.'

"Thereupon Mr. Lincoln wrote on a visiting card the following:—

"'*Let Betsy Ann Doughterty alone as long as she behaves herself.*
'A. Lincoln'

"Handing this card to her advocate, he said, 'Give this to
Betsy Ann.'

"'But Mr. President, couldn't you write a few words to the officers that would insure her protection?'

"'No,' said the President, 'officers have no time now to read letters. Tell Betsy Ann to put a string in this card and hang it round her neck. When the officers see this, they will keep their hands off your Betsy Ann.'"

In this instance, Lincoln responded creatively with characteristic compassion, thus neutralizing a situation that could have otherwise proved profoundly mortifying to his imperceptive visitors. Of the incident, Lincoln remarked afterward he wished he had no more serious issues to deal with than Betsy Ann. "If there were more Betsy Anns and fewer fellows like her husband, we should be better off," he observed. "She seems to have laundered the governor to his full satisfaction, but I am sorry she didn't keep her husband washed cleaner."[83]

❤ ❤ ❤ ❤ ❤ ❤ ❤ ❤

COMPASSION PAYS ITS DUES

"Never hesitate to hold out your hand; never hesitate to accept the outstretched hand of another," urges Pope John XXIII.[84]

As the pope's observation implies, compassion recognizes that as fellow travelers taking the same perilous life trek, we have responsibility toward those who need comfort and aid in traversing life's arduous obstacles. Speaking to this point, Albert Schweitzer emphasized, "Tenderness toward those weaker than ourselves strengthens the heart toward life itself. The moment we understand and feel sorry for the next man and forgive him, we wash ourselves, and it is a cleaner world."

Schweitzer, who, throughout his lifetime as a physician, freely served his fellow men, also urged others to give of their intangible wealth: "Whatever you have received more than others—in health, in talents, in ability, in success—all this you must not take to yourself as a matter of course. In gratitude for your good fortune, you must render in return some sacrifice."[85] Extending the same theme, Wilfred Grenfell says, "The service we render to others is really the rent we pay for our room on this earth."[86]

Writings of Dr. Tom Dooley, a young doctor who sacrificed his life for others, embody this sense of dedicated service to mankind. Dooley, who served as a physician in northern Laos, wrote a letter shortly before his death to a young graduate from medical school coming to intern under his tutelage. In this letter, Dooley described where he practiced medicine:

"This valley in Laos, prior to our Medico hospital, had nothing to offer the sick but black magic, necromancy, witchcraft, clay images, sorcery and betel juice. The villagers wallowed in monkeys' blood, cobwebs, tigers' teeth and incantation. . . . Here in Laos, there are three million people and only one Laos doctor.

"Though this is sometimes called 'the age of the shrug,'" Dooley continues, "I do not believe you would say, as some do, 'So what, it's not my problem.' You and I, Bart, are the heirs of all ages. We have been born and raised in freedom. We have justice, law and equality. But we have overlooked another side of our inheritance. We have also the legacy of hatred, bred by careless men before us. We have the legacy of abuse, degradation and the inhumanity of men blinded by prejudice and ignorance. . . . To people like you and me, richer in educational opportunities than many, this is a challenge. To accept it is a privilege and a responsibility."

Continuing, Dooley urges Bart, "Bring your gadgets and the armamentarium of drugs, to be sure, but most of all bring your human spirit. Bring your youthful enthusiasm, your drive, your energy, your dedication to help the sick. Bring your wonderful spontaneity, your belief in the good and the right. Bring along a sense of humor. . . . You'll certainly need it when the roof leaks, the patients eat all the pills the first dosage and the witch doctors put cow dung over your sterile compresses."

Above all, Dooley finishes, "Splash some of your human warmth and goodness on people who heretofore have known little of this element in the Western man. . . . Use your profession and your heart as a cable to bind men together."[87]

Dooley understood what we must all realize if we are to discover our soul—that all men are universally one in spirit. To this point, Daphne Rose Kingma reflects, "Every human being is your counterpart. Every other human being possesses and embodies aspects of yourself: your dreams, your sorrows, your hope(s). . . . For each of us there was a time when the world was young, a springtime of spirit that was later tested by the winters of discontent; and in the midst of each of our lives lies the haunting shadow of death.

"Therefore we are all quite alike; indeed at the core we are all one, all lost—and found—in the same mysterious enterprise that is life. Hold this in your heart as you go about your day, and the world will cease to be inhabited by strangers, and the burden of life itself will no longer be a process of loneliness."[88]

❤ ❤ ❤ ❤ ❤ ❤ ❤ ❤ ❤

COMPASSION NEEDS NO JUSTIFICATION

Compassion rests upon the premise that people are intrinsically valuable simply because they are, and thus compassion treats no one with callous disregard. There need not be, then, any further justification for compassion other than there are suffering people, who, by reason of their humanity, deserve such respect. Such is the essence of the true story "Night Watch," written by Roy Popkin, which began as a nurse took the tired, anxious serviceman to a hospital bedside:

"'Your son is here,' she told the patient. She had to repeat the words several times before the man's eyes opened. Heavily sedated because of the pain of his heart attack, he dimly saw the young man in the Marine Corps uniform standing outside the opaque walls of the oxygen tent. He reached out his hand. The Marine wrapped his toughened fingers around the old man's limp one, squeezing a message of love and encouragement. The nurse brought a chair, so that the Marine could sit alongside the bed.

"Nights are long in hospitals, but all through the night the young Marine sat there in the poorly lit ward, holding the old man's hand and offering words of hope and strength. . . . Occasionally, the nurse suggested that the Marine move away and rest awhile. He refused.

"Whenever the nurse came into the ward, the Marine was there, oblivious of her and the night noises of the hospital—the clanking of an oxygen tank, the laughter of night staff members exchanging greetings, the cries and moans and snores of other patients. Occasionally, she heard him say a few gentle words. The dying man said nothing, only held tightly to his son.

"Along toward dawn, the patient died. The Marine placed on the bed the lifeless hand he had been holding and went to tell the nurse." While she did what she had to, he waited. Finally, she returned. She started to offer words of sympathy, but the Marine interrupted her.

"'Who was that man?' he asked.

"The nurse was startled. 'Wasn't he your father?' she queried.

"'No, he wasn't,' the Marine replied. 'I never saw him before in my life.'"

The nurse asked why he hadn't said something when she took him to the wrong room.

"'I knew right off there'd been a mistake, but I also knew he needed his son, and his son just wasn't here. When I realized he was too sick to tell whether or not I was his son, I figured he really needed *me*, so I stayed.'"[89]

This young Marine recognized the dying man's acute need to have his son at his bedside during his last few hours on earth. And he might have even imagined the son's intensified grief had he realized his father died alone and without the comfort of another human being.

Inherent in this young man's actions was a deep-seated respect for the intrinsic value of another human being—in this case, a stranger—which prompted him to play an indispensable part in the unfolding drama of a fading human life. His actions also demonstrated that intuitively he understood—as it were—that compassion makes no distinctions.

To understand the concept of human value is to begin to understand the fragile nature of one's own and others' souls. This, in turn, commands the need to treat such souls with gentleness, and with the same tenderness and care, that one extends to a newborn baby, the holding of whom, in itself, is a deeply soul-satisfying and wondrous experience.

The word *wondrous*, with all that it implies, is applicable to the growth of compassion for others. When one is wondrous of the very existence of life and of the universe and of the mysterious realms of the human soul and spirit, one cannot at the same time be angry, or abrasive, or preoccupied with satisfying the needs of the ego. Nor can one treat another person as an object, to be brushed aside as an inconvenience, or verbally or physically battered and bruised at a whim.

Rather, if one is wondrous of the preciousness of life, one

becomes extremely protective of others, who, in their own innermost depths, duplicate one's self. The need to treat others with
the respect and care due them as invaluable human beings is
inherent in this piercing observation: Love people, and use
things, and never confuse the two.

▾ ▾ ▾ ▾ ▾ ▾ ▾ ▾ ▾

COMPASSION COMPELS ACTION

Inherent in compassion is a deep-seated wish to quell pain and
eliminate the world's vast suffering. Thus, compassion takes
action. From this grander perspective, Peter De Vries notes, "We
are not primarily put on the earth to see through one another,
but to see one another through."[90]

Compassion took action "to see another through" during
World War II, embodied in Helen Keller's decision to visit and
aid recently blinded and deafened servicemen. Although vehemently opposed to war, Keller's heart opened to help after a pivotal conversation with a friend, whose penetrating insight
released her to follow her heart.

Of her friend, Keller relays that she "realized how World
War II had coiled itself about my mind with burning anguish,
and without preface or apology she blurted out on her fingers to
me, 'Why not go to the wounded soldiers and find out yourself
what you can do for them? You have your two hands, your heart,
and your faith in their strength to rise above circumstances.
Remember, they have adjustments to make just as you had when
you were a child. You have forgotten the very traces of the dark
and silent horror that clutched you. You owe a debt to the soldiers. We all do. Perhaps you can pay yours. Paying it will enable
you to accept their sacrifice—their sacrifice for us, for each other,
and the unrealized dream we call civilization.'"

Responding to her friend's encouragement, for more than two years Keller visited disabled servicemen in more than seventy hospitals, truly rendering "compassion in action."[91]

"Compassion in action" also made its entrance in Sue Monk Kidd's life late one evening in a hospital elevator. Restless and distraught as she attended to her intensely ill husband, she left his bedside soon after midnight. Darkness alone pressed against the window pane, and to Kidd, the very night seemingly conspired to darken her soul. Anguished, she slipped on her shoes and stepped out to a shadowy hospital corridor. As her fears intensified, unbidden tears spilled over and sobs crowded her throat.

Seeing the hospital elevator doors open, Kidd darted inside, fumbling for the buttons. Her now ungovernable sobs—echoing anonymously in the elevator—gave gargantuan expression to her deepening fears. How many elevator rides she took, she couldn't count—but no matter. She was at last alone, in this solace able to release her overwhelming grief and despair. But then a ping— and the elevator opened, revealing an elderly man with thinning white hair. Entering, the man pushed a button, his attention riveted on Kidd's disheveled condition.

As he handed Kidd a neatly folded handkerchief, his eyes searched her face, piercing the deep reaches of her soul. All the while, his kind, steady gaze conveyed deep sorrow over her suffering. Like the first rays of the morning sun, the man's soothing demeanor dispelled the darkness and the night, warming Kidd's spirit and firing her hopes. Feeling connected, centered, received, she felt strangely as if God was in the elevator, working through this man's generous and bountiful soul.

As the door swished open, Kidd thanked the stranger and handed him back his well-used handkerchief. Nodding, and with a gentle smile, he slipped away. Now bolstered, she returned to her husband, sustained by a strength beyond herself—the product of soul meeting soul in the elevator.[92]

In a final instance, compassion took action in salvaging the life and spirits of a purebred border collie. After purchasing a neglected piece of range land on Vancouver Island, Canada, Phillip Keller urgently needed a sheep dog to herd his grazing ewes and lambs. Scouring the newspaper advertisements one day, Keller read an ad: "Wanted—Good country home for purebred border collie. Chases cars and bicycles." When he hurriedly phoned the owner, she pled, "Please do come quickly. No one else wants her."

When he arrived at the woman's home some thirty miles away, Keller followed her into the backyard. There, he was suddenly beset by "a flying, leaping bundle of a dog" who lunged at him, snarling and snapping. Stunned, he realized the dog was chained from her collar to a steel post and—by another chain—hobbled from her neck to back leg. Reacting as he edged closer, laying her ears back, she growled menacingly at him. Keller grasped the scene: a dog "'gone wrong' . . . totally useless . . . a sad spectacle . . . almost beyond help." Yet, she was a superb creature with splendid breeding and remarkable learning potential.

Keller took the collie, oddly convinced this torn and twisted creature could be redeemed. In a clean kennel, the collie refused to eat or drink and rejected Keller's every approach. Finally, with the dog's health deteriorating, Keller took daring action, setting her free. In moments she disappeared, and subsequent efforts to locate her proved fruitless. One day, at the top of a large outcrop he saw her—crouched like a cougar—watching him. As he called to her, she quickly withdrew. After that, Keller left food out every day.

A few weeks later Keller again saw the collie, this time

keenly observing the sheep, her inbred instincts surfacing. Throughout, Keller experienced intense compassion for the collie, longing for her to love and trust him. Then one evening as Keller stood entranced by a glowing sunset, the collie's soft warm nose touched his hand. Lass—for he had named her that—had come! He was ecstatic, and rightly so, for her soul-stirring action spawned the beginning of an enduring companionship.

As mutual affection and trust grew, Keller began teaching Lass essential sheepherding commands, and she soon skillfully managed the sheep. Quickly becoming totally devoted, she readily assumed even tough or trying tasks. Further, she became Keller's virtual shadow, "his presence her peace and pleasure." In exchange for Keller's compassion, Lass became the mainstay of his entire operation, their ever-deepening partnership gracing his life and hers.[93]

♥ ♥ ♥ ♥ ♥ ♥ ♥ ♥ ♥

COMPASSION SEES THROUGH THE HEART

Compassion knows, as Antoine de Saint Exupéry advises, that "it is only with the heart that one can see rightly; what is essential is invisible to the eye."[94] Thus, searching beyond trappings and appearances, compassion sees through the heart—its wish, in any stricken being, to reach and nurture that being's timeless soul.

Many years ago, Arthur Gordon tells, compassion "saw through the heart" in an English setting. At the time, a poverty-stricken young boy obtained a low-paying twelve-hour-a-day job in a print shop. Passionately interested in books but unable to buy any, he deliberately passed a dingy secondhand bookstore each day on his way to work. If a book lay open in the window, he would stop and read the two visible pages.

"One day he noticed that the book he had scanned the day before was open to the *next* two pages. The day after that, the same thing happened. He read on and on, two pages a day, until he came to the last page. On that day the old man who ran the store came out and told him, with a smile, that he could come in and read anything at any time, with no obligation to buy."

Thus, a kindly old man behind a dusty window contributed to a boy's life. He also contributed to the world, because the boy, Benjamin Farjeon, subsequently became an eminent author.[95]

Likewise, another person who compassionately "saw through the heart" was Kermit, Theodore Roosevelt's fifteen-year-old son. Having unearthed a book—*The Children of the Night*—by an obscure poet named Edwin Arlington Robinson, Kermit sent a copy to his father, who was as impressed as Kermit with the freshness and originality of the work. Exploring the origination of the book and the circumstances of the author, Kermit found that Robinson was working as a timekeeper in the construction of the New York subway. This was no place for a poet, Kermit told his father. Couldn't he arranged a job for Robinson in which the poet could make a living and yet still have time to write poetry?

Although Theodore Roosevelt had strict views about the Civil Service, he agreed with Kermit's view and found a position for Robinson in the New York Custom House. Responding to Kermit's insistent proddings, the president went further, convincing a major book company to publish Robinson's book, and he and Kermit wrote a book review for *Outlook*. The subsequent review caused a sensation in the American literary as well as political world. For his part, Theodore Roosevelt "was patronized by critics, derided, scolded, put in his place." However,

Roosevelt's unequivocal support sparked Robinson's eventual rise as a major American poet.[96]

Finally, "seeing through the heart" was President Abraham Lincoln shortly after the second battle of Bull Run. The day was the last Saturday of September 1862, and all forty-odd hospitals in Washington were filled with sick and wounded Union and Confederate soldiers. Determined to visit every hospital before the day's end, early that morning President Lincoln had left the White House. It was now late afternoon, and the president had just finished praying for a dying Confederate soldier at whose bedside he had knelt.

As he stepped into a waiting carriage, the weary president was interrupted by a hospital nurse telling him the soldier was pleading for his return. Returning immediately to his bedside, he quietly asked how he might assist.

"'I am so lonely and friendless, Mr. Lincoln,' the boy whispered, 'and I am hoping that you can tell me what my mother would want me to say and do now.'"

Lincoln reassured the soldier he knew exactly what action his mother would have him take, adding that he was glad the soldier had again asked for him. "'Now,' he said, 'as I kneel here, please repeat the words after me.'"

Then, "the lad, facing eternity with recollections of a good mother," prayed with Lincoln. Head resting upon the president's arm, he repeated the following words—words he had learned at bedtime at his mother's knee:

> Now I lay me down to sleep;
> I pray the Lord my soul to keep.
> If I should die before I wake,
> I pray the Lord my soul to take.
> And this I ask for Jesus' sake.[97]

♥ ♥ ♥ ♥ ♥ ♥ ♥ ♥ ♥

COMPASSION HAS ULTIMATE REGARD

Inherent in compassion is the capacity to treat others as you would if you knew and loved them, and therefore cared about their well-being. James Michener, who never knew his own parents or anything about his family, speaks poignantly regarding ultimate regard: "I was born to a woman I never knew and raised by another who took in orphans," he relates. "I do not know my background, my lineage, my biological or cultural heritage. But when I meet someone new, I treat them with respect. For after all, they could be my people."[98]

Accepting the perspective that other people could be our people, we thus respond with compassion to alleviate suffering in others *as if they were our own.* Such compassion, which springs from our very core, seemingly comes from a well of common human experience, tapping the greater spirit and understanding of collective man. Serving to illustrate is a couple who became lost while exploring the back roads of rural Ireland. Relates the wife: "My husband and I lost our way. We spotted a farmer leading his cow to pasture and stopped him. 'Excuse me,' I said. 'Could you direct us to Mohill? We're lost.'

"A lovely smile creased the man's leathery face. 'You're not lost at all, do y'see, for you've found me,' he answered, 'and I know the way.'"[99]

In this vein, we've all experienced sudden relief and restored security because we've found one of "our people," a person who knew the way, who rescued us in a tense moment or in a time of trouble or loss. We've even experienced being momentarily pampered simply because a stranger cared about our comfort. Such are the gifts we can return to other human beings crossing our paths, whether strangers or not, simply because we share a common human bond and because they are "our people."

Also illustrating the concept that "other people could be our people" is Sam Rayburn, a former longtime Speaker of the House. Although Rayburn "could be hard and cold on business matters," he always manifested gentleness when dealing with helpers or personal acquaintances, writes D. B. Hardeman in *Life*.

Taken with Rayburn's gentle, as well as kind, demeanor, Hardeman once commented on his extreme politeness toward waitresses and bellhops. And what was Rayburn's response? That he wouldn't be unfeeling toward any youth waiting on him "for all the gold in Fort Knox," reminding Hardeman that any waitress "might be your sister or mine." Snapping his fingers, he added, "What we do in this life is often determined by a mighty small margin. I missed being a tenant farmer by just that much—but someone was kind to me in my youth."[100]

When compassion has ultimate regard, it is able to generalize and extend feelings of tenderness felt toward loved ones to other people. Separately driving along a busy interstate, for example, two men each passed an older woman who had a flat tire, and both turned around to help. Both also understood why, and one, a little chagrined, articulated out loud the reason: "I turned back because this woman might have been my own mother."

In similar instance many years ago, H. G. Wells was showing a friend his lavish new home in London. As he opened a door on the third floor to a small room, he said, "Here is my bedroom."

Asked why he didn't occupy one of the larger downstairs bedrooms, Wells replied that those rooms belonged to his housemaid and cook, who had served him for over two decades.

"But in most homes the servants have the small rooms,"

Wells's friend pointed out. To this, Wells replied, "That's why mine haven't. My mother was a maid in a London house."[101]

In extending ultimate regard, compassion projects itself into another's place and acts accordingly. Such was the case of the father of Catherine Marshall, a prolific Christian writer. Marshall's father, a preacher, was neither eloquent at the pulpit or a particularly adept theologian, Marshall relates. Rather, his forte was people.

One day, he sought out a new member of his congregation, locating the man working at an enormous railroad roundhouse. In extending his hand to the worker, the worker deferred: "Can't shake hands with you," he said apologetically. "They're too grimy."

Leaning down, Marshall's father rubbed his hands in coal soot and then, standing up, he again offered a hand: "How about it now?" he inquired of the worker.[102]

Similarly, Cecil John Rhodes—whose large fortune endowed the Rhodes scholarships—once leveled and equalized a relationship. As the story tells, Rhodes was a stickler for correct dress and behavior, but he once refused to impose his standards at another's expense. Instead, in that person's behalf, he took decided and compassionate action to neutralize an otherwise embarrassing situation.

Residing in Kimberely, Africa, Rhodes had invited a young man from another city to a dinner party. Traveling by train, and arriving at the exact time of the party's outset, the young man went directly to Rhodes's house in travel-stained clothes. There he was understandably appalled when he found the assembled guests in full evening dress.

With the other guests, the apprehensive young man waited for their host. When Rhodes finally did appear, he was not sporting resplendent evening wear. Instead, he wore a shabby old blue suit. The young man later learned that Rhodes, in evening wear, had been poised to welcome his guests. Informed of his traveling guest's plight, however, he had quickly withdrawn to his dressing room and changed clothes.[103]

Foremost, extending ultimate regard to others embodies embracing a truth to which Herman Melville speaks: "We cannot live only for ourselves. A thousand fibers connect us with our fellow men."[104] In essence, then, all human beings are "our people." We thus extend ultimate regard to others because of our intrinsic kinship to them and to a Father in Heaven who responds with ultimate regard toward all.

But offering of ultimate regard extends even further—to God's creatures. Illustrating is Henry David Thoreau, who, in adoration, once wrote, "I had a sparrow alight upon my shoulder for a moment while I was hoeing in a village garden, and I felt that I was more distinguished by that circumstance than I should have been by any epaulette I could have worn."[105]

By virtue of breath of life and divinity of origin, we are also kin to God's creatures, to whom mankind owes its very survival. Of such vital human-creature bonding, Susan Chernak McElroy reflects, "Our intended place is not that of overlord or master, but one of a respectful and loving partnership." In such partnerships, God's creatures bestow upon us immense powers and gifts, transforming "our everyday lives, taking us outside of ourselves and into the here and now of their own being. And through their presence, we come to feel the divine presence that dwells within all Creation."[106]

♥ ♥ ♥ ♥ ♥ ♥ ♥ ♥

COMPASSION HAS INSIGHT

Compassion perceives the dilemmas of others and wishes to buffer them in circumstances that might bring pain. However, sometimes such insight does not come easily or immediately. Nor may such insight develop until people interact with and comprehend the dilemmas of other persons for whom they have felt distaste or even hatred. A pioneer story illustrates:

The Fredricksons were early settlers in southern Utah. Having come before the main company of pioneers, they were the first and only family in the area for a period of time. Because their food supply was nearly depleted, John Fredrickson had gone to see what was delaying the main company.

The day the food supply was finally exhausted, he still had not returned. In desperation his wife, Rachael, began praying that somehow she and her four young children would not starve. Then, glancing out the window, she saw Indians coming toward the house. She instinctively sent the children into the back room and reached for a gun. Then she remembered a religious leader's earlier counsel: "Feed the Indians; don't fight them." Offering a short prayer for protection, Rachael put the gun away.

Walking into her small home, the Indians demanded food. After Rachael explained she had no food, they thoroughly searched the house. To their dismay, they found only a sack of clover stored for spring and a sack of flour so bitter that—after tasting it—they went outside and spit it out. They then left, hurting no one.

The next morning Rachael Fredrickson found fresh deer meat at the door.[107]

Through this simple act, the Indians sensitively expressed compassion for Rachael and her children, who, they determined, had so little—and such intolerable—food to eat. In leaving a supply of meat, the Indians must have concluded that what they themselves wouldn't eat surely shouldn't be required eating for another.

Compassion also demonstrated insight when a four-year-old

child responded to the racial violence—and the publicity over it—in Birmingham, Alabama. She and her mother were sitting at a soda fountain when a black youth, entering the drugstore, sat down beside her. Leaning over, the child patted his hand. Speaking softly, she said she was sorry about Birmingham. Smiling sadly, the young man squeezed her hand. He, too, was sorry, he replied.

Compassion further had insight in the instance of Sharon Salzberg, who describes an overseas trip during which she handed her passport to a uniformed Soviet official. The suspicious official inordinately studied her picture and, with a demeanor of "icy rage," gave her "the most hateful stare" she had ever encountered. Never having experienced such toxic energy, Salzberg stood stunned, enduring the official's silent interrogation until—returning her passport—he dismissed her.

A shaken Salzberg retreated to the airport's transit lounge, her entire being consumed by the infectious malevolence. Then came a sudden flash of insight: If exposure to this man's toxic energy could so quickly sicken her, how did he survive it always? Now comprehending his inescapable malignancy of soul, she felt only compassion. She viewed him no longer as a threatening enemy, but, instead, as an intensely suffering fellow being.[108]

Finally, many years ago compassion had insight on two fronts when a small dog disappeared from home. His whereabouts were discovered when a neighbor heard faint barking coming from a fifty-foot-deep dry well on an abandoned property. To the rescue, the owner—carrying a sack and flashlight—was lowered down the shaft, where he found the dog, weak and hungry but uninjured.

As the owner put the dog into the sack, he felt something brushing his leg. Shining his flashlight on the well floor, to his amazement he discovered a large rabbit, which he caught and also put into the sack. As the trio were being hauled up, however, the sack hit a crosspiece, and as the sack opened, the rabbit fell out. Continuing the ascent to the top, the owner fed and watered the ravenously hungry dog. Then, intending to return home, he called the dog to follow. The dog, however, refused to leave the well site.

Comprehending the dog's apparent concern, a neighbor, experiencing compassion for both animals, retrieved the rabbit. Once rescued, the dog sniffed the rabbit eagerly and then—assured of its well-being—willingly followed his owner home.

♥　♥　♥　♥　♥　♥　♥　♥

COMPASSION MAKES NO JUDGMENTS

"It is amazing how the habit of searching out the best in others enlarges our own souls," reflects an unknown author. In a reverse twist, the habit of malicious judgment, if practiced, can potentially have a withering effect on those same souls.

Another unknown author tells of one woman whose soul could have used a little ironing out. This woman, who was forever complaining about the untidiness of her neighbor, gleefully drew her friend to her window one day and said, "Look at those clothes on the line, gray and streaked!" The friend replied gently, "If you'll look more closely, you'll see that it's your windows, not her clothes, that are dirty."[109]

This woman was in the unenviable position of needing such advice as Sarah Brown imparts: "Only God is in a position to look down on anyone."[110] And she also might have benefited from the insights of Anne McCaffrey, who wrote, "Make no judgments where you have no compassion."[111] Even William Arthur Ward could have admonished her, "It is fair to judge people and stained-glass windows only in their best light."[112]

Illustrating the absence of judgment *and* the presence of compassion is actor and dramatist Peter Ustinov, who presented prizes at a Speech Day in an English school. In response to the announcement that two boys had failed their examinations, Ustinov took the sting out of the public remark by personalizing the boys' situation to himself: "I do not have a single qualification to my name, and the world has a great need for unqualified people," Ustinov proclaimed. "I'm as drawn to the two who didn't pass as I am toward any minority. Had I been a member of this school, the number would almost certainly have been three. All those who don't reach the heights in life still have a value in this world."[113]

Alluding to the necessity of not humiliating others, Ustinov took advantage of a public teaching moment that could prove to have many reverberations. In addressing the boys' plight publicly, Ustinov conveyed sympathy for—and to—the boys, implicitly assuring them that, in this life, mistakes or failures were not out of order. And, by personalizing the boys' situation, he also took the sting out of their public reprimand and assured them of their intrinsic worth. He and the boys belonged in the same category, he inferred—and though he did not add it, the boys surely recognized that he was widely viewed as being of worth, and thus were they also.

As in the preceding story, compassion represents those who, by reason of their lower positions or status, have no power or clout. It also recognizes their plight and, whenever possible, looks after them. While teaching a course at Yale in television news, Tom Brokaw drew on this principle in agonizing over having to assign grades. He reports:

"Each time I attempted to record a grade that I knew would

be a disappointment, I could see this earnest young face, listening attentively during class or, with hand raised, eagerly waiting to share an insight. I wanted to put an asterisk beside the grade with the notation: 'If your parents or a prospective employer question this, please have them call me collect. I'll explain that you really did try hard.'"[114]

As with Ustinov, Brokaw separated intrinsic worth from earthly performance. Although he knew he could do little about the situation, he still rendered compassion to those who received the lower grades, hoping that others would see their efforts and not judge them as deficient in value.

Both Ustinov and Brokaw knew how to temper judgment. Telling of when his father taught him much about such tempering, an adult son observes, "Once on a railway journey my father unintentionally perpetrated some slight infraction and was unmercifully bawled out by a minor train employee. I was young then and hotly told my father afterward that he should have given the man a piece of his mind.

"My father smiled. 'Oh,' he said, 'if a man like that can stand himself all his life, surely I can stand him for five minutes.'"[115]

This boy's father wryly taught his son an object lesson—that it was not his son's place to judge others. If, through bad habits or abrasive behavior, others made a spectacle of themselves, this was not his or his son's problem. Nor was it up to himself or his son to correct the behavior. Others, his father inferred, are responsible for their own behavior, which will ultimately reap for them their own benefits or consequences.

Inaccurate information is often a primary factor causing lack of compassion and imposition of harsh judgment. It was without accurate information or compassionate eyes of her neighbors that one needy woman incurred their unsparing criticism. Clarence W. Hall tells of an attractive widow with three children who moved to a small town and "in a few weeks she was the most talked-about pretty woman in town. She was too pretty. . . . Several men had been seen visiting her. . . . She was a poor housekeeper. . . . Her children ran the streets and ate at the neighbors'. . . . She was lazy and spent most of her time lying on the sofa reading."

But what was the truth about this woman? Hall continues his story: "One morning our pretty neighbor collapsed in the post office, and the truth soon came out. She was suffering from an incurable disease and couldn't do her housework. She sent the children away when the drugs could not control her pain." The woman later explained she had wanted to be happy and light-hearted around her children. And she emphasized that when she died, she wanted to do so alone to shield them from her suffering.

And who were the men who had visited her? "Her old family doctor, the lawyer who looked after her estate, and her husband's brother."

The townspeople were kind to the woman for the last months of her life, says Hall, but those who had judged her so harshly never forgave themselves.[116] In this respect, the towns-people initially might have benefited from the words of an anonymous author: "There is a vast difference between putting your nose in other people's business and putting your heart in other people's problems."[117]

Offering further sage advice, St. John of the Cross said, "Never listen to accounts of the frailties of others; and if anyone should complain to you of another, humbly ask him not to speak about him at all."[118]

In checking any tendency to render contrary judgment, we benefit by holding in our hearts the words of a Chinese proverb:

"Be not disturbed by being misunderstood; be disturbed rather at not being understanding."

Also of worth is the thought of leaving all judgments of others to God. Advises Hall, "Arrogating to ourselves the functions of the Deity is as presumptuous as it is irreverent." And Hall quotes Bishop Fulton J. Sheen, who once said, "The separation of people into sheep and goats will take place only on the Last Day. Until then we are forbidden to make the classification."[119]

♥ ♥ ♥ ♥ ♥ ♥ ♥ ♥ ♥

COMPASSION EXERCISES DISCRETION

Compassion for others—and for ourselves—is often best expressed in the things we do not say—or in the tact we exercise to allow others to avoid humiliation. Compassion thus exercises discretion.

Composer Johannes Brahms modeled discretion in enabling his elderly father to save face. Although near poverty, Brahms' father steadfastly refused to take any money from his son, and it required all of Brahms' tact and diplomacy to support him.

One time, when Brahms and his father parted, Brahms said to him, "Believe me, Father, music in every situation is the greatest comforter. Whenever you are discouraged and feel you need something to lift you up, just take my old score of Handel's *Saul* and read it over. I'm sure you'll find there whatever you need."

Remembering sometime later his son's words, Brahms' father looked through Brahms' old score. What he discovered was indeed the one thing he needed: his son had placed a bank note between each page.[120]

"Discretion is many things: prudence, tact, circumspection, restraint, moderation," emphasizes novelist Max Ehrlich. "But basically, and above all, it is the art—one of the most important social arts we can possess—of knowing how to retain a confidence, to handle privileged information."[121]

One man who did so was a senior newspaper editor who, many years ago, scraped together enough money to achieve a lifelong dream of owning and operating a small-town newspaper. During his second year as editor, a blank column appeared on the second page; after that, through the next several years, other blank columns infrequently appeared; and, once, a blank column appeared on the first page.

Although tremendous curiosity regarding the blank columns abounded among the townspeople, no amount of their prying uncovered a satisfactory explanation; nor would the editor explain. As the blank columns sporadically appeared, some townspeople began to suspect that the editor was becoming mentally unbalanced. Rumors also began circulating that the editor was extorting money from people who feared certain stories would ruin their reputations. Worried about the editor's own reputation, a friend came to him regarding the rumors, but even then—although pained—the editor refused to reveal why he published the blank columns because, as he said, "some good folks would get hurt."

But when rumors persisted, it was an elderly man, deemed an outsider in the community, who came forward to set the record straight; and although it took tremendous courage, this man publicly announced indignantly and angrily that the editor had never extorted money from people. He knew the truth because, as he explained, he had once been the absent subject of a blank column.

And then the man told his story. Propelled by desperate financial circumstances, and with the fear of financial failure weighing down his soul, he had once committed a dishonest act. He had stolen, and ultimately sold, a tool from the supply room of a large tool company where he was employed. After that, stealing and selling tools came more and more easily. And he had been caught.

In the sheriff's office when the man was questioned, the editor listened as he shamefully spoke of the fear that had prompted his dishonesty. Instead of writing down the man's story, the editor closed his notebook, noting that the man's wife was a woman of integrity who didn't deserve disgrace. Normally, he said, he would publish a story of such a theft. However, this time he was going to run a blank column to protect the man's wife. This column would also serve as a warning that, if the man ever again committed another dishonest act, his story would be revealed.

Elaborating, the editor explained that the blank column was an opportunity for erring persons to have a second chance to redeem themselves, thus avoiding publicly humiliating their families and subjecting themselves to scrutiny. The blank columns also symbolized the editor's confidence that those in question would not become repeat offenders. Instead, they would hopefully learn from their folly and thereafter embrace integrity.

And so it was—as they understood the real reason for the blank columns—that the townspeople regarded the editor with renewed respect and even greater admiration than before. And although there was much speculation as to the sources inspiring the columns—when the editor died, eight of the eleven empty columns still remained a mystery.[122]

In this instance, the editor exercised prudence and constraint, discreetly protecting the identities of nearly a dozen people, thereby protecting their families and their reputations. At the same time, by running a blank column, the editor provided a mock experience reminding offenders of the humiliation that could have accrued—and that could still accrue through future poor judgment—to themselves and their families. While preserving others' dignity and aiding them to save face, he never-theless helped them to rise to a higher level of maturity and character development.

The editor's actions were thus a lesson in the art of discre-tion—in essence, of sensitively and soulfully responding to and caring for the needs of his fellow beings.

♥ ♥ ♥ ♥ ♥ ♥ ♥ ♥ ♥

COMPASSION LOVES GENTLENESS

"A profusion of pink roses bending ragged in the rain speaks to me of all gentleness and its enduring," reflects William Carlos Williams.[123] In such gentleness, compassion often finds form.

Gentleness gives gentleness in return for itself. "For every action, there is an equal and opposite reaction," observes Paul G. Hewitt. Essentially, he notes, if you touch the world gently, the world will touch you gently in return.[124]

The concept of "gentleness begetting gentleness" prevailed during a morning rush at a Chicago subway station, a time in which harried commuters jammed and shoved their way onto the train. Describing what happened in the resulting chaos is an observant commuter: "When it seemed as if every inch of space had been filled, I spied a panic-stricken young man at the car door. Realizing that the train would soon pull away without him, he cried out, 'There's room for all six hundred of us if we'll just love one another a little!'

"The human sea parted and he slipped onto the train. Despite the crowding and the long ride ahead, we all relaxed a little; the incident had set a new tone of gentleness for the day."[125]

Through utilizing a positive and creative approach to resolve his problem, this young man instantly catalyzed feelings of gentleness that rippled through a crowd of strangers.

In some instances, a crowd of strangers may instantaneously begin sharing similar positive sentiments as they engage in an event so drawing to their souls that they bond as one. It was such a crowd of strangers that extended gentleness to a master—Russian poet Boris Pasternak—and thus paid the man great homage.

The event in question occurred one evening many years ago in a filled auditorium. Pasternak had begun reading aloud a long poem from his works when a sheet of paper slipped from his grasp. Embarrassed at his fumble, he bent to pick up the sheet, only to hear a voice from the audience calling out the next phrase; and then another voice, and another phrase; and soon hundreds of voices in unison were repeating the lingering words of his poem, until—in a tide of tribute—the entire hall reverberated with his lyrics.[126]

In yet another instance, also occurring many years ago, a crowd—again through gentleness—paid ultimate respect to another master—this time cellist Pablo Casals. Casals had performed in every European capital but one, the great capital of Vienna, for which, incongruously, he felt the most musical affinity. But, finally, because he had so longed to perform in Vienna, with great apprehension he accepted an invitation to play there.

That night, with the concert hall overflowing, Casals positioned his violin to begin his performance. However, as he first drew his bow across the strings, it slipped from his fingers. Desperately trying to retrieve the bow, he watched, mortified, as it nevertheless shot from his grasp and flew over the heads of the audience in the first row. Says Casals of his harrowing experience, "There was not a sound in the hall. Someone retrieved the bow. It was handed with tender care from person to person—still in utter silence—and as I followed its slow passage, a strange thing happened. My nervousness completely vanished. When the bow reached me, I began the concerto again . . . with absolute confidence. . . . From then on, I visited Vienna every year."[127]

In reverse, through gentleness and long-suffering, a lone man affected a group of strangers—for some, probably indelibly challenging their prejudiced attitudes. During the French occupation of the Saar in the 1920s, the German population was incensed over alleged harsh treatment by black colonial troops. Facing a noisy and hostile audience in Berlin, the renowned black singer Roland Hayes stood quietly and resolutely by his piano, waiting for the audience's hissing to cease. Only when the auditorium became silent did Hayes, after signaling his accompanist, began to sing softly Schubert's "Du bist die Ruh" ("Thou Art Peace"). With the first words of his song, a profound hush overcame the crowd—Hayes's artistry and poise had transcended their anger—and a fathomless communion of spirit took place between singer and audience.[128]

One person's lifetime gentleness toward others may also permanently affect such others for the better, as in the instance of Ardis Whitman's father. Whitman speaks of her father, who, many years ago, was a kind and gentle country minister in Nova Scotia. Within the framework of worldly wealth or fame, he had no power, but he did have a power of much more importance. He very quietly affected lives for the good throughout his ministry, attracting parishioners to him largely because they experienced no risk in sharing, or, in his presence, being deemed flawed human beings.

Upon his retirement as an elder, this minister received a letter from a church official residing in a former parish. "We hear that you will soon be retiring," the official wrote. "Would you come and settle here? We feel that we'd be a better community and better neighbors for having a man whose life is so genuine living among us."[129]

Imagine, if you will, a man whose life was so exemplary and so gentle that people felt their lives would be blessed by having him within their midst. And imagine people reaching out to this man—from the tenderness of their hearts—to extend to him the honor of such an invitation. Indeed, gentleness does beget gentleness.

♥ ♥ ♥ ♥ ♥ ♥ ♥ ♥ ♥

COMPASSION MAY BE CULTIVATED

Compassion may be cultivated, just as one cultivates a garden. Alexandra Stoddard writes of a gray-haired older man sitting next to her on an airplane, who related this story: "My older sister thinks the world has passed her by," he mused. "She has no friends, no social life. Her children are too busy to be bothered with her. I told Helen that she should think of her life as a garden, her family and friends as her flowers. Everything needs nurturing. You have to tend your garden in order to have your life blossom in fragrant, colorful abundance."[130]

In one's garden, compassion is among those human qualities that need tending, and, when rightly tended, compassion blooms and unfolds in a quiet but brilliant display of one's humanity to man. What occurs, in essence, is a "flowering of the heart," as depicted in pop star Cliff Richard's description of a visit to a Bihari refugee camp in Bangladesh:

"That first morning I must have washed my hands a dozen times. . . . I didn't want to touch anything, least of all the people," he recounts. "Everyone in those camps was covered in sores and scabs."

But then Richard had a startling experience forcing him to face, by virtue of his own humanity, that he shared a common denominator with this hungry and beleaguered group of refugees. He continues his story:

"I was bending down to one little mite, mainly for the photographer's benefit, and trying hard not to have too close a contact. Just then someone accidentally stood on the child's fingers. He screamed and, as a reflex, I grabbed him, forgetting his dirt and his sores. I remember that warm little body clinging to me and the crying instantly stopping. In that moment I knew I had [much] to learn about practical Christian loving, but that at least I'd started."[131]

In this instance, his exterior trappings crumbled, Richard felt deeply inward an unfamiliar stirring of compassionate and tender feelings toward another human being. He also recognized he had momentarily spiritually bonded with another being and that, with effort, he could repeat his experience by nurturing compassion toward others. As with Richard, we too can cultivate compassion, and it appears that the more compassionate we become, the more our souls mature and become godly in nature.

❖ ❖ ❖ ❖ ❖ ❖ ❖ ❖ ❖

COMPASSION IS SOUL SATISFYING

Unbidden, our souls swell when we see the lives of others touched by our benevolence. A case in point is that of former Surgeon General C. Everett Koop, who describes his frantic efforts years ago to save a dying baby with a diaphragmatic hernia. Responding to an urgent phone call, Koop rushed to pick up the baby at a nearby hospital. When he got there and realized the elevators weren't working, he retrieved the baby by running up, and then down, nine flights of stairs. After driving the baby to the children's hospital, he hurried up two floors and laid him on an operating table.

By now, the baby was dark blue and apparently lifeless. With no time for sterile precautions, Koop opened up the baby's chest and with a finger massaged his tiny heart until it started beating. Then he finished the operation.

Says Koop of his dedicated effort, "About twenty-five years later, my secretary ushered into my office a young man about six feet four inches tall who stood somewhat embarrassedly before me and said, 'My father thought you'd like to meet me. You operated on me when I was fifty-five minutes old.' I ran around the desk and hugged him."[132]

Inherent in Koop's warm and magnanimous greeting seems an instinctive recognition that this young man would be forever grateful to him for this gift of life. Perhaps, too, he recognized that, in saving the young man's life, he had also touched other lives—the young man's parents, brothers and sisters, and extended family—as well as many others who knew and loved him. Generations, in fact, would be affected by his life-saving actions.

Finally, Koop probably comprehended that this young man would, as he himself had done, ultimately contribute to mankind. In thus perceiving the many eternal nuances of his life-saving deed years ago, the physician's overwhelming rush of feelings indescribably permeated his heart, transforming and greatly warming his own soul.

III

❦ ❦ ❦ ❦ ❦ ❦ ❦ ❦ ❦

ON KINDNESS

After a person had hurt a woman's feelings, a friend advised her, "Go out and do the nicest thing you can think of for someone else. That will restore the balance in the universe."[1]

Acts of kindness obviously fall within the category of some of the nicest things someone could do for another. Perhaps it is fanciful to think of kindness as capable of restoring the balance of the universe, but it's not so fanciful to regard kindness as capable of restoring the balance—or the very health—of soul.

In reality, kindness indelibly imprints itself on many dimensions of the soul. Kindness creates immediate intimate and compassionate connections between people, momentarily bonding even strangers together as common members of humanity. Assuredly kindness, endowed with such bonding potency, will "win and preserve the heart," Humphrey Davy advises.[2]

Moreover, kindness helps guide us through relationships without stumbling and may even lubricate our way. Indeed, regarding kindness's role in facilitating good will and cooperation, a Persian proverb advises, "With a sweet tongue and kindness, you can drag an elephant by a hair."[3] Kindness also compensates for the ills that beset us, restoring and fortifying our belief that goodness still prevails on this earth. As Charles Kuralt observes, "The everyday kindness of the back roads more than makes up for the acts of greed in the headlines."[4]

And it is kindness that provides us with a universal language understood by all men, as Mark Twain was quick to recognize: "Kindness," he said, "is a language the deaf can hear and the blind can read."[5]

But kindness's most important function is that of soothing others' souls and protecting the tender hearts and fragile feelings of those who are easily wounded. There is no tranquilizer more effective in comforting the soul, nor any medication more potent in restoring or bolstering self-esteem or belief in self, than a few kind words.

Kind words may even soften those who appear more resistive and tougher than the norm, for most people who are overlaid with dense layers of protection have a vulnerable core that soothing words may penetrate. Indeed, Frederick William Faber notes, as the "music of the world," kind words "have a power that seems to be beyond natural causes, as if they were some angel's song that had lost its way and come on earth. It seems as if they could almost do what in reality God alone can do—soften the hard and angry hearts of men."[6]

Kindness's vital role in soothing man's wounds and in comforting his soul is highlighted by Sir Kenneth Clark, who concludes, "Ask any decent person what he thinks matters most in human conduct [and] five to one his answer will be 'kindness.'"[7] In this vein, urges Ian Maclaren, "Be kind. Everyone you meet is fighting a hard battle."[8] In overcoming those battles, others everywhere crave and are fortified by such kindnesses as an encouraging word, a sensitive deed, or a gesture affirming their inherent worth.

Recognizing the stalwart nature of kindness in buoying the

spirit of the common man was Princess Diana, who died in an August 1997 car accident. Delivering a eulogy at Princess Diana's funeral in Westminster Abbey, Earl Spencer, Diana's brother, quoted favorite lines of Diana's—written by Adam Lindsay Gordon—which read as follows:

> Life is largely froth and bubble,
> But two things stand like stone.
> Kindness in someone else's trouble,
> Courage in your own.[9]

❧ ❧ ❧ ❧ ❧ ❧ ❧ ❧

KINDNESS PUTS ON NEW LENSES

Kindness requires an alternative perception, challenging us to look through different, and much expanded, lenses, and to stretch ourselves and our conceptions of our worlds and the people in it. Eleanor Roosevelt captures the resulting emotional and intellectual growth and stimulation that accrue to people who engage openly with others, of such gains: "If you approach each new person you meet in a spirit of adventure, you will find yourself endlessly fascinated by the new channels of thought and experience and personality that you encounter. I do not mean simply the famous people of the world, but people from every walk and condition of life."[10]

Augmenting is Daphne Rose Kingma, who describes more specifically the "people from every walk and condition of life" to whom Roosevelt is referring. Says Kingma, "The person who doesn't fit in with our notions of who is worthy of our love—the bag lady at the corner, the strange old man who rides through town on a three-wheel bike all strung up with flags—is just the person who, by not fitting into our patterns, insists that we expand not only our views but also our capacity to love."[11]

Describing what she terms the "joy of diversity," Jane W. Lund speaks of an experience that stretched her perception when she encountered someone totally unlike herself. This person did not belong to the same category of people with whom she ordinarily associated, and was someone whom she might ordinarily have avoided. Undoubtedly, by giving this man an audience in a world in which he often experienced rejection or scorn, Lund extended a kindness. By listening, however, Lund discovered that becoming aware of this man's broadening although not altogether enviable life trek actually enriched her own life. Here—as Lund tells it—is her experience:

"I didn't expect him to be gentle," she reflects. "What I noticed, really, was his hat . . . brown, broad-brimmed, studded with silver, and graced with a long, slender feather. Beneath its brim, a mass of curly blond hair cascaded and merged with a flowing beard. His body was close-coupled . . . his face, cherubic. He had a charming way of holding his head to one side . . . then smiling . . . a sigh . . . a pause . . . his blue eyes glanced up . . . then to the side as if in search of the perfect way to express himself. He smiled, tears formed, and I was riveted. He spoke softly, emotionally, insightfully. He *was gentle*.

"Here was a man of simple needs and rich experience . . . one who drank deeply from his cup of life. He had spent the 60's as a minstrel . . . roaming from place to place, creating and singing ballads . . . and seeking to become one with the universe.

"He was gifted with a primal, undisciplined talent. He respected 'work' only as a necessary means to an end, he told me as he exhibited that becoming, self-effacing gesture.

"'For me,' he explained, 'The kind of work that most men do would be like hitching a deer to a plow. . . . If I pursued it long enough, it would break my legs!'

"I listened, fascinated, as he . . . told me of the 'flower children' in Haight-Ashbury. . . .

"He spoke of the thrill of achieving a synchronization of thought, spirit, and emotion; and of enjoying the delicious awareness of being an original and essential part of something *very* large and exquisitely wonderful!

"He told me of the subtle beauties of the desert . . . of flowers so elegant, but so fragile that they bloomed and died in a single hour! He told of monolithic shafts of red stone that pierced the sky . . . of clouds that subdued the sun, and of morning mists that probed each craggy rock with wet, inquisitive fingers.

"I listened, fascinated . . . silent . . . secure in the creature comforts that had kept me hitched to my plow. But for an hour I had known the adventure of soaring on unfamiliar wings, into worlds I had never known!"[12]

Throughout her mental and emotional journey with this man, Lund discovered the often surprising attributes and complexities of another human being—a happening she could easily have missed had she not persevered in her discovery process. Through her unusual experience of entering a world of which she knew little, intuitively Lund also became more acutely attuned to her own humanity.

Lund further became more attuned to her similarity to another, seemingly starkly different and perhaps—to the world—inferior human being, and, as well, more attuned to common spiritual beginnings flowing from a universal divine source.

She also may have realized that, in every human, fortunate or unfortunate, is a story—a work of fact and experience waiting to be shared and to be fed into the pool of common human knowledge.

There is intrinsic value in reaching out in kindness to many individuals unlike ourselves. Experiences such as Lund's make us more cognizant of one of life's truths, as captured by an unknown author:

"The worth of life is not in the number and bulk of its possessions, but in the number, and pleasantness, and the varieties of experiences and consciousness to the mind. A man may have a richer life experience out of a tent on a vacant lot than another has out of a . . . [lavish] mansion in the midst of a magnificent estate. Invariably, it is those who seek the value of life rather than wealth who have the most satisfying and most stimulating experiences."[13]

♥ ♥ ♥ ♥ ♥ ♥ ♥ ♥ ♥

KINDNESS IS COURTEOUS

Kindness is courteous—and sometimes even a bit courageous—as in an instance Dan Rather relates regarding a rather mortifying elevator ride in a large hotel. Having arrived late in the evening to the hotel, and having had to arise early in order to deliver a speech to several thousand people, Rather was not in a particularly good mood. Thus, his ire was piqued in the elevator as he felt all eyes on him. And—he confesses—he thought, *Didn't any of these people's mothers teach them that it's rude to stare?*

After the elevator had reached the lobby, one of riders, a "crisply and immaculately groomed" woman, approached Rather, gently touching his sleeve, and said quietly, "Mr. Rather, I don't mean to intrude." Rather admits to thinking, *Then why are you?* But the woman's next words set him on his heels. Tells Rather, "She looks first to one side, then to the other, making sure no one else is listening."

And then she continues: "'I don't want this to be awkward or embarrassing in any way.' Pause. 'But your fly is unzipped and a piece of your shirttail is sticking through it.'"

After that, finishes Rather, the woman simply smiled and strode away.[14]

In this instance, Rather was pulled up short, forced by another's courteous behavior to evaluate his own lack of such civility. He also inherently acknowledged his error in not extending courtesy to someone who—as it turned out—had centered on his own welfare. After evaluating his actions, Rather might have readily even taken to heart what Ralph Waldo Emerson once admonished: "Life is not so short but that there is always room for courtesy."[15]

In another instance, during the 1972 Fischer-Spassky world-championship chess match, courtesy—as a form of kindness—also prevailed. Writing in *Life*, Brad Darrach notes that, although Fischer had once listed Spassky among the ten world's greatest chess players of all time, during the match he spoke of him contemptuously. Yet, after the sixth match, in which Fischer, with admirable precision, had beaten Spassky, Spassky joined with the audience in applauding Fischer. Stunned and somewhat disoriented by Spassky's applause, Fischer rushed offstage, and only as he was being driven back to his hotel did he reveal how deeply Spassky's gesture had moved him. Of those accompanying him, Fischer incredulously asked over and over, "Did you see what Spassky did?" "Did you see him applaud?" Then, with great admiration in his own voice, he added, 'That's sportsmanship. That shows he's a true sportsman.'"[16]

For Fischer to have had such a stunned reaction would suggest that he may typically have been unaffected by the positive actions of others. Yet, in this case, kindness, in the form of courtesy, seemingly had the ability to penetrate Fischer's soul, offering him core nourishment he badly needed.

Even if Fischer had been impervious to Spassky's courtesy, Spassky's actions were not misspent. To the contrary, Spassky actually inadvertently fed his own soul. Opening up the possibility of such gain, an anonymous author observes, "Kindness is never wasted. If it has no effect on the recipient, at least it benefits the bestower."[17]

A story of Abraham Lincoln—whose name is inextricably equated to kindness and courtesy—illustrates the extensive generosity with which courtesy can take form. At Gettysburg, the audience, it appears, generally perceived that Edward Everett had spoken too long. But by that era's standards, Everett, at seventy years of age, was an elderly man and his speech that day represented the culminating glory of a long career. However, perceiving the classic qualities of Lincoln's address, Everett sent the President a note that read, "I should be glad if I could flatter myself that I came as near to the central idea of the occasion in two hours as you did in two minutes."

With customary graciousness, President Lincoln replied, "In our respective parts yesterday, you could not have been excused to make a short address, nor I a long one."[18]

At times courtesy prevails in the form of tact, a condition defined by O. A. Battista as "the ability to make a person see the lightning without letting him feel the bolt."[19] On a long overseas flight that was to deplane in New York City, for instance, a passenger asked the stewardess for a cup of tea and was much, and loudly, annoyed when the stewardess reported the tea supply was exhausted. As the man spewed out abrasive criticism of the airline and the service, she said sweetly, "Let me explain, sir. Before takeoff, we had a briefing to decide whether to take along five thousand five-hundred ninety tea bags or you. I voted for you." With that, the stewardess heard no more.[20]

Sometimes the will to be courteous is sorely tested, as in an incident occurring many years ago. On this occasion, Jed Carver had spent most of a day in the woods gathering a good-sized load of firewood. Tired and anxious to get home to a hot meal, he felt almost betrayed when his wagon wheel broke.

A short time after Carver jumped off the wagon and began to unload the wood, a neighbor happened by. Stopping momentarily, he commented, "I can see that you need help, Jed, but I do hate to be late for supper." Without another word he drove off, leaving Carver by himself to unload the wood, repair the wheel, and then reload the wagon.

Several days later, on a Sunday afternoon, Carver came upon this same neighbor with his buggy firmly stuck in the mud. Without saying a word, Carver got down from his wagon, took off his shoes and socks, rolled up his pant legs, and helped push the buggy out of the mud. He then went to the nearby stream, sat down on a rock, washed his feet, and dried them.

Finally, the astonished and rather embarrassed neighbor got up enough nerve to ask, "Why did you stop to help me after I left you with that broken wheel?"

"Because," said Carver, "I'm not going to let your behavior dictate what I do for my fellow man."[21]

In this instance, Carver remained impervious to his neighbor's actions and, despite negative circumstances, remained courteous and true to his kind nature, choosing to perpetuate good, for goodness' sake. He refused to be deterred, or pulled off center, simply because someone else chose to behave badly. Perhaps Carver also instinctively grasped a life principle that John Prutting, a physician, puts forth: "It is . . . true that sometimes, simply by acting, the appropriate emotions will follow. If we are generous and kind toward others, we usually find that we begin to *feel* good toward them."[22]

❤ ❤ ❤ ❤ ❤ ❤ ❤ ❤ ❤

KINDNESS RESPECTS VULNERABILITY

Kindness treats vulnerability with a soft touch, preserving the fragile nature of others and protecting them from emotional harm. In this regard, Joyce Brothers reflects, "There is a rule in sailing where the more maneuverable ship should give way to the less maneuverable. I think this is sometimes a good rule to follow in human relationships as well."[23]

The sense of "giving way"—and protecting those whose tender feelings can easily be bruised—was evident in an instance when Italian-Catholic Sonia Mamo became engaged to Rajiv Gandhi, who was to become India's prime minister. In meeting her future daughter-in-law for the first time, Indira Gandhi was sympathetic to the young woman's position and recounted her own controversial marriage to Rajiv's father, a middle-class Parsi. Indira's family were Brahmins.

"Sonia, I am a mother," she said. "You need not be afraid of me. I was also a girl like you in love with a boy from a different community and religion. I can understand your love."

As Sonia turned to leave, Indira, reinforcing her kind words, motioned Sonia to come to her. Then, asking Sonia to turn around, Indira, taking a needle and thread, mended a loose hem on her dress.

A number of years ago, kindness protected vulnerability when Yankee pitching star Ron Gundry went hunting with teammate Catfish Hunter. Gundry recalls, "We were separated, and I was just waiting for a deer by the tree. I didn't really know whether I could kill one or not. Well, when I turned around, there was this deer, almost staring me in the face. We startled each other; I hadn't heard him, and he hadn't caught my scent. For a moment it seemed that neither of us knew what to do."

Finishes Gundry, "I couldn't shoot him. So I just looked at him and said, 'Boo!' and he ran away. I never did tell Catfish about it."[24]

A story of the Great Babe Ruth, related by Norman Vincent Peale, tells of kindness again protecting vulnerability, this time several decades ago. At Babe's career's peak, Peale recalls, Babe although large in stature, was "graceful, even rhythmic, in his motions. When he batted, it was like a symphony of beauty— the crack of the bat on the ball, the run, the tag on the base. He hit seven hundred fourteen home runs, and the multitudes loved him."

But Babe Ruth eventually became older, and in his decline, the Yankees traded him to the Boston Braves. In Cincinnati, at one of Babe's final games, Peale sat with a large crowd watching the Braves play the Reds. This day, Babe wasn't doing well. Neither was his rhythm intact. After twice fumbling the ball and several times throwing balls off-target, he enabled the Cincinnati Reds to make five runs. At game's end, with head down—and to the booing of fans "who once cheered him riotously"—Babe walked toward the dugout.

But then, over the railing and across the field, came running a small boy, who threw his arms around his hero's knees. Bending down, Babe picked up the boy and, after setting him down and tousling his head, walked with him, hand-in-hand, off the field. At this, a hushed silence fell over the crowd, those present awed by this galvanizing moment. Thus, a small child's kind thoughtfulness ultimately overruled a crowd's cruel thoughtlessness. The child's actions enabled Babe—with head held and heart unfettered—to exit the playing field with unmitigated dignity.

Writing of yet another instance of kindness protecting vulnerability is news reporter Tom Zucco. The date was August 7, 1993, the setting a minor league baseball park in Dunedin,

Florida. During a night game, in the stadium were twenty-two hundred fans cheering on the hometown Blue Jays playing against the Fort Lauderdale Red Sox. The Blue Jays led 4–0 as Dunedin started Denise Gray, a twenty-three old pitcher, who had a one-hitter after six innings. Of Gray's game performance, writes Zucco, he "was mowing down the Red Sox like so many blades of grass."

But as the Red Sox were about to play out their inning, the home-plate umpire called time. Glancing around, Gray saw the reason. After stumbling onto the field, a young boy had initiated a conversation with the players. "The next thing you know, he turned and started coming toward me," he relates.

As the boy approached the mound, Gray recognized he was mentally handicapped, therein incurring a dilemma. "I didn't want to be mean to him," he recalls. "He didn't understand the rules. So I handed him the ball. And he promptly threw a strike!" And then another pitch—as the security guards stood aside and the organist played music to accompany the throw. At that point, "the crowd in the stand went wild and gave the boy a standing ovation."

Tugging on Gray's glove, now the smiling boy reached up for a hug. That's when Gray—the man who had spent years fighting to enter the big leagues, the man who always stayed focused and serious—lost his composure and started to cry.

After the boy's mother had come for him, Gray could not regain his composure or finish his team's winning game. Of his deeply-felt emotions, Gray recounts that although the incident interrupted a game in which he was playing exceptionally well, he wouldn't trade his soul-penetrating experience "for anything in the world."[25] And also of the boy's own experience, the organist later observed, "The kid was in heaven. It was like the world stopped for a little while, and everybody was able to love him."

In this instance, Gray was kind to a vulnerable child who, by unknowingly breaching cultural norms, stood to be castigated. Through his receptivity, Gray saved the child from profound embarrassment and confusion. As well, the entire crowd—touched by the poignancy of the event—joined Gray in protecting the boy's fragile ego.

In respecting vulnerability, kindness does not exact penalties, trying instead to be pliable in difficult situations. Illustrating is an instance in which a teenage daughter tentatively approached her mother one day. Describing her daughter's uncomfortable demeanor, the mother relates, "I could tell she was agitated and burdened by something. Finally she blurted it out, 'I got an *F* on my report card.'

"I stayed on automatic pilot," the mother reports. "The first thing out of my mouth was, 'Does that mean you did *nothing?*' I began the intimidation parents use when something their child has done raises insecurities regarding their adequacy as parents. Finally I said to my daughter, 'You go finish your jobs. I have to think about this,' giving her the impression her fate was in my hands. I hoped my disapproval would motivate her to do better. With head hung down, she left the room.

"Then I began thinking. My husband and I had always aspired to have our children become self-motivators rather than their being motivated out of fear, guilt, or physical retribution. The thought popped into my head: 'The times I needed love most was when I made mistakes. Those were the times I wished some significant person would put his or her arms around me and say, 'Everyone makes mistakes.'

"I also remembered she had been agonizing over this *F* for a week. And I thought of how hard she works and how committed she is to doing well. I knew then it wasn't my job to make her feel any more responsible or sad about her grade. She was imposing her own suffering. So I decided that, if her job was to be a self-motivator, my job was to love and support her."

At that, the mother called her daughter back into the room and said to her, "When golfers play golf, they are entitled to one mulligan—one bad stroke that doesn't have to go into their score. I'm going to give you this mulligan." Instantly, a wave of relief crossed the daughter's face.

The daughter left the room and a short time later she was back. "I've already figured it out," she announced, proceeding to tell her mother what action she planned to take to obtain a better grade. After that, the mother left for the evening. When she returned, she found on her bed a poem her daughter had written, several lines of which read:

> Though it seems we may stray and darken your day, our hearts
>   will never turn away.
> If you ever feel low because of a blow you've received in this
>   world we live in,
> Remember the people who love you so—
> your five understanding children.[26]

♥ ♥ ♥ ♥ ♥ ♥ ♥ ♥

KINDNESS SCREENS ITS WORDS

Abraham Lincoln's secretary of war Edwin Stanton once wrote an angry letter to a general who had publicly struck out at Lincoln, accusing him of favoritism. Stanton read the letter to Lincoln, who pronounced it—with great enthusiasm—as making its mark: "First rate, Stanton!" he exclaimed. "You've scored him well! Just right!"

However, as Lincoln saw Stanton slipping the letter into an envelope, he quickly asked him, "What are you going to do with the letter now?"

"Mail it," came Stanton's reply.

"No, no, that would spoil it," Lincoln advised. "File it away. That is the kind of filing that keeps it sharp—and doesn't wound the other fellow."[27]

In this instance, Lincoln screened his words. He was kind to two people—first, to the man to whom the letter was intended, and second, to his secretary—for Lincoln, aware of the potential personal and political reverberations of such a letter, could have criticized Stanton for his actions.

In acting kindly, Lincoln also intuitively knew what Blaise Pascal has captured in words:

"Cold words freeze people, and hot words scorch them, and bitter words make them bitter, and wrathful words make them wrathful." But kind words have a very different impact, projecting their "own image on men's souls; and a beautiful image it is. They soothe, quiet and comforter the hearer."[28]

Sometimes, however, a word not spoken is the choicest word of all; and, in fact, such restraint represents an act of goodness. In an anonymous anecdote, Socrates—while conversing with a fellow being—inherently expresses this view:

"Have you heard, O Socrates—"

"Just a moment, friend. Have you made sure that all you are going to tell me is true?"

"Well, no, I just heard others say it."

"I see. Then we can scarcely bother with it unless it is something good. Will it stand the test of goodness?"

"Oh, no, indeed. On the contrary."

"Hmmm. Perhaps, somehow, it is necessary that I know this in order to prevent harm to others."

"Well, no—"

"Very well, then. Let us forget about it. There are so many

worthwhile things in life; we can't afford to bother with what is so worthless as to be neither true nor good nor needful."

Adding a slightly different bent, Henry Van Dyke adds to the wisdom of screening one's words: "There are two good rules which ought to be written on every heart—never to believe anything bad about anybody unless you positively know it to be true; never to tell even that unless you feel that it is absolutely necessary, and that God is listening while you tell it."[29]

And another author also advises, "One of the first things which a physician says to his patient is, 'Let me see your tongue,' A spiritual adviser might often do the same."[30]

In screening one's words, choosing silence is an attractive option. "If a word spoken in its time is worth one piece of money, silence in its time is worth two," advises the Talmud.[31] Also applauding silence are several philosophers: "As you go through life you are going to have many opportunities to keep your mouth shut. Take advantage of all of them," reflects one.[32] "Say the best. Think the rest," says another. And still another offers, "Silence is not only golden; it's seldom misquoted."[33]

Offering further perspective regarding silence, James Alexander Thom observes, "We suggest an addition to the usual college speech-department curriculum: a course to teach people when to keep still. It could be called Silence 101, or perhaps Basic Reticence, maybe Social Circumspection.

"For every time we regret keeping still, there are about ten times we regret speaking up. Common reasons that words get us in trouble: 1) we don't express what we mean; 2) we speak at the wrong moment; 3) people react not to what we said, but to what they thought we said.

"In our non-speech course, we might quote Thomas Carlyle: 'Speech is great, but silence is greater.' And Plutarch: 'He can never speak well, who knows not how to hold his peace.' And we'd send our students away with the maxim, 'A closed mouth gathers no foot.'"[34]

When kindness does speak, it meticulously screens words, as in the meritorious instance of a college professor who told a worried student that he had just barely flunked. Kindness realizes that, as Robert Fulghum notes, "Sticks and stones may break our bones, but words will break our hearts."[35] Bearing on this thought is a sign in a little shop that reads, "Kindness spoken here." Perhaps this message could be a motto for people everywhere.

Most of us can afford to more often screen our words and follow the wisdom contained in an Islamic proverb, which proposes that each word we think of uttering should pass through three gates. At the first gate, the gatekeeper asks, "Is it true?" At the second gate, he asks, "Is it necessary?" and at the third gate, "Is it kind?"[36]

Sometimes, however—though kindness must screen its words—our own moral values compel us to speak out. Writing of "regrettable silences," Seattle *Times* columnist Dale E. Turner tells of having agonizing regrets at times he failed to speak at all. In particular, he writes of a person who heard others assassinating a friend's character. Afterwards, this person observed, "I am sorry that I did not heed the dictum to 'defend the absent.' My silence seemed to give assent to what they were saying."[37]

Once courageously "speaking out" was Jakob Ludwig Mendelssohn—a celebrated nineteenth-century composer. Of gentle disposition and a kindly critic, on one occasion Meldelssohn's sterling qualities emerged counterpoint to abrasive and undue criticism of Gaetano Donizetti, an Italian composer of light opera. Although Mendelssohn's convictions regarding music vigorously opposed Donizetti's, he emphatically defended him.

On this occasion, accompanying Mendelssohn were persons

who, idolizing him, sought to court his favor by capitalizing upon his sentiments. Mendelssohn became incensed, however, when those present began "flinging . . . harsh and contemptuous criticisms" toward Donizetti. Finally, indignantly responding to "attempts to curry favor . . . at the expense of another composer," Mendelssohn cried out, "I like it; and do you know I should like to have composed such music myself!"[38]

In screening its words, kindness offers many benefits to the receiver, including enhanced self-confidence. Such was the case when Richard Merrifield, singing in a cantata, was unable—with his untrained second bass voice—to reach middle C. Recognizing the problem, the conductor encouraged Merrifield to change chorus sections rather than transpose an octave down, explaining, "We'll need you in the lower range." Merrifield appreciated that the conductor thus preserved for him "a sense of particular usefulness. To leave another secure in a special area may be as great a principle of ethics as the Golden Rule."[39]

In screening its words, kindness also enables people to save face. Years ago, relates Louis Nizer, he enjoyed watching a particular comedian when others told him "new" jokes. And, of the comedian's response, he recalls, "Inevitably he knew [the joke], but not once did he embarrass the teller by stopping him. He would listen appreciatively and comment, 'Isn't that wonderful!' He was like a lover of opera, who can enjoy the same music over and over again. When he was challenged to admit that he had known the story all the time, he would reply, 'But I like the way you told it.'"[40]

Another story of Abraham Lincoln also provides an interesting twist to kindness's screening its words. "How can you speak kindly of your enemies when you should rather destroy them?" an elderly woman once asked Lincoln. To her inquiry, Lincoln responded, "Madam, do I not destroy them when I make them my friends?"[41]

Summarizing the wisdom of screening one's words, an unknown author finalizes, "You may be sorry that you spoke, sorry you stayed or went, sorry you won or lost, sorry so much was spent. But as you go through life, you'll find—you're never sorry you were kind."[42]

♥ ♥ ♥ ♥ ♥ ♥ ♥ ♥

KINDNESS SPEAKS KIND WORDS

"'T'was a thief said the last kind word to Christ. Christ took the kindness and forgave the theft," tells Robert Browning.[43]

In the world's most defining moment—the crucifixion of Christ—kindness, in its own words, and from an entirely unexpected source, made an indelible mark. Yet never again to entertain such a divine moment, nevertheless, across the ages kind words have possessed a divinity of their own, often cutting to the quick and touching others at their soul's innermost reaches. Indeed, Blaise Pascal notes, kind words "produce their own image on men's souls, and a beautiful image it is."[44]

Inevitably, a few chosen words can make a difference, buoying a heart, comforting a soul, or even changing a life. And often simply the willingness to speak out is sufficient to nurture a human soul. Such kind words may also have reverberating effects, as Mother Teresa observes: "Kind words can be short and easy to speak, but their echoes are truly endless."[45]

Despite their necessity to the soul's health and well-being, kind words are foreign, or of low count. In her classic 1852 novel *Uncle Tom's Cabin*, Harriet Beecher Stowe poignantly captures such deprivation of kind words upon soul. She writes of Eva, who stood looking at Topsy: "There stood the two children, representatives of the two extremes of society. The fair, high-bred child, with her golden head, her deep eyes, her spiritual, noble brow . . . ; and her black, keen, subtle, cringing, yet acute neighbor," the first child born of cultivation; the second, of oppression. In Stowe's dialogue, Topsy is being severely reprimanded by Miss Ophelia.

" . . . When Miss Ophelia expatiated on Topsy's naughty, wicked conduct, the child looked perplexed and sorrowful, but [Eva] said sweetly,

" 'Poor Topsy, why need you steal? You're going to be taken good care of, now. I'm sure I'd rather give you anything of mine, than have you steal it.'

"It was the first word of kindness the child ever heard in her life; and the sweet tone and manner struck strangely on the wild, rude heart, and a sparkle of something like a tear shown in the keen, round, glittering eye; but it was followed by a short laugh. . . . No! the ear that has never heard anything but abuse is strangely incredulous of anything so heavenly as kindness; and Topsy only thought Eva's speech something funny and inexplicable,—she did not believe it."[46]

The world is full of Topsys, of people, some perhaps less strangers to kind words, who nevertheless yearn for them, want them, need them, and—by virtue of destiny—are gravely deprived of them. Yet through kind words, spoken wherever we go, we may lessen the deprivation of many. In this regard, our opportunities are unfathomable, for as Seneca expresses, "Whenever there is a human being there is a chance for kindness."[47]

Particularly of kind words, Jeremy Bentham advises, "Kind words cost no more than unkind ones . . . and we may scatter the seeds of courtesy and kindliness around us at so little expense. If you would fall into any extreme let it be on the side of gentleness. The human mind is so constructed that it resists vigor and yields to softness."[48]

With such kind words a well-respected baseball player responded to a small boy who, after a game, approached him in the clubhouse. Born without a right hand, the player was taken aback as the child candidly began speaking of the player's disability. With tears in his eyes, the child—himself having one hand with only parts of two fingers—said his peers called him "crab." Then the player pointed out that he, who was playing in the majors, was just like the boy. Thus—as he himself had done—the boy could overcome his handicap.

"Yes," said the player. When he was young, other kids used to say his hand looked like a foot. But, he asked the boy, was there anything he, the boy, couldn't do? "No," the boy replied. Then said the player, "Look at me. I'm playing in the Majors and I'm just like you."[49]

To this boy, the player's kind words may have struck a deep chord, perhaps diminishing the ever-present anguish of his short yet painful childhood. Perhaps, too, those kind words would initiate a more productive and hopeful life for a boy.

In another instance, kind words spoke up when Katherine Hepburn was acting in a film. Two boys appearing with Hepburn were initially in awe of her, but she instinctively put them at ease. Then, on the filming's third day, one boy bungled his lines and Hepburn assured, "My fault, my fault." "How could it be your fault?" the startled boy asked. "I forgot the line."

"Because," replied Hepburn, "I delivered *my* line too fast. That made you forget."[50]

Speaking of kind words' potency, Jane Lindstrom also tells of a time when, convalescing from surgery, she felt lonely, unimportant, and unforgotten. Then she received a card from a casual acquaintance she often passed going to school. Each day she missed Jane's smile and wave and prayed she would soon be well, the acquaintance wrote. "You're probably surprised at receiving this note," she added, "but the world for me is a less happy place without you. And how will you know unless I tell you?"

Reading and rereading the words, Lindstrom savored the essence of each, but the writer's question—"How will you know unless I tell you?"—repeatedly drew her attention. Cognizant of the card's positive impact on her morale, Lindstrom thus poses her own question: "How can any of us know what's in the mind and hearts of others—unless we receive some word, some gesture?"

In a sophisticated, sterile world, most people check their emotions, withholding words of love, admiration and approval, reflects Lindstrom. And yet such words might bring "some unhappy person a moment of joy or help him cope with deep despair. They might even become the few bright threads in the dull fabric of this life."

Essentially, Lindstrom's message is that words of kindness locked in our hearts don't reach others, that they are like letters written but not sent. Going on record with caring words, she adds, will help us "defeat those two arch enemies of human happiness—loneliness and insignificance."[51]

♥ ♥ ♥ ♥ ♥ ♥ ♥ ♥

KINDNESS UNDERSTANDS

Coming from a neighbor's house where her little friend had died, a small child was stopped by her father:

"Why did you go?" he questioned.

"To comfort her mother," said the child.

"What could you do to comfort her?" the father questioned again.

"I climbed into her lap and cried with her," was her reply.

This child exhibited deep understanding of another human being's pain and, in kindness, acted in her own simple but profound way to console the mother.

Also demonstrating penetrating understanding, and thus kindness, is Roberto De Vicenzo, who, upon completing a golf tournament, was approached by a woman who stated her daughter had leukemia and pled for money to pay medical bills—money he produced. Later, a friend told De Vicenzo the woman's daughter wasn't ill—she had lied to him. In response, Roberto replied, "My friend, that is the best news I ever heard in my life!"[52]

As in the preceding instance, kindness has the good sense to overlook the follies and frailties of other human beings that another might penalize to the extreme. Kindness also realizes that the entire human race makes errors every day and that errors inevitably foster the growing process. Thus, kindness allows flunks and is even gracious enough to compensate for errors, protecting self-esteem and facilitating others ' recovery from their mistakes. As such, kindness is consistent with the poignant reflection of Baruch Spinoza, who said, "I have striven not to laugh at human actions, not to weep at them, not to hate them, but to understand them."[53]

Further illustrating penetrating understanding was Brigadier General Theodore Roosevelt Jr., who, during World War II, was waiting at the airport for his plane's departure. Stepping to a ticket window, a sailor asked for a seat on the same plane, explaining, "I want to see my mother. I haven't much time."

Not impressed, the reservations clerk coolly conveyed her indifference: "There's a war on, you know," she replied.

Then General Roosevelt, having overheard the conversation, stepped to the window and requested his ticket be transferred to the sailor. Thereafter, a friend asked, "Teddy, aren't you in a hurry, too?"

"'It's a matter of rank,' came the reply. 'I'm only a general; he's a son!'"[54]

Also showing penetrating understanding was General Dwight D. Eisenhower, who paid a visit to front-line troops during World War II and braved rain and ankle-deep mud to address the men from a makeshift platform. After finishing, as he turned to go, Eisenhower slipped from the platform and sprawled in the mud, sparking the soldiers to roar with laughter.

Covering his confusion, the commanding major general accompanying Eisenhower helped him to his feet, apologizing profusely for his men's behavior. "It's all right," the general responded. "That fall probably helped their morale more than the speech."[55]

In another instance, in descending the stairs in his headquarters, Eisenhower was bowled over by a private intent on an errand. As Eisenhower calmly uncrumpled himself, he managed to save the day for the horrified private. Brushing himself off, Eisenhower remarked something like, "Wouldn't you think an old man like me would be smart enough to wear his glasses so I could see where I was going?"[56]

In the preceding, Eisenhower had keen insight into the soul needs of soldiers under his command. He was acutely aware of the life-threatening and fear-producing situations these soldiers constantly faced. And, he also realized their enormous need for momentary respite from their grim situation—a respite only comic relief could provide. It was kindness, at its elegant best, that Eisenhower offered the GIs.

A final instance of deeper understanding occurred in a story Terry Dobson tells through a young man's eyes. This man, an American, was on a train on drowsy spring afternoon traveling through the suburbs of Tokyo. But the security and comfort of the near-empty car was suddenly shattered when, at one station, the doors opened and a big man—drunk and dirty—staggered in. Bellowing violent curses, the man struck a woman holding a baby, both of whom fell spinning—fortunately unharmed—into the laps of an elderly couple.

Still enraged and continuing to wreak havoc, the drunk swung and kicked at the terrified, retreating people as they moved as far from him as they could. Looking for a weapon, the drunk tried to wrench a metal pole from its stanchion. At this, the young American stood up, ready to fight the drunk; and the drunk, centering his rage on the American, moved toward him, shouting that the man needed a lesson in Japanese manners.

Extremely angered by the drunk's action, the young man was strangely eager to fight the intruder; in fact, he incensed the drunk through his looks of disgust and dismissal. Then he pursed his lips and blew the drunken man an insolent kiss.

The young man was strong and lithe from daily aikido training the past three years. However, because in Aikido training students are not allowed to fight, he had never used his martial skills in combat. As he rose to meet the drunk, the young man tried to ignore his teacher's frequently emphasized words: "Aikido is the art of reconciliation. Whoever has the mind to fight has broken his connection with the universe. If you try to dominate people, you are already defeated. We study how to resolve conflict, not to start it."

As the young man stood poised and the drunk prepared to lunge at him, both men heard an earsplitting shout—"Hey!" Recalls the young man: "I remember the strangely joyous, lilting quality of it—as though you and a friend had been searching diligently for something, and he had suddenly stumbled upon it. 'Hey!'"

Whirling around in opposite directions, both men stared down at a little old Japanese man in his seventies, sitting immaculate in his kimono. Ignoring the young man, the elder beckoned to the drunk, and the young man watched, astounded, as the drunk blindly obeyed. As the drunk stood in front of the elder, blatantly challenging him, the elder began to speak to the drunk ever so softly and with keen interest.

Enraptured and captured by the lilting voice, the drunk listened as the older man engaged him in conversation, the elder telling of himself and inquiring about the other man. As he did so, the drunk's face—and his clenched fists—slowly began to soften. In response to the elder's inquiry about his wife, the drunk replied his wife had died. Relates the young man, "Very gently, swaying with the motion of the train, the big man began to sob. 'I don't got no *wife*. I don't got no *home*. I don't got no *job*. I'm so *ashamed* of myself.' Tears rolled down his cheeks; a spasm of despair rippled through his body."

And as he heard the elder man chuckle sympathetically and invite the man to sit next to him—it was then the American's turn to cry. As he reached his destination, the young man turned one more time to look at the pair. As he stepped off the train, he saw the drunk's head nested in the elder's lap, with the elder softly stroking his filthy, matted hair.

"As the train pulled away, I sat down on a bench," reports the young man. "What I had wanted to do with muscle had been accomplished with kind words. I had just seen aikido tried in combat, and the essence of it was love. I would have to practice the art with an entirely different spirit. It would be a long time before I could speak about the resolution of conflict."[57]

❤ ❤ ❤ ❤ ❤ ❤ ❤ ❤ ❤

KINDNESS IS THOUGHTFUL

Kindness is cognizant of the living creatures—both man and animal—that co-exist or pass through its earthly space. Whenever possible, then, the kindly human spirit extends thoughtfulness to bring comfort and succor to those in need. A case in point is thoughtful action of Abraham Lincoln, who "once, while visiting the army's telegraph hut in Washington . . . saw three tiny kittens wandering around and mewing as if lost."

Lincoln then "picked up one of them and said, 'Where is your mother?' 'The mother is dead,' someone told him. 'Then,' said Lincoln, petting the little one, 'she can't grieve as many a poor mother is grieving for a son lost in battle.' Gathering the other two kittens in his hands, he put them on his lap, stroked their fur, and, according to General Horace Porter, said gently, 'Kitties, thank God you are cats, and can't understand this terrible strife that is going on.' And to Colonel Theodore Bowers he said, 'Colonel, I hope you will see that these poor little motherless waifs are given plenty of milk and treated kindly.'

"On several occasions afterward Porter noticed Lincoln fondling these kittens. 'He would smooth their coats' according to Porter, 'and listen to them purring their gratitude to him.' A curious sight it was, Porter thought, 'at an army headquarters, upon the eve of a great military crisis in the nation's history, to see the hand which had affixed the signature to the Emancipation Proclamation and had signed the commissions from the general-in-chief to the lowest lieutenant tenderly caressing three stray kittens.'"[58]

Relative to kindness, yet again did Lincoln demonstrate his unerring and lifetime thoughtfulness. After the war, Lincoln was responding to thousands of appeals for pardon. Ordinarily, each soldier's appeal was supported by letters from influential people. However, one day a single sheet came before him without any supporting documents. "What!" exclaimed the President. "Has this man no friends?" "No sir, not one," said the adjutant. "Then," said Lincoln, "I will be his friend."[59]

In the late 1700s, kindness was further thoughtful relative to actions of Arthur Wellesley Wellington, a British general and statesman. As the story goes, "Wellington came upon a small boy sitting at the side of the road, crying as if his heart would break. 'Come now, that's no way for a young gentleman to behave. What's the matter?' he asked. 'I have to go away to school tomorrow,' sobbed the child, 'and I'm worried about my pet toad. There's no one else to care for it and I shan't know how it is.' The duke reassured him, promising to attend to the matter personally.

"After the boy had been at school for little more than a week, he received the following letter: 'Field Marshal the Duke of Wellington presents his compliments to Master _____ and has the pleasure to inform him that his toad is well.'"[60]

On a grave note is also an instance of kindness expressing thoughtfulness which involved American Pat Frank, during World War II a wartime correspondent on the Italian Front. In 1945, following the allied armies in their final thrust through Italy, he and other correspondents were flown to Berlin to cover the Potsdam conference. With other Americans, he was housed in the suburb of Zehlendorf, "billeted in a typical middle-class home on a shady street." His roommate was Ed Murrow and the two were the only occupants of the house. Living over the garage, they discovered, was the elderly couple who had occupied the home.

Earlier, the Russians had occupied Zehlendorf and had largely stripped the house to which the pair was assigned. Because the Russians had said Americans were barbarians, the couple were at first extremely leery of the men, fearing for their safety and their few remaining possessions.

Instead, the Americans—telling the couple to return to their house—gave the two access to all "the staples that in those days correspondents did not forget—chocolate, coffee, soap, tea, K-rations, and canned meat and butter." In return, tells Frank, the couple was "pitifully and almost incoherently grateful."

The next day, Frank and Murrow discovered flowers in their room and knew they had made two friends. Ends Frank, "In the ruin and bitterness of Berlin . . . a vase of flowers was a wondrous thing."[61]

In the most stirring of incidents, a sheriff's deputy in Lane County, Oregon—Robert Gross—did what he could to cushion a couple's unbearable loss of their daughter Katie. As columnist Karen McCowan writes, Gross had been present when Katie died, and wishing her parents to know what had happened, he wrote the following letter:

"Mr. and Mrs. Weinman," he began, "I am sorry for your loss. I am writing this letter to you because I have three teen-age children of my own, a son and two daughters. If any of them died, I would want to know the things that I am going to tell you."

In the letter, Gross told of coming upon the accident scene after the auto collision on an icy stretch of road. "Katie was in the driver's seat. She had received a severe blow to the left side of her head, and the force had rendered her unconscious. I lifted her head to ease her breathing; then I held her gently and kindly until the rescue personnel arrived.

"After a few minutes, it was clear that Katie did not survive, but we did not stop helping her breathe until an electronic monitor was connected to her and verified that she was gone.

"I wanted you to know that Katie was not awake and frightened and suffering—she never regained consciousness. I also wanted you to know that she did not die alone. She died being held by a father who loves his own teen-age daughters, and knows how precious children are. I am sorry this happened to your little girl. Please call me if you should ever wish to talk about that day."

Later, the Weinmans met Gross at Katie's funeral and they did want to speak with him. Thus, a few weeks later, Gross went to the Weinman's home where he spent several hours answering their questions. Says Diane Weinman of Gross's thoughtful actions, "It helped because he's a dad and he knew my pain. He was direct and honest—and he has strong faith. He made a big difference."[62]

Of such elegant actions, reflects Bob Greene, "The human spirit can be an amazing thing, and sometimes you encounter it at its very best when you aren't even looking."[63]

* * * * * * * * *

KINDNESS IS BENEVOLENT

"Kindness," reflects Randolph Ray, "comes very close to the benevolence of God."[64]

Speaking of kindness's benevolence, Mother Teresa advises, "Be kind and merciful. Let no one ever come to you without coming away better and happier. Be the living expression of God's kindness: kindness in your face, kindness in your eyes, kindness in your smile, kindness in your warm greeting. . . . To children, to the poor, to all who suffer and are lonely, give always a happy smile—Give them not only your care, but also your heart."[65]

As Mother Teresa infers, much of the warmth and tenderness of kindness's benevolence is conveyed not through words but through radiance of the soul. Of her father, whose soul-stirring touch divulged his keenly felt emotions, Freya Stark relates, "All the feeling which my father could not put into words was in his hand—any dog, child or horse would recognize the kindness of it."[66]

Additionally, kindness's benevolence gives generous invitation through a receptive and inviting demeanor. Assuming such posture was Sam Rayburn, who held the U.S. House of Representatives' gavel longer than any other person. Well-known for his kindness, Rayburn was sorely missed when he died in November of 1961. Once a small girl visiting Rayburn's grave was about to pick a flower at his graveside when she was stopped by an officer. An onlooker observed, "If Mr. Sam had been there, he would have said, 'Let her have the flower.'"[67]

Also striking—besides his receptive and inviting demeanor—is Rayburn's perceived benevolence in protecting another's sense of value. Illustrating this laudable characteristic is another observer, who reported that Rayburn had "a peculiar rule about his mail. If a woman wrote to him in pencil, he answered in pencil; if in ink, he answered in ink. He never upstaged anyone."[68]

Kindness's benevolence further rises to the occasion through impeccable etiquette. "Etiquette is also part of the spiritual practice of kindness," advise Frederic and Mary Ann Brussat. "In Earth etiquette, we don't walk on flowers or leave trash in parks. In house etiquette, we don't ignore or abuse our possessions. In animal etiquette, we don't ridicule our pets or frighten them."[69]

Many years ago, in New York City, etiquette benevolently stepped forward in sleety and slushy weather to assist someone in need. Hurrying along 42nd Street, with collars tucked about their ears, most pedestrians were preoccupied with reaching shelter. Yet, one pedestrian noticed a young black man struggling with a heavy valise in one hand, a huge suitcase in the other, slipping and sliding as he hurried toward Grand Central Station.

"Suddenly," goes the story, "a hand reached out and took the valise, and at the same time a pleasant but positive voice said, 'Let me take one, brother! Bad weather makes it too hard to carry things.' The black man was reluctant, but the young white man insisted, with the remark, 'I'm going your way.' All the way to the station the two chatted like old friends.

"Years later, Booker T. Washington, who told the story, said, 'That was my introduction to Theodore Roosevelt.'"[70]

Additionally, kindness's benevolence is delightfully conveyed through humor and lightness of heart and mind, both characteristic of Henry Adams. Adams, a renowned nineteenth century novelist, is remembered by biographer and relative Marjorie Chanler as being "delightful with children." Of Adams, she tells a revealing experience: "I took my youngest son, Theodore, to lunch with him one day, and as I was presenting him I said, 'This is your Uncle Henry (all my children called him that), and he knows everything.' Teddy looked at him in round-eyed silence through part of the meal, watching for his opportunity. During a pause in the conversation of the grownups the little boy leaned forward respectfully and said, 'Uncle Henry, how do you feed a chameleon?'"[71]

Kindness's benevolence, moreover, constitutes a golden chain, the links of which, ever so delicately, tenderly interlace and interlock God's creatures, one to another. For example, naturalist Jane Goodall's seminal writings of her chimpanzee studies reflect a benevolence enabling her to transcend even the species barrier. Such benevolence is reflected in Goodall's description of a momentary and intense spiritual bonding with the chimp colony's patriarch:

"One day as I was sitting near him, I picked up a ripe palm nut and held it out to him on my open hand. He turned his head away. When I moved my hand closer, he looked at it and then at me. He took the fruit and at the same time held my hand firmly and gently with his own.

"At that moment there was no need of any scientific knowledge to understand his communication of reassurance. The soft pressure of his fingers spoke to me not through my intellect but through a more primitive emotional channel. . . . It was a reward far beyond my greatest hopes."[72]

The benevolence of kindness also reigns as people respect and protect God's creatures, as did Henry David Thoreau. On one occasion, Thoreau—an eminent nineteenth-century writer and a dedicated nature lover—was having difficulty educating woodchucks to avoid his garden. Of his problem, he observed, "My enemies are worms, cool days, and most of all woodchucks. They have nibbled for me an eighth of an acre clean. I plant in faith, and they reap."

Though the woodchucks were savoring his patch, Thoreau respected their foremost position, recognizing they "had prior claims as residents." However, if they remained, he also realized, he would be gardenless. Ultimately, he consulted a veteran trapper who, in colorful language, advised him to shoot the creatures. Disdaining this advice, Thoreau found matters getting worse instead of better.

Later, a desperate Thoreau "procured a trap and captured the grandfather of all the woodchucks. After retaining it for several hours, he delivered it a severe lecture and released it, hoping never to see it again. But it was a vain delusion. Within a few days [the woodchuck] was back at its old stand, nibbling heartily as ever at his beans. Accordingly he set the trap again, and this time when he caught the villain he carried it some two miles away . . . and let it depart in peace."[73]

Too, kindness's benevolence manifests itself in compassionately aiding strangers, as Niccolo Paganini so did many years ago. As the story goes, Paganini, an eighteenth-century Italian violin virtuoso, "happened, in the course of a walk on the streets of Vienna, to come across a miserable little fellow sawing away on an old fiddle. On inquiry the great violinist learned that the boy was trying to maintain an invalid mother and several little brothers and sisters by his street playing.

"Paganini, touched by the boy's destitute circumstances, took the old fiddle and began to play in his marvelous manner; and after a crowd had collected he himself passed around the hat and collected a goodly sum from the bystanders, adding to it all the money he had in his own pockets."[74]

Finally, in universal form, kindness's benevolence once manifest its brilliance through an older American couple's sympathy and sorrow for fallen street fighters. Years ago, in visiting Paris, the couple encountered marble plaques, set in the walls of many Paris buildings, with flower boxes underneath. Inquiring of this oddity, they learned that every plaque was engraved with a name, commemorated the spot where—in the bitter battle in 1944 to liberate Paris—a young resistance fighter had died. After conferring, the two thereafter walked around the corner, returning shortly with several flower bouquets. Locating all the plaques embedded in surrounding buildings, they selected and meticulously placed a flower in each adjoining flower box.[75]

Through such benevolent acts as the preceding, kindness often finds a home. Such acts, Frederick W. Farrar emphasizes, when silently combined, represent "the silent threads of gold which, when woven together, gleam out so brightly in the pattern of life that God approved."[76]

♥ ♥ ♥ ♥ ♥ ♥ ♥ ♥ ♥

KINDNESS OFTEN RECIPROCATES

"One of the most difficult things to give away is kindness—it is usually returned," reflects Cort Flint.[77] To offer kindness, in fact, is to ultimately incur intrinsic benefits in the form of increased self-esteem and personal growth. With respect to the latter, Eric Hoffer observes, "Kindness can become its own motive. We are made kind by being kind."[78]

By being kind, people may provide a model that has enduring effects on others, and such people may ultimately return the kindness. A classic case is that of Robert Louis Stevenson, who lived out his last years on the island of Samoa. When European authorities imprisoned his friend Mataafa, the Samoan chieftain, Stevenson—although in very ill health—returned again and again to visit him in his captivity, always bringing him a small gift. The Samoans themselves, deeply moved by Stevenson's enduring kindness, through long labor gave a gift of love by building Stevenson a road. And when Stevenson died, the Samoans buried him on a high hilltop and created the law that there were to be no firearms shot on the hill, for Stevenson was to forever sleep in peace.[79]

Practicing kindness can also reciprocate in the form of later, unexpected help, as when a woman stopped along a barren stretch of road to aid a family with a flat tire. Twelve miles later, stranded with a blowout herself, she was rescued by the very family she had earlier helped. In another instance, a man who had stopped on his way to a job interview, taking time to aid a stranger revive his stalled automobile, walked into the interview only to encounter the man he had helped.

In a third instance, a businessman arrived at a hotel late one night without a reservation. With all the rooms booked, the night clerk on duty offered the man the other twin bed in his small room which, without hesitation, the weary man accepted. Thanking the clerk the next morning, the man remarked that if he were to ever establish a hotel he would like the clerk to manage it. Some years later, the clerk received a call from this man—

John Jacob Aster—who now did own a new hotel. And the hotel was the Waldorf Astoria.

To this end, Ralph Waldo Emerson notes, "It is one of the most beautiful compensations of life that no man can sincerely try to help another without helping himself."[80]

On the other hand, sometimes *not* rendering a kindness can have unanticipated repercussions. Charles G. Dawes, who knew U.S. President William McKinley well, tells of a happening many years ago in the president's life. At the time, President McKinley was having difficulty deciding which of two men who had equal qualifications to appoint to a vacant cabinet post. One night, a telling event occurred when both McKinley and one of candidates were riding in a streetcar.

The car was crowded the night McKinley boarded, and he had moved to the rear, where he took the last available seat. Soon thereafter, an elderly washerwoman carrying a heavy basket boarded the car. Although the woman, standing near the front, looked extremely exhausted, no one offered her a seat. Sitting nearby was the candidate in question, who, ignoring the woman, shifted his position and kept his eyes on his newspaper.

Moving to the front of the car, McKinley reached the woman, took the basket from her, and escorted her back to his seat. With his head buried in his newspaper, the candidate did not see McKinley or observe his actions.

"The candidate never knew," Dawes tells, "that this little act of selfishness, or rather this little omission of kindness, had deprived him that which would have crowned his ambition of a lifetime."[81]

❤ ❤ ❤ ❤ ❤ ❤ ❤ ❤

KINDNESS CHANGES LIVES

"With kindness you can give a man back his self-respect, you can bring life to smothered dreams, you can mend broken hearts, you can bring heaven down to earth," reflects an anonymous author.[82]

In this regard, a kindness may have a lingering effect, quantitatively bettering a person's life perspective. Rendering such kindness was cellist Pablo Casals, who heightened and salvaged the morale of a distinguished violinist. Several months before the 1927 Barcelona music festival commemorating the hundredth anniversary of Beethoven's death, Casals visited his dear friend Eugène Ysaÿe in Brussels. Almost seventy, Ysaÿe had quit playing the violin, grieving over his last, disappointing public appearance. Convinced that Ysaÿe could still render a magnificent performance, Casals urged him to participate in the Beethoven centennial. "Eugène," Casals said, "you must come and play the Beethoven violin concerto at our festival."

Ysaÿe stared at Casals in astonishment. "But, Pablo," he protested, "that's impossible!. . . . I haven't played the Beethoven concerto in fourteen years."

"'No matter. You can play.'

"'You really believe so?'

"'I know it. You can and you will.'

His face suddenly appearing youthful, Ysaÿe responded, "Perhaps the miracle will happen!"—and agreed to play.

Several weeks later, Casals received a letter from Ysaÿe's son Antoine, who was greatly disturbed that Casals had raised his father's hopes of playing again. "If only you could see my dear father," he wrote, "if you could see him working every day, playing scales slowly and laboriously hour after hour. It is a tragedy, and we cannot help weeping over it."

After arriving in Barcelona, Ysaÿe was exceedingly nervous at the festival's rehearsal, which quietly worried Casals. Casal's apprehension grew on the evening of Ysaÿe's performance as Ysaÿe moved slowly and seemed weary. Casals suddenly thought, *He is old; have I done my friend a great injustice?*

But then Casals tells of Ysaÿe's stunning formal performance, "I lifted my baton, and he raised his violin to his chin . . . and, with the first notes, I knew that all was well! In some passages it seemed he might falter, and I felt his nervousness throughout. But there were many movements of the great Ysaÿe, and the effect as a whole was overwhelming.

"Once again, as so often in the past, I was lost in the wonder of his music. The ovation at the end was frenzied. Then Ysaÿe took my place on the podium and conducted Beethoven's 'Eroica' Symphony and afterwards the Triple concerto with Cortot, Thibaud and me playing. . . .

"In the dressing room after the concert Ysaÿe was overcome with emotion. He kissed my hands and wept, exclaiming 'Resurrection!'"

The next day Casals took his friend to the train station. Leaning out of the carriage window—obviously not wanting to separate—Ysaÿe talked to Casals and clasped his hands tightly as Casals moved along the platform with the slowly moving train. Then, as the train gathered speed, Ysaÿe suddenly thrust something into Casals hands. Realizing Ysaÿe wished to leave with him something—anything—that represented himself, Casals curiously glanced down at the object. It was Ysaÿe's pipe.[83]

Finally, endowed with potential and powerful soul-altering quality, kindness may utterly transform another's life through the simplest of actions. Such was kindness's impact in the following story:

In 1887 in an almshouse in Stockholm, an orphaned six-year-old girl lived in the care of an unkind elderly woman. As the story goes, "when her guardian went out to earn her daily pittance, she locked the little maid in the house to prevent her wandering about; and so the lonesome little Johanne was deprived of the bright sunshine and sight of the beautiful trees and flowers so beloved by every Swedish heart.

"One day she had worked over the little tasks assigned her until she was tired, and oh! how she longed to get out into the open air. But no, the door was locked. No wonder she poured out her childish grief in tears. Soon her sole companion caught her eyes, and, taking her half-starved cat, she rocked her until they both feel asleep. When she awoke the sun had gone well down. Fearing the scolding she was sure to get when the guardian came home, the child caught up her work and began to sing in a sweet voice that seemed far too old for a girl of her age.

"While she went on with her singing, it happened that a lady of high rank was passing the house; and so struck was she by the clear, sweet tones, that she stopped her carriage to listen. On caroled the little songstress, perfectly unconscious of her audience, till she was startled by a knock at the door. She could not open it, but some kind neighbor told the fair visitor about the little prisoner. The kind-hearted lady came back afterward and secured the child admission to a school and later to the Royal Theater classes. As the girl grew older her talent developed, until as the 'Swedish Nightingale' she was known the world over." Her name—Jenny Lind.[84]

In yet a third story, the kindness of one man—Abraham Lincoln—actually prevented a consummate life change that would have reverberated throughout generations. One day, an elderly man approached President Lincoln, pleading for a pardon for his son. Responding, Lincoln, gently but firmly, indicated he was sorry. "I can do nothing for you," he said. "Listen to this telegram I received from General Butler yesterday: 'President Lincoln, I pray you not to interfere with the court-martials of the army. You will destroy all discipline among our soldiers.'"

At that, "the old man's face fell; but when Lincoln saw his hopeless despair, he cried, 'By jingo! Butler or not Butler, here goes!' He wrote an order and showed it to the old man: 'Joe Smith is not to be shot until further orders from me. A. Lincoln'

"'Why, I thought it was a pardon,' said the father disconsolately. 'You may order him to be shot next week.'

"'My old friend,' said Lincoln, 'I see you are not very well acquainted with me. If your son never dies until orders come from me to shoot him, he will live to be a great deal older than Methuselah.'"[85]

Kindness thus has the potency to change an enduring perspective, profoundly alter a life course, or even preserve a life. As illustrated, kindness is endowed with a life-altering strength and a vast sphere of influence not commonly recognized. As Frances J. Roberts advises, "Kindness is like a rose, which though easily crushed and fragile, yet speaks a language of silent power."[86]

♥ ♥ ♥ ♥ ♥ ♥ ♥ ♥

KINDNESS PREVAILS IN DARK TIMES

"The greatness of a man can nearly always be measured by his willingness to be kind," G. Young imparts.[87] A man's greatness may become all the more evident when such kindnesses occur in desperate circumstances. Attesting to this point is Gerda Weissmann Klein, a Jew and former Nazi prisoner:

"Most . . . people think [the Holocaust camps were] like snake pits—that people stepped on each other for survival. It wasn't like that at all." Instead, she says, there was kindness, support, and understanding.

Of the camp, Klein speaks particularly of a childhood friend who one time found a raspberry and carried it in her pocket all day, that evening to present the raspberry to Klein on a leaf. Says Klein of her experience, "Imagine a world in which your entire possession is one raspberry, and you give it to a friend. Those were moments I want to remember. . . . People did behave nobly under unspeakable circumstances."[88]

Victor Frankl, also once interned in a Nazi concentration camp, explains how people, even as they themselves suffered, could maintain their humanity and extend kindnesses to others in the worst of circumstances: "We who have lived in concentration camps can remember the men who walked through the huts comforting others, giving away their last piece of bread. They may have been few in number, but they offer sufficient proof that everything can be taken from man but one thing: the last of the human freedoms—to choose one's attitude in any given set of circumstances—to choose one's own way."[89]

Of note is that visionary acts of kindness in dark times profoundly aided in healing the Civil War scars. In *American Places*, William Zinsser tells of these kindnesses, which occurred during the surrender of the South to the North. Of circumstances leading to the April 9, 1865, surrender, Zinsser writes that General Robert E. Lee's 55,000-strong Army of Northern Virginia had been entrenched for nine months near Petersburg, south of Richmond. On April 2, his railroad lifeline cut by the North, Lee retreated, but General Ulysses S. Grant was in close pursuit, and by April 6 the battle was over. First, Union troops captured almost a fifth of Lee's army at Sayler's Creek and took some six thousand prisoners.

And, then, pushed beyond their limits, huge numbers of hungry and exhausted soldiers fell out of ranks. The Confederate army had dwindled to thirty thousand men when Lee, speeding west, received a note from Grant calling for surrender.

Pondering his dwindling options, Lee chose not to inflict further useless pain and suffering on either side. Although Grant said that he would "rather die a thousand deaths" than meet with Lee, he nevertheless sent an aide to find, in a nearby village, a suitable meeting place for the surrender.

Wilmer McLean's home in Appomattox, Virginia, ultimately provided the meeting site. Lee arrived first in dress uniform, and Grant, whose baggage wagon had fallen behind, arrived second in his muddy field uniform. In a parlor setting, the two men amiably discussed extraneous subjects until eventually Lee brought up "the object of our present meeting." To Lee's request, Grant took out a pen and rapidly wrote out the surrender terms, which, in reading, Lee was astonished to find no hint of reprisal. His men were simply to surrender their arms and go home. These very liberal terms, Grant apprised, would have "a very happy effect" on his army and foster the two sides reuniting. Also at Lee's request, Grant instantly agreed Lee's soldiers—most small farmers—could keep their horses to plant the crops their families so desperately needed through the next winter.

Lee stated he was releasing his Union prisoners, his provisions being impoverished for soldiers of either side. In response, Grant said he would send twenty-five thousand rations to Lee's army. After the meeting, Grant also ordered an immediate stop to a spree of cannon firing instigated by jubilant officers at nearby Union headquarters. "The war is over—the rebels are our countrymen again," he said, emphatically demonstrating intolerance of further wounding of "a foe who had fought so long and valiantly."

Comprehending the mood of clemency, many Union soldiers themselves went to the Confederate camps, emptying
haversacks of their own food, including "delicacies that the
rebels had long gone without." But the next action of the Union,
informs Zinsser, was to set "in motion the final act of healing."
As Confederate troops marched into the village to stack their
arms, they were met by Union troops, who lined up and, at
attention, gave them the soldier's salutation as they passed by.

Responding to this magnanimous and deeply respectful gesture, the commander general of the Confederate troops ordered
his own brigades, as they passed through, to return the salute—
"honor answering honor." Of this moment, the Union general
designated to receive the surrender—Joshua L. Chamberlain—
later wrote, "On our part not a sound of trumpet more, nor role
of drum; nor a cheer, nor word nor whisper of vain-glorying, but
of an awed stillness rather, and breath-holding, as if it were the
passing of the dead!"

And so it was, continues Zinsser, that on April 12, four years
to the day from the war's beginning, "from early morning until
late afternoon the saluting soldiers of the South marched past the
saluting Union soldiers, stacked their rifles and tattered
Confederate flags and started for home. Counting the Union
troops, almost one hundred thousand men had been in
Appomattox Court House that day. Seventy-two hours later
they were all gone."

Grant's generous and nonvindictive actions set the stage for
the war's final end. After Appomattox, two hundred thousand
Confederate troops were still fighting and these men would not
"have laid down their arms if Grant had taken a hard line with
Lee," Zinsser notes. "Grant's surrender terms gave the rest of the
Southern soldiers a good reason to go home."

It was to three men Zinsser gives credit for the prevailing

theme of forgiveness and reconciliation after the war. The first two were Lee and Grant, who radiated honor and valor. The third was Abraham Lincoln, always known and greatly respected for his kindness. Lincoln, says Zinsser, "had often spoken of wanting a merciful peace," and Lincoln had—two weeks before the surrender—instructed Grant as to his wishes regarding reconciliation after the war's rapidly approaching end.

Speaking more broadly of Lincoln's compassionate nature, Zinsser refers to his second inaugural address. This address, he writes, "delivered only five weeks before his consuming war finally ended and six weeks before he himself was killed, moves me more than any American document—a continuing astonishment in its wisdom and compassion, in its plea for a reconciliation that would have charity for all, and in the Biblical grandeur of its language."[90]

Ever foremost, it was the indomitable Lincoln—in evincing consummate kindness and compassion—who provided the forgiving tenor so integral to healing a shattered nation. In so doing, Lincoln expressed in practice what he believed in principle and at one time had written: "I shall do nothing through malice. What I deal with is too vast for malicious dealing."[91]

❦ ❦ ❦ ❦ ❦ ❦ ❦ ❦ ❦

KINDNESS RESTORES HOPE

Hope is an element that Emily Dickinson calls the "thing with feathers that perches in the soul."[92] Hope is tenuous and fragile, but enduring in the sense that most people have an instinctive sense of compassion and will reach out to others. Be such a person, Rabbi Harold S. Kushner urges: "Be among those who reach out, who assist, who comfort, who bind wounds and dry tears.

... Remind people whose lives have been shadowed by evil that there is still plenty of goodness in the world."[93]

Helen Hayes tells of such goodness in relating how, in her darkest hour, hope came in the form of kindness. That darkest hour was in 1944, a period in which she was mourning the tragic death of her daughter, Mary, who had died of polio. At that time, Hayes was wrought with unanswerable questions—Why Mary?—Mary, her daughter, who had been so young and lovely, so alive with the world—her only child. Why had Mary suffered such a needless, cruel illness?

Although Hayes recognized her enduring depressed state, she could find no relief, nor could she create beauty and meaning on stage when she could find none in her own life. To save herself, she tried to search for God through reading the Bible and other works, but that search failed. She could not bring back her daughter and, she reports, "that brutal fact overwhelmed me, blinded my heart."

During this dark period, Hayes withdrew from her outer world, refusing to accept professional or social engagements and restricting her contacts to family and intimate friends. She was dimly aware of a Mr. Isaac Franz, who phoned every day, trying to reach her. "He has just lost a little boy with polio and he seems to think it would help his wife if she could see you," Hayes's husband reported after he had finally personally taken the man's call. Aghast, Hayes told him she could not see the woman. She had no strength to buoy up another person; she had barely enough for herself. "Of course, Darling, that's what I told him," her husband responded. But the calls kept coming.

Finally, Hayes agreed to see Mr. Isaac Franz and his wife, and the day came when she steeled herself for the ordeal. In their Sunday best, the other couple came, "with a quiet dignity that surmounted their painful self-consciousness." Hayes and her husband tried to put the couple at ease, both recognizing the enormous courage the couple had mustered to make this visit.

"Now," says Hayes, "I discovered the truth about their visit. It had been the husband's idea entirely and he had arranged it without his wife's knowledge. But he was so sure that a meeting would bring some comfort to his wife that he forced himself to ask it. As for his wife, she was appalled when she heard of the completed arrangements, but knowing how difficult it had been for her husband, and how important to him, she consented to come. Each was doing this for the other—in the moment of great need."

As the discussion proceeded, Hayes learned details regarding the couple's life; they owned a tiny stationery store and it was obvious that they lived modestly. The Hayes family, by contrast, were wealthy. Says Hayes, "I had never known anything but success, fame, luxury. And yet the four of us suddenly had one thing to share, the tragic loss of our children."

It was Mrs. Franz who first began talking, but Hayes soon began reciprocating, revealing stories of Mary, whose name, since her death, she had not mentioned. However, she now took her memory out of hiding, and she realized she felt better for it.

But it was a stunned Hayes who listened when Mrs. Franz told her the couple was going to adopt an orphan from Israel. How could the Franz family ever replace their child? she wondered. Guessing Hayes's thought, Mrs. Franz responded she could not. However, she had love and wisdom to give—should she let those go to waste?

"I—I don't know," stammered Hayes, who listened as Mrs. Franz elaborated: "No, my dear, we cannot die because our children die. I should not love less because the one I loved is gone—but more should I love because my heart knows the suffering of others."

Pondering, Hayes realized Mrs. Franz was right. Although her daughter had been a vital and integral part of her life, that part was gone, yet she was a better person for having been Mary's mother, and "for having hoped and dreamed and worked for her." She further realized the irony, because she feared her strength being drained, of not wanting to see Mrs. Franz. Exactly the opposite had occurred—she had been fortified by this woman. "When they finally rose to leave," recalls Hayes, "I realized why my search for God had been fruitless—I had looked in the wrong places. He was not to be found between covers of a book, but in the human heart."

Although Hayes and her husband invited the Franzes to come back, the couple never returned, always busy with their small store and their new son, perhaps, says Hayes, who understood "that our worlds were meant to touch but briefly." But through the Franzes, Hayes gives credit, she learned humility and another important lesson: that the celebrated are as vulnerable to affliction as those of other social status. In essence, reflects Hayes, her experience taught her that in God's eyes, none is privileged; all are equal.[94]

❖ ❖ ❖ ❖ ❖ ❖ ❖ ❖ ❖

KINDNESS IS A CHOICE

When Clare Boothe Luce was seventy-five, she was asked whether she had any regrets about her life. Her response? "Yes, I should have been a better person. Kinder. More tolerant. Sometimes I wake up in the middle of the night and I remember a girlfriend of mine who had a brain tumor and called me three times to come and see her. I was always too busy, and when she died I was profoundly ashamed. I remember that after fifty-six years."[95]

Luce realized that throughout her life, she had had ever-present a daily choice to be kinder and more caring to others. And that any such proactive choice would have made her a better person. Just as with Luce, we have life choices waiting in the wing: Can we open our minds, hearts, and resources to others and extend ourselves to make kindness a way of life?

Richard Rhodes, a prolific author and Pulitzer Prize winner, is a man who urges others to choose such kindness. In *A Hole in the World: An American Boyhood*, Rhodes tells how he and his brother Stanley survived a terrible childhood ordeal. His message to readers? That we all possess power to influence events and to change lives for the better. And he challenges us to make that investment, particularly through observant kindness.

In the summer of 1938, Rhodes's twenty-nine-year-old mother committed suicide, from his perspective "a Depression casualty." Surviving her were a husband and three young sons, the oldest of whom Rhodes's father sent to live with relatives; the other two boys he kept himself. When his mother died, Rhodes was still in his crib.

For the next ten years, Rhodes and his brother Stanley lived in a series of boardinghouses, sharing a room with their father, a boilermaker's helper for the railroad. For six of those years, Rhodes and his brother were the fortunate recipients of love and warmth. They lived in a house operated by a kind immigrant German couple whose daughter—a polio victim confined to a wheelchair—nurtured the two boys as if they were her own. From there, the threesome moved on to deteriorating boardinghouses, until Rhodes's tenth birthday, when his father remarried.

Rhodes describes his stepmother, a woman from an impoverished Texas mining background, as relentlessly and capriciously cruel; and his father—after his marriage—as too cowardly to defend Rhodes and his brother from brutalization.

Thus, they suffered through a nightmare of extreme child abuse in which, devoid of their father's protection, they were vulnerable to a stepmother for whom "everything became possible."

Propelled by fear of ultimate beatings should their stepmother be displeased, the boys were also forced to sell trinkets from door to door and to collect soft-drink bottles for the deposit money. On weekends, they were often ordered to leave the house early and not return until dark. Even in sub-zero weather, and wearing only thin rags, they were forced to sell their wares. Their stepmother taunted them that if they "got cold they might quit being lazy and find some work to do to get warm." In the end, the boys' meager earnings were permanently conscripted by their stepmother—half, she pronounced, to contribute to their board and room; the rest, for safekeeping so the boys wouldn't squander the money.

Worst of all, tells Rhodes, while his stepmother and his dad dined on steak and fresh fruit, the boys lived almost exclusively on black-eyed peas, mashed to bitter gruel, and burned, sometimes rotten hard-boiled eggs. They learned to scavenge from the garbage cans behind grocery stores and drive-ins and to steal and beg for food. Both boys' weight dropped to skeletal proportions, and, of one of few existing childhood snapshots, Rhodes describes himself as appearing "like an Auschwitz child."[96]

Looking back at those hellish years over four decades ago, Rhodes wonders why he and his brother survived with the capacity to love still intact; and, as the recipients of horrific abuse, why neither became child abusers themselves. Having repeatedly mulled over this ravaging abuse, Rhodes has also repeatedly concluded that he and his brother are today healthy human beings because of the unsolicited kindness of strangers. Writing of these persons in *Parade Magazine*, Rhodes remarks, "They could have looked the other way, pretended they didn't see the abuse, chosen not to become involved. My own father chose that response. Stanley and I were resourceful enough to keep ourselves from bare starvation. But the kindness of strangers gave us hope."

Of kindnesses extended, Rhodes speaks particularly of his first-grade teacher, who was Stanley's teacher the year before. Cognizant of his meager and shriveled lunches, several times a week his teacher—as she had previously done with Stanley—asked a favor at lunch break. Would he go to the grocery store and buy her a half-pint of milk? And, "as if in afterthought" she would say, "Here's another dime. Buy some milk for yourself." As Rhodes emphasizes, despite her meager salary, this teacher repeatedly sacrificed to supplement his, and his brother's, lunches.

Rhodes credits Stanley as a hero who finally saved them. After a particularly severe beating with a belt, thirteen-year-old Stanley ran away and hid for the day in a huge storm sewer. With nowhere else to go, and with no one who cared about him and his brother, Stanley walked to the police station, where he related his story.

In the years of 1948–1949, children had no rights, nor did agencies exist to intercede on their behalf. With the principle of "family authority" prevailing, courts were reluctant—except in the most extreme of cases—to intervene. But during the two weeks Stanley was in juvenile detention, he relentlessly insisted he and his brother be removed from their abusive home and together placed elsewhere. Stanley prevailed in court and the pair were subsequently relegated to a privately endowed boys' home, where—incidentally—Rhodes later became a trustee. There, over time, the boys recovered their health, staying until graduating from high school.

Of his harrowing experience, Rhodes urges, "Don't be a

bystander. If you see something happening that you think is wrong, get involved. Speak up. Do something. The kindnesses of strangers helped my brother and me survive our childhood ordeal. It can help other victims today as well."[97]

IV

♥ ♥ ♥ ♥ ♥ ♥ ♥ ♥ ♥

ON GIVING

After lecturing her six-year-old son on the Golden Rule, a mother concluded, "Always remember that we are in this world to help others." Mulling over his mother's words for a minute, the young child then asked, "What are the others here for?"[1]

We're all acquainted with people who *don't* think they're in this world to give to others. A rich man, for example, once asked a friend why he was being criticized for being miserly, pointing out that it was common knowledge he would leave everything to charity when he died.

At that, the friend commenced telling the man a story about a pig and a cow who were speaking together. Lamenting over his unpopularity, the pig noted people were basically unfair in contrasting his and the cow's contributions. "Yes, you give milk and cream, but I give more," he pointed out. "I give bacon, ham, bristles. They even pickle my feet! Still, nobody likes me. Why is this?"

After a momentary pause, the cow responded, "Well, maybe it's because I give while I'm still living."[2]

Not "giving while you're living" is an issue one advertising

tycoon attacked head-on, making the inconsistency of this position laser-sharp. In responding to a top executive's refusal to
move from California to a New York office, the tycoon took a
new tack. Stressing that upon his death, the executive would succeed him as company president, the tycoon reasoned with him,
asking if he wouldn't have to move to California at such time.

The executive agreed to do so.

"You will do this for me when I'm dead?" asked the tycoon.

"Yes."

"Then, why," demanded the tycoon, "won't you do it for me
while I'm alive?"

At this juncture—as the story goes—the executive capitu-
lated.[3]

Consistent with the preceding, people sometimes procrastinate giving until a confrontive situation shocks them into thinking differently. In this instance, the executive obviously felt
coerced into complying with the tycoon's wishes. Thus, the story
does not fully apply because capitulation does not constitute true
giving. Coercion aside, however, the point the tycoon makes
here—If you'd do something good for me when I'm dead, why
won't you do the same while I'm alive?—applies aptly to personal
relationships. Such actions, however, must be given freely by,
not wrenched from, the heart.

Sometimes people don't give because of a "I'm not going to
give if I'm not going to get" attitude, as in a discussion between
two local residents of a small town in Maine. Speaking of the
virtues and shortcomings of an old-timer who had just died, one
man asked the other if he was going to the funeral. "Nope," he
replied. "He ain't comin' to mine, so I ain't goin' to his."

Some may refrain from giving for another reason. Culturally,
a giving nature—as a personality attribute—is often viewed as
an "add-on," and inferior to such marketable attributes as

strength, intelligence, and power. And yet, giving is a spiritual necessity and a trait to be valued and treasured. Reflecting on his maturation in this respect is George Gissing, who confesses, "I used to judge the worth of a person by his intellectual power and attainment. I could see no good where there was no logic, no charm where there was no learning. Now I think that one has to distinguish between two forms of intelligence, that of the brain and that of the heart, and I have come to regard the second by far the most important."[4]

Others may not give because they've relegated their lives to obscurity and routine, thus becoming oblivious to the desperate needs of others in an outer world. Too, emphasizes one source, "We are often victims of our own fears and rationalizations—that the world is too dangerous a place to connect with, that one person cannot make a difference. Too many of us suffer from social shrinkage, reducing the boundaries within which we are willing to act from our hearts to smaller and smaller circles of friends and family."[5]

Perhaps the most insidious reason for not giving is that, sadly, our culture generally celebrates selfishness, superficiality, lack of compassion, and utter self-absorption. Speaking particularly of a media that perpetuates such shallowness, Tim Goodman, a television critic, writes of one program, "Meanness is celebrated. Nobody is living an examined life. Getting yours is the goal. Anger and bitterness supplant happiness. Emotion over love, and the mundane is king."

Having quoted Goodman, news reporter Stephanie Salter herself observes that in a culture of excesses, "people . . . reduce human beings to one-dimensional objects and dismiss them because of the way they look. Wall Street and politics celebrate meanness. . . . The popular entertainment media belittle intellectual and spiritual depth . . . self examination, enlightenment

and the assumption of personal responsibility. . . . Anger and bitterness are encouraged by us in the news media, [and] by much
of popular music and literature."

And what is Salter's conclusion regarding the media's presentation of the good life? "To make a regular comedy festival of
[such fare] is my idea of slowly poisoning the human soul and
buying into the belief that people are just no . . . good."[6]

Inadvertently, a life-pattern of not giving is insidious, block-
ing nourishment vital to our emotional health, as John C.
Cornelius emphasizes: "To deny ourselves the joy of giving is to
deny our basic needs. People want to give. People instinctively
want to serve their fellow man. And if we deny that instinct, we
risk emotional death, just as a man who denies his hunger
instinct risks physical death."[7]

Not giving may also penalize us in material ways, as one
farmer found when he discovered, and subsequently planted, a
progressive new seed corn. When the farmer's neighbors, noticing the greater yield of corn, asked him to share his seed crop,
the farmer refused, electing to maintain his competitive edge.

However, to the farmer's consternation, the second year the
new seed didn't produce as abundant a crop; and the third year,
the crop's yield was even less. Then, to his dismay, he realized
his prize corn was being pollinated by the inferior grade of corn
from his neighbor's fields.[8] In short-changing his neighbors, the
farmer had ultimately short-changed himself.

❧ ❧ ❧ ❧ ❧ ❧ ❧ ❧

GIVING BEARS A "DO DISTURB" SIGN

"Once," says a mother, "when we were in the living room with a
guest, my small daughter came and sat close to me on the sofa

and whispered, 'Will you look at me, too, some of the times, and smile, and speak to me?'"⁹

This child appealed to her mother to grant her the precious gift of her "emotional presence." As this child knew, being there is perhaps the ultimate expression of love.

Children are the world's most adept teachers of the concept of being there, as also illustrated by another child, a young son, who kept coming into his father's study, constantly interrupting his work. Offering his son a number of diversions—the loan of his knife, a pencil, a quarter—the father found nothing that would occupy him. Finally, somewhat frustrated, the father asked, "Son, what do you want?"

Replied the boy, "Daddy, I just want you."

Borrowing a concept from financiers who speak of "available funds," philosopher Gabriel Marcel wrote of emotional generosity, regarding it as a rare human quality entailing "opening a line of credit" to other people. Giving, in this sense, involves making ourselves available to others, not by what we own, but by who we are. Marcel speaks of people, burdened by egos, money, or academic degrees, who allow no one else to enter their inner world. Closing themselves off to others, they become crisped like dry autumn leaves.¹⁰

Nothing "crispates" a person's soul as much as having a "Do Not Disturb" sign hanging over his or her heart. In this respect, many writers converge to identify a core truth regarding the human condition: that in freely giving to others, we add to our own essence. Louis Ginsburg, for example, reflects, "The only things we ever keep are what we give away."¹¹ And Leonard Nimoy adds, "The miracle is this—the more we share, the more we have."¹²

Boyd Ware vividly remembers the moment when he learned the meaning of such giving: "When I was a boy," he recalls, "my parents asked me and my two brothers to help create a Christmas for a family in need by choosing among our own toys ones that would be just right for the children in this family. After choosing, we would work as a family to repair and clean up the toys. And at first the project sounded like fun.

"But, to be honest, when it came to giving up our own personal toys, we began to lose enthusiasm. Silently, we boys thought, 'Why do we have to do this?' However, once we became involved in the project, we became excited—almost as though we were experiencing what the family would feel on Christmas morning.

"The weeks of preparation went by quickly and soon it was Christmas Eve. Just after dark we loaded boxes of presents and food into the car and drove to the family's home. Dad let us take the boxes to the door while he and Mom remained in the car. Dad parked the car just out of sight, but close enough to the scene that he and Mom could see what happened."

Ware and his brothers placed the boxes on the porch, knocked, and then ran, diving behind some nearby bushes. They were out of breath as the porch light came on. Describing subsequent events, Ware relates:

"As we watched, I saw one head peak out through the glass pane in the door. Soon more heads appeared and the door opened a little, then closed. Not long after, the door opened again and I could hear excited voices. Once more the door closed, and when it opened this time, even more heads appeared. Then the door opened a final time and the kids scampered out. They surrounded the boxes placed on the porch, excitedly talking about them. Finally, they took the boxes inside.

"It seemed like forever, but it was probably only a few moments later that the door opened again, this time just part way. The mother of the family appeared and, with a voice that conveyed deep gratitude, she called out into the night: 'Thank you! thank you! Whoever you are!'

"Her words lingered in the air for a moment and then the door closed, the light went out, and she was gone. Tears were pouring down my face as I turned to my brothers and discovered they were also crying."

Ware continues: "After remaining in the bushes a few minutes to compose ourselves, we went back to the car. Very little was said for we, as a family, had seen and felt the same things and what we witnessed seemed almost sacred. I'll never forget my feelings when the mother called out to us. Her words penetrated my heart, forever changing the way I felt about life. It was at that moment I discovered how good it felt to give. I'd never really ever sacrificed anything before, or given of myself, and this was the first time I'd ever done something important for someone else.

"I don't remember the toys I received that Christmas—it hardly seemed important. I had received the most precious gift. I had received the gift of giving."[13]

❖ ❖ ❖ ❖ ❖ ❖ ❖ ❖ ❖

GIVING HAS NO EXPECTATIONS

One day a number of years ago, the world was indelibly enriched through the modest contributions of several men who will never know the enduring implications of their actions. It was during the 1920s that Frederic Loewe, Vienna-born composer of *My Fair Lady*, arrived in the United States. At the time, Loewe, a gifted pianist unable to find a market for his talent, was discouraged and depressed. And because he had no money to make further payments, his one prized possession, his piano, was about to be repossessed. This looming event represented a final blow to his musical aspirations.

On the morning the movers were to arrive for his piano, and while he gloomily waited, Loewe decided to play one last time and did so with rare inspiration. Bent over the keyboard and intent on his music, Loewe did not hear the moving men enter the room. When at last finished, he glanced up and was startled to see an audience—three moving men seated on the floor.

The men said nothing and made no movement toward the piano. Instead, they opened their wallets and pooled enough money to pay the overdue installment. Placing the money on the piano, they left empty-handed.

These men, themselves probably existing on meager wages, gave because they recognized Loewe's musical genius and realized they could not, in good conscience, take from Loewe the one thing that gave him comfort or offered hope. Deeming the needs of another human being superordinate to their own, they walked away, never to know, through their humble giving, the gift they bestowed upon mankind.

It is as Helen Keller has said: "When we do the best that we can, we never know what miracle is wrought in our life or in the life of another."[14]

Just as in the preceding instance, over the course of human existence, stresses Myles Connolly, "countless, obscure, good people have quietly affected the lives of those about them without even being aware they are doing it, willing no commendation, expecting none."

We have all known such persons—strangers as well as friends—who have enhanced the quality of our day, Connolly continues. Such persons "come into a room in a dark hour—a sickroom, say, or a death room, a room without hope, or merely in an hour when we are lonely or discouraged. They may say little, if anything. But the shining quality of goodness radiates from them, and where there was dark there is light, or the beginning of light; where there was cowardice there is courage; where there was listlessness there is love of life."

And Connolly finishes, "These friends—or wonderful strangers, met at a picnic, in a lifeboat, in a hospital waiting room—all these, humble and aware, carry with them the kindness and generosity of their lives. These, it seems to me, are the greatest artists for they practice the highest of the arts—the art of life itself."[15]

As Connolly underscores, perhaps the most rewarding form of giving is to bestow a gift upon another—a gift with no attachments, and no expectation that one's actions will be reciprocated.

Regarding giving without expectation, Anne Morrow Lindbergh adds, "To give without any reward, or any notice, has a special quality of its own. It is like presents made for older people when you were a child. So much went into them—dreams and prayers and hours of knotted fingers and frozen effort. But you knew, even if they didn't, that you were giving them something worthy of them."

And Lindbergh continues, "There is something of worship or prayer in laying down an offering at someone's feet and then going away quickly. The nicest gifts are those left, nameless and quiet, unburdened with love, or vanity, or the desire for attention."[16]

Further illustrating giving without expecting reward is R. Lee Sharpe, who recalls a childhood story. One spring day long ago, he and his father went to "old man Trussell's blacksmith shop" to pick up a rake and a hoe his father had earlier left for repair. Upon arrival, the tools were ready, and Sharpe's father handed a silver dollar to Mr. Trussell, who refused it. "No," he said. "There is no charge for that little job," to which Sharpe's father insisted Mr. Trussell take the money.

Regarding what happened next, Sharpe recalls, "If I should

live a thousand years, I'll never forget that blacksmith's reply. 'Sid,' he said to my father, 'Can't you let a man do something— just to stretch his soul?'"[17]

Sharpe's story illustrated a principle Mr. Trussell well knew, that giving to others is nutrition to our souls, the fodder upon which they thrive. Fed by such giving, our souls slowly move toward maturity and we gradually achieve a sense of purpose and life mission leading to ultimate happiness.

Giving without expectation, however, is sometimes obscured when friends ask to borrow money. Pondering the issue of lending versus giving money to such intimates is Roy H. Barnacle. Ultimately, Barnacle established a decision that, in giving money, he would expect nothing in return. He vividly recalls his decision point: Once seeking the advice of a friend, he described being torn between two principles—his reluctance to lend money to friends and his commitment to helping them. His friend's advice was simple: "Never lend anything to anyone you wouldn't want to give him in the first place." That brought closure to the matter for Barnacle, who learned a lesson regarding true giving.

"'True giving,'" he emphasizes, "is free from any obligation that makes giving a 'loan.' Gifts become debts when not given freely. And shouldn't our true gifts be given freely, and presented to another in the same way? Then charity will be free of finances, love unburdened with personal claims, and giving and receiving, all that we will ever require, will be ours for the asking."[18]

Troubling feelings related to giving without expectation can also emerge in giving to a homeless person or, in Arthur Gordon's words from an earlier era, to "a beggar or panhandler." In New York City, walking to work, Gordon and a friend were approached by a faded, poorly dressed woman asking for money for her hungry children. From his pocket, Gordon's friend pulled change that he gave to the woman.

Gordon subsequently disparaged his friend, noting the woman stood on the same street corner every day and would probably just spend the money on liquor. Perhaps so, his friend replied, but he observed that perhaps God sometimes provides such experiences just to test our mettle. And as he moved on, he added quietly, almost to himself, "The act of giving is more important than the merit of the receiver." This, notes Gordon, represented a life truth to remember and to apply.[19]

Feeling similarly was Walt Whitman's mother, as Whitman, a nineteenth-century poet, tells: "There in Brooklyn, we were coming down what was called Washington Hill together . . . one of the many walks I delighted to take with my dear, dear mother. I can see it all, all, even now: the two of us there, the man approaching—my mother's voice: her hand as it was laid on my arm. . . . The fellow came up—asked me for ten cents: he had not eaten, etc. I growled out: 'I'll give you nothing': turned away."

Whitman knew the man was drunk, but his mother said, "'I know you feel it would only add to his misery to give him ten cents more now: I know about such men: when they get into that state then nothing can be done for the moment but give them the drink: it is but mercy to give it to them.' . . . She was quiet, tender."

As Whitman "looked at her as if to ask, What?" his mother continued: "'I wish you had given him the money: I would have you go back and give it to him yet.' So I went back, complied—we resumed our walk."[20]

Writing in the third century A.D., Aristotle perhaps best conceives the issue of giving to beggars. Upon being censured for giving alms to a "bad man," Aristotle said, "I did not give it to this man, I gave it to humanity."[21]

❤ ❤ ❤ ❤ ❤ ❤ ❤ ❤

GIVING GIVES GENEROUSLY

"As a child I understood how to give; I have forgotten this grace once I became civilized," observes Ohiyesa.

To give is to give generously, as would a child—with purity of heart and intentions—of one's time, talent, and of every resource, to this generation and the next. As illustrated below, to give generously has many dimensions:

Giving is generous in sharing its worldly wealth. Of note is an instance occurring many years ago in composer Johannes Brahm's life. When informed an English admirer had willed him one thousand pounds, Brahm received the gift ecstatically. "That a perfect stranger, who has, as far as I know, never even written me, should remember me thus, touches me most deeply and intimately," he exclaimed. "All exterior honors are nothing in comparison." Not himself in need, Brahm continued, "I am enjoying [the gift] in the most agreeable manner, by taking pleasure in its distribution."[22]

When giving is consummately generous, giving becomes magnanimous. In the early 1700s, moving words of Alexander Pope to Jonathan Swift convey magnanimity's attitude. Said Pope, "I am rich enough and can afford to give away a hundred pounds a year. I would not crawl upon the earth without doing good. I will enjoy the pleasure of what I give by giving it alive and seeing another enjoy it. When I die I should be ashamed to leave enough for a monument if a wanting friend was above ground."[23]

Giving is further generous in endowing future generations as did former Governor Hogg of Texas. On his deathbed, the governor declined a monument, instead requesting there be "planted, 'at my head a pecan tree, and at my feet an old fashioned walnut and when these trees shall bear, let the pecans and walnuts be given out among the Plains people of Texas, so that they may plant them and make Texas a land of trees.'"

Governor Hogg's wishes were respected and, in 1926, the first nut harvest was planted in nursery rows. For many years thereafter, virgin nuts were similarly planted and, each year when the saplings were mature enough to transplant, they were distributed to school and county boards.[24]

In its generosity, giving often steps back, as did W. H. Auden with Dorothy Day, founder of the Catholic Worker Movement and editor of the *Catholic Worker*. A notable early 1900s social reformer, Miss Day had been fined two hundred fifty dollars because her hostel for derelicts failed city code. In leaving for court the next day—reported the New York *Times*—Day walked past a gathering of beggars looking for handouts. Stepping from their midst, a man told Day he knew of her difficulty and wanted to assist with the fine. So, he said, handing her a check, "Here's two-fifty." Thanking him, and elated over having two dollars and fifty cents, Day hurried on to keep her court appointment. On her way, however, glancing at the check she was stunned in comprehending its amount: two hundred fifty dollars—enough to cover the entire fine. And, the check had W. H. Auden's signature. "Miss Day was apologetic for not having recognized him," the *Times* noted. "'Poets do look a bit unpressed, don't they?' she said."[25]

Generosity of giving includes graciously responding in ways that enhance others' self-esteem. Such was the habit of Henry Clay, a nineteenth-century statesman and orator known for his impeccable manners. Upon a chance meeting with Clay, a lady once questioned him, "You do not remember my name?" "No," Clay's prompt and gallant response, "for when we last met long ago I was sure your beauty and accomplishments would very soon compel you to change it."[26]

Giving's generosity also includes generosity of spirit—that indomitable manner of graciously managing others without ruffling feathers or causing pain. Such generosity led out when acclaimed poet Robert Browning once attended a dinner given in his honor. A young man—an unfamiliar guest to everyone—maneuvered the poet into a position behind the grand pianoforte, monopolizing his time. In a literal corner, from which there seemed no escape, Browning solved his own difficulty: "'But I'm monopolizing you,' he said, laying on the youth's shoulder a friendly hand which left him no choice but to yield to the pass."[27]

Additionally, giving generously extends to strangers. "If a man be gracious to strangers, it shows that he is a citizen of the world, and his heart is no island, cut off from other islands, but a continent that joins them," tells Francis Bacon.[28]

Such was the generosity graced upon a stranger by Saint Aidan, an Irish monk who, in the sixth century A.D., became bishop of Northumbria and pursued missionary endeavors in northern England. On this occasion, King Oswin, ruler of a British province and a friend of Aidan's, gave the bishop a horse of splendid breeding. Soon thereafter, in meeting a beggar who asked for alms, Aidan at once dismounted and gave the horse, with all its costly trappings, to the man.

The king—extremely hurt and angry upon hearing of Aidan's action—called Aidan before him, perhaps intent on slaying him. "Why did you give away the horse that we especially chose for your personal use when we knew that you had need of one for your journeys?" he asked. "We have many less valuable horses that would have been suitable for beggars." To this, Aidan replied, "Is this foal of a mare more valuable to you than a child of God?" Pondering Aidan's words, the king suddenly cast his sword aside and, kneeling at Aidan's feet, beseeched his forgiveness. At this, "Aidan, greatly moved, begged the king to go to his dinner and be merry."[29]

Further, giving is generous in sharing touching or brilliant displays of God's creation, as years ago did a missionary in India. Taking with her a young girl to watch a sunset, standing on a ridge, the two watched the sun slowly dropping beneath the horizon. As it slowly dipped, the sunset endowed the heavens with "its reddened rays across the landscape—touching it with magic loveliness." Enraptured, the girl said excitedly, "I must run and tell my mother!" "But," queried the missionary, "surely your mother had seen the sunset?" "Oh yes," replied the girl, "but she doesn't know how beautiful it is."[30]

Moreover, giving generously extends overflowing love to others. Poignantly illustrating is a small boy, who repeatedly entered the Church on Christmas Day. While there, a priest asked him, "What gift did you ask of the Christ Child?"

"Oh," came the reply, "I didn't ask Him for anything. I was just in there loving Him a while."[31]

Finally, giving generously forgives; and, indeed, notes E. H. Chapin, "never does the human soul appear so strong and noble as when it forgoes revenge and dares to forgive an injury."[32] In the 1200s, however, generosity of spirit nearly flunked in the case of Frederick the Great of Prussia. Seized with a mortal illness, Frederick inquired of proper spiritual authorities whether he was mandated to forgive *all* his enemies. After receiving an affirmative reply, Frederick instructed his wife, the queen, "Dorothy, write to your brother that I forgive him all the evil he has done me; but wait till I am dead first."[33]

By contrast generosity of spirit wore the crown of forgiveness in the instance of several Southern women. Relates Coronet, "The Civil War was over, but the news brought little joy to the sleepy town of Columbus, Mississippi. Of the hundreds of Confederate soldiers who had marched away, only a few returned. But this was a time for work, not tears.

"Columbus had stood in the path of bloody campaigns, and the dead must be given a last resting place. Soon the cemetery held hundreds of Confederate soldiers and some forty men who had worn the Blue.

"One spring day in the late 1860s," relates Coronet, "three southern young women of Columbus, their arms full of flowers, began to tend the graves of husbands and sweethearts. On this day they invited the young widow of a Confederate soldier to join them.

"As her three companions knelt to place their bouquets, the widow stood erect, gazing over the other bare and forlorn graves. What a pity that these should be forgotten!

" 'Why don't we break our bouquets and place a flower on each grave,' she suggested." The women hesitated, then quietly untangled the bouquets and placed a blossom on each mound.

"Soon thereafter, Columbus saw an unusual procession: a long line of young women in white and matrons in mourning, arms heaped with flowers, walking to pay homage to their country's dead. And that day, for the first time, every grave received a floral tribute.

Finishes Coronet, "The ceremony became a yearly custom, they spread to other towns and cities. And thus was born one of our great traditions—the solemn ceremony of Memorial Day."[34]

❤ ❤ ❤ ❤ ❤ ❤ ❤ ❤ ❤

GIVING GIVES BACK

At times, when someone gives, the other gives back a gift—often with overflowing gratitude—to repay the gift given earlier. Ralph

Kinney Bennett, for example, tells of a magical childhood in which his mother read to him and his twin brother every night, a spellbinding event that left both boys with a capacity for imagination, wonder, and gratitude; and a sense of aliveness and joy. Bennett also conveys the lasting impact of their enthralling adventures upon their lives. And he tells of returning—on the eve of his mother's life—the same generous gift of enchantment and love given him so long ago. Bennett's story begins with a description of the boys' memorizing adventures always instigated by their mother:

"'Okay, kids, it's time for bed.'

"My twin brother Roger and I would rush upstairs to get into our pajamas. Mom would come up with books under her arm. After our prayers we'd hike up on one elbow, while she sat on the edge of the bed. I see her still, smoothing the pages open with her hand, drawing a deep breath and beginning to read.

"We had no idea whom we'd meet on those wonderful nights. It might be the mysterious horseman galloping in the ominous cadences of Robert Louis Stevenson's poem; the strange Rumpelstilskin or the humble Abou Ben Adhem; the courageous David poised before Goliath or the serene Jesus standing before Pilate. It might be Paul Revere riding for freedom or Ichabod Crane riding for his life.

"Soon we were sitting beside her, following the tiny black words across the pages as she transformed them into vivid pictures with her voice. There was Billy Whiskers, the peripatetic goat, escaping the San Francisco earthquake with his 'chums,' a black cat and a yellow dog. There was Captain Nemo on the bottom of the sea; Tom Sawyer on the half-painted fence; Horatius, sword flashing, at the Roman bridge.

"By the time Roger and I went to first grade, we could read. We led double literary lives. By day we made our way through bland schoolbooks in which sunny-faced boys and girls tossed balls in well-groomed yards, visited dairy farms and chatted with smiling policemen. By night—like ancient kings cradling their chins in the thrall of court storytellers—we reveled in Mother's reading. She took us adventuring through Edgar Allen Poe's Paris to solve the murders in the Rue Morgue. We walked the misty streets of London with Dr. Fu Manchu, and the fearful blackness of the Bordge with Count Dracula. We hadn't the faintest notion of the respect she was according us, of the muscle she was putting in our intellects, by what she chose to read— Shakespeare, Dickens, O. Henry. And with every pause, inflection and turn of phrase, she taught us how to make words smile or cry or thump you on the forehead.

"By the time we were eight or nine, the bedtime readings had passed. We had our own stack of books. In the evening we'd do our homework at the oilcloth-covered kitchen table, until Mom—book in hand—would interrupt. "Listen to this!" she'd say. Schoolwork would be set aside, and we'd soon be laughing as we tilted ourselves precariously on the kitchen chairs and listened to Mom read of alarms in the night at James Thurber's household.

"As the years passed, Roger and I grew up and away, off to college and then work. I became a newspaper reporter, my brother an English professor. Mom had only a high school diploma, but it was a mere footnote to the education she acquired through reading. She had worked as a secretary, laundress, door-to-door cosmetic saleswoman, school cook and auto-parts-store bookkeeper. Finally she 'followed me into the business.' She took a job as a proofreader for a chain of weekly newspapers and worked her way up to become editor of the *Ligonier Echo*, the weekly newspaper in our town.

"Then Mom contracted diabetes. Eventually there were

several strokes. Now she is an invalid, small, white-haired, confined to bed and chair. Her speech is slow and uncertain, and she is virtually blind. But her mind is bright as ever. Her faith and patience through all this are as heroic as anything she once read to me.

"So it is now my pleasure to read to her. I'll call and say, 'Mom, I'm coming tomorrow.' I hear her struggling for a second on the long-distance line. 'Oh, boy! That's good.'

"I make the three-hour drive with a pile of books on the back seat—some the well-worn ones she read to me long ago. When I arrive, she is sitting by her bed, hands clasped. We chat. Then there is a pause, and she asks with halting speech, 'What did . . . you bring?'

"Sometimes I read some of her own poems, printed in the annuals from the Fort Ligonier Poetry Society. Sometimes it's a chapter from the Bible or some article I've written. Once again we plumb the depths and reach the heights—from the inspiration of Milton's poetry and Paul's letters to the sentimentality of James Whitcomb Riley and the humor of Mark Twain.

"There is nothing quite so pleasurable as to hear my mother laugh at stories that amused us more than forty years ago. So we trot out Thurber again, or Benchley. She sits, eyes closed, hands clasped, nodding as the words smile and cry and thump us on the forehead. Like travelers anticipating the sight of home just around the bend, we tiptoe along the old familiar path of little black words to rediscover moments ever fresh and funny.

"Sometimes, on my way home, I think back to nights when Mom's old Plymouth pulled into the driveway. She'd be weary from the thirty-mile trip from her job, but never so tired that she could not open a book and share it with us. And as I drive, I thank God for words and books, and for the exquisite pleasure of returning the precious gift of a mother who read to me."[35]

❤ ❤ ❤ ❤ ❤ ❤ ❤ ❤

GIVING REWARDS THE BESTOWER

In many ways giving often rewards the bestower. Perhaps no more powerful example can be found than that of Carolyn Tanaka, a nurse who served in the Vietnam War. At one time, Tanaka was assigned to care for Rory Bailey, a newly arrived Army private, in the emergency room of the 24th Evacuation Hospital in Long Binh. Both were twenty-one years old. At that time, Bailey remembers only "searing pain and then darkness." Tanaka, however, remembers a sight that would haunt her forever: "The man did not have a face."

Over the years, Bailey, who is blind, endured over two hundred operations, and Judith Newman and Giovanna Breu, who have written Bailey's story, describe his appearance after these efforts: "His face is dignified but masklike. The destruction of all facial muscles have left him unable to move his cheeks or eyelids. Fortunately, he can move his lower jaw and tongue . . . enabling him to talk. If he has made it through tough times, he says, 'it's because God is helping me.'"

These authors continue, "Although he reaches out to God, Bailey accepts help from few others. In earlier years, Bailey lived with relatives, but today resides alone in a home outside Valparaiso, Indiana. Bailey is self-sufficient, supplementing his veteran's pension by selling afghans and hats he has knitted. He also listens to country music, fishes, and tinkers with a CB radio."

For years, Tanaka—the nurse who had saved Bailey's life and cared for him—wondered if the man without a face hated her for saving him. And for years, there was no answer to that question. But twenty-five years after their experience in the evacuation hospital, Tanaka was to find out. It was at the official dedication

of the Vietnam Women's Memorial on Veteran's Day—
November 11, 1993—that the two met again.

As Bailey waited by the memorial that day, Tanaka walked
over to him and identified herself. She then immediately hugged
and held him tight for what seemed forever. And in a choked
voice, Tanaka whispered to Bailey, "It's a miracle." Initially, say
the authors, Bailey, "always adept at hiding his feelings, held her
tight and said nothing. Then, quietly, he volunteered the words
she longed to hear: 'Thank you.'"[36]

Similarly, another long-ago act of giving came back in a most
surprising way to reward the giver, again forever binding giver
and receiver. It was the year 1957, in New York City, when, on a
blind date, a young Jewish woman named Roma met a young
Polish man—also Jewish—named Herman. In gradually sharing
their pasts, Herman told Roma he had been in a concentration
camp during the last World War.

Shuddering, Roma told Herman of her own traumatic experience during the war of daily working in a field located near a
concentration camp. She had a lingering memory of a boy
interred there, she said. It was wintertime and she described
standing in the snow-covered field, snug in her own warm clothing and boots, aware of the boy, clad only in a thin prison uniform, his feet bound with rags. She used to throw bread and
apples over the fence to him, she told Herman.

In an almost disbelieving tone, Herman leaned closer to
Roma and asked, "What was the name of the camp?" Roma
couldn't remember, but she described the camp—it was in
Germany, not too far from Berlin. At the time she had not been
imprisoned, she explained, because her father had bought fake
passports certifying she and her family were Christians. In
response to Herman's intense questioning, Roma told of feeding
the boy for seven months, until he disappeared, which caused

her to fear for his life. She added other descriptive details of her experience that, to her puzzlement, seemed to galvanize Herman. Finally, with tears flowing, Herman took Roma's hand in his own and, filling in other details himself, he told Roma he knew of her experience firsthand. Why? Because he had been there. *He was that boy.* It was then that Roma knew that angels had orchestrated the circumstances that had twice brought the couple together and that were to bind them together forever.[37]

Giving rewards the bestower in many ways, but, as in the preceding instances, perhaps the greatest reward constitutes the binding of souls. Regarding this phenomenon, Eric Hoffer expounds: "There is sublime thieving in all giving. Someone gives us all he has and we are his."[38] And writing five centuries ago of such propensity, Machiavelli, a famous Florentine states-man, adds, "It is in the nature of men to feel as much bound by the favors they do as by those they receive."[39]

That giving has such binding power is also illustrated in a story Jo Ann Able relates: "Several years after building our home, we became keenly aware that the location, or neighborhood, in which we had built was affecting our lives in totally unantici-pated ways. We were the youngest couple on the block, the other families being at least as old as our parents.

"For some now-forgotten reason we became good friends with Donna, the elderly widow who lived up the street from us on a large corner lot. Her only child, Judith, lived out of the state, and family members, particularly brothers and sisters, who tried to help with her home and yard were all older than she was.

"Year after year, as my husband and I walked around our neighborhood, we frequently commented that someone should do something about Donn'a weedy parking strip. Green grass and trees flourished along the remaining length of the street. One day we noticed that soil—although of somewhat questionable quality—had been dumped along the area. With sudden insight, we decided that we could level and plant the area. After all, we were young and strong, and hadn't we built our own home and landscaped our own lot?

"For several weeks during spare moments we weeded, leveled, hauled off extra soil, planted, fertilized, and then watered. We carefully placed our own sprinklers so that the entire length of newly planted lawn could be adequately and frequently watered. We felt nothing short of childish glee when that first tinge of green turned into thick, mowable blades of grass. We thought with satisfaction that our project was completed.

"But it wasn't. We now had a bond with Donna, as strong as any we had to our own families. Fall meant raking leaves for her—not because she asked us to, but because we wanted to. Wintertime found us shoveling her walks and driveway. Spring and summer were times to help her plant and water her flowers. And always there was visiting—and listening—and learning. Over ten years have come and gone, but the bond is as strong as ever."[40]

❤ ❤ ❤ ❤ ❤ ❤ ❤ ❤

GIVING MAKES NO DISTINCTIONS

Giving gives for giving's sake, any time, anywhere a person has resources that momentarily fit another's needs. An engaging instance of such spontaneous and generous giving involves naturalist Andrew Simmons. While on a road trip, he once spotted on the highway a woodchuck that had just been run over by a car. Thinking that this woodchuck would be a delicious treat for his owl or eagle, Simmons pulled to the roadside and began stuffing the woodchuck into a paper bag. Realizing that a car had stopped beside him, Simmons looked up just in time to see a woman rolling down her car window. Then, he recalls, "A matron with sympathetic eyes reached out and stuffed a ten-dollar bill in my pocket. 'Here,' she said, 'go get yourself a decent meal.'"[41]

A more serious instance of spontaneous giving involved a family who assumed their own Sub-for-Santa project to help a family in need. This family's story is related by Richard M. Siddoway, a neighbor, who writes of this event. Recalls Siddoway: "One barrier to gathering the information needed to assure the family's needs and wishes were being met was the fact that while the family members spoke Spanish fluently, they spoke very little English. A bilingual co-worker of my neighbor volunteered to visit the family and make a list of their Christmas desires. He returned with the list and a rather dismal description of their circumstances. The Hernandez family consisted of a single mother with five small children. They were living in a rather rundown apartment building with apparently little furniture or food."

The family vigorously went to work gathering requested items, continues Siddoway, and two days before Christmas, they loaded their minivan with presents and drove to the Hernandez family's address. But the family found "the apartment building was shabbier than they had been led to believe. The paint on the front door was peeling, and the door fit poorly in its frame." Sent to locate the Hernandez family were two teenage girls, who "entered the hallway of the building, shut the door and felt the icy draft flowing under it. They searched the hallway for the Hernandez family's name, but the mailboxes were marked only with apartment numbers. Tentatively they knocked on the door of No. 1. There was no answer. A bare bulb hanging on a piece of twisted wire from the ceiling gave little light to the hallway. They knocked at No. 2. Again, no answer.

"The would-be-Santas tentatively climbed the creaking stairway to the second floor. One handrail was missing, the other hung loosely from the wall. The ceiling tile was stained from leaking water. Warily the girls knocked on the door of No. 3. They heard the sound of small feet running across a bare wood floor. The door opened slowly, revealing a small boy with chocolate eyes. The girls looked beyond him and saw three other children sitting on the bare floor near a small, scraggly, undecorated Christmas tree. A woman sat on a wooden rocking chair holding a baby in her arms.

" 'Merry Christmas' called out the girls, and they began placing the gifts under the Christmas tree. Tears began streaming down the face of the woman in the rocking chair.

"Quickly the girls raced up and down the rickety stairs delivering the brightly wrapped gifts. The boxes of food were placed in the kitchen. The children sat wide-eyed near their mother. She struggled to her feet and handed the baby to the oldest child. As the girls finished placing the last gift beneath the tree, she hugged each one. With tears streaming down her cheeks one of the girls whispered, 'Merry Christmas, Mrs. Hernandez.'

"There was a sharp intake of breath. The woman drew back and stared at the floor, then she shook her head.

" 'Hernandez,' she said pointing out her open door at the door of No. 4. 'Lopez,' she said pointing to herself. A thin smile flitted across her face, then she picked up the baby and sank back down in the rocking chair. A few words of Spanish were exchanged with the children and they began picking up the gifts and handing them back to the girls. In total silence the presents were carried across the hall to the Hernandez family."

Finishes Siddoway: After that, "Christmas Eve became an even busier day for my neighbor's family as gifts were purchased so that Santa Claus could make a second visit to the Lopez family. This time there was no difficulty finding the right apartment."[42]

True to the preceding instance, pure giving makes no distinctions with respect to race, ethnic group, religion, or any other factor that artificially separates people into different categories. Emma Lou Thayne writes of another such instance, telling of Jan Cook and her husband, who lived for three years in deepest Africa, where his work had taken him.

From the time the couple and their three small children had moved to Africa, Thayne tells, "any church meetings they attended took place in their own living room with only themselves as participants. By their third Christmas, Jan was very homesick. She confessed this to a good friend, a Mennonite; Jan told her how she missed her own people, their traditions, even snow. Her friend sympathized and invited her to go with her the next month to the Christmas services being held in the only Protestant church in the area, saying there would be a reunion there of all the Mennonite missionaries on the continent.

"It took some talking for Jan to persuade her husband, but there they were, being swept genially to the front of a small chapel. It felt good being in a church again on Christmas. The minister gave a poignant sermon on Christ; the congregation sang familiar carols with great vitality. Then, at the very end of the meeting, a choir of Mennonite missionaries from all over Africa rose from their benches and made their way to stand just in front of Jan and her family. Without a word, they began singing. Without a leader, without music, without text, they sang, 'Come, Come, Ye Saints.' Every verse.

"Disbelieving, totally taken by surprise, Jan and her husband drenched the fronts of their Sunday best clothes while being carried home on Christmas. When the choir finished, Jan's friend said simply, 'For You. Our gift.'

"Jan's Mennonite friend had sent to Salt Lake City for the music to the Mormon hymn that she knew Jan loved, had had it duplicated and distributed to every Mennonite missionary in Africa; they in turn had learned it very carefully to bring the spirit of Christ to their own reunion, where foreigners to their faith would be waiting to hear."[43]

• • • • • • • • •

GIVING EMBRACES ANONYMITY

"The work of an unknown good man is like a vein of water flowing hidden underground, secretly making the ground green," reflects Thomas Carlyle.[44]

The following letter comes from one such unknown good man who made "the ground green" for many people. This letter was found in a can wired to the handle of an old pump at a site offering the only possibility of drinking water on a very long and seldom-used trail across Nevada's Amargosa Desert. The letter reads:

"This pump is all right as of June 1932. I put a new sucker washer into it and it ought to last five years. But the washer dries out and the pump has got to be primed. Under the white rock I buried a bottle of water, out of the sun and cork end up. There's enough water in it to prime the pump, but not if you drink some first. Pour about one-fourth and let her soak to wet the leather. Then pour in the rest medium fast and pump like crazy. You'll git water. The well has never run dry. Have faith. When you git watered up, fill the bottle and put it back like you found it for the next feller. [Signed] Desert Pete

"P. S. Don't go drinking the water first. Prime the pump with it and you'll git all you can hold."[45]

Desert Pete signed his name to personalize the letter and to give it authenticity. He knew, however, the near improbability of his ever coming face-to-face with any of the letter's beneficiaries. Neither was he concerned that his actions be recognized, but only that they ensured that those next using the pump could obtain desperately needed water. In urging those who drew water from the pump site, in turn, to leave the site as they found it, he created a legacy of anonymous giving, each traveler to the next—a legacy that quenched the thirst, and perhaps even saved the lives of, many who journeyed this lonely desert trail.

In another instance, the famous cowboy-humorist Will Rogers anonymously gave something under circumstances he never expected. Albert P. Hout, who authors this incident in Rogers's life, sets the context of his story with one of Rogers's best-known observations: "I never met a man I didn't like." But, as Hout explains, an occasion did occur in Rogers's life when, as a young cowboy, he came close to not liking a man he hadn't yet met.

It was the winter of 1898 and Rogers had just recently settled in at a Wyoming ranch that he had inherited. His life was going rather smoothly until one day when a nearby farmer shot one of Rogers's steers that had broken down his fence and eaten some stored hay. Inasmuch as the farmer had violated range custom by not informing Rogers of his deed or the reason for it, when notified of the incident Rogers became extremely angry. In his wrath, he solicited a hired hand to accompany him to the farmer's home, determined there to confront the man.

On the way, a blue norther struck, coating Rogers and his hired hand with a frozen layer of ice. When they reached the farmer's home, his wife greeted them at the door. Her husband was absent, she explained, but the two freezing men were indeed welcome to wait inside by the fire for his return, an invitation they gratefully accepted. While Rogers was warming himself, he noticed how thin and work-worn the woman appeared and how scrawny the children were who shyly peeked at him from behind the furniture.

When the farmer returned, his wife introduced the men and informed him they had been caught in the storm. As she finished speaking, Rogers opened his mouth to wreak his vengeance, but then suddenly shut it again, his harsh words catching in his throat. In lieu of an onslaught of unchecked anger, Rogers instead extended his hand to the farmer. The farmer, unaware of the reason for the men's visit, invited them to dinner. "You'll have to eat beans," he apologized, "for the storm has interrupted the butchering of my steer."

After dinner, inasmuch as the storm was still raging, the couple insisted that the two men stay overnight, another invitation gratefully accepted. The next morning, after a warm and hearty breakfast of biscuits, beans, and coffee, the two men rode toward home. Having noticed that Rogers hadn't mentioned the reason for his visit, the hired hand challenged Rogers' resolve: "I thought you were going to lay that sodbuster low about your steer," he chided.

Momentarily, Rogers remained silent, but thereafter responded: "I intended to, but then I got to thinking. You know, I really didn't lose that steer. I just traded it for a little human happiness. There are millions of steers in the world but human happiness is kinda scarce."[46]

❤ ❤ ❤ ❤ ❤ ❤ ❤ ❤

GIVING SHARES THE SELF

Giving knows that the greatest gift is, as Ralph Waldo Emerson once wrote, "a portion of thyself."[47]

At times, sharing a portion of self has stirring and long-lasting ramifications, significantly feeding the soul of both giver and receiver. Elaborating on this point, Richard Jefferies observes, "To reflect that another human being, if at a distance of ten thousand years from the year 1883, would enjoy one hour's more life, in the sense of fullness of life, in consequence of anything I have done in my little span, would be to give me peace of soul."[48]

Such significant sharing of self occurred when Jimmy Durante accompanied Ed Sullivan to a hospital on Staten Island, New York, to entertain World War II wounded. In order to meet his next commitment, Durante would have to catch a certain ferry back to New York; thus prior scheduling precluded his performing any more than one routine at the hospital. Even then, he would have to rush to catch the ferry.

Not expecting Durante, the men went wild and when he finished his especially energetic routine, they broke into thunderous applause. As Sullivan started to announce Durante's exit, the comic inexplicably took the mike and performed two more complete routines. Backstage afterwards Sullivan chided Durante, concluding, "Now you'll never make your ferry."

Guiding Sullivan to the curtain, Durante soberly told him to look at the front row of the audience. Thrusting his head through the curtain, Sullivan saw two young lieutenants on the center divan. Each having lost an arm, they were applauding by clapping their two remaining hands together.[49] For Durante, giving of himself to soldiers who had themselves given so much, and so permanently, for the sake of their nation had supreme priority. Durante responded from his heart, sharing what he had to give—himself—for a few more precious moments.

Cellist Mstislav Rostopovich also shared a portion of himself in an act related by Henry Fogel, former executive director of the National Symphony in Washington, D.C. Fogel and his wife, along with Rostopovich attended the wake of a Kennedy Center stagehand. Fogel tells of driving Slava and his cello to the funeral home, where Fogel "schlepped the cello inside." Inside they found the bereaved family and several of the symphony's staff and stagehands.

Moving to the open casket, Slava knelt and put his hand on the hand of the deceased. Asking Fogel to bring him a chair and cello, he then played, with eloquence, the Saraband from Bach's Second Cello Suite.

Says Fogel of this stirring event, "Here is the greatest cellist in the world playing, without publicity, for this man. The stagehands had tears in their eyes, and one said to me, 'I didn't realize a cello could speak.'"[50]

Similarly, when Jerome Kern collapsed from a cerebral hemorrhage on a New York City street and was taken to a hospital, Oscar Hammerstein II shared a portion of himself. As Kerns—who gave the world such glorious melodies as "Smoke Gets in Your Eyes" and all the *Showboat* tunes—lay dying, among those at his bedside trying to rouse him from a deep coma was Hammerstein. Lifting a corner of the oxygen tent, Hammerstein put his mouth to Kern's ear and said softly, "Listen, Jerry," after which he sang a favorite composition of Kerns—"I've Told Every Little Star."

A smile crossed Kern's lips as, simultaneously, his tortured breathing subsided. Then, sighing deeply, he died.[51]

A further instance of sharing a portion of self involved Walt Whitman. When a baby in a crowded Washington horse car was screaming, Whitman took the baby from its mother and cradled him in his own arms until the baby fell asleep. When the conductor left the car for supper, for the remainder of the trip Whitman acted as conductor, still holding the sleeping baby.[52]

In a final instance, Albert Einstein also belatedly shared a portion of himself. A friend had informed Einstein that his barber intensely wished to meet him, and, further, that on every occasion the friend received a haircut, the barber inquired again about this possibility. Having written down the barber's name and address, Einstein intended to contact him, but before this happened, the man died. Upon receiving this news, Einstein made a trip from Princeton to New York to visit the barber's grave—his farewell salute to an admirer and ardent fan.

In the preceding, each giving person's soul responded, providing a personal human touch at a crucial time. All of us have a desire to blend our lives with others—a desire as natural to us as taking our next breath. Our essential life purpose is thus to share, to love, to cooperate, and to assist one another. And when we blend our lives with others, giving of who we are, reflects Roy Cook, "there are no limits to the bridges or harbors one can build."

• • • • • • • • •

GIVING GIVES WHAT IT CAN

Giving a little when you can't give much has been encouraged by many philosophers across the ages. Advises Mother Teresa, "If you can't feed a hundred people, then just feed one." Sidney Smith also observes, "It is the greatest of all mistakes to do nothing because you can do only a little. Do what you can."

And Henry Wadsworth Longfellow comments, "No man is so poor as to have nothing worth giving: as well might the mountain streamlets say they have nothing to give the sea because they are not rivers. Give what you have. To someone it may be better than you dare to think."[53]

A heart-rending instance of humble giving concerned Mother Teresa who—in the House of the Dying—nursed a newly arrived woman whose condition was profoundly wretched and terminal. Asking the Sisters to aid other patients, Mother Teresa, who personally attended to the woman, tells her story:

"I did for her all that my love can do. I put her in bed, and there was such a beautiful smile on her face. She took hold of my hand, as she said one word only, 'Thank you'—and she died."

Mother Teresa offered this woman all she had—her abiding love. But, in the exchange, the woman also offered Mother Teresa all she had—her utter gratitude and her beautiful smile. Both benefitted from this moving experience. Says Mother Teresa of the woman's poignant gift:

"I could not help examining my conscience before her, and I asked what would I say if I was in her place. And my answer was very simple. I would have tried to draw a little attention to myself. I would have said, 'I am hungry, that I am dying, I am cold, I am in pain,' or something, but she gave me much more— she gave me her grateful love. And she died with a smile on her face."

Mother Teresa speaks further of the miraculous gift such dying bestows, relating "how so many of them, loved and cared for in their last hours, pass into eternity with a look of peace on their faces, and a word of thanks on their lips."[54]

Another instance of "giving gives what it can," placed in a much earlier era, concerns Jake, who lived in an orphanage with nine other boys. In the winter, any extra money went for coal to heat the old buildings so that the food the children ate was very basic and, at times, sparse. But at Christmas, each child received an orange. It was the only time of year such a rare treat was provided, and it was coveted by each boy like no other thing they had ever possessed.

Because the oranges were so prized, it was an unspoken habit that each boy would save his orange for several days—admiring it, feeling it, loving it, and contemplating the moment he would eat it. Some would even save the orange until New Year's Day or later, much like many people relish saving their Christmas trees and decorations until the new year, just to remind them of the joy of Christmas.

This particular Christmas day, Jake had broken the orphanage rules by starting a fight, and as a consequence, the orphanage director took back Jake's orange. Jake spent Christmas day empty and alone, and when nighttime came, he could not sleep. Sobbing silently, he mourned the orange he could not now savor with the other boys.

As he lay awake, quietly crying, a soft hand placed on Jake's shoulder startled him, and he felt an object quickly shoved into his hands. A child then disappeared into the darkness, leaving Jake alone to discover a strange looking orange—an orange made from the segments of nine other oranges, nine highly prized oranges that had to be eaten that Christmas night, instead of their being saved, admired, and cherished until another day.[55]

Further demonstrating "giving gives what it can" is a story related by a young man, a volunteer in a Latin American refugee camp. As he tells, he had befriended a small boy who always wore the same ragged and dirty shirt. To aid the boy, he searched through a box of used clothing and located two shirts roughly the boy's size in reasonably good repair. After having given the excited boy the shirts, he was later surprised to see another boy wearing one of them. When he next saw his small friend, he explained the shirts were meant for him. "But," exclaimed the boy, "you gave me two!"[56]

In a final example, in a long-ago intriguing twist of events, a woman of Utah pioneer stock gave all she had—despite her earlier protestations. The treasured story is of Eulalie Leavitt

Taggart, who writes of her experience, preserved below in her own imperfect and limited writing:

"Behold I stand at the Door, and Knock.

"These words of a hymn brings to me something, I will never forget it, It was [Easter Sunday, April 8, 1906] we had spent the day at my Father's. They told us of one of my neighbor that had taken a little boy 12 years old to raise and my first remark was, Well I would never take a nothers child to raise those that want them can have them I don't want them,

"My Father said you don't know what you would do.

"Well that night we had gone to bed it was about 11 o'clock, a knock came on the door I went and their stood Estella Bernhisel Bell with a little baby in her arms, it was her sister Annie B. Beck's and wanted to know if I would take it and nurse it as its Mother was in convulchings the baby was borned Saturday.

"Well the first thing came to me was what I had said that day, I wouldent take some one elses Baby to raise.

"Well I just reached out my arms and took that tiny little thing and said, yes and I will do all I can, I had a baby 6 weeks old she weighed 8 lbs and was a fat butter ball and was their a difference in these babies, My baby was Ruey, the little baby was 6 weeks old it weighed 5 lbs, well I took it and loved it and done all I could till it was 3 months old. I gave it a good start, that was some thing I will never for get, We should be very careful what we say because we may be called to do the things we think we just can't do. And we never know how far our help will go and to who.

"One experience that happened, Hyrum Bear and Dr Adamson came in to see the baby, Dr. took a hold of her little hand and said 'look that baby can die any minut there is nothing to hold her.' Hyrum said, 'Now you might be surprised if she grew to be one of the biggest women in Cache Co,' and then he 'said this good girl is giving her all the strength she can to help her, she is not going to die '.

"It was hard to Watch the little thing knowing she was some one elses baby it was a big responcibabley I had to perform, but I done all I could for her. The Lord blessed me so I could give her a good start in life, I was 21 years old when I had her. We always called them the Big baby and the Little baby. She will always be Little Annie to me. I took care of her 3 months then my health gave away having to much to do, so I took the baby to her GrandMother Beck,where she lived till she was married, she has growed till now she is much bigger than my daughter her age. I have a picture of her when she went to school and about the time she was married,

"The baby's Father has never remarried as he dont believe in taking another wife, he wanted to live to met the dear one that he had here, she was a jewel and a very sweet girl, she loved every little child she met. her first baby died then her."[57]

● ● ● ● ● ● ● ● ●

GIVING CREATES EARTHLY ANGELS

Jane W. Lund tells of two earthly angels who saved her son. These were young men, she alludes, she would never have conceived as capable of giving to her. However, due to these earthly angels' efforts, her son—although badly hurt in a serious automobile accident—ultimately survived. Of these angels, she writes:

> I thought when I saw angels,
> They would be
> Personages of spirit,
> Clothed in white
> And surrounded by glory.

I did not know
They would be mere boys
With long hair,
And ragged jeans . . .

But, not long ago
Two such angels
Lifted a car
From my son's broken body
And revived, and comforted him
Until help came.[58]

As with these young men, it's not surprising that earth angels come in every form and perform services of all types. In *How to Find Your Angels*, Karen Goldman speaks of such angels, ones we are perhaps too preoccupied to see. Our encounter with these angels—often precious people in our lives—are marked by beautiful moments, tender gestures, and sweet gifts to the soul.

To find your angels, just remember the mark of an angel is love, advises Goldman. Angels are everywhere, manifesting their love with every gracious heart, every honest smile, every act of kindness, every constructive thought, every selfless desire. And you can find them by asking yourself, Who helps me grow? Makes me laugh? Brings out the best in me? And by looking for "angel" signs.

You can spot an angel, continues Goldman, in finding someone who warms your heart, raises your spirits, or helps you grow. Angels are those people who make you feel welcome; encourage you to express your best self, give you gentle pats on the back, or remind you of your value. Most important, an angel brings out the angel in you.

In actuality, an angel could be you. So, in addition to spotting and appreciating your own earthly angels, why not become an angel yourself, finishes Goldman: "If we were all a little more like angels, Earth would be a little more like heaven."[59]

In actuality, becoming an earthly angel may be as simple as following the instinctive response of an open heart, say Ram Dass and Paul Gorman: "Caring is a reflex. Someone slips, your arm goes out. A car is in a ditch, you join the others and push. A colleague at work has the blues, you let her know you care. It all seems natural and appropriate. You live, you help."[60]

Sometimes, we may take such pleasure in what we did, and how we did it, and our effort may seem so natural that we may be surprised that, in someone else's eyes, we achieved the status of an earthly angel.

Not surprisingly, earthly angels are not always people, as Susan Chernak McElroy tells. McElroy, author of the article "The Angel Who Fetched" and the book *Animals as Teachers and Healers*, asserts that animals, too, can be "angels." Relating events prompting her book, she speaks in more detail: Immediately after a pet magazine published her article, McElroy was astonished to receive letters "pouring in from all over the world about 'other angels': the lives they had changed, the teachings they had offered, and the love and mercy they had shared." McElroy published these stories in her book, including one contributed by Judy Seay, who speaks below of a transcendental moment in which Buddy, her border collie, became an earthly angel.

One day, a deep sadness settled over Seay in pondering her mother's recent health decline from chronic emphysema. Although her mother had rallied once, Seay and her mother "both knew on some deeper level that death would be coming to call soon." The sadness clinging tightly, Seay "took off up the mountainside to find a place to pray." Buddy immediately followed, and Seay wondered about his motives: "'What does he want?' I thought as I climbed and Buddy followed, leaping from ledge to log to rock along with me as I cried out my anguish in the canyon and prayed for help to heal the wound inside of me.

"Then, without preamble or warning, I understood that Buddy was my help. . . . He was sent on this day . . . obeying a voice deeper than the canyon and lighter than the mountain air—a voice my own sadness wouldn't let me hear."

Concludes Seay: "Buddy was pulling angel duty and I understood. Peace settled like a butterfly in my heart. I looked at Buddy and he grinned his best goofy-dog grin, ears pinned back, stump tail wagging. Like old, dear pals, we walked together back down to the ranch."[61]

Many stories of earthly angels abound, sometimes dramatic, such as that of Clara Barton, founder of the Red Cross. As an anonymous author tells, "Disdainful of bullets, and riding a mule, she rode through battle smoke of the Civil War to deliver surgical dressings, clothing and food.

"Her greatest tribute was as in the words of an Army sergeant: 'I thought that night if heaven ever sent out a holy angel, she must be the one, her assistance was so timely.'

"Someone else said: 'She has done her work with the skill of a statesman, the heart of a woman, and the final perseverance of a saint.'"[62]

In another dramatic instance, an earthly angel appeared in a most unusual form—that of an enemy. A German soldier, Karl, was captured in World War II after the American army invaded Germany. Wounded and an invalid confined to his own village, he was rounded up for questioning before being sent to a prisoner-of-war camp. Taken before an American officer, Karl tells, the officer and he "faced each other, victor and vanquished. The officer's boots were polished, his uniform neat. He was young and healthy. I was ragged, defeated, wounded. His glance took in my clothes, my shoes, my arm in its sling."

When questioned, Karl said he was a sheepherder. "There is in my village no one to take care of the land or the animals. My brothers . . . "

"What about your brothers?" the officer queried.

"Killed," Karl said to the officer. "All three of them."

"And the rest of your family?"

"My father died during the war. There is only my mother left, and my young sisters."

In his village, empty of able-bodied men, Karl explained, someone had to bring order to the land and provide food for the villagers and refugees who fled the railroad towns during the bombing.

Karls' face flinched as pain closed in, and his wound and fear of imprisonment made perspiration roll down his face. Would the young man understand, he wondered, about the shearing and lambing, the crops and farm seasons? The loss of even a week could bring hunger. The sensible thing, he knew, would be to be allowed to go home. But he also realized things were different during wartime.

The officer, rubbing his hand over his eyes, suddenly also seemed weary. "Then," relates Karl, "he spoke sharply. 'Go home,' he said. 'Go home.'" Faint and swaying a little, Karl could hardly comprehend his good fortune. He stumbled out the door, without even the strength to say thanks, but no sooner had he left than came a sharp rapping at the windows—a soldier motioning for his return. "So I was not free after all! They had been joking!" Karl thought. Once again inside, however, Karl saw the officer was smiling, his military air gone. To the soldier standing at the window, the officer ordered, "See that this man gets a ride home."[63]

Sometimes the actions of earthly angels have eternal implications. Telling of a defining moment in his life when he was permanently shaped by an "angel" is the late Bishop Fulton J. Sheen, an eminent Roman Catholic clergyman. After completing college, Sheen won a coveted national scholarship worth several thousand dollars that could underwrite his earning a Ph.D. "But, at the same time," he says, "ever since my earliest recollection, I had wanted to be a priest." Thus, Sheen was torn: "Accepting the university scholarship would have meant postponing my call to the priesthood and maybe endangering it."

Soon after college graduation, Sheen visited a former professor of philosophy and enthusiastically shared the news. Grabbing Sheen by the shoulders, the professor asked, "Do you believe in God?" What a silly question, Sheen replied. Of course he believed in God. "But do you believe in God practically?" the professor challenged. Yes, came the answer. Then said the professor, "You know your duty. Go to the seminary now and begin studies for the priesthood. Tear up the scholarship."

Sheen protested. Why couldn't he work now for his Ph.D. and then later enter the seminary? Retorted his professor, "If you make that sacrifice, I promise you that after your ordination to the priesthood you will receive a far better university education than before." At that, Sheen says, "I tore up the scholarship, and after ordination as a priest, I spent almost five years in graduate studies—most of them in some of the great universities of Europe. The professor was my angel. I saw it then, but I see it more clearly now."

When earthly angels intervene, recipients—glancing back— sometimes sense that some deeper process may have been at work, as Bishop Sheen asserts: "God is generally operating behind secondary causes, like an anonymous benefactor. God's direction of our lives is so hidden that most of us are unaware of how we were made an angel to help a neighbor, or how a neighbor was made an angel for us." Sheen speaks of Dr. Paul Tournier, "one of the greatest of modern psychiatrists," who wrote that, for years, his life was confused and without direction "and never entrusted clearly to the guidance of God."

After spiritually committing to such guidance, notes Sheen, Tournier wrote, "God led us step by step, from event to event. Only afterwards, as we look back over the way we have come and reconsider certain important moments in our lives in the light of what followed them or when we survey the whole progress of our lives, do we experience the feeling of having been led without knowing it, the feeling that God has mysteriously guided us. We did not perhaps know it at the time. Time had to elapse to enable us to see it. But He opened the unexpected horizon to us."

Speaking of the universality of "earth angels," Francis Thomson once said, "Stir but a stone and start a wing." Citing Thomas's observation, Sheen concludes of such angels, "They are everywhere—only we do not recognize them as such."[64]

❤ ❤ ❤ ❤ ❤ ❤ ❤ ❤

GIVING ATTRACTS HEAVENLY ANGELS

Throughout history, angelic assistance has been reported by people of almost every faith, and the sacred books of the three monotheistic faiths of the East and West—Judaism, Christianity, and Islam—contain many references to angels in heaven and on earth.

In Christianity, in particular, "The empire of angels is as vast as God's creation," reflects Billy Graham in *Angels: God's Secret Agents*. "They crisscross the Old and New testaments, being mentioned directly or indirectly nearly three hundred times."[65]

Until recently, angel appearances have been generally regarded as events of the past. However, the 1990s ground swell of publicity over angels in TV programs and a plethora of angel books "flying out of the stores"[66] have convinced many people otherwise. As a result, more and more people are stepping forward to share soul-warming, personal stories of angels who have rescued or comforted them. And, indeed, a *Time* magazine poll indicates almost seventy percent of Americans believe in the existence of angels.[67]

Other than a faith in God, what can be more comforting—in an unpredictable world, profoundly beset with violence and strife—than to think angels are there, watching out for us (despite, at times, our getting in their way)? And consider that these angels have our long-range, even heavenly, welfare in mind. The literal presence of angels in our midst, in fact, may have been what prompted the writer of Hebrews to caution, "Be not forgetful to entertain strangers: for thereby some have entertained angels unawares" (Hebrews 13:2).

Why should there not be angels? asks Sophy Burnham, author of *A Book of Angels* and *Angel Letters*. Their stories are legion: "William Blake saw angels in the trees. He was merely a ten-year-old boy who one day looked up and saw angels and afterward could not stop drawing them and writing his ecstatic poetry in homage of them. . . . Jacob wrestled with an angel. . . . And an angel came to Abraham. . . . And today a little child will see an angel, or an angel will unexpectedly swoop in to save an adult's life, as happened once with me."[68]

Burnham didn't grow up believing in miracles or angels, but when she was twenty-eight, she relates, an angel miraculously saved her life. For years, she kept her story to herself, but in finally going public, she was surprised—not only did many people believe her, they themselves had angel stories.

Of her own story, Burnham tells of being abroad on a skiing vacation and deciding to try a challenging slope. Losing control, she "was hurtling downhill when a mysterious, black-clad figure cut in front of her, stopping her fall. Shaken, Burnham got up and discovered she was just inches from the edge of a cliff. Her rescuer had vanished. There was simply nowhere he could have gone."[69]

In "Angels All Around Us," Dawn Raffel tells of Marlene Wiechmann and her daughter Emily, who having had a stroke at seven months old, was partially handicapped. As the family was on their way back from a vacation in Yellowstone National Park and traveling through Wyoming, Emily didn't feel well. When she started throwing up and her eyes weren't focusing, the family knew they needed a hospital, but the nearest town, Rock Springs, was seventy miles away.

As the family approached Rock Springs and Emily's condition continued deteriorating, her mother desperately prayed for help. Just then, the family saw a blue-and-white hospital sign, and, as they followed three or four others, the signs led them directly to the emergency room. Quickly diagnosing Emily as having a seizure, doctors stabilized her with an anticonvulsant, after which Wiechmann acknowledged her gratitude for the signs leading them to the hospital.

Of events following, she reports, "The doctor looked at me and said, 'What signs?' He traveled that road every day and there were no hospital signs, he noted. But all four adults in our van had seen them. We went back and looked again. They were gone. I called someone at the chamber of commerce, who said there had never been any hospital signs on that route. I believe they were put there for us by God or his angels."[70]

Writing the angel story of four-year-old Anjee Uhlenkott of Asotin, Washington, is David Johnson, Associated Press news reporter. From Anjee's and her parents' perspective, she was "guarded by an angel" when she encountered danger. In December, 1996, Anjee slipped out of her house, manipulating a deadbolt lock to enter the family's swimming pool area. Riding her tricycle around the pool, she rode too close to the pool's edge and fell in. Returning home from watching an older daughter's basketball game, Anjee's mother asked Anjee's father where she was. "In her room," was the reply.

Hurrying to Anjee's room, her mother discovered her gone and an immediate pool check revealed something at the bottom of its deepest end—Anjee's tricycle. Anjee's mother dove into the pool and pulled Anjee's lifeless body from the water. Hearing her screams for help, Anjee's father burst out of the house and, while the two parents frantically tried to revive Anjee with CPR, the oldest daughter called 911. A physician arrived just behind an Austin County Sheriff, both followed by the paramedics. "For all intents and purposes, Anjee was dead," reports the physician. "She was as cold and lifeless as anybody you'll see in a morgue."

From the hospital, Anjee was flown by helicopter to Spokane's Sacred Heart Medical Center, where the prognosis remained grim. The next morning—as Anjee remained on life support—doctors talked to her parents about disconnecting the equipment. However, a subsequent brain wave test showed wave activity and no swelling of the brain. On the fifth day, Anjee began waking up and breathing on her own. Further tests showed near-normal brain activity, and a week after the accident the Uhlenkotts were told, "We think you're going to get your daughter back." And Anjee's consistent progress each day came to bear out the doctors' assessment.

"Medical experts estimate Anjee was under water for between ten and twenty minutes—more than enough time to cause brain damage or death," writes Johnson. Doctors can only conclude divine intervention saved Anjee, Anjee's mother reports. Ask Anjee what happened and she'll tell you: "I fell in the water and died and the angels brought me back." And, ends Johnson, "No one is arguing her point."[71]

Additionally, Pamela Johnson believes an angel saved her toddler. "It was dusk when my toddler disappeared," she relates. "Frantically we searched the house, the yard, the neighborhood. As darkness fell upon us we hadn't found my Amber.

"My best friend held me tightly and reassured me gently, 'It's okay, honey. We'll find her.'

"'Where?' I sobbed. 'Where? If anything happens to her it will be my fault. I'm blind.'

"'Don't blame yourself. My Elizabeth gets away from me as fast and I can see. Pam, pray right now, pray.'

"I sank to my knees and pleaded, 'Please God . . . where is my baby? You are the only one who knows. Can you help us find her? Please Lord!' I got up from my knees, composed and enfolded in a blanket of peace and warmth.

"I followed Debbie into the house. Numbly, I answered the policeman's questions, which he asked in a monotone. I wanted to shout at him, 'Don't you know my little girl is out there some-where in the dark, frightened and alone and maybe hurt?' I laid my head wearily on Debbie's shoulder and wept quietly. I had faith that God would protect Amber, but he had to understand that I am a mother, too. I felt helpless. What else could I do? Only God could work the miracle. He did this in a matter of sec-onds by a soft knock at the back door.

"At the door stood the miracle, my Amber. I scooped her up in my arms and hugged her to me. Tears streamed down my face for a different reason this time. 'Thank you, God.' I said over and over. Then, after the excitement settled down as I rocked Amber to sleep, it hit me. She had been alone and serene at the door, not even a whimper. It didn't make sense. If a neighbor had been with her, we would have seen him and he would have brought her to the front door. She was not sleeping in the backyard. Several of us checked earlier. How could a one-year-old find her way home at night all by herself? The answer came simply: God sent one of his angels to watch over my baby and bring her back to me."[72]

Finally, Joan Wester Anderson, author of *Where Angels Walk* and *Where Miracles Happen,* tells of the Reverend John G. Paton, a missionary in the Southwest Pacific New Hebrides Islands. Of the story, set in a previous era, Anderson relates, "One night, hostile natives surrounded his headquarters, intent on burning out the Patons and killing them. John Paton and his wife, alone and defenseless, prayed all night that God would deliver them. When daylight came, they were amazed to see the attackers leave!

"Eventually, the tribe's chief became a Christian, and Reverend Paton asked him what had kept the chief and his men from burning down the Patons' home that night.

"The chief explained that he had seen many men standing guard—hundreds in shining garments with drawn swords in their hands. They seemed to circle the mission station so that the natives were afraid to attack. Only then did John Paton realize that God had sent His angels to protect them."[73]

In considering these and thousands of other angel stories—both ones current and those abiding throughout the ages—words of the writer of Psalms take on brilliance: "For he has charged his angels to guard you wherever you go, to lift you on their hands for fear you should strike your foot against a stone" (Psalm 91:11–12).

♥ ♥ ♥ ♥ ♥ ♥ ♥ ♥ ♥

GIVING MAKES SACRIFICES

Giving involves making sacrifices, sometimes small ones such as commitment of time, an inconvenience, or money spent. Sometimes, however, the sacrifices are much larger, as in the instance of comedian Joe E. Brown, who, in 1943, was the first entertainer to visit a marine battalion on Midway Island. Entertaining for hours, Brown was never funnier, perhaps giving the greatest performance of his life to the troops. And when later surrounded by the soldiers after his performance, Brown extended himself, emanating empathy for men who lived daily under the unrelenting threat of death. He knew their feelings, Brown said, because he, too, had a son in the service.

It was not until after Brown's cheerful and energized exit did the company commander inform the soldiers of Brown's sacrifice, noting the circumstances under which he had arrived. On his way to Midway for the performance, Brown received a radio message: his own son had been killed in action.

In the 1500s, giving sacrificed, this time through actions of Sir Philip Sidney, an English writer, soldier, and courtier who ultimately died fighting the Spaniards in the Netherlands. At Zutphen, having been wounded in the thigh, Sidney was being carried by stretcher to have the wound dressed. Knowing, because of loss of blood, that he was suffering greatly from thirst, someone found a water bottle for him. As the bottle was put to his lips, Sidney caught sight of another wounded man, a foot soldier, who looked longingly at the water. At once, Sidney passed the bottle to the soldier with the words, "Thy need is yet greater than mine."[74]

A. J. Cronin tells of another instance of sacrifice many years ago. Cronin relates practicing with a nurse who labored twenty years single-handedly—without adequate medical facilities—in a small, rural, and backward community in South Wales. Describing the nurse, Cronin says she was a plain woman "with a solid figure and a lined face. Yet, there was a steady frankness in her clear, gray eyes which lit up her quite ordinary features."

And, continues Cronin of the nurse, "her work was dreadfully hard, a ten-mile round, a never-ending day. Often I marveled at her fortitude and patience, her calmness and cheerfulness. Her supreme unconscious selflessness, above all, seemed the keynote of her character. She was never too busy to speak a word of sympathy, nor too tired at night to rise for an urgent call."

Deeming the nurse's salary extremely inadequate in light of her circumstances and adversities, Cronin approached her after finishing one night a particularly strenuous case, asking her why she didn't insist she receive a higher salary. She was worth at least an extra pound a week, and if anyone knew she was worth it, God did.

Pausing, then smiling, the nurse gazed at the Cronin with an intensity that startled him.

"'Doctor,' she replied, 'if God knows I'm worth it, that's all that matters to me.'"[75]

In a final instance, giving sacrificed in the case of both father and son. In a personal story, "The Old Hitching Tree," Ewart A. Autry tells of many years ago burying his father on a bleak March day. On that occasion, in a rickety wagon, Autry's family rode with his father's body twelve miles to the cemetery ground beside the country church. There, for so many years, his father had been the church's pastor, and, indeed, had given his last sermon only a few short days before. Looking back, Autry remembered other trips over the same path, trips full of family laughter and song, but solemnity now prevailed. For Autry—as the wagon rolled on toward the cemetery—"the rattling of the trace chains were like the tolling of bells, and the whine of wind in the pines was a dirge that would be forever sung."

Accompanying Autry's sorrow was bitterness regarding his father's passing. He was yet not a man, and he yearned for his father. But his bitterness stemmed from observations of many paying their last respects to his father that he had "shortened his own life by riding horseback through rain and sleet and snow to preach, to minister to the sick, and bury the dead."

His mind mulling over his loss, Autry remembered the lonely nights his mother kept vigil for his father's safe return. And the terrible storm one night when he and his siblings huddled around his mother, "terrorized by the lightning, the crashing thunder, and the roaring wind," tells Autry. "Then came a lull, and we heard his song—faint at first, but growing louder as he rode down the hill, singing that we might know of his nearness and not be afraid."

Preoccupying Autry's mind were two questions: Given his father's dedicated sacrifice, what had he accomplished? And were these accomplishments worth the price his father, and now his family, had incurred? He was soon to receive his answer. As the church came into view, Autry was stunned by the panoramic sight of horses and buggies, wagons, cars, and people filling the church and yard, even overflowing into the cemetery. Recalls Autry, "As we slowly approached, men took off their hats; women and children wept. The scene was so foreign to the bitterness I had nurtured that I felt a strangling tightness in my throat."

Though the surrounding grounds seemed completely filled, one vacancy did still remain—the old hitching tree where Autry's father had always tethered his horses. One final time, the crowd knew, his father would need the hitching tree, a tree to which, without touch of rein, the horses headed and then halted. Awed and humbled by the crowd's inconsolable mourning for his father—the one who had ridden through rain and sleet and snow to bring a message—Autry's bitterness subsided, "washed away by the tears of the multitude." Of his ride home that day, Autry, who was then rejuvenated, recalls, "The rattling of the trace chains was like bells of victory, and the mockingbirds and the wind in the pines united in a triumphant chorus."

In 1968, at his story's telling, Autry now stood as pastor at the same pulpit his father once occupied. And when preaching, he often looked outward at the indelibly etched symbols of his father's sacrifice—his gravestone and the gnarled old hitching tree. Too, Autry now fully understood his father's resplendent sacrifice, one that came of "riding through rain and sleet and snow . . . [and] singing in the storms so others might not be afraid."[76]

▾ ▾ ▾ ▾ ▾ ▾ ▾ ▾ ▾

GIVING GRACIOUSLY RECEIVES

"It is more blessed to give than to receive," assures Halford Luccock. However, he adds, "givers who cannot take in return miss one of the finest graces in life, the grace of receiving. . . . To receive gratefully from others is to enhance their sense of worth. It puts them on a give-and-take level, the only level on which real fellowship can be sustained." And "it changes one of the ugliest things in the world, patronage, into one of the richest things in the world, friendship."[77]

In the following instance, a woman graciously received. Having adopted a teenager who had been, for years, in the state social welfare system, she changed jobs so she could be home more with her new daughter, going from an administrative assistant to a college department secretary with an accompanying decrease in pay. So, for several years, she and her adopted daughter lived on a very modest budget, one not allowing any savings for a down payment on a house. This woman tells her story, which she has entitled "A Hundred Dollar Thingee":

"'Mom?' whispered my daughter in her after school check-in call. Her quiet tone was very unusual because she has an enthusiastic, booming voice.

"'Yes, dear.'

"'Mom, we got a hundred dollar thingee in the mail today,' the whispering continued.

"'Oh, honey, it's just a scam. Look at it. We'd probably have to buy a thousand dollars worth of something we don't need to get the hundred dollars off.'

"'No, Mom, it's a real hundred dollar thingee. Like a dollar.'

"'You mean like real money?'

"'Yeah, Mom, it's real money. It came in the mail to both of us.' She had to tell me it was addressed to her as well as me, as we'd been working on not opening other people's mail.

"'Well, dear, hide it somewhere and don't tell anyone that we got it.'

"Indeed it was a real hundred dollar bill that had been mailed to us with just a short note inside, saying it was from friends. From there on, we received money—at irregular intervals all summer and into the fall—a total of about seven hundred dollars. Sometimes with a note, often wrapped in plain paper. The envelopes were hand-addressed and I tried to match the handwriting to any sample I had among all my friends, including the envelopes from previous Christmas cards. I could not find a match.

"Then, in the middle of November we received another envelope with another hundred dollar bill in it—but this time there was a typed letter included. The letter said that our 'friends' knew that we wanted to buy a house but did not have the down payment for one. They, as a family, would give us enough for a down payment, five to six thousand dollars. Overwhelmed with the immense generosity of the gift, I nevertheless started looking for a house immediately, but the housing situation was bleak. I hunted all through November and into the first part of December with no luck. Toward the middle of December, another envelope with a typed letter arrived—in the envelope was a six thousand dollar cashier's check. The writer of this letter apologized for holding us to a down payment on a house and released us to do with the money whatever we wanted. However, within two weeks we had found a little house to buy and soon moved into it.

"No, we haven't a clue who gave us the money," this woman relates. "Our 'friends' will remain anonymous but their benevolence won't. They didn't ask us to keep this quiet and we have not. There is so much negative broadcast in our world that I want to do my part in letting it be known there is plenty good being done, too."[78]

♥ ♥ ♥ ♥ ♥ ♥ ♥ ♥

GIVING MAKES A DIFFERENCE

"I want it said of me by those who knew me best, that I always plucked a thistle and planted a flower where I thought a flower would grow," conveys Abraham Lincoln.[79]

In this life, we all have opportunities to "pluck thistles and plant flowers," and, in that sense, to find purpose through giving; even, ultimately, to feel our lives are worth living because of such purpose. Feeling worthwhile, in fact, may be much more important than feeling happy. "I cannot believe that the purpose of life is to be 'happy,'" Leo Rosten stresses. "I think the purpose of life is to be useful, to be responsible, to be compassionate. It is, above all, to matter; to count, to stand for something, to have made some difference that you lived at all."[80]

Lidia Rawska tells of a man who, through his generous giving, did make a difference:

"I knew a Jewish lady named Helen in a Jewish nursing home in Chicago," she relates. "Despite my visits, she was lonely and had a great desire to die. (I am not sure that visits can change that, but at least they can make the stay less bleak.)

"One day Helen was unexpectedly visited by a man who was a Christian, although I've never learned of what religion or how he had heard of my friend. This man became a great ray of sunshine in this 95-year-old woman's life. He took Helen for rides, for ice cream, to doctor's offices, and for special hospital tests. She had ugly tumors on her neck, which, because they were not malignant, were ignored by the nursing home staff. So this man took Helen to a clinic to have them removed. When her blood was drawn for analysis, he gently slid his hand under her elbow, so the elbow wouldn't get bruised on the hard table. His visits were frequent and filled with laughter, fun and surprises. Helen always reported to me what they did and often commented, 'If only I was younger.'

"The man's visits continued for about six months, at which time he went back home to another state, saying he had a family problem, and didn't write to her. After three months, the man's sister wrote to Helen and told her he had just died of cancer and how much and how beautifully he always spoke of her. We both cried at the news. Helen went into a rapid decline after that and she, too, soon died. They're both gone now, but the example of the dying man who used up his last months of life to bring cheer to someone else will stay with me forever."[81]

Another instance of "giving makes a difference" occurred on

Christmas Eve of the year 1818, at Oberndorf, a village in the Austrian mountains. At St. Nicholas' Church, the parishioners were preparing music for the Christmas services when the church organ broke down. Not wanting to disappoint the church members, and enthusiastic about the program himself, Josef Mohr, the assistant pastor, searched intently for a solution. Inspired as he glanced at an old guitar, he sat down at his desk and wrote a litany of warm, soul-rending words.

In a short time, Mohr knocked on the door of Franz Gruber, the church organist, greeting him with a sparkle in his eyes and a piece of paper in his hands. Explaining he had written a Christmas song, Mohr asked Gruber if for tomorrow's program he could compose for it a suitable air. To this creation, Mohr elaborated, he would add two solo voices, a chorus, and a guitar accompaniment. Feeling less than adequate to the task, Gruber nevertheless assumed the challenge, the joy he felt in reading Mohr's verses prompting and guiding his work. Sitting at his spinet, he searched for the appropriate chords and laboriously completed the written score.

After Gruber delivered the score, Mohr played the piece on his guitar. The two then sang the beautiful and immortal melody—"Silent Night, Holy Night"—unaware that the dearest song known to Christendom had just been created.[82]

A further instance of "giving making a difference" concerns Reverend Henry Francis Lyte, whose heart was sad and burdened. As a preacher, he had dedicated his entire life to teaching love of God and man. Yet, today, a Sunday, was typical of so many others during his long years of preaching—a half empty church, "tight hard faces listening without hearing, minds far away, hearts locked against the meaning of his words."

For Lyte, his failure—a bitter failure—rested in the animosities, the cruelty and greed, and the petty jealousies between peti-

tioners that persisted despite his continued efforts to teach otherwise. And now he was old and knew, through his physician,
that within several months he would die. From his discouraged
perspective, his life appeared to have yielded no enduring meaning.

For comfort, Lyte reached for the well-worn Bible on his
desk, which fell open to a favorite passage: "Abide with us; for it
is toward evening and the day is far spent." In the midst of reading and rereading the familiar soothing words, however, Lyte
suddenly felt joyous. No longer feeling discouraged, he concentrated on committing to paper the uplifting and unbidden words
singing through his mind: "Abide with me; fast falls the eventide;
The darkness deepens; Lord, with me abide . . . " In an astound-
ingly short time, Lyte created, in five verses, one of the most
inspiring and beautiful hymns of all time.

Of his work, it is written, "Few people today know the name
of Henry Francis Lyte. But the soul-stirring hymn he wrote in
less than an hour, a hundred years ago, is known and loved all
over the world—has given comfort and courage to millions.

"When the famous nurse, Edith Cavell, went before a
German firing squad, she whispered the words of 'Abide with
Me.' When the R.M.S. *Stella* was sinking with one hundred and
five victims during the Second World War, a woman—one of the
noble unidentified of the world—stood on the bridge and sang
'Abide with Me' until the others were singing with her, and they
went down bravely. . . . So out of a great heart came a great
hymn. At the end of his life, in a moment of shining faith and
inspiration, Henry Francis Lyte created a sentiment that lives on
and on—words of enduring power and influence."[83]

Finally, tells William F. McDermott, giving made a difference
through the works of Warner Sallman, a young commercial
artist. As a biblical institute student, Sallman heard a visiting

presenter speak of a needed portrait of Christ portraying him as a man who lived among ordinary people. "We oughtn't set Him apart," the presenter emphasized. "I hope some day an artist will give us a picture of Him as such a man of strength, courage and ideals, cheerfulness, and hope."

Needing to design, by the next day, a cover for a religious youth publication, Sallman listened attentively. He also remembered a ministry administrator emphasizing that no artist had ever conceived the *real* Christ. Having always wanted to do religious art, Sallman wondered whether he dare try to portray Christ. He decided to pray. Perhaps God would aid him in creating a portrait that was "vital, strong and arresting, so necessary to draw the eye and stir the heart."

Sallman withdrew to his attic studio that evening to work, only to produce a number of failed sketches. He prayed again, but still received no inspiration. Discouraged, he went to bed, but images of Christ kept running through his mind. Then, at 2 A.M., "suddenly there flashed to his mind a vision—the face of Christ as it should be!"

Grasping a pencil, Sallman made a thumbnail sketch before the image faded. Then, after several hours of sleep, he arose and made a charcoal drawing of the portrait. That day he made his deadline. However, although over the years Sallman received a trickling of requests for his portrait, public response was slow in coming. Close to ten years after the portrait's origination, a seminary student entered it "in a class competition for the most appealing likeness of the Nazarene." There, the portrait drew a large majority of the votes.

After a decade of shouldering the expense of printing and distributing perhaps a thousand drawings, Sallman was now encouraged. Making an oil painting of the portrait, which he called "The Head of Christ," he placed it on the mantel in his home. There, two representatives of a religious publishing house were elated with the portrait and eager to print the painting. The painting's first run of one hundred thousand copies were snapped up by a public that demanded more and more. The flood tide roared, from one edition to another of the painting, until, in 1942, three million had been sold. By 1956, Sallman had sold approximately one hundred million pictures of "The Head of Christ" and other religious paintings.

Of the painting's spiritual image of Christ, relates McDermott, "Many critics believe Sallman's painting already has won a place among the great religious works of all time. It is lofty in concept and realization, yet there is an earthiness about it that inspires the run-of-mill people of all races and positions to acts of kindness, decency and good will."

Personal stories abound regarding the portrait, which has affected millions of people. In one instance, set during World War II, a GI of Japanese-American ancestry discovered while aboard a train in North Dakota that he had lost his ticket. As he pulled out his billfold, the conductor recognized his small "Head of Christ" picture. "I'll take your word for it that you lost your ticket, son," the conductor said. "We'll let that picture be your passport." In another instance, an intruder who broke into the home of a terrified woman spotted the portrait on her wall. Suddenly, he lowered his gun. Rushing to leave, he told the shocked woman she could keep her money. "I can't look at *that* picture and steal. I saw things like that when I was a kid."

A final instance occurred when the Japanese were marching captured Americans at bayonet point to uncertain fate. After one American began whistling a gospel hymn, a captor sidled up and asked if he was Christian. He himself was Christian, he said, and his mission at home had a big picture of Jesus. Inspired, the American pulled from his wallet a small picture of Sallman's "The

Head of Christ." Recognizing the picture as identical to that he had seen, the Japanese told the American they would be friends. Ends McDermott, "The two 'enemies' became friends—reconciled by the Prince of Peace through the ministry of a picture."[84]

❤ ❤ ❤ ❤ ❤ ❤ ❤ ❤ ❤

GIVING IS CONTAGIOUS

In rendering gifts of spirit, giving often sparks others to give similarly until a glowing wildfire engulfs all surrounding hearts. Experiencing such soul-touching momentum some fifty years ago was U.S. Air Force lieutenant Gail S. Halvorsen. During the 1948–49 Soviet siege of West Berlin following World War II, Halvorsen, among hundreds of allied pilots, airlifted supplies to the city. Nicknamed "The Candy Bomber," Halvorsen dropped candy and gum attached to handkerchief parachutes to West Berlin children, ultimately a momentous effort that came to symbolize the airlift.

Pivotal to allied intervention and Halvorsen's presence on the scene was Russia's June 1948 total blockage of surface routes to West Berlin, a population of two million. The West forcefully countered the Soviets, who intended, through starvation and economic collapse, to force Berlin's capitulation to communism. "In the Cold War's first nervy showdown," the Allies—using treaty-guaranteed air corridors—continuously airlifted fuel, food, and medical supplies to Berlin the next fifteen months.

Launching the airlift from Germany's Tempelhof Airport, Allies supplied Berlin with 2.3 million tons of supplies in more than 277,000 flights. In round-the-clock deliveries, aircraft were taking off and landing almost every minute at the airlift's peak. Ultimately, through accidental death, the airlift claimed thirty-nine Briton and forty-one American lives.

During the siege, grateful Berliners called the constant roar of planes overhead "a symphony of freedom." During the airlift's fiftieth anniversary in May 1998, voicing Germany's continuing gratitude was Chancellor Helmut Kohl. Kohl, speaking at Tempelhof Airport, stated that Berlin owed its survival and freedom to firm Allied resolve and to an enduring airlift representing to Berliners "a symbol of democracy's durability."[85]

In the airlift saga, Gail Halvorsen's own story began one fateful day when innocently conversing with thirty-odd children through a barbed wire fence near the Tempelhof base. After an hour—his driver waiting—Halvorsen realized he needed to leave immediately or risk missing his return flight to the Rhein-Main air base where he was stationed.

But something about the children huddling along the fence intrigued Halvorsen. They were different. Unlike children in other countries, these children did not beg. Although deprived of candy and gum for years, relates Halvorsen, they "refused to tarnish their feelings of gratitude for something so nonessential and so extravagant." Now hurrying toward his driver, something compelled Halvorsen to stop. Instinctively reaching into his pocket, he discovered two sticks of gum.

"Thirty kids and only two sticks of gum, there will be a fight," thought Halvorsen. For a moment he stood poised. "Now was the moment of truth. To the jeep or back to the fence?" He turned back, a forever life-changing decision. "Now it was too late to turn back. I was committed," Halvorsen relates. "In the last few steps to the fence I broke the two sticks of gum in half and headed for the children who had been the translators. . . . In all my experiences, including Christmases past, I had never witnessed such an expression of surprise, joy, and sheer pleasure that I beheld in the eyes and faces of those four young people. Nor do I remember seeing such disappointment, as was evident in the eyes of those who came so close."

Tempered by earlier deprivations, the children's disappointment quickly diminished and no fighting broke out. Then, those given no gum began "requesting a share in the tin foil or the outer wrapper. Strips were torn off and passed around. The recipients' eyes grew large as they smelled the bits of wrapper and recalled better times." Deeply touched, Halvorsen had sudden inspiration: "Why not drop some gum and even chocolate to these kids out of our airplane the next daylight trip to Berlin?" he thought. Despite reservation, Halvorsen next astonished himself by telling the children his plan and establishing ground rules: "I will do this thing only if the persons who catch the packets will share equally with everyone in the group."

With the translated news came sound of joy and celebration. And then "the little girl with the wistful blue eyes was prodded to be the spokesperson. They want to know which aircraft you will be flying,'" she translated. Not to be stymied, Halvorsen replied the children should watch for a plane that several times wiggled its wings. "'What is viggle?' she asked with a wrinkle on her nose," at which Halvorsen produced "a demonstration that could have won an Oscar."

Suddenly remembering the driver, Halvorsen was greatly relieved he was still waiting. Preoccupied during the return ride, he wrestled with whether to request permission. No, too much red tape, too much wasted time, he decided. Only once—one careful drop shouldn't hurt—he'd just have to be careful. Now, back at base, he realized his strictly controlled ration card would tender only a few morsels. So, how could he obtain the promised gum? Of course!—by using his two fellow flyers' ration cards. After explaining his plan, the two—with eagerness mixed with reluctance—handed over their cards. But, how would they drop the candy? Now, all conspired to solve the problem. They would make parachutes with handkerchiefs, tying candy to each corner.

After making "a firm pact of utmost secrecy," the men left for Berlin. Near the arriving base Halvorsen, spotting the waiting group, wiggled the plane's wings. And "the recognition was instant. That little band literally blew up, waving, jumping, circling, and sending, we were sure, a few silent prayers." The first drop was a huge success and the children's enthusiasm catching. So, why not execute one more drop of candy? Just one more wouldn't hurt. But they would need more ration cards and additional contributors, and these were forthcoming. And thus, for the next two weeks, ecstatic men dropped growing bundles of candy to a growing group of children, each time being "treated with a remarkable spontaneous demonstration of sheer joy."

But their secret did not prevail. For one thing, Halvorsen—having been dubbed "Uncle Wackelflugel [Wiggly Wings]"—was receiving each day a growing and obvious stack of letters from children expressing gratitude or requesting drops in other areas. For another, the word was out. One day an officer met their arriving plane—not a normal procedure, Halvorsen knew. With sinking heart, he responded to the officer's request that the pilot join the commander in his headquarters. His fellow flyers, he noted, were quick to point out just who was the pilot.

Braced for a scotch blessing and more, Halvorsen held his breath. But what was the commander doing? With an irritation that stemmed from his receiving information belatedly, the commander was nevertheless congratulating Halvorsen for his actions. A candy parachute had nearly hit a reporter on the head, the commander relayed. The reporter had written an article, the news was all over Europe, the general had called to congratulate the uninformed commander, the general wanted to see

Halvorsen, and there was an International Press conference set up for him in Frankfurt. "Fit them into your schedule," ordered the commander. "And Lieutenant, keep flying, keep dropping, and keep me informed." In finishing, a now smiling commander shook Halvorsen's hand.

Now more and more candy was showing up on Halvorsen's cot, and other flyers were asking to become candy bombers in "Operation Little Vittles," as the project was affectionately dubbed. As the world received news of the candy bombing, more and more stacks of mail piled up, all requiring responses. And both American and West German children were requesting pen pals from their counterparts.

In attempting to solve a growing problem of a diminishing number of parachutes in ratio to a growing candy pile, the men attached notes to the parachutes, giving an address, and asking the West Berlin children for their return. To their surprise, back came the old parachutes, accompanied by a growing number of newly made parachutes usually accompanied by requests for drops in other city areas. Further, the shortage having been broadcast, many American radio stations, particularly on the East coast, were honoring requests for tunes in exchange for parachutes.

The parachute shortage was now more than solved. Now, because of a *Weekly Reader* notice, a growing number of American elementary schools were becoming involved. Twenty-two schools were organized in full support of candy, parachutes, and packaging, and across the country city leaders were mobilizing assembly stations. Businesses, too, were contributing thousands of yards of cloth and tons of candy for the parachutes. To accommodate the increased benevolence, from a central location the men began a massive effort to coordinate flight schedules and drop areas with candy supplies and parachutes.

But now Halvorsen was getting requests from *East* Berlin children to make drops. Why discriminate, thought Halvorsen—"the law of gravity is the same on both sides of the border." And so a drop was made; and the Russians objected; and people all over the world protested the Russian objection; and "Operation Little Vittles" almost got canceled; and, subsequently, very clear orders were issued—absolutely no more candy bombing over East Berlin.

At Air Force request, Halvorsen next was off to the United States to appear on TV's *We the People* and to engage in other media coverage. There he was contacted by a member of the American Confectioners Association, who faced him with a staggering request: How much candy would he like for his operation? Says Halvorsen, "If I ever heard of a blank check this was it. I thought of how big each drop should be, how many guys were in our squadron, how many trips they would make to Berlin in twenty-four hours, multiplied that by thirty days, to put it on a monthly basis, and gave him a number that I thought would give him indigestion. . . . He didn't bat an eye." Further staggering Halvorsen's mind was that the offering member was Jewish, ready to abandon the past and focus on the kids, "the hope of the future."

"Operation Little Vittles" ignited innumerable touching moments and connecting hearts. As they wept, children and parents randomly delivered flowers on the streets to uniformed men—all strangers. A small girl insisted Halvorsen, as a token of gratitude, take "her most cherished and perhaps last remaining personal possession, her little fuzzy teddy bear." Knowing the bear had comforted her during the Allied bombing raids and the last Battle for Berlin, Halvorsen resisted, but the child prevailed and he accepted the gift.

Also, Halvorsen and company visited a children's hospital

with a supply of bubble gum, and soon children everywhere were popping bubbles. And elsewhere, a saddened father sat staring into the night, realizing he had no birthday present for his son. As he looked "out of the broken and patched window of their top floor apartment," he found on the roof and within reach a gift—a heretofore unnoticed candy parachute. Additionally, six thousand five-hundred tons of candy, packaged in small quantities, were arduously flown into Berlin barely in time for planned Christmas parties for the children.

And so it went until June 1949, when the blockade ended. "But," says Halvorsen, "the memory of Uncle Wiggly Wings and the candy-filled parachutes . . . had become a symbol of man's love and concern for others."[86]

♥ ♥ ♥ ♥ ♥ ♥ ♥ ♥

GIVING CREATES A LEGACY

Perhaps of all that man creates in this world, reflects W. Somerset Maugham, "the richest in beauty" is a life well lived.[87] And a life well lived is one that leaves a legacy for those who follow.

Margaret Lee Runbeck speaks of such legacy as she observes that a man leaves "all kinds of footprints" when he walks through life, some of which "you can see, like his children and his house." Others are invisible, like the prints a man "leaves across other people's lives, the help he gives them and what he has said . . . his jokes, gossip that has hurt others, encouragement. A man doesn't think about it . . . but everywhere he passes, he leaves some kind of mark. These marks added together are what man means."[88]

All human beings need to know that their lives have had meaning to others—a need Harold Kushner has put into words: "Our souls are hungry for meaning, for the sense that we have figured out how to live so that our lives matter, so that the world [will] be at least a bit different for our having passed through."[89] Also expressing the innate wish of men to make a difference in the lives of others is George Macdonald, who says, "If I can put one touch of rosy sunset into the life of any man or woman, I shall feel that I have worked with God."[90] And Emily Dickinson adds, "If I can stop one heart from breaking, I shall not live in vain."[91]

In giving, we may thus leave a legacy. And we secure such a legacy by choosing to account for our lives and to deliberately decide how to allocate the contained allotment of time we have on this earth. To this point, a Scouting poster reads, "A hundred years from now it will not matter what my bank account was, the sort of house I lived in, or the kind of car I drove. But the world may be different because I was important in the life of a boy."

A question we all might ask is, "A hundred years from now will the world be any different because I was important in the life of someone?"

Were she on earth today, in all modesty Anne Sullivan, the teacher of Helen Keller, could have answered a resounding yes.

During her lifetime, Helen—blind, deaf, and mute from nineteen months on—rose above her triple handicap to astound the world both with the conquest of her afflictions and her inspirational writings. And it was Anne Sullivan, whom Helen called her beloved "Teacher," who led her out of this darkness.

In *Journey into Light*, Ishbel Ross tells Helen and Teacher's early story. Deemed by several an idiot, Helen herself speaks of her profound loss of function, the result of a debilitating illness—a "fever of brain and stomach." With "appalling suddenness," tells Helen, her world became completely dark and still· "My few words wilted, my mind was chained in darkness and my growing body was governed largely by animal impulses."

For the next four and a half years, Helen lived in darkness, often, because of her entrapment of soul, having wild gusts of rage. Helen was to write, years later, of this early time: "I felt as if invisible hands were holding me. I made frantic efforts to free myself."

Cowed by her violence, Helen's gentle mother repeatedly deferred to Helen's demands, giving her all-encompassing power. Finally, at near-breaking point, Helen's mother found Charles Dickens' *American Notes*, a book telling of a young deaf, mute, and blind girl whose darkness of mind had been penetrated by Samuel Gridley Howe. Subsequently Helen was taken to the Perkins Institute, where Howe's successor recommended as a tutor Anne Sullivan, a recent graduate.

Ross describes Sullivan, the child of Irish immigrants, as having a life with "a Dickinson touch." Having been "starved, bruised, neglected," and routinely beaten by a drunken father, Sullivan finally entered an almshouse as a state charge. Later entering Perkins in 1880, and blind from trachoma, Sullivan endured two operations restoring her sight. However, throughout her life, her vision gradually diminished until toward life's end, she became blind again.

Unlike the stereotypical schoolmarm of the day, Sullivan was a lively young woman who ultimately dedicated herself to molding, "out of the animalistic creature she first encountered," a fully functioning person. And, in arriving at Helen's home, Sullivan met her first challenge in so doing. Writes Ross, "Helen rushed at her as she stepped from the carriage, felt her dress and face, repulsed a caress, tried to open Miss Sullivan's bag and staged a scene on the doorstep when Mrs. Keller attempted to take it from her." In response, Sullivan brought out a doll and, after Helen had briefly played with it, spelled into her hand the letters *d-o-l-l*. Her attention attracted, Helen tried to imitate the finger motions. "This," writes Ross, "was the first conscious effort ever made to teach Helen."

When Sullivan attempted to take the doll from Helen, the first of what were to become many tussles began. Decisively, Sullivan moved Helen and herself into a cottage away from her parents, where "a Herculean battle of wills raged for several days." Says Ross of this battle, "It was a physical as well as a mental struggle, but Miss Sullivan won, even though she had to hold Helen down by force for two hours at a time to quell her fierce resistance. 'Her restless spirit gropes in the dark,' Teacher commented. 'Her untaught, unsatisfied hands destroy whatever they touch because they do not know what else to do with things.'"

Within two weeks, Helen experienced a miraculous event heralding the beginning of her journey out of darkness. Attempting to build associations, Sullivan started having Helen touch objects, at the same time spelling out their letters in Helen's hand. But the breakthrough was to occur at the pump house. As Sullivan drew water that flowed over Helen's right hand, she spelled w-a-t-e-r into her left, and suddenly Helen understood the word's meaning.

"'The word coming so close upon the sensation of cold water rushing over her hand, seemed to startle her,' Miss Sullivan wrote. 'She dropped the mug and stood as one transfixed. A new light came into her face.'" Helen's own recollection is: "Somehow the mystery of language was revealed to me. I knew then that w-a-t-e-r meant the wonderful cool something that was flowing over my hand. That living word awakened my soul; gave it light, hope, joy; set it free!"

Within the day, Helen had learned more than thirty words and, at the end of three months, more than four hundred; and soon she had conquered over six hundred. As Helen's vocabulary quantitatively expanded, so did her education, starting with counting, numbers, and writing. Her unquenchable desire for learning consumed and exhausted Helen, and she was deemed by some as being "overtaxed and driven." To this, says Ross, "the teacher's immediate comment was: 'So far nobody seems to have thought of chloroforming her, which is, I think, the only effective way of stopping the natural exercise of her faculties.'"

At eight, Helen learned Braille and began to consume books, while Sullivan worked out for her a systematic program to study arithmetic, geography, zoology, botany, and reading. With Sullivan at her side, Helen went to college and, at twenty-four, graduated with high honors in English. Having throughout her later childhood astounded the intellectuals of Boston and other places, Helen began writing to famous men throughout the world, both in French and English. And now requests were flowing in for appearances and magazine articles. Books that she was to generate were translated into many languages, as well as Braille.[92]

Over the course of her life, Helen labored diligently to speak naturally. In her own book, *Teacher*, Helen says of Sullivan's committed efforts to improve her diction: "By nature she was a conceiver, a trail-breaker, a pilgrim of life's wholeness. So day by day, month after month, year in and year out, she labored to provide me with a diction and a voice sufficient for my service to the blind." In this regard, Helen credits Sullivan's unrelenting efforts until her death in 1936 as multiplying her powers of service, rendering her a priceless gift.

Of other priceless gifts endowed, Helen credits Teacher as designating, as her lifework, Helen's "development as a human being." "Thus," she relays, "Teacher opened unimaginable channels for the faculties with which God had endowed me—love, thought, action, and speech. . . . Four modes of life. And to others besides myself she was a fountain of encouragement to unfold their finer selves. In her best moods she enveloped everyone with her sympathy, [viewing them] as undreamed depository of joys, sorrows, affections, and forces of creation, and often they were responsive to her."

As Teacher's eyes and health increasingly failed her and death neared, to Helen she said of the deaf-blind, whose cause she had ever espoused, "Hold out your arms to them, forget yourself in them, and be faithful to their cause. That will be your true memorial to me, Helen. There may be a wall between you and them, but hammer it down, stone by stone, even if you are broken by the effort, just as some of Florence Nightingale's nurses died of exhaustion."

The preceding is illustrative of what Helen calls "such virtue and power of communication in Teacher's personality" that, after Teacher's death, they emboldened Helen to preserve aiding others beset by darkness and silence. At times, wrote Helen, it seemed that God was using Teacher, "who touched my night to flame, to kindle other fires of good."

In finishing her book, Helen notes that although her beloved Teacher was dead and she herself was growing older, she could "yet experience new birth and youth in the soul of Teacher." Says Helen of Sullivan's lingering legacy, "The certainty that her creative intelligence and truly human quality of mind do not perish, but continue their vivifying work, sweetens my loneliness and is like the warm spring air in my heart."[93]

❤ ❤ ❤ ❤ ❤ ❤ ❤ ❤ ❤

GIVING SETS A STANDARD

Ralph W. Sockman tells the story of Julia Ward Howe, who was speaking to Charles Sumner, a distinguished senator from Massachusetts. As they spoke, she asked him to extend aid to a needy person. Responding, the senator answered, "Julia, I have become so busy, I can no longer concern myself with individuals." To this, Julia sweepingly replied, "Charles, that is quite remarkable. Even God hasn't reached that stage yet."[94]

God's position regarding giving is all-encompassing and unequivocal, as taught in the Old Testament: "Every man shall give as he is able, according to the blessing of the Lord thy God which he hath given thee" (Deuteronomy 16:17).

Thus, God himself has set an unqualified standard of giving for his children—a standard difficult, by virtue of our own fallibility, to achieve. Germane to this is an observation of Soren Kierkegaard: "Most people really believe that the Christian commandments (e.g., to love one's neighbor as oneself) are intentionally a little too severe—like putting the clock ahead half an hour to make sure of not being late in the morning."[95]

Of sobering consequence are the words of Mohandas Gandhi, whose 1948 assassination partially resulted from friendship with Christians, whom some fellow Hindus resented. Asked once by an eminent American preacher what he considered Christianity's biggest problem, Gandhi instantly answered, "Christians."[96] If Christians truly lived Christianity, Gandhi is also reputed to have said, all the Hindus in India would be Christians.

Of magnanimous giving, John Ruskin observes of this Christian ethic: "It is not written, blessed is he that *feedeth* the poor, but he that *considereth* the poor."[97] In the following instances, two young boys learned the meaning of the word *considereth*. In one, recalling an incident indelibly printed on his memory, Comedian Dick Gregory tells how, as a youth, one day he was particularly successful in selling papers and shining shoes. Deciding to celebrate, he entered a restaurant and ordered a veritable feast of his favorite foods. As he ate, an elderly alcoholic

also came in, ordered twenty-six cents worth of food and subsequently savored each morsel he consumed.

Flying into a tumultuous rage when the man admitted to
being penniless, the restaurant's owner knocked him down with
a bottle and began kicking him. At this, Gregory intervened,
imploring the owner to restrain himself and offering to pay the
bill. Surprisingly, the downed man addressed Gregory: "Keep
your twenty-six cents," he admonished. "You don't have to pay
now. I just finished paying for it." Moreover, in leaving, he placed
his hand on the boy's shoulder. Gregory's actions came too late,
he informed him. Why did he not offer earlier?[98] With piercing
chagrin, Gregory realized he had neglected to give what was
needed when it was needed.

Reporting similar chagrin is Archibald T. Davison, who, with
respect to spontaneous giving, calls his own learning experience
"one tragically unforgettable moment." At home one bitter winter's day, he recalls answering the door, where on the porch
stood a man without overcoat or gloves. When asked by the
man if he might gain work shoveling snow from the steps and
sidewalk, Davison, a child at the time, momentarily stood
silently, his eyes set fixedly on him. Then, slowly, he closed the
door "without even a courteous word of refusal." As the man
turned away, Davison remembers the utter resignation on his
face.

Davison was suddenly smitten by that haunting look—a look
that vividly plagued and grieved him. He relates of his memory:
"Many a night, lying in the dark, I have looked into that man's
eyes and have literally sweated with longing to be a child again
and to atone for those ten black seconds of time."

Fortunately, Davison's unobliterable experience resulted in an
overarching moral philosophy that guided his entire life's conduct. Embracing all animal and human life, Davison became

infinitely careful to avoid inflicting hurt on live creatures and—with respect to fellow beings—to infinitely carefully measure his words.[99]

As Gregory and Davison provide testimony, our supreme challenge, Christian or not, is to dilute the misery of our fellow men. Phillips Brooks offers a striking example of a magnanimous person who qualified. Many years ago, shortly after Brooks's death, his oldest brother told his physician, "Phillips might have saved himself, and so prolonged his life. Others do; but he was always giving himself to any who wanted him." Replied the physician, "Yes, indeed, he might have saved himself, but in so doing he would not have been Phillips Brooks. The glory of his life was that he did not save himself."

Of this interaction, the author, listed only as Tidings, reflects, "Ah! the glory of any life is that is does not save itself. Like Mary, Bishop Brooks gave the best he had to God and humanity, and that is why the fragrance of his life has filled two continents with its sweetness."[100]

Of such consummate giving the words of Cicero, a Roman orator and statesman, ring true: "In nothing do men more nearly approach the Gods than by doing good to their fellow men."[101] And, he adds, "It is our special duty that if anyone needs our help, we should give him such help to the utmost of our power."[102]

Such was the case of Fiorello La Guardia, one-time mayor of New York, who, earlier in his life, spontaneously offered help when presiding over a police court. One bitter cold day, a trembling elderly man was brought before La Guardia, charged with stealing a loaf of bread—by all indications because his family was starving. Nevertheless, La Guardia declared that, with the law making no exception, he had no choice but to fine the man ten dollars.

But as he spoke, LaGuardia reached for his wallet and added that he was remitting the man's fine. Tossing a ten-dollar bill into his famous sombrero, he further ruled he was "going to fine everybody in this courtroom fifty cents for living in a town where a man has to steal bread in order to eat. 'Mr. Bailiff, collect the fines and give them to this defendant!'" he ordered. After the hat was passed, "an incredulous old man, with a light of heaven in his eyes, left the courtroom with a stake of forty-seven dollars and fifty cents."[103]

Also did Lafayette magnanimously address the needs of the unfortunate. Although the year's harvest in 1783 was scarce, the bailiff of Lafayette's estate in Chavanic had been successful in filling the barns with wheat. Addressing Lafayette, the bailiff advised that because of the inferior harvest, the price of wheat had risen. Thus, it was time to sell. However, remembering the hungry peasants in surrounding villages, Lafayette responded, "No, this is the time to give."[104]

And, Jacob Bright, the father of John Bright, a famous nineteenth-century British politician and orator, provides another example of magnanimous giving. Walking up the hill from town to his home, he encountered a distraught farmer whose horse had just broken a leg and had thus been destroyed. Onlookers stood around the farmer, expressing their condolences at his great loss. Grasping the situation, Jacob removed his hat, put five pounds in it, and then addressed the sympathetic bystanders: "I"m five pounds sorry. How sorry are you?" After passing the hat, Jacob had collected enough money for the farmer to obtain another horse.[105]

Finally is a story of Gandhi. Ever sensitive to the needs of the less fortunate, Gandhi was boarding a moving train when one shoe slipped off, falling on the track. Unable to retrieve the shoe, Gandhi calmly took off his other shoe and threw it close to the first. When an amazed companion inquired about his action, Gandhi answered, "The poor man who finds the shoe lying on the track will now have a pair he can use."[106] Gandhi's actions were thus consistent with the inscription on his tombstone that reads "Think of the poorest person you have ever seen and ask if your next act will be of any use to him."[107]

With respect to magnanimous giving, newspaper columnist Dale Turner sums up our challenge: "There are millions of people today at the counter of life, hungry, but with no money to pay and no food within reach. There are millions who need others to help them move toward some form of 'equality.' Those of us who can help cannot do it all, but we can do something."[108]

V

• • • • • • • • •

ON CARING

Caring is another ingredient—an investment of the heart—
that connects us to other people. In fact, the theme of caring runs throughout the Bible and, emphasizes Arthur Gordon,
"what the Bible seems to be saying is that if you take this one
ingredient out of life, nothing has much meaning.

"The Bible is full of the importance of caring," he continues.
"The Good Samaritan is concerned about the victim of the rob-
bers, so he acts. The other travelers, afraid that if they acted they
might get into trouble, 'passed by on the other side.'

"Conversely, what got the Prodigal Son into trouble was not
caring. He didn't care what he did to himself, or how his behavior affected others. But his father cared—and kept on caring.
And this was the salvation of the boy, because when he finally
hit bottom, he knew where to turn. 'I will arise,' he said, 'and go
to my father.'"[1]

In this instance, the prodigal son's father had what might be
called a gracious heart.

♥ ♥ ♥ ♥ ♥ ♥ ♥ ♥ ♥

CARING HAS A GRACIOUS HEART

Caring has a gracious heart, and such a heart has a unique function, the essence of which is illustrated in the story of a small-town physician who was asked—with all the difficulties attendant to his choice of locations—why he didn't move to a big city where he could have regular hours, make a substantial income, and specialize.

To this query, the physician responded that he did specialize—he specialized in people.

As with the physician, the gracious heart likewise specializes in people. And, as with the physician, the gracious heart works around the clock, serves many purposes, and has many distinctive marks.

One mark of such a heart is that it focuses keenly on people in ways that make them feel unique, invaluable, and fully validated as human beings. With respect to performance—analogous to the high regard and intense interest the gracious heart conveys—is the manner in which cellist and conductor Mstislav Rostropovich performs for an audience: "If you are playing for eighteen thousand people," he says, "play as if for one—with seventeen thousand nine hundred ninety-nine eavesdroppers."[2]

Describing the moment in her life she was shocked into recognizing the need to extend high regard to others is Joann C. Jones. Jones describes an instance in nursing school in which a professor administered an unexpected quiz to herself and her classmates. She buzzed through the test until she came to the last question, which completely stymied her. The question: What was the first name of the school's head custodian?

Jones didn't know, nor did anyone else. When asked by a classmate whether the last question would count toward their grade, the professor was absolute, emphasizing to the class that, as nurses, they would cross paths with people from every walk of life, all of whom had ultimate value. And, thus, all people were worthy of the nurses' utmost care and consideration, even if their efforts consisted of a gesture so small as a smile and a greeting. Describing her experience as a lesson never forgotten, Jones relates that she also still remembers the custodian's name, which she later learned. It was Dorothy.[3]

Another mark of a gracious heart is a keen and poignant understanding of other people and the burdens they carry. Illustrating such a discerning heart was the mother of Ardis Whitman. Recalling a childhood event of many years ago, Whitman tells of being a small girl in a parsonage and watching people coming to her mother, streaming "into our home by the score, bringing their troubles and joys and hopes." She speaks of one young woman in particular.

"One day, from my favorite perch in the poplar tree, I saw a girl plodding up the sidewalk. She wore scuffed shoes, red with the clay dust of our Nova Scotia country, and her lipstick was too bright for her tired face. I guessed that she must work in the lobster cannery on the Gulf shore five miles away and, of course, she had walked the whole distance. She rang the bell and disappeared.

"An hour later, she came out on the doorstep with my mother. The girl's voice, sounding full of tears, drifted back to me: 'Sure was a long way. But I had to talk to somebody who would understand, and you did. I'd walk it all over again if I had to.'"[4]

Whitman's mother was a person possessing a gracious heart—a heart open and receptive to others and with the ability to discern, with penetrating understanding, the deepest feelings and fears of others.

Too, the gracious heart is always generous with its time and caring actions toward others. In this respect, Ruth Stafford Peale tells of an African boy who gave his missionary teacher an exquisite seashell for Christmas. The teacher, who realized the boy had walked miles to retrieve the shell, knew the significance of the gift, and in thanking the boy the teacher mentioned how overwhelmed he was with this exceptional effort. Eyes lighting up at the teacher's response, the boy replied, "Long walk, part of gift."[5]

The gracious heart also knows people matter most. In "Gardenias for Mama," Faye Field tells of a young girl with such a heart. The girl—having visited a friend in a wealthy section of Houston—was enroute to Dallas via a streamlined Zephyr train. During the visit, her friend had given her a generous armful of gardenias for her mother on Mother's Day.

The girl now carefully held the gardenias, protected in damp paper towels and an outer covering of waxed florists' paper. Sitting there, she imagined her mother's joy in receiving the gardenias, as she had always loved them. Having repeatedly failed in attempts to grow the flowers herself, her mother once remarked she would never have gardenias on the coffee table.

But, on the train, the girl's gracious heart was to be tested, first by the elderly man who wistfully spoke of having his own gardenias long ago. "Here, take a gardenia for your boutonniere," she offered, and the man walked away with a gardenia and a lighter step. Then came the nurse in uniform who, in smelling the flowers, explained she was caring for a crippled four-year-old girl in the next car. Would the girl mind if she took several gardenias to the child? She had so many. The nurse walked off with the several gardenias, looking less weary as she left.

Next came an elderly couple, who, smelling the flowers, smiled and moved on to the car's rear. Having seated his wife, the man returned, explaining this day was their fifticth wedding anniversary. He always gave his wife flowers on their anniversary, but he had none today. Could he buy several gardenias from her? The girl gave the man half the remaining gardenias, and he walked off with the flowers and a rare expression of happiness and gratitude.

As the train pulled into the station, the girl moved into the aisle, where beside her sat a tiny middle-aged Mexican woman. "Are those flowers for your mother?" she inquired, wishing the girls' mother a good Mother's Day. "Nobody remembers me on this holiday," she added. In the last struggle of her heart—for her heart had struggled each time a gardenia left her hand—with little hesitation the girl placed the remaining flowers in the woman's lap, leaving the train with a gracious heart fully intact.[6]

It is the gracious heart that offers emotional generosity of spirit enabling a beneficiary to feel more valued or enhanced by the one extending the gift. And it is the gracious heart, through its nurturing attention to others' needs and feelings, that provides life direction, often smoothing their paths and guiding their way in difficult circumstances. And, finally, it is the gracious heart— lending others strength to ultimately and triumphantly bear their burdens—that provides temporary sanctuary until those others can face life on lifted wings.

❤ ❤ ❤ ❤ ❤ ❤ ❤ ❤

CARING LISTENS

Caring opens up its ears as well as its heart to discover and embrace the inner soul of another. And thus caring commits to listening to the words and actions of others and goes in search of their feelings. One man whose very life exemplified the art of listening to others was Clarence Day.

"The best listener I ever knew was the late Clarence Day, author of *Life with Father*," reveals Alice Duer Miller. "He did not listen in silence. He laughed, he groaned, he roared; his eyes shone with surprise and delight. However mild the anecdote you might be relating, it became significant through his exciting interest. The consequence was that I don't believe anyone knew more of the human heart—knew more about what people were doing and feeling and how the world was wagging—than he did."

Clarence Day *cared*—and those around him had daily living proof of his caring through the vigorous and intense interest he took in everything they said to him. This Day did although he was crippled with arthritis and never outside the walls of his room for the last fifteen years of his life. Just as Day had a choice, we have that same choice of whether to listen with the same keen interest. Says Miller, "You can listen like a blank wall or like a splendid auditorium where every sound comes back fuller and richer."[7]

Caring knows that if it truly wants to connect with or to aid another human being, it needs to listen attentively. Indeed, Sue Atcheley Ebaugh notes, "The greatest gift we can give one another is rapt attention to one another's existence."[8] But even under the best of circumstances, listening is difficult to achieve. "Being a good listener isn't as easy as it sounds," quips Jane Goodsell. "Looking interested for a long time is very tiring on the eyebrows."

William Stringfellow has his own thoughts regarding listening: "Listening is a rare happening among human beings," he emphasizes. "You cannot listen to the word another is speaking if you are preoccupied with your appearance or with impressing the other, or are trying to decide what you are going to say when the other stops talking, or are debating about whether what is being said is true or relevant or agreeable. Such matters have their place, but only after listening to the word as the word is being uttered."⁹

But listening is not so difficult if someone becomes still—still enough to listen with the heart. Only by having had the experience of "being still" could William Butler Yeats have so eloquently written what he did about listening: "I hear [the words] in the deep heart's core."¹⁰

When, through the gift of listening, people are given the opportunity to share "the last words in their heart, they also receive a gift—the gift of healing," observes Catherine de Hueck Doherty. And such listening may figuratively offer even another gift: "Someone has said that it is possible 'to listen a person's soul into existence.' I like that."¹¹ Appending is Quaker Douglas Steere, who adds, "To 'listen' another's soul into life, into a condition of disclosure and discovery, may be almost the greatest service that any human being ever performs for another."¹²

Years ago, a nursing home staff member "listened another's soul into existence" when assigned to aid a totally withdrawn elderly woman who, with eyes closed, day after day incessantly rocked in her rocking chair. The staff member nonverbally "listened" to this woman by pulling up a rocking chair along side her and—radiating love—rocking with her for two days. On the third day, the woman opened her eyes and said the first words she had spoken for two years—"You're so kind." Within two weeks, she had left the nursing home with her family.

In an era when potent psychotropic medications were not available to aid the emotionally ill, a chaplain also committed himself "to listening another person's soul into existence." Telling this story is Donald E. Smith, who writes of a severely depressed and withdrawn young man in a mental hospital. Therapy had been of no avail and nothing, it appeared, could penetrate the psychic barriers between himself and the outside world.

Something about the young man touched and intrigued a chaplain working as a part-time volunteer at the hospital. Determined to make emotional contact with the young man, the chaplain kept trying day after day—sometimes reading from books or newspapers; at others, asking questions or telling stories. But the young man's response—always the same—was silence.

Months passed. Then one day the chaplain went to the window and started describing the scene outside: the summer sky, the leaves blowing in the wind, a squirrel running through the tree branches. All at once, in a halting, husky voice, the young man hesitantly whispered his first words: "I . . . had a pet squirrel once."

In this instance, the great chasm between the young man's inner and outer worlds was temporarily bridged because someone cared enough to "listen his soul back into existence." Although there were no opportunities to mirror back the young man's verbal speech—for he kept his silence—the chaplain attempted through absolute attention to dismantle the young man's psychological, and perhaps spiritual, barriers and to nudge his soul, inch by inch, back into the real world.

Says Smith of the chaplain's caring actions and the young man's first faltering steps back toward reality: "At last the barriers had been breached—because one person was able to make his ego hold its breath long enough for a lost, tormented soul to feel the healing touch of attention."[13]

As the preceding illustrates, listening to another is capable of inducing a soul experience. From Brenda Ueland's perspective, listening is a magnetic and creative force enabling the minds and spirits of others to unfold and expand. "Ideas actually begin to grow within us and come to life," she relates. "When we listen to people there is an alternating current, and this recharges us so that we never get tired of each other. We are constantly being recreated."

Ueland "listens with affection" when someone speaks to her. The reason? Because she believes that person is revealing his soul. Of the gradual emergence of soul, Ueland wryly reflects, initially when one listens, the soul "is a little dry and meager and full of grinding talk," but, with attentive listening the other person begins to show his or her true self and becomes wonderfully alive.

The more deeply we listen, the more we attune ourselves to the roots of others' suffering and ways of alleviating it. To listen most deeply requires our warmly inviting others to express their innermost thoughts and engaging our own souls to receive—in purity of form—those thoughts. "It is with the soul that we grasp the essence of another human being, not with the mind, not even with the heart," Henry Miller emphasizes.[14] And when, through soul, we engage others, we offer others a priceless gift, as Jean Shinoda Bolen tells: "To voice something you're feeling and put observations into words with another person who is totally present is a creative act embodying soul and love."[15]

To listen with one's own soul and thereby possibly engage another's soul, one must become fully present. To listen is thus to pay absolute attention, to enter others' worlds, to try seeing things from the inside out. To listen is also to verbally walk with people, to emotionally hold hands, and to experience what they experience. Finally, to listen is to refrain from adding to, or changing, others' perspectives. In listening, one does not judge, twist, or embellish information. One simply receives the thoughts and feelings flowing from others' minds and hearts.

To reach such purity of receivership is an act of maturity, and from Andrew V. Mason's perspective, "Sainthood emerges when you can listen to someone's tale of woe and not respond with a description of your own."[16]

To be ultimately effective, listening needs to be active, rather than passive, verbally reflecting another person's thoughts and feelings and capturing their essence in fresh words. Such listening involves direct eye contact, an attentive posture, and warmth that emanates from the heart. Through our active listening, others may bring their thoughts into focus and ponder and clarify them. When confident they have been heard, others may almost magically shed hurts and pains, change views, or even resolve problems. And almost magically, if *both* parties mutually attend and attune to each other carefully, they truly begin to understand each other, for listening promotes reciprocity and trust.

Illustrating how one person can make a difference by truly listening is Roy H. Barnacle. Barnacle, a father, tells of becoming concerned about his young, usually happy-go-lucky daughter, who came home from school in a depleted and withdrawn mood, refusing to participate in any usual activities. A worried Barnacle lifted his daughter on his lap, where, in a soothing voice, he began to ask her questions about her day and tried listening to her answers. For a time, nothing seemed to displace his daughter's somber mood. And then he noticed that both her shoelaces were untied and asked her whether they bothered her. Yes, answered his daughter, noting that she kept tripping over them.

Sitting his daughter on the sofa, Barnacle knelt in front of her and, taking the laces in his hands, pulled them even and tied each shoe tight. When he looked up at his daughter, she was watching him "with an almost rapturous look on her face."

"How does that feel?" Barnacle asked.

"Good, Dad—really good."

"I knew the feeling," relates Barnacle. "We had had no lengthy talk of how to get along with people or the importance of improved grades, or growing up. It was a resolution of that background drip of irritation that comes when we walk around all day with a lace undone, or a small piece of gravel in our shoe, or a leaky pair of shoes in the wet grass. Sometimes all that takes place is a very small thing; something adjusted, something simple, something cared for."[17]

❤ ❤ ❤ ❤ ❤ ❤ ❤ ❤

CARING ACCENTUATES POSITIVES

Several decades ago, the *Sunday Times* in London, England, took on the challenge—for one week—of running each day a front-page column of good news. Among the items reported were the following: 92 percent of first-class mail was delivered on time; twelve thousand babies were born; no banks collapsed; there were eight thousand marriages; and 176 million pounds in tax revenues were collected from one oil field. And for good measure, the suicide rate went down.[18]

Consistent with this unusual media coverage, James Reston, a former vice president of the *New York Times*, reflects upon the pressing need for newspapers to print uplifting news: "I have occasionally flirted with the idea that every responsible newspaper should have one competent editor in charge of nothing but good news," he says. "I am not talking about silly Pollyanna drivel, but about hard, factual news about the accomplishments and decencies of our people, which all too often get buried under the daily torrent of gloom."[19]

Such positives quantitatively add to the goodness in the world. And positives also bind relationships together. That positives work better than negatives in securing low-risk, trusting, and open relationships is no secret. Speaking of the superior effects of positives over negatives in human relations, one woman reflects, "You catch more flies with honey than with vinegar"—a point illustrated below.

An elderly man remembers a 1907 environmental cleanup in Brooklyn, New York—a story Atlanta columnist Leo Aikman tells. The man's family of eight owned a plot with a vegetable garden bordered by lilac bushes. Back of their house was a tenement, populated by a dozen families who habitually threw their trash into the family's garden. Incensed, he and his older brother wanted to "tell off" the polluters.

But their mother, a woman who had never even finished grammar school in the Old Country and who hadn't ever heard of "psychology," refused to let her sons complain. Directing her sons to pick lilacs, she instructed them to give a bouquet to each tenant family and to say their mother thought they might enjoy them. "Somehow, a miracle happened," the man relates. "No more pollution."[20]

Telling of another instance some years back in which "positives" prevailed is J. Wallace Hamilton, who speaks of an Indiana sheepman, troubled because neighbors' dogs were killing his sheep. "Sheepmen usually counter that problem with law suits or barbed wire fences or even shotguns, but this man went to work on his neighbors with a better idea," relates Hamilton. "To every neighbor's child he gave a lamb or two as pets; and in due time when all his neighbors had their own small flocks they began to tie up their dogs and that put an end to the problem."[21]

Several lessons appear inherent in the preceding stories. First, people have a way of living up or down to the opinions of others. Second, they respond willingly to and even thrive on positive responses. Third, in a world organized to highlight the negatives, most of us could better serve ourselves and the world by increasing our flow of positives to friends and strangers alike. Reinforcing these observations is John Masefield, who says, "Once in a century a man may be ruined or made insufferable by praises. But surely once in a minute something generous dies for want of it."[22]

In focusing on positives, the challenge is to acknowledge what people *are* doing—from their own framework, not ours—and to give them credit for trying and for growing, even if their actions aren't consistent with our preferences. Such did a mother of a twelve-year-old boy, who ordinarily begrudged wiping dishes. One night while he was drying a large meat platter, the platter slipped from the boy's hands, shattering on the floor. There was a pregnant pause. Then said the boy's mother, "You know, Robert, of all the times you have dried dishes for me, this is the first time you have dropped one. I think you have set some kind of record." Relief crossed the boy's face and he grinned. At that moment, he also became a much more willing dish dryer.[23]

Focusing on positives and interrupting negatives often takes considerable effort, but such effort has its reward, as one man revealed. Asked by a friend about the reason for his obvious popularity, he confided that when he disagreed with someone, he used to say, "Hogwash." But one day he began substituting the word *amazing* for *hogwash*, and ever since, he has had "people drawing power."

Speaking of accentuating positives is Arthur Gordon, who tells of drowsily listening to a sermon "in a back pew of a little country church." Gordon was suddenly jarred out of his sleepy trance as he dimly heard the preacher urge his congregation to "stop worrying about your own halo and shine up your neighbor's!" This golden piece of advice captured Gordon's imagination, leaving him "sitting up, wide-awake" because he had perhaps just heard the best eleven-word formula for getting along with people he'd ever come across.

The preacher's advice impressed Gordon, first, because it implied every person "has a halo that's worth watching for and acknowledging." He also enjoyed the "droll celestial picture the advice conjured up: everybody industriously polishing away at everybody else's little circle of divine light." Finally, the advice was apropos "because it reflects a deep psychological truth: that people have a tendency to become what you expect them to be."[24]

In the late 1800s, an acclaimed British statesman and novelist, Benjamin Disraeli, came radiantly shining through himself as he polished someone else's halo. Alan Loy McGinnis tells Disraeli's story: "A young woman was taken to dinner one night by William E. Gladstone, a distinguished British statesman, and the following night by Benjamin Disraeli, his equally distinguished opponent. Asked later what impression these two celebrated men had made on her, she replied thoughtfully: 'When I left the dining room after sitting next to Mr. Gladstone, I thought he was the cleverest man in England. But after sitting next to Mr. Disraeli, I thought I was the cleverest woman in England.'"[25]

In this world, almost as many ways of accentuating positives exist as do situations, in some instances complete with an opportunity to be creative. One day, for example, Ralph Waldo Emerson, assisted by his son Edward, tried to lead a young heifer into his barn. Grasping the animal's ear, Edward pulled from the front as his father pushed from behind, but the heifer stayed put.

In the midst of their pulling and pushing they were interrupted by a laughing Irish servant girl, who—motioning the two men aside—thrust a finger into the heifer's mouth. Expecting to find nourishment from the proffered digit, the heifer obediently followed her into the barn.

That night, Emerson, who entertained a profound respect for the practical side of life, gleefully wrote in his journal, "I like people who can do things."[26]

In another creative instance, an elderly woman, having boarded a New York bus and put her half-fare into the coin box, was immediately challenged by the driver. Indignantly, she waved her "Reduced Fare for the Elderly" card at him, protesting to another passenger that she was eighty years old. Why would the bus driver want proof? A few thoughtful seconds later, her annoyance turned to amusement. "Well, that really makes my day," she told the passenger.

When the woman had exited the bus, the driver turned to the other passenger, explaining his behavior: "I do that once in a while," he said. "And it always works like magic."[27]

A final creative instance involved General Ulysses Grant, who, during the Civil War, had moved his occupying army into Shiloh, ordering a seven o'clock P.M. curfew. A staff member, however, reported a distinguished Southern lady, a Mrs. Johnson, had been seen near the downtown headquarters close to curfew limit.

Approaching Mrs. Johnson, Grant told her two of his officers would escort her home. Mrs. Johnson's determined response was that she would not budge. Smiling, Grant retreated to his headquarters, returning with an overcoat covering his insignia and rank. "May I walk with you, Mrs. Johnson?" he asked.

"Yes," was her reply. "I'm always glad to have a gentleman as an escort."[28]

Overall, accentuating positives can become a way of living and loving if we commit to acquiring this perspective, as did one woman who lived long ago. Telling another story, Arthur

Gordon speaks of visiting an old forgotten cemetery in the Deep South one lazy Sunday afternoon and finding the weathered stone that marked the grave of a "beloved wife" who died in 1865 "of a fever." The line of script below her name, almost indistinguishable, read, "Ever she sought the best, ever found it."

These eight words profoundly stirred Gordon, who reminisced regarding this woman's life a century ago. He imagined her living through the civil war—a hideous war that might have taken her husband, or perhaps her sons, from her. She had lived in a beaten, broken country, in which she must have experienced humiliation and despair. Yet, it struck Gordon that despite her adversity, those she loved had written she had ever anticipated the positive and had ever found it.

Gordon pondered the words the remainder of the day, sensing their inherent courage and dignity. For him, they also contained "a kind of triumph, too, as if they contained a secret of inestimable value. What you look for in life, they seemed to say, you will surely find."[29]

❧ ❧ ❧ ❧ ❧ ❧ ❧ ❧ ❧

CARING GIVES COMPLIMENTS

"A compliment is verbal sunshine," says Robert Orben, referring to a compliment's capacity to warm a person's entire being.[30]

Despite the remarkable effect compliments can have, they are always in short supply, a point to which Phyllis Theroux attests: "One of the commodities in life that people can't get enough of is compliments. The ego is never so intact that one can't find a hole in which to plug a little praise. But compliments, by their nature, are highly biodegradable and tend to dissolve hours or days after we first receive them—which is why we can always use another."[31]

We all possess the extraordinary power to compliment others, a power that requires almost nothing but the will to communicate. The spontaneous act of saluting another's skill or talent, or his or her excellence, intelligence, or character traits, is nourishing to the human spirit. Recognizing this, Mark Twain once remarked he could live for two months on one good compliment.

And what constitutes a good compliment—one on which you could live two months? The answer: A compliment bestowed from the heart, with a bow of love tied around it. Describing the most eloquent compliment she'd ever encountered, Doris Ann Krupinski tells of an incident involving Joseph Choate, one-time United States ambassador to Great Britain. Asked who he'd like to be if he could die and then return to earth as someone else, without a moment's hesitation Choate responded, "Mrs. Choate's second husband."[32]

Compliments may address admirable attributes or the honors or accomplishments of another. However, perhaps the most powerful and savorable of compliments is one that says simply—as did that of Choate's—"Thank you for being who you are."

Phyllis McGinley cites what she considers the essential ingredients of a compliment: spontaneity, uniqueness, and wit. She also identifies two compliments she deems as meeting those criteria. One, in an earlier era, is the oft-repeated remark made by Charles MacArthur to Helen Hayes when they first met: he offered her a bag of salted peanuts, regretting that they weren't emeralds. McGinley also tells of a personal compliment she considered just as elegant as that received by Helen Hayes. In this instance, it was her husband-to-be who shared the limelight after rescuing McGinley from a wasp, a creature she had "always feared with the terror other people reserve for mice or sharks or snarling dogs.

"Alerted by my girlish screams of terror," she tells, "he captured the ravening insect in a handkerchief and dropped it out the window. When I turned to him with murmurs of gratitude, he managed to gild the moment.

"'Think nothing of it,' he said. 'I wish it had been a dragon.'"

No wonder, says McGinley, that she married the man three months later.

McGinley further cites a treasured compliment written in a letter to her by her young daughter while the daughter was out of town visiting relatives. Reads the letter: "Dear Mommy, I am having fun. But I am sad because you are so far away. I miss you with my arms and my legs and my whole stomach." And finally, another compliment held dear is this one given McGinley by an adored, and older friend who believed her, "however wrong-headedly, to be comely, clever and destined for high places."

One thing this friend could never convince McGinley of was that she owned "a brilliant and bewitching smile," McGinley's doubts originating, in part, because she had been brought up on the Colorado prairies where there were no orthodontists. However, one day a convincing compliment of the friend made its mark: "But, 'Phyllis,' she told me dreamily one day, 'you have fascinating teeth. They're so individual—no two alike.'"[33]

"There are two ways of spreading light: to be the candle, or the mirror that reflects it," observes Edith Wharton.[34] In complimenting another, a person becomes "the mirror that reflects the light." In a story Margaret Cousins tells, a stranger is the mirror reflecting the attractive image of another.

Cousins describes standing in line with a friend early one morning for a White House tour. Never at her best at an early hour, Cousins absent-mindedly admired her friend's immaculate grooming and her well-pressed, attractive outfit. After they had been waiting about half an hour, they saw a distinguished-looking woman, hands full of documents and in deep concentration, walking down the corridor. As she passed the two, her face suddenly brightened. Says Cousins of the woman's response, "Pausing for an infinitesimal second, she smiled at my friend and said, 'My, you look nice!'" After that, she went briskly on down the corridor.

Cousins reports her friend blushed with pleasure, obviously heartened by the woman's compliment, even to the point that her friend experienced physical effects: "Buoyed up by a stranger's recognition of her efforts to look attractive, she lifted her chin, straightened her shoulders and forgot that her feet were tired." Taken with her friend's reaction, Cousins wondered why she had never complimented her regarding her appearance. She'd always valued her friend's impeccable presentation of self, but had never openly expressed her admiration of this trait.[35]

Cousins highlights the importance of responding to the positive attributes we perceive in others. We never know when our observations may uplift others, fortifying their self-confidence and gracing their lives with comfort and sweetness.

♥ ♥ ♥ ♥ ♥ ♥ ♥ ♥

CARING IS APPRECIATIVE

Martin Buxbaum tells a story about Dr. William Stidger, who took the time to write a letter of thanks to a schoolteacher for the strong encouragement she had given him in her class thirty years before. Not long after, Stidger received a letter, written in a very shaky hand, which read:

"My dear Willie: I want you to know what your note meant to me. I am an old lady in my eighties, living alone in a small room, cooking my own meals, lonely, and seeming like the last leaf on the tree. You will be interested to know, Willie, that I taught school for fifty years and in all that time, yours is the first letter of appreciation I have ever received. It came on a cold, blue morning and cheered my lonely old heart as nothing has cheered me in many years."[36]

Consistent with this vignette, William James—who has poignantly captured in words people's soul needs to be appreciated—reflects: "The deepest hunger of Human Nature is the craving to be appreciated."[37] And Hilaire Belloc adds, "I never yet knew a man so blasé that his face did not change when he heard that some action or creation of his had been praised; yes, even when that praise came from men most insignificant."[38]

People thus have an intrinsic hunger to be acknowledged or validated by others—to know that their presence on this planet is recognized and that their actions make a difference. While active appreciation is in short supply, it significantly magnifies the heart and soul of any receiver. Appreciation affirms that a giver's efforts are helpful, and the appreciative person makes a point of describing the impact of the giver's actions, upon him- or herself. Appreciation is thus the receiver's means of saying, "Thank you for your goodness."

In a story called "Thank You for Asking Me," Pamela Johnson tells of communicating to givers a deeply-felt message of appreciation for their goodness. Writes Johnson: "I walk briskly three miles a day around a ball park. I think this is no big deal even though I have only about five-percent vision. Surroundings are mostly blurry, and I can barely read large print.

"Each summer evening before sundown, I clip along at a fast pace for about an hour around the sidewalk surrounding a baseball field. Anyone who darts across my path and gets in my way may not survive the impact.

"One night my steps seem to slow as I watch the sunset colors fade into night. For some reason my eyes are stronger and

God allows me to see clearly the splendor of his glorious creation. . . . I savor this moment of seeing.

"I continue on my way enjoying the cool breeze and smelling the greenery near by. Soon it is pitch black and the field lights go on to light my path.

"I pass by some young men involved in a game. Their ball hits the fence hard close to me.

"Suddenly one of the players yells, 'Can you get our ball?'

"No one seems to be around except me, so I call back, 'Sure,' as I scramble for the ball. It takes me a few minutes to find it nestled in the grass where I grope for it, but the players patiently wait. They don't send someone after it who might spot it quicker with his eye. . . . I toss the ball back over the fence. To these players, this is an ordinary simple action, but I knew the game must go on and they had counted on me.

"When one of the players yelled, 'Thanks,' a warm sense of well-being washed over me. I have been treated like a capable human being; I am like them inside—needing approval and friendship.

"The players would never know the significance of my smile as I responded, 'Thank you for asking me.'"[39]

For Johnson, the words of Samuel Johnson aptly apply: "The applause of a single human being is of great consequence."[40]

Indeed, applause is one way of showing appreciation, as in the instance of Walt Whitman. Once, when little known, Whitman was engaged to read a poem at an exhibition, but advance poems he supplied to several newspapers yielded him mostly negative publicity; and when he arrived at the exhibition hall, workmen were still noisily building or arranging the exhibits. Despite the slurs and attacks in anonymous papers both before and during the event, a New York correspondent reported that Whitman's reading received a large, welcoming reception.

When the poet began reading, the correspondent wrote, "five or six hundred carpenters, machinists and other workmen paused with their tools in their hands to listen, and . . . the audience of two or three thousand people several times interrupted with applause."[41]

Interestingly, *no* applause may also manifest deep and moving appreciation, as in a magnetic moment spawned by Pacchierotti, a nineteenth century vocalist. As the story goes, "when singing at Rome in a certain opera, he sang with so much beauty of tone and true feeling that, at a certain place where a solo passage was followed by a short orchestral symphony, the orchestra was so moved by his singing as to forget to go on with their playing. Pacchierotti turned to the conductor, saying, 'What are you about?'

"The leader stared as if from a dream, and could only say, 'Pray forgive me.' The whole orchestra were sitting with tears in their eyes, oblivious of their duties."[42]

Tales are legion of delightful ways people have formerly expressed appreciation. Years ago, for example, a Pacific Gas and Electric Company received this letter from a customer: "There I was on the highway, standing bewildered in front of my wrecked-by-a-deer car. Along came a PG&E lineman. He radioed for the highway patrol. It was a very cold night. He offered his jacket, then turned on the heater in the pickup. After the highway patrol came, he drove me home to a worried wife. He was very helpful, thoughtful and considerate. He would accept nothing. So the least I can do is write a letter of appreciation.

"P.S. To help pay for the gasoline, oil and pickup depreciation, I left our front porch light on all night."

Also years ago, sent to the editor of the Sacramento *Bee* was this letter: "Sir: We would like to express our gratitutde to the farmer near Sycamore Slough, who assisted us when the battery went dead in our houseboat; to Mike of New Hope Landing who got us running again after our steerage broke on the Mokelumne; to the boatload of people who pulled us out of the mud at low tide at the Cosumnes; and to the three boys who pushed us broadside off the sand bar near Guist's. They all helped make our weekend a success." The letter was signed, "The Four Women in the Houseboat."

Last, and deeply touching, is the instance of a four-year-old girl who, after a wonderful day of playing with friends, asked permission to say her own evening prayer. "Then she said, 'Thank you, God, for a pleasant day,' hesitated a moment while she thought what should come next, then in complete sincerity added, 'I hope You've had a good time too.'"[43]

In their own way, animals may also express appreciation, as described by Jeffrey Moussaieff Masson, author of *Dogs Never Lie about Love*. Masson tells of taking his two dogs to a new park, a wetlands, where there resided huge numbers of ground squirrels and large jackrabbits. In an isolated area, the dogs could run free, and after Masson opened the car door, they were off and running. A few moments later they were back, eyes expressing "visible excitement" at being allowed to roam this outdoor dog paradise. They looked at Masson, he says, "as if grateful, as if saying to me, 'Yes, this is exactly the kind of place we love. Thank you for taking us here. Thank you, thank you, thank you.'"[44]

Most of us could afford to demonstrate more appreciation to people who give quietly to us in ways we take for granted. To gauge the importance of appreciation, think about these questions regarding any important person in your life: What would I be missing if that person were no longer in my life? In what specific ways would I miss that person? And, What would I like to say to this person if I only had one more chance?

Pensively, James A. Farley adds other questions he asks of

himself and others: "How much do most of us appreciate the countless little daily acts of . . . kindness by others that make our lives more comfortable? How grateful are we, really, for the privilege of living in a country where most of us can take freedom, justice and security for granted? How much thankfulness do most of us feel for the marvelous gift of life itself, and how adequately do we express this to the Giver?"

In honestly assessing his own answers, Farley faced the painful truth: He was not nearly as appreciative as he should, or would, like to be. So he committed to the following resolutions:

"To thank the people who make my world run smoothly . . . not just with a casual word or an impersonal tip, but with some expression of genuine interest in them as fellow human beings.

"To make myself more aware of the miraculous privileges involved simply in being an American, and to show my thankfulness by working without thought of reward to make [my] country . . . better.

"To remind myself every day of the infinitely precious value of every minute of existence, and to show my gratitude to God not only with prayers of thanksgiving but by living as close as possible to the way He wants me to live."

And Farley finishes: "A basic rule in showing appreciation, I have found, is this: *do it now*. Do it while your sense of gratitude is fresh and strong. If you feel a flash of thankfulness, act on it before the impulse dies away."[45]

❤ ❤ ❤ ❤ ❤ ❤ ❤ ❤

CARING ENCOURAGES

"Some buffalo were placidly grazing on the open range when a cowboy rode up. He stared at them for several minutes and then blurted out, 'You are such ugly creatures! Your hind legs are longer than your front ones; you have humps on your backs, shaggy hair, beady eyes and tails with bushes on the end. Ugh! Disgusting!' Then he rode away.

"'Gee,' one buffalo remarked to another, 'I think we just heard a discouraging word.'"[46]

In life, as with these buffalo, you don't have to go very far or wait very long to "hear a discouraging word." And it's not hard, either, for most of us to be like the cowboy and to offer others a few unsolicited words ourselves.

The challenge we face is to encourage, rather than discourage, others, and—for instance—to be capable of riding up to any old buffalo and blurting out something like, "I've been noticing your hind legs, and your humps, and your tails with the bushes on the end, and I've been thinking, 'What a creative arrangement.'"

Can you just imagine those buffalo kicking up their heels at those encouraging words? The right words at the right time can do wonders for anyone. And among the most powerful words are those that essentially convey the message: You can do that.

Without exception, everyone requires encouragement, even those who might appear otherwise. Presenting a vivid example is Norman Rockwell, who could likely be viewed as self-contained and assured. However, Ken Stuart, *Saturday Evening Post*'s art editor, knew differently. Having worked closely with Rockwell, Stuart was amazed to discover Rockwell's strong need for encouragement. He observes, "Though the years, critics faulted Rockwell for not being something he never thought he was—an artist like Vermeer or Matisse. Norman knew he was a marvelous limner of the nicer side of American life, a man whose love for the unabashedly wholesome brought pleasure to an enormous number of people. As such he had no equal. But the critics annoyed him just the same, and accusations that his work was overly sentimental or shallow would occasionally throw him into a spell of depression. At such times, I found myself in the curious position of trying to give encouragement to the most beloved artist in America."[47]

A story of Phillips Brooks, a late nineteenth-century theologican, illustrates the power of encouragement in buoying the spirits and hopes of others. After having secured an interview with Brooks, a struggling young man repeatedly reviewed his problem before meeting with Brooks to assure himself Brooks would understand. Telling what then happened, Robert W. Youngs reports, "The interview was a glorious experience. He came away inspired. Halfway home, it occurred to him that he had forgotten to mention his problem to Brooks. 'But,' he said, 'it did not matter. What I needed was not the answer to my problem so much as the contagion of a great spirit.'"[48]

With such encouragement, people's souls flourish. Without it, they may suffer significantly. Emphasizes Celeste Holm, "We live by encouragement and die without—slowly, sadly, angrily."[49] Despite its redeeming value, encouragement is in short supply. Rarely do we give or receive enough of this basic soul-fortifying substance, to other people or to other creatures. Emphasizes Douglas Woodruff, even "animals, like human beings, have to be encouraged, petted, and above all, made to feel important if they are to do their best work."[50]

Illustrating encouragement's potential is Mary Ann Bird, who tells how a teacher's tender response indelibly enhanced her self-esteem when she was a lonely child. Relates Bird, "I grew up knowing I was different, and I hated it. I was born with a cleft palate, and when I started . . . school my classmates—who were constantly teasing—made it clear to me how I must look to others: a little girl with a misshapen lip, crooked nose, lopsided teeth . . . and garbled speech.

"When schoolmates would ask, 'What happened to your lip?,' I'd tell them I'd fallen and cut it on a piece of glass. Somehow it seemed more acceptable to have suffered an accident than to have been *born* different. I was convinced that no one outside my family could love me. Or even like me.

"Then I entered Mrs. Leonard's second grade class.

"I never knew what her first name was—just Mrs. Leonard. She was round and pretty and fragrant, with chubby arms and shining brown hair and warm, dark eyes. . . . Everyone adored her. But no one came to love her more than I did. And for a special reason.

"The time came for the annual 'hearing tests' given at our school," continues Bird. "I was barely able to hear anything out of one ear, and was not about to reveal yet another problem that would single me out as different. And so I cheated."

The "whisper test," as it was known, required that each child walk to the classroom door, turn sideways, and close one ear with a finger. From her desk the teacher would whisper something the child was to repeat. Each ear, in turn, was tested.

"As usual, I was last," Bird recalls. "But all through the testing I wondered what Mrs. Leonard might say to me. I knew from previous years that the teacher whispered things such as 'the sky is blue' or 'do you have new shoes?'

"My turn came. I turned my bad ear to her, plugging up the other solidly with my finger, then gently backed my finger out enough to be able to hear. I waited, and then came the words that God had surely put into her mouth, seven words that changed my life forever.

"Mrs. Leonard, the teacher I adored, said softly, 'I wish you were my little girl.'"[51]

❤ ❤ ❤ ❤ ❤ ❤ ❤ ❤

CARING IS A TALENT SCOUT

As a talent scout, caring believes in looking for the positive attributes in others. "The greatest good you can do for another is not just to share your riches but to reveal to him his own," observes Benjamin Disraeli.[52]

The wife of Nathaniel Hawthorne was a talent scout for her own husband—a woman who fully believed in his ability to write. One day in 1849, Hawthorne, shattered by his dismissal from his government job in the customhouse, returned home in despair. How, now, would he support his family? Where else might he find a job? What would become of him in the future? Responding to his agony, his wife encircled him in her arms and comforted him. It was then she suggested that, with his time now his own, he could now focus on the novel he had always wanted to write. And what was the outcome? Hawthorne's literary classic, *The Scarlet Letter.*[53]

Being a talent scout involves perpetually viewing people through positive lenses, as was the habit of Duke Ellington. "Ellington talked to me about his music," remembers a friend. "He composed with each musician in the band particularly in mind. 'You keep their weaknesses in your head as you write,' he said, 'and that way you astonish them with their strengths.'"[54]

Another time, Robert Burns, the Scottish poet, was the talent scout. Burns met Sir Walter Scott when Scott was twelve years old and considered by many to be a "dullard." Fortuitously, however, Scott accompanied his parents to a party gathering of famous literary guests. There, he noticed Burns admiring a picture, complete with an engraved couplet of a stanza.

Inquiring about the couplet's author, Burns was met with silence until Scott tentatively spoke up, naming the author and finishing the poem. Putting his hand on Scott's head, Burns insightfully pronounced, "Ah, bairnie, ye will be a great man in Scotland some day." Thus, in one telling moment, Scott found purpose and definition, ultimately fulfilling Burns's prophetic prediction.[55]

Beethoven once acted as a talent scout to Franz Liszt, in the mid-1800s an esteemed pianist and composer. In 1823, at twelve years of age, Liszt, a youthful prodigy, was scheduled to give a concert. And, upon the encouragement of another composer, Beethoven attended the concert to hear and encourage Liszt:

"When the little Liszt came out on the platform, he saw Beethoven sitting in the front row. Instead of being unnerved by the great man's presence, it was an inspiration to him and he played with great fire and abandon. In the storm of applause which followed, the great master was seen to step up on the platform and catch up the little fellow in his arms and kiss him on both cheeks. Liszt never forgot this incident and used to repeat it with great pride, for he felt that the master had set the seal of greatness upon him with that kiss."[56]

Vladimir Horowitz, in the early to mid-1900s a gifted and celebrated pianist, also tells of giving his first American recital when he was twenty-four. At performance's end, many renowned colleagues were waiting to see him—his manager informed him—but compelling was an elderly man from Horowitz's district in Russia. Horowitz invited the man, who had been deeply moved by his performance, into his dressing room.

Tells Horowitz, "He came in with tears in his eyes and took my hands and kissed them and said, 'Horowitz, Horowitz, it was wonderful, it was beautiful . . . but you must continue to play like today. Never change. . . . All the great ones are outside your door, wanting to see you. Hoffman—why he didn't like the way you played the Chopin, and Rachmaninoff hated the G-Minor

Prelude, and Rosenthal was upset with the Brahms. Keep playing just the way you do!'"[57]

Yet another time, a discerning teacher served as a talent scout, having profound impact on a youth who later became a widely acclaimed surgeon. Wild and unruly in high school, in his senior year the surgeon faced a pending suspension. But then a teacher whose class he was failing made a remark irrevocably reversing his life's course and proving seminal to his choice of vocation. In contrast to frequent cajoling, her unexpected comment "rang out like a clarion." She said, "You have the most marvelous, sensitive hands. Surely you will do important work with them."[58]

With wisdom, this teacher focused on the youth's promise— not his problems. Had she not then recognized his potential, the world would have been deprived of a man with great healing power. So, too, may the world often be deprived of others' talents—famous or not—if those around them don't perceive and relay to them their gifts. The vital role of such talent scouting is reflected in John L. Elliott's words: "Most of us, all of us, have finer things of which we are capable than we ever do. Every man and woman has a finer person in him than the world ever knows."[59]

Sobering are the experiences of many gifted people whose associates intervened in ways to discourage their ultimate life paths. Six-year-old Thomas Edison, for example, came home from school with a note saying he was "too stupid to learn." Alfred Tennyson's grandfather handed him ten shillings for writing a eulogy to his grandmother, with the words, "There, that's the first money you ever earned by your poetry, and take my word for it, it will be the last." Benjamin Franklin's mother-in-law also hesitated to let her daughter marry a printer, fearing that with two printing offices in the United States already, the country could not support a third.[60]

Also sobering is that our vision of others' talents is often obscured by factors, cultural or otherwise, of which we are totally unaware. Thus, critical to talent scouting is an open-mindedness that precludes judgment and allows others the right of discovery. Speaking in the late 1950s, Henry J. Allen, a former governor of Kansas, describes how others might have viewed Abraham Lincoln as a boy. Henry illustrates how we may inaccurately perceive others' potential or even how cultural factors may rob a person of such potential:

"Had Abraham Lincoln been living today, the Rotary Club would supply him with a set of books; the Lions Club with a good reading lamp; the Cosmopolitan Club with writing equipment; and the Kiwanis Club with a wooden terrazzo for the cabin.

"He would have the protection of child labor insurance. A kindly philanthropist would send him to college with a scholarship.

"Incidentally, a caseworker would see that his father received a monthly check from the county. He would receive a subsidy for rail splitting, another one for raising a crop he was going to raise anyway, and still another subsidy for not raising a crop he had no intention of raising.

"Result: There would have been no Abraham Lincoln!"[61]

Neither, in the 1920s, without a father's consistent positive feedback, may Calvin Coolidge have become the thirtieth United States president. Reminiscing once about his son, Coolidge's father said, "It always seemed as though Cal could get more sap out of a maple tree than any other boy I knew."[62]

As with Coolidge's father, we can proactively affect people's lives by acquiring positive lenses. Focusing on others' capabilities may fire hopes and dreams and ignite self-confidence. In this regard, Tony Parker observes, searching for others' talents is akin to searching for gold: As a gold prospector, you find precious metal in people when you least expect it.[63]

Ralph Waldo Emerson likens the challenge of uncovering talents to that of viewing others as plants, not weeds.

And what is a weed? Emerson explains: "A plant whose virtues have not yet been discovered."[64]

❤ ❤ ❤ ❤ ❤ ❤ ❤ ❤

CARING HAS MANNERS

Intriguing is a true story of two orchestra conductors, both of whom habitually closed their eyes to enhance their concentration when orchestrating music. After the first time they performed together in a concert, one reported of their experience: "We understood each other perfectly. There was only one critical moment when I opened my eyes and I saw that my friend was conducting with closed eyes. I promptly closed mine so as not to spoil anything."[65]

This conductor manifested an impeccable sense of timing that allowed him to attune to the moment, with absolute concentration upon his music. To him, it was thus vital he stay synchronized with his friend, whom he presumed felt and acted similarly. To do less would have—for him—constituted shockingly poor manners in the form of interrupting the other conductor's perfect "soul" experience.

Another case of heightened (as well as perhaps overwrought) sensitivity to another's circumstances is the true story—set in the early 1900s—of two geologists who headed an expedition to the South Pole. These geologists were accompanied by an aide who, busy in a tent one night, heard one of the geologists—in a muffled voice—calling to him, "Mawson, are you very busy?"

"'Yes I am,' replied Mawson. 'What's the matter?'

"'Are you really very busy?'

"'Yes,' said Mawson, then doing some intricate computation. 'What is it you want?'

After a moment of silence, again came the other man's muffled voice: "'Well, I am down a crevasse, and I don't think I can hang on much longer.'"[66]

Finally is an old story of a famous pianist who observed, as he began his concert, that a woman in the front row had dozed off; moreover, she slept through the entire performance. When a standing ovation at the concert's end woke up the woman, the pianist leaned forward and said apologetically, "It was the applause, madam. I played as softly as possible."[67]

In the preceding instances, one person demonstrated heightened awareness to another's experiencing and circumstances—a necessity in manifesting manners. Defining manners, Emily Post says, "Manners are a sensitive awareness of the feelings of others. If you have that awareness, you have good manners, no matter what fork you use."[68] Also addressing the vital importance of manners, Freya Stark comments, "Manners are like the zero in arithmetic; they may not be much in themselves, but they are capable of adding a great deal to the value of everything else."[69] And adding a finishing touch is Phyllis McGinley, who emphasizes that manners are actually morals—"exercises of the body for the sake of the soul."[70]

Manners, as well, are guidelines for relating to others in ways that perpetuate, in relationships, peace of mind, congeniality, and civility. "Manners are society's way of oiling the machinery," points out Michael Korda. "If you don't lubricate relationships . . . tempers rise and people fight unnecessary battles."[71]

Jo Coudert also adds, "I used to think manners, like paint, were designed to make the surface look good. But one day I learned the real value of paint the hard way—when I investigated a parade of black ants climbing the side of my house. I discovered they had tunneled through the unpainted bottom of a windowsill and were attacking the wooden under-pinnings. And I suspect we're now learning the hard way that manners aren't merely decorative but serve to keep the foundations of society intact."[72]

Appending is Owen Edwards, who observes that "the point of manners is clarity and simplicity. A code of conduct makes it possible to understand vexing situations without starting from scratch each time." Manners give us bearings in yet other ways, he continues. In a world that is suffering from "etiquette deprivation," the presence of manners in another person may suggest an inherent sign of morality, or perhaps a commitment to smoothing life's path for all, or maybe even "a determination to champion respect in an increasingly disrespectful world."

Foremost, Edwards advises, "when you meet someone with good manners, or even exquisite manners (a far more rare encounter), you can't know immediately if you're meeting a good person. You may not know for years, or ever. But you will know instantly that *something* is right about them. The world is well supplied with rude people spouting high moral positions about human rights, but it is noticeably lacking in those who worry about the human being waiting in line behind them at the automatic teller machine while they balance their checkbooks."[73]

Annoyed by others' bad manners is Mark Twain, who wryly observes, "It is a mistake that there is no bath that will cure people's manners, but drowning would help."[74]

Bad manners—often based on a false sense of entitlement and an insensitivity to others—create immediate schisms in relationships and low-grade chaos in social situations. By contrast, good manners are facilitative, giving clean passage anywhere, as illustrated in an instance occurring at an airport. As an impeccable Englishman stood in line at a reservations counter, a woman abruptly crowded in front of him, curtly demanding a ticket upgrade to first class. Resisting the woman's intrusion, the Englishman picked up the woman's ticket and pressed it back in her hand. "Madam," he noted, "first class is not a boarding pass. It is a way of life."[75]

Similarly, to extend manners at all times, "as a way of life," people must perceive all others as intrinsically valuable human beings who are worthy of thoughtful consideration. In George Bernard Shaw's play *Pygmalion* (from which the musical *My Fair Lady* was adapted), Professor Higgins conveys this point to Eliza, a young cockney-speaking flower girl. Intending—through teaching Eliza manners—to transform her into a lady, Higgins instructs, "The great secret, Eliza, is not having bad manners or good manners or any particular sort of manners, but having the same manner for all human souls."

When people respond naturally with good manners, they can confidently face any situation. Illustrating this point, Elizabeth Post tells of a time a woman was unexpectedly presented to Queen Elizabeth. Friends asked how she had known what to do. And, they also asked, hadn't she been scared to death? To the contrary, the woman responded, "It was very simple. I have only one set of manners."[76]

Possessing good manners includes the willingness to apologize. Referring to the vital role apologizing plays in the recovery of good will and positive feelings, Eda LeShan observes, "The more I think about it, the more it seems that the capacity to apologize is probably one of the most civilized attributes of being human."[77]

An apology is also a wonderfully cleansing and healing experience, Norman Vincent Peale suggests, "because some deep wisdom in us knows that when even a small wrong has been committed, some mysterious ethical equilibrium is disturbed; and it stays out of balance until fault is acknowledged and regret expressed."[78]

As well, from the perspective of Mstislav Rostropovich, apologizing when one has wronged another is a soul-enhancing experience. Viewing his capacity to apologize when appropriate as his life's greatest achievement, Rostropovich urges others to also commit to apologizing: "Everyone should realize that, far from humiliating, [apologizing] elevates the soul."[79]

If an apology aids the person who apologizes, it also aids the person who receives it, as Robert Conklin illustrates. Conklin vividly recalls a time he took an early morning breakfast flight that was late in both departing and arriving. Adding insult to injury, the weather was turbulent and by the time the plane landed, admits Conklin, he was grumpy.

But then, over the intercom, came an apology by the captain for the choppy ride; and, soon after, the stewardess added an apology for the delay. At that, Conklin's annoyance immediately abated: "About this time I wanted to say, 'Aw heck, it wasn't your fault the air was bumpy and the plane was late. You don't have to apologize.'" Conklin's mood was brighter, he acknowledges, "as if the unpleasantries had been bagged and placed aside."

Apologizing is an emotional pacifier that soothes "the jagged corners of someone's feelings," continues Conklin. It's also a way of communicating care for others—a message they sometimes ache to hear. "The world keeps putting pebbles in one's shoes. It's nice to have someone come along and take a few out."

Finishing, Conklin concludes that apologies may "seem to be verbal trifles, throwaway words that some don't consider of enough significance to bother saying. But life is a mass of specks and drops, tiny happenings that are pluses or minuses. Anything, no matter how small, that you can contribute to a plus nature to those around you makes you a special quantity in their lives."[80]

❤ ❤ ❤ ❤ ❤ ❤ ❤ ❤ ❤

CARING WEARS A SMILE

Several decades ago, in a cold-war era wherein Soviet long-range bombers were photographing American warships, American aircraft were sent up to get pictures of the bombers. After several failed attempts, an American pilot succeeded in closing in on a bomber and began snapping photographs. A flustered Soviet pilot broke air silence asking for orders from home as to what to do. "Smile," came back the pointed answer.[81]

Everybody loves a smile. Smiling is a potent way to say, "I care," "I've noticed you," or, "Even though you're a stranger, you're an important person to me." A smile thus communicates approachability and establishes or enhances emotional connections with others. Describing the warmth of a smile, Joseph Addison reflects, "What sunshine is to flowers, smiles are to humanity." And, of their importance, he adds, "They are but trifles, to be sure, but scattered along life's pathway, the good they do is inconceivable."[82]

One woman recognized the vital importance of a smile, and another woman, Jean Schwartzstein, tells of her, "When the subway train I was riding on stopped at Grand Central Terminal, two people got on. They were strangers to each other. I heard the man say, 'I never expect to find one on the subway.' The woman answered, 'Oh, I always pick one up. If you look you'll find one. I collect them.'

"I couldn't figure out what they were talking about until the train pulled into my station and the woman got up to depart as well. She gave me a great big, bright smile and, of course, I smiled at her. Whereupon the woman turned back to the man and said, 'See, there's another one!'" At that—with an air of satisfaction—she exited the train.[83]

This woman knew that, in life, a smile counts—a bunch. Everyone loves smiles, particularly kids, who genuinely appreciate such simple and inviting communication. Says Peg Bracken of one child who particularly admired smiles, "When someone once asked my brother, as a little boy, what was his favorite vegetable, he said punkins, because they smile a lot."[84]

Capturing the essence of smiles, an anonymous author says, "A smile costs nothing but creates much. It enriches those who receive without impoverishing those who give. It happens in a flash and the memory of it sometimes lasts forever. None are so rich they can get along without it and none so poor but both are richer for its benefits."

Further, relates this author, "a smile creates happiness in the home, fosters good will in a business and is the countersign of friends. It is rest to the weary, daylight to the discouraged, sunshine to the sad and nature's best antidote for trouble. Yet it cannot be bought, begged, borrowed or stolen, for it is something that is no earthly good to anyone until it is given away. Nobody needs a smile so much as those who have none left to give."[85]

Smiles can create a positive mood in, and even emotional ties to, an entire crowd, as Bob Elliott, of the Bob and Ray comedy team, tells. Describing an unusual experience on a New York City bus, Elliott recalls how the driver greeted new passengers: "We don't allow smiling on this bus!" he would say. Or, as the bus got under way again, "No smiling while the bus is in motion, please." Taken by the driver's surprising gesture, entering passengers looked at him in amazement. Then, in response, even the grumpiest of passengers began to smile.

Elliott describes the bus driver's approach as infectious, its effects rippling among passengers throughout the bus. Strangers with smiles—turning to talk to other smiling strangers sitting in the next seat—chuckled at the amazed reaction of new riders to the driver's boarding instructions.

Reaching their stops, many passengers deliberately exited through the forward door, thanking the driver for the positive experience and wishing him a good day. "Of course everybody says that," observes Elliott. But, of this particular experience, he emphasizes, "I really do believe it made everybody's day."[86]

Years ago, a smile also made the day—and perhaps even the life—of Gus Kasico. Harold Helfer tells of Kasico, a humble man who, from his cart, for years sold roasted peanuts on a sidewalk corner of the White House. One day Kasico was transferring to a new location, a move that indeed made him sad.

"You must understand," says Helfer, "that Gus Kasico did not mind having to move himself and his cart of roasted peanuts from this corner because of the money he might lose by transferring to a new location." Gus knew he could probably sell just as many peanuts in another park. "No, the reason that Gus Kasico . . . felt sad [was that] it had made him feel so good to be located on this corner, on the same corner with the President of the whole United States! But after today he would not be here.

"The location of his peanut cart had always given Gus such a nice, warm glow inside himself," Helfer continues. "Whenever anyone asked him what he did, he never said, simply, 'I sell peanuts on a corner.' He always said, instead, 'I am at The White House'— and he might add as a murmured afterthought, 'with peanuts.'

"When he sent letters back to the old country, he always mentioned about being in business 'at the same location' with the President of the whole United States. 'We get along fine,' he would also add from time to time.

"And Gus Kasico, the peanut vendor, was convinced that this was so. Of course, he only saw the President through the heavy, grilled, iron fence. But still it seemed to Gus that sometimes he would discover the President—maybe from somewhere on the lawn beyond, or from the window in the White House—smiling at him. It always seemed to be such a nice, friendly smile that it filled Gus through and through with the warmest of feeling."

Where Gus came from, people weren't treated equally—sometimes they were snubbed or ignored—but "this country was different. Everyone was the same as everyone else. Why, even the President of the whole United States smiled at him from beyond the iron fence!

"This had been such a big thing to Gus. Because sometimes he did get lonely and homesick. There weren't very many people who spoke his native language here, and many of the ways seemed strange to him. And there was such a rush here, too—everyone in such a hurry.

"But the friendly smile from the other side of the iron fence somehow told him that everything was all right; that he belonged and was welcome; and that he would find himself fitting into the scene, happy and satisfied."

In a few minutes he'd have to start pushing his cart away for the last time. But now, his life changed forever, Gus was thinking that despite the lack of freedom and autonomy in the old country, he might go back. Such consideration was new to Gus, who'd always said "that he would rather be a peanut vendor in the United States of America than a big bureaucrat with a chauffeur and a limousine back there."

Gus wished he was just having a bad dream, but he knew he wasn't, for sure. His landlady had read aloud a morning newspaper story about him even containing a picture of him and his cart on The White House corner. In Washington, the story said, vendors were no longer permitted on corners near public buildings. And—after some six years—today was Gus Kasico's last day on The White House corner.

Gus's heart was heavy as he stooped to remove the wood under the front wheel that kept his pushcart from rolling. As he straightened up, he felt a gentle tap on his shoulder.

"He turned around, and there it was—that wonderful smile! Only—fantastically, incredibly, miraculously—it didn't come from somewhere beyond the iron fence this time! It was right beside him!

"The President of the whole United States was standing there before him! And his smile, if anything, was even more genuine and wonderful than he had imagined it to be when seeing it from a distance through the iron fence."

And then he heard the voice: "I'd like to buy some peanuts, a dollar's worth." With a "Yes—sure" that caught in his throat, Gus was handing the President of the United States some bags of peanuts! "And, with his smile almost as beamingly broad as the whole expanse of The White House lawn, the man from The White House now shook Gus's hand with an affectionate warmth." He had read of Gus's leaving his corner, he said, and he would miss Gus, adding he wished him well wherever he went.

"Gus Kasico didn't even seem to *push* his cart to his rooming house that evening, but to *float* there with it. He wondered how he could ever have thought that he might leave the United States of America. Why, this was his home; this was his land! He was part of it, and this was where he belonged! In the twinkling of an eye he had now seemed to become part and parcel of everything about him. The iron fence had melted away."[87]

❤ ❤ ❤ ❤ ❤ ❤ ❤ ❤

CARING VALUES HUMOR

A saying attributed to Will Rogers gives perspective to the role of humor in our lives: "We are all here for only a spell. Get all the good laughs you can."[88]

Most of us can afford to take Rogers' light-hearted advice. We intuitively recognize that we need humor. It's good for our health, it's good for our souls, and it's good for our relationships. And what is humor?

"Humor is laughing at what you haven't got when you ought to have it," says Langston Hughes.[89]

"Humor is a spontaneous, wonderful bit of an outburst that just comes," adds Erma Bombeck. "It's unbridled, it's unplanned, it's full of surprises."[90]

And, finishes Romain Gary, "Humor is an affirmation of dignity, a declaration of man's superiority to all that befalls him."[91]

In life, humor plays itself out in many ways that create, for each of us, a better life. Humor can make us laugh heartily with, and feel deeply for, those we love. Humor strengthens bonds, diffuses volatile situations, heals wounded feelings, keeps communication harmonious and open, and represents a subtle way of lobbying for change.

Leo Rosten adds, "Humor is the affectionate communication of insight,"[92] a point Will Rogers illustrated. When visiting Paris, Rogers sent a postcard of the famed armless statue of Venus de Milo to his niece, scribbling on the back, "This is what will happen to you if you don't stop biting your fingernails."[93] Whether Rogers was seriously trying to influence his niece to quit biting her fingernails is unknown, but if so, she undoubtedly thought about restraining herself, and if so, with his benign and subtle humor, Rogers wouldn't have hurt her feelings.

Humor also translates to any language. Jeff Wheelwright illustrates with a story involving Alaska's Governor Jay Hammond, "a wry and bearlike man," who visited Peking in 1979. During a televised meeting between Hammond and China's vice premier, "the wry and diminutive Den Xiaoping," through an interpreter Deng posed a question to Hammond:

What did Hammond think of the Chinese system of government? "What was I supposed to say to that—especially with people back home watching?" recalls Hammond. "Finally I said, 'Any regime that manages to do away with the necktie can't be all bad.'"

After an ensuing exchange between Deng and the interpreter, the latter turned and told Hammond, with no expression at all, "The vice premier says you crack him up."[94]

That humor translates into any language is also illustrated in the story of Cab Calloway, who starred in *Hello Dolly!* several decades ago. Once honored by a Hebrew organization for his efforts in promoting interfaith cooperation, Calloway attended the awards banquet where the toastmaster told a joke in Yiddish. When Calloway joined in the ensuing laughter, he surprised the toastmaster, who observed, "I didn't know you understood Yiddish."

"I don't," said Cab, with a chuckle. "But I have confidence in you fellows!"[95]

In a reverse twist, while lecturing to a group of Korean officers an American general took several minutes to tell his favorite joke. Then translating, using only seven or eight words, the interpreter told the general's joke, at which the entire group burst into hearty laughter. Curious, later the general asked the interpreter how he could so quickly tell such a long joke. "Well sir," confessed the Korean, "I didn't think anyone would get the point so I just said, 'The General has just told a joke. Everyone will please laugh.'"[96]

Humor gives us glimpses of ourselves in ways that help us laugh about life events we all experience—life events over which, most of the time, we have little or no control. Comedian Tim Conway, in fact, was a master at poking fun of such events. Once, on NBC's *Today* show, Johnny Carson asked Conway where he had obtained his off-the-wall sense of humor. Responding, Conway attributed his style to his father, illustrating with a typical childhood scenario: "My father and I were sitting in the living room when suddenly a tornado touched down, uprooting a large tree in the front yard and demolishing the house across the street. Dad went to the door, opened it, surveyed the damage, muttered 'darn kids' and closed the door."[97]

Although Conway told this story in a humorous context, in this once real situation, Conway's father's humor had inherently made the unbearable bearable. A vital function of humor, in fact, says Peggy Noonan, is that it "allows us to step out of the moment, look at it and sum it up with no great reverence."[98] In another instance, humor took a similar form when, in 1976, an earthen dam broke in southeastern Idaho, washing away or breaking into piles of rubbish and splinters the homes of most of the people in the valley. The few houses left standing were damaged almost beyond recognition.

A sign hanging from a house in a town where damage was extensive conveyed how one family approached the catastrophe. The family's house was newly built, and before the flood it had had two stories. After the flood the first story was entirely washed away, leaving the second floor balanced on what looked like four stilts. Knowing that friends and neighbors had experienced similar fates, and realizing that a little levity might go a long way in helping the community, this family penned these words: "Around here, we build our houses from the top down."[99]

Finally, during the Persian Gulf conflict a sign observed in a Tèl Aviv back yard next to a Scud-missile crater read, "Actually we wanted the pool a little to the right."[100] This light-hearted play on tragedy suggests the viability of James Thurber's own apt definition of humor, that of "emotional chaos remembered in tranquillity."[101]

In daily news replete with tragedies occurring in our own backyard and in every corner of the earth, humor gives us both relief from pain and hope for the future. Capturing the relief that can spring from taking ourselves and our struggles less seriously, Langston Hughes speaks of humor's possible refreshing effect: "Like a welcome summer rain," he says, "humor may suddenly cleanse and cool the earth, the air and you."[102]

Where there is good humor, there is usually laughter. And what is laughter? Perhaps it might be best defined as "the tinkling of the soul." Sir James M. Barrie captures laughter's tinkling, or lilt, as he couples the origin of fairies with the sounds of the first baby laughing: "When the first baby laughed for the first time, the laugh broke into a thousand pieces and they all went skipping about, and that was the beginning of fairies."[103]

The laughter that springs from humor may even be a God-given gift, designed to soothe man's soul. In laughing, man experiences a healthy, full-bodied physical rejuvenation that cuts through stress and shortcuts suffering, representing what Arnold Glasow terms "a tranquillizer with no side effects."[104] Laughter also provides warmth and comfort to the soul, as captured by Victor Hugo: "Laughter is the sun that drives winter from the human face."[105] And Mort Walker augments, "Laughter is the brush that sweeps away the cobwebs of the heart."[106]

Peter Ustinov also views "the sound of laughter . . . as the most civilized music in the universe."[107] And laughter does have implications for men-at-large, aiding even strangers to establish emotional connections. Often, in fact, laughter becomes contagious, stirring entire crowds, bringing into synchrony the positive reverberations of the souls of the many. One cannot help but wonder that even the angels in heaven—in their state of complete goodness—at times may share with each other, through laughter, an intermixed tinkling of their own souls.

❤ ❤ ❤ ❤ ❤ ❤ ❤ ❤ ❤

CARING IS PATIENT

Once a mother committed to a New Year's resolution to be patient with her daughter, a teen, no matter how irritating or grumpy she got. And then she came across her own daughter's list of resolutions. Among them? To be patient with her mother no matter how irritating or grumpy she got.

As in this instance caring knows the importance of patience in creating an atmosphere of good will, a gesture that subsequently encourages others to respond from the heart. Germane to the importance of patience in creating such ambiance, a Chinese proverb reflects that "with time and patience the mulberry leaf becomes a silk gown."[108]

A mulberry leaf did became a silk gown in an instance in which one young man exercised patience. In an article called "Falling in Love," newspaper writers Elaine Jarvik and Susan Whitney describe how the young man's patience paid off in the world of romance: "Elaine Pine was carrying a bag of garbage the first time she met Kurt Peterson," these authors relate. "He was standing on her porch looking for some friends who lived next door.

"Elaine had just been at a party down the street, at the home of people who didn't recycle. So she brought the bag of soda cans back home with her, and that's when she ran into Kurt, whom she'd never seen before.

"'Can you just hold this for a second,' she said, handing him the bag of garbage. Then she opened her door and went inside with some other packages. Five minutes later, as she was watching TV with her roommate, she suddenly remembered the guy on the porch. 'Oh my gosh,' she said.

"When she opened her front door, the guy was still there. She invited him in.

"Her wedding ring, eighteen months later, was inscribed with the words, 'Hold this.'"[109]

Paul Sweeney views today's lack of patience as reflective of the intensive stress of the Western culture. "How can a society that exists on instant mashed potatoes, packaged cake mixes, frozen dinners and instant cameras teach patience to its young?"[110]

And Vaughn Monroe appends, "This would be a fine world if all men showed as much patience all the time as they do while they're waiting for a fish to bite."[111]

Nevertheless, although the world is short on patience, patience is vital to caring and to the ability to extend self to others. An anonymous author, for example, views interruptions from a unique perspective: "When you are exasperated by interruptions, try to remember that their very frequency may indicate the valuableness of your life. Only the people who are full of help and strength are burdened by other people's needs."

This author continues, "The interruptions which we chafe at are the credentials of our indispensability. The greatest condemnation that anybody could incur—and it is a danger to guard against—is to be so independent, so unhelpful, that nobody ever interrupts us and we are left comfortably alone."[112]

An added dimension of patience is that of developing encompassing tolerance of others' idiosyncrasies. Such patience is based partially on the premise of Joseph Fort Newton: "We cannot make people over. Our business is to make ourselves better and others happy, and that is enough to keep us busy."[113]

Further providing perspective regarding tolerance is Thomas á Kempis, who advises, "Endeavor to be always patient of the faults and imperfections of others, for thou hast many faults and imperfections of thy own that require a

reciprocation of forbearance. If thou art not able to make thyself that which thou wishest to be, how canst thou expect to
mould another into conformity to thy will?"[114] And Richard
Whatley appends, "Ten thousand of the greatest faults in our
neighbors are of less consequence to us than one of the smallest of our own."[115]

Providing the clincher in aiding patience to take root is
Goethe's mother, who reflects, "I always seek the good that is in
people and leave the bad to Him who made mankind and knows
how to round off the corners."[116]

Patience with others includes patience with God's creatures,
as demonstrated by Isaac Newton, a prestigious scientist who in
the early 1700s conceptualized the law of gravity. If the story is
true, most of us would be hard pressed to emulate Newton's classic presentation of patience. Yet, it must be emphasized, the animal in question was innocent in his actions (as is usually the case
of people) and therefore not deserving of wrath. As the story
goes, Newton owned a pet dog named Diamond who one day
accidentally knocked over the candle on his desk, starting a
blaze destroying records of many years of research. Newton,
viewing the destruction, said only, 'O Diamond, Diamond, thou
little knowest the damage thou hast done.'"[117]

British anthropologist Louis Leakey, the son of British missionaries, tells how he, as a boy, developed the patience for which
he became so famous. Born in Kenya and brought up in an African
tribe with other Kikuyu youths, Leakey identifies two attributes
that contributed to his subsequent career as a fossil hunter:

"Patience—especially patience—and observation" were these
factors, he says. "In Africa, survival depends upon your reaction
to irregularities in your surroundings—a torn leaf, a paw print, a
bush that rustles. And patience. I can still hear the Kikuyu elders

telling the boys over and over, 'Be patient, be careful, don't hurry. Try again and again and again.'"[118]

To have patience is to slow down enough to notice the people and problems in our lives, observations that often save the day. As Charlie W. Shedd observes, "Patience is a particular requirement. Without it you can destroy in an hour what it might take you weeks to repair."[119] And Arnold Glasow cautions, "The key to everything is patience. You get the chicken by hatching the egg—not smashing it."[120]

In this regard, patience can award a person with increased perception, as Elspeth Huxley highlights: "The best way to find things out . . . is not to ask questions at all. If you fire off a question, it is like firing off a gun; bang it goes, and everything takes flight and runs for shelter. But if you sit quite still and pretend not to be looking, all the little facts will come and peck round your feet, situations will venture forth from thickets, and intentions will creep out and sun themselves on a stone; and if you are very patient, you will see and understand a great deal more than a man with a gun."[121]

If a caring person adds—in addition to love—the element of patience, that person creates in relationships a powerful means of positive influence, for as George Washington Carver observes, "Anything will give up its secrets if you love it enough."[122]

Prize-winning novelist Louise Erdrich tells about the surprising and definitive day in her life that she acquired patience, and patience and love wedded. She speaks of her mother, who had seven children by age thirty. Her mother, notes Erdrich, found ways of sublimating her tension and frustration and never lashed out at a child. However, Erdrich acknowledges that she somehow did not acquire her mother's patience.

When she became a mother, Erdrich yearned for her

mother's high level of patience, which, surprisingly, one day suddenly seemed to be bestowed upon her. Telling of the occasion she "was invested mysteriously with [her] mother's grace," Erdrich describes being alone with fussy children who were not sleeping through the night. As a result of four straight sleepless nights, she missed a work deadline, and at the same time, her fussy baby continued to cry. The tension and acute stress seemed merciless. "Then," she says, "I broke through a level of sleep-deprived frustration so intense I thought I'd burst, into a dimension of surprising calm. I know exactly when this happened.

"My hand reached down, trembling with anger toward the needy child, but instead of roughly managing her, my hands closed gently as a whisper on her body. At that moment, I was invested not with my own thin-worn endurance, but with my mother's patience. I knew that was a gift she had given me . . . [one that] had lain with me all my life, like a bird in a nest, waiting until the moment my hands needed the soft strength of wings."[123]

Erdrich was fortunate in that patience—as an attribute— finally became her own, almost as though it was instantly bestowed by creative powers from above. In acquiring patience, most of us are not so fortunate, and for those of us who want to increase patience, Mother Teresa is a sterling model. Although known as a devout and serious person, Mother Teresa's good sense of humor came shining through during a news conference. When asked whether she objected to being photographed constantly, a smiling Mother Teresa responded she had made a contract with God—"For every time someone takes my picture, he takes one sould out of purgatory." After enduring a full day of numerous shutters clicking, she wryly added that "purgatory must be empty today."[124]

❤ ❤ ❤ ❤ ❤ ❤ ❤ ❤

CARING INFLUENCES

Caring has influence and also commands respect, as in an entertaining story Charles Kettering tells. Kettering's story illustrates how caring's influence can be soft and delicate and—in this case—can even tease a bit. Says Kettering, "I bet a friend of mine that if I gave him a bird cage and hung it up in his house he would have to buy a bird. He took the bet. So I got him a very attractive bird cage made in Switzerland, and he hung it near his dining room table. Of course you know what happened. People would come in and say, 'Joe, when did your bird die?'

"'I never had a bird,' he would say.

"'Well, then what have you got a bird cage for?'

"He said it was simpler to go and buy a bird than have to explain why he had the bird cage."[125]

Of Kettering's story, it might be said that in wielding influence, one has to hang bird cages in the minds of others and then wait for them to go out and obtain something to put in them.

Although caring has influence, whenever possible, caring avoids force. Unfortunately, the gain of power through leadership can corrupt the natural man, who may wield such power to his own advantage. As Abraham Lincoln has observed, "Nearly all men can stand adversity, but if you want to test a man's character, give him power."[126] Indirectly, Lincoln is referring to the responsibility of men to use power judiciously.

Speaking to the judicious use of power is Peter Rucker, who says, "Rank does not confer privilege or give power. It imposes responsibility."[127] Consistent with this point, General Dwight D. Eisenhower once observed, "You do not lead by hitting people over the head—that's assault, not leadership."[128] Eisenhower, in fact, used to demonstrate the art of effective leadership with a simple piece of string. Putting a string on the table, the general would say, "Pull it and it'll follow wherever you wish. Push it and it will go nowhere at all."[129] Finally, in explaining his approach to leadership, Eisenhower said, "I am not one of the desk-pounding type that likes to stick out his jaw and look as if he is bossing the show. I would far rather get in the background and, recognizing the frailties and requirements of human nature, try to persuade a man to go along—because once I have persuaded him, he will stick. If I scare him, he will stay just as long as he is scared and then he is gone."[130]

"Power is all perception," adds Peter Guber. "Its non-use is its most powerful use. The trick is to use the least amount of power to create the maximum amount of change. Someone who has elegance can apply power selectively like a laser, and carefully, almost unobtrusively, so that you don't feel you're being overpowered. You feel like you're being motivated."[131]

As to the power of effective influence in the work place, consider this excerpt from a factory worker's letter: "My foreman thinks I have more ability than I think I have. So I consistently do better work than I thought I could."[132]

Capturing the essence of effective influence, John Churton Collins urges, "Never claim as a right what you could ask as a favor." Essentially, effective influence invites, rather than demands, what it wants or needs from others. "When a dog runs at you, whistle for him," advises Henry David Thoreau, who, tongue-in-cheek, describes through analogy how influence gives an invitation.[133]

Complementing Thoreau's thought, Emily Ann Smith, a former college professor, observes, "I've learned a lot from dogs. Years ago, I forced a daily spoonful of cod-liver oil down the throat of my German shepherd puppy. The dog slipped from my grasp one day, spilling the potion. Then he began licking the spoon. He liked the oil, but not my method of giving it to him.

"I've often put that over into teaching. What the teacher has, maybe the student wants, if you just give it to him the right way."[134]

As Smith alludes to, control tactics never inspire in other people any motivation or interest in pursuing the controller's objectives or designs. Rather, such tactics serve to stir rebellion and steer others toward behavior and attitudes directly counter to those being imposed.

In achieving vested objectives in human relationships, we thus have only one viable alternative—to operate from an "influence base," that is, a position to which others through invitation are attracted, and thus motivated, to fulfill our needs or to even espouse our personal values. In the absence of control, these others are so drawn to the extent that they love and respect us and want to freely offer us "gifts of self." Such an influence base is not easily earned, necessarily emanating from many small encounters over time based on trust and good will.

In achieving its goals, influence always looks for unusual or imaginative ways to accomplish its objectives. Illustrating is a creative approach a symphony conductor incorporated to teach music appreciation to the very young. Recognizing that three- and four-year-olds want to touch whatever attracts them, the conductor "set the children on small chairs in the center of the orchestra. Each instrument was demonstrated alone, and then the children were invited to take their chairs and sit next to whichever instrument they liked. The final number was played with each child sitting alongside . . . of the musician playing the instrument of choice."[135]

As a means of creatively appealing to others, influence often utilizes subtle humor, as occurred many years ago at a stage play during which many women wore hats obscuring the vision of others in the audience. At the end of the first act, the manager gracefully pled for the removal of hats, and then—after a moment's hesitation—made an exception: "Of course," he said, "this request doesn't apply to elderly ladies." At that, every hat came off.

In addition, influence attempts to enter others' worlds and may even "lean into" resistance to thereby solidify relationships. Such action occurred when Lillian Carter addressed a group of college students who, she had been warned in advance, would probably be rowdy. Unexpectedly, Carter invited students to throw toward her paper airplanes with their names on them so she could take them home to her two sons, Jimmy and Billy. The students obliged Mrs. Carter, who, having once been a fraternity housemother, was adept at managing college boys.[136]

Influence further assists people to save face, as it did many years ago at a dinner for Commonwealth heads of state. Seeing a guest pocket a gold salt shaker, the chief of protocol asked Winston Churchill what to do. "Leave it to me," said Sir Winston, who proceeded to pocket the matching gold pepper shaker. Turning then to the thief, Winston whispered, "Oh dear, the chief of protocol saw us. We'd better put them both back."[137]

Influence also takes a positive approach, as illustrated in a story regarding Flora Isabel MacDonald, some years ago Canada's minister for external affairs. Once, when MacDonald was involved in a public debate with other candidates in her district, a supporter, obviously intoxicated, persistently heckled and interrupted the other candidates. The audience openly fidgeted, but no one wanted to tackle the hazardous task of ejecting or silencing him.

Decisively taking charge of the situation, MacDonald moved from the stage to the floor, greeting her supporter with a smile. Putting an arm around his shoulders, she earnestly talked to him, charming him from the auditorium. She returned alone to the audience's appreciative applause.[138]

Finally, influence commits to everyone winning, as illustrated in a story Francis Gay tells: "Two small boys in front of me were walking slowly, deep in conversation, when they stopped to share an apple. 'You cut and I'll choose,' said one to the other. A penknife appeared, the cut was made and the choice decided.

"What a splendid way of ensuring an apple is equally shared!" Gay emphasizes. "Perhaps this world could get along with fewer conferences and agreements, I reflected, if only the powers that be had the simple solution that schoolboys worked out centuries ago."[139]

♥ ♥ ♥ ♥ ♥ ♥ ♥ ♥

CARING ALLOWS MISTAKES

A woman tells of a letter she found taped to her front door one morning:

"Dear Sir (or Madam)," read the letter, "I am substituting for the regular paper boy and am not highly skilled in throwing newspapers. In fact, I threw yours on your roof.

"I could not give you another paper because someone else would have been shorted. I couldn't see how I could get the paper down, and then saw that you have a door on your second story leading to the roof and realized you would be able to get it relatively easily. I am really sorry for the trouble. Aren't you glad I'm not the regular boy?"[140]

In this instance, the substituting delivery boy made a mistake. One must wonder what the reaction was of the woman who found the note. Did she get angry? Or did she laugh? In her mind, what latitude—if any—did she offer to the perpetrator of a blunder that would, at least slightly, inconvenience her? If she chose a tempered view of the mistake made, she added a bit to the world's goodness.

In the context of goodness, caring offers a wide margin of error to everyone it encounters, realizing that mistakes constitute not exposure of character flaws but opportunities for growth. Caring also commits to protecting the fragile egos of those who err in its presence.

Such caring is personified in the form of Thomas Edison, who knew that people, rather than mistakes, matter. As Edison worked on improving his first light bulb, he gave a finished bulb to a young employee to take upstairs. Nervously, the employee carried the bulb up the stairs, step by step, only to drop it at the last moment. His error required the entire staff to work another twenty-four hours to make a second bulb. When the bulb was finished, Edison turned and handed it again to the same young man for transport. Says James Newton, who tells the story, "The gesture probably changed the boy's life. Edison knew that more than the bulb was at stake."[141]

Edison also well knew, as William D. Brown captures, that "failure is an event, never a person."[142] To this perspective, Buckminster Fuller adds, "We were deliberately designed to learn only by trial and error. We're brought up, unfortunately, to think that nobody should make mistakes. Most children get de-geniused by the love and fear of their parents—that they might make a mistake. But all my advances were made by mistakes. You uncover what is when you get rid of what isn't."[143]

And, to these observations Charles F. Kettering appends, "Virtually nothing comes out right the first time. Failures, repeated failures, are finger posts on the road to achievement. The only time you don't fail is the last time you try something, and it works. One fails forward toward success."[144]

Modeling the ease of making a mistake—and not demeaning herself for it—is TV chef Julia Child. Relates *Universal Press International* editor John DeMers: Viewers of Child's "French Chef" remember best "the spills, the potato pancake scooped back into the skillet after falling on the counter, the legendary Roast Suckling Pig that defied all efforts at carving. In addition to Child's candor and dry wit ('Nobody's looking,' she said, calmly replacing the potato pancake), what impressed viewers most was the warm reassurance that mistakes were all right."

Explaining her attitude toward calamities occurring on her TV shows, Child explains that being a good cook includes being able to recover.[145] Child's presentation as a fallible human being who makes mistakes—and indeed, as a being who *expects* to make mistakes—is worth emulating.

Imperviousness to others' judgments when one makes a mistake is also an acquired attribute worth considering. Illustrating is an observation Alice Duer Miller makes of her father, Clarence Day: "My father cared less for other people's opinion than anyone I have ever known," she tells. "The most characteristic story of him is this. He and my mother were dining at a large formal dinner. My mother was horrified to see her husband suddenly disappear under the table. The fact was that the dining-room chairs had been too few, and my father had been given a chair with castors; leaning back, the castors had slid, and he had fallen under the table.

"On the way home, my mother, asking and hearing this explanation, said to him: 'I hope, Jimmie, you explained to the people next to you what happened.' My father looked at her in slight surprise. 'No,' he said, 'It wasn't any of their business.'"[146]

To penalize others, or even oneself, for common mistakes is to ignore the fragility and vulnerability of the human condition. Everyone on this planet makes mistakes every day, and in this respect, there are no special cases. Robert Townsend speaks of the propensity—and necessity—of making frequent errors:

"Admit your own mistakes openly, maybe even joyfully. Encourage your associates to do likewise by commiserating with them. Never castigate. Babies learn to walk by falling down. If you beat a baby every time he falls down, he'll never care much for walking."[147]

Mark Twain humorously adds, "Always acknowledge a fault frankly. This will throw those in authority off their guard and give you opportunity to commit more [mistakes]."[148] Twain's advice is somewhat epitomized in the actions of Mohandas Gandhi, who had a reputation of changing his mind publicly. Asked by an aide how he could so freely contradict this week what he had said the previous one, Gandhi replied, "Because this week I know better."[149]

In managing our reactions to mistakes—those of others, as well as our own—we can opt for the same humorous or benign perspective reflected in the observations of Twain and Gandhi. Further illustrating such perspective is Tug McGraw, who had an ingenious philosophy of pitching which he called his "frozen snowball theory." He explains:

"If I come in to pitch with the bases loaded and Willie Stargell is at bat, there's no rational reason I would want to throw the ball. As long as I hold on to it, nothing bad can happen. But I'm aware that eventually I have to pitch. So . . . I remind myself that in approximately a billion years the sun is going to burn out and the earth will become a frozen snowball hurtling through space. And when that happens, nobody's going to care what Willie Stargell did with the bases loaded."[150]

And, so—if we remain consistent with Tug McGraw's posturing—when it comes to making or allowing mistakes, we can ask ourselves whether the mistake really matters. And, for tight spots, when we're in danger of blowing our cool, we might even repeat in our minds a question especially designed for such moments: "In the overarching, cosmic view of things, with death at our left shoulder, what difference does it really make?"

❤ ❤ ❤ ❤ ❤ ❤ ❤ ❤ ❤

CARING DOESN'T CRITICIZE

In life, among the most bothersome of the "small-time" negatives that gnaw and chew at us is criticism. Although we may view this affliction as besetting other people, we may sometimes not regard ourselves as suffering from this rampant habit. However, when we are honest with ourselves we usually realize the probability is high that we, too, struggle with downloading on others.

Unfortunately, with respect to criticism, says Leo Aikman, "most of us are umpires at heart; we like to call balls and strikes on somebody else."[151] In this regard, perhaps our situation is similar to that in a Calvin and Hobbes cartoon. After a disastrous encounter, Calvin concludes, "My whole problem is my lips move when I think."

However, when we do offer criticism, we may believe it is obviously for the other person's good. And, of course, when we deem it proper to improve someone else—as a self-appointed improvement committee of one—we may employ only what we believe is constructive criticism, believing that we "care enough to say the very worst."

But, the question must be asked, "Is there such a thing as constructive criticism?" The very phrase seems to involve a contradiction in terms. How can one be "constructive" and "critical" at the same time when, by definition, criticism involves the act of finding fault, censuring, and disapproval?

It's hard then to see what's so constructive about criticism of any kind. Most of us would emphasize, in instances of our being the *recipient* of such silliness, "Don't give me any of that 'constructive' business!"

Mignon McLaughlin, in fact, probably represents the attitude of most of us: "No one wants constructive criticism. It's all we can do to put up with constructive praise."[152]

And Hal Chadwick expands our perspective, observing, "No one so thoroughly appreciates the value of constructive criticism as the one who's giving it."[153]

Judith Martin, who writes the "Miss Manners" column, provides the clincher: "Perhaps the greatest rudeness of our time comes not from callousness of strangers but from the solicitousness of intimates who think that their frank criticisms are welcome."[154]

Why is constructive criticism such a flop? First, being critical simply doesn't work if one's goal is to influence others in ways that are palatable, helpful, and effective: "I have seen many amazing things in my life, but I have never seen anyone who could take criticism well," informs Roger Rosenblatt. "All criticism, be it casual or vicious or constructive, is unpalatable. Sure, you can profit from criticism in the long and painful run. But taking it is something else. Taking it means letting it go down like custard— no blinking, no flinching, no wishing you were dead."[155]

Secondly, critics don't get good press. "The trouble with critics is that they have not been in the kitchen where the things are cooked," says J. B. Priestley.[156] And Kenneth Tyman chimes in, "A critic is a man who knows the way but can't drive the car."[157]

Third, there exists a high correlation between a sender's giving constructive criticism and a recipient's reacting defensively. Give a dose of constructive criticism and what do you get? Voilá! An instant negative reaction and an immediate impediment to effective communication. A note from an advertising executive to a writer in another agency, written after the executive had been criticized by the other man, serves to illustrate. The note read, "Dear Pot, Yes I am black. Kettle."[158]

As in this instance, a person on the defensive often counter-attacks, which serves to escalate an argument, with each party blaming the other for starting the conflict and neither party assuming responsibility for perpetuating the same.

An alternative to constructive criticism is that of giving people feedback about what they are doing right or what they have accomplished. Praise has power, notes Bern Williams: "Praise can give criticism a lead around the first turn and still win the race."[159] Praise also motivates, observes Jocco Grand: "The attention span of a typical human is ten praises, six promises or one preachment."[160] And people prefer praise, as Norman Vincent Peale assures us: "Most of us would rather be ruined by praise than saved by criticism."[161]

Another alternative to criticism is to become a person who has the best interests of another at heart, something that must occur over time, and with many affirming acts. "He has a right to criticize who has a heart to help," advises Abraham Lincoln.[162] And James Dobson adds, "The right to criticize must be earned, even if the advice is constructive in nature. Before you are en-titled to tinker with another person's self-esteem, you are oblig-ated first to demonstrate your respect for him as a person. . . . When a relationship of confidence has been carefully con-structed, you will have earned the right to discuss a potentially threatening topic. Your motives have been thereby clarified."[163]

Still another alternative to criticism is becoming open, in a relationship gone awry, to being the one who makes the neces-sary adjustments. Illustrating is an instance of a husband who said to his wife, "I'm uncomfortable about something, but in talking to you about this, I am not presuming you're the one who needs to change. That, in fact, may be my task."

An even further—and much admired—alternative to criticism is silence, for, as Israel's former Prime Minister, Golda Meir, once said, "You can't improve on saying nothing."[164]

A final alternative to criticism is to suggest positive solutions that appeal to another person. "There is nothing as easy as denouncing," emphasizes Will Rogers. "It doesn't take much to see that something is wrong, but it does take some eyesight to see what will put it right again."[165] And, Henry Ford counsels, "Don't find a fault. Find a remedy."[166]

♥ ♥ ♥ ♥ ♥ ♥ ♥ ♥

CARING CHECKS ANGER

Caring knows that anger pushes people away and lessens their motivation to change, as in the instance of Johnny, a first-grader whose school teacher told him to sit down. When the boy didn't sit down, the teacher spoke more strongly: "Johnny, sit down!" When that didn't work, the teacher spoke again—this time with anger—"*Johnny, sit down!*" Johnny responded, "All right, teacher, I'll sit down. But in my heart I'll still be standing up."

As in this instance, when anger is used as a weapon of force, people will "still stand up" in their hearts and subtly or even forcefully resist change. Underscoring the propensity of people, when assailed with anger, to nevertheless hold tight to their positions is John Morley, who observes, "You have not converted a man because you have silenced him."[167]

There is no end to people's creativity in finding ways to resist being diminished by others' anger. At the airline ticket counter, for example, an agent endured a tirade from a customer unhappy with his reservations. Calmly correcting the problem, the agent then leaned over the counter, put a colorful and official-looking tag on the man's lapel, telling him to show the tag to the flight attendant immediately after boarding.

Anticipating the tag was one entitling him to special privilege, the man did as instructed, only to learn the tag was reserved for children requiring special attention.

Some years ago, in another instance of passive resistance, a small girl—being punished for a minor misdemeanor—was compelled to eat dinner alone at a little table in a dining room corner. Others in the family ignored her until they heard her audibly saying grace over her food. Prayed the girl, "I thank Thee, Lord, for preparing a table before me in the presence of mine enemies."[168]

Finally, Mark Twain provides a classic case of passive resistance to anger. Strenuously objecting to her husband's going visiting without a collar or tie, Twain's wife once scolded him for visiting a particular neighbor in such diminished dress. Consequently, Twain wrapped up a collar and tie and sent them to his neighbor's with a note. "A little while ago I visited you without my collar and tie for about a half-hour. The missing articles are enclosed. Will you kindly gaze at them for thirty minutes and then return them to me?"[169]

In passively resisting others' anger, people may strike back more dramatically. During basic army training, for example, recruits' tempers were flaring after weeks of the sergeant's daily, and severe, tongue-lashings. When—out of the blue—a rock buzzed by the sergeant's head, the sergeant turned to a recruit known for his antics, asking him if he could prove he didn't throw that rock. Yes, replied the recruit, who continued by saying that if he'd thrown the rock, he would have used a bigger one, thrown it harder—and he wouldn't have missed.[170]

Very rarely, anger is warranted when other people or other

creatures are being mistreated. Such was the case with Ulysses S. Grant. Horace Porter, on Grant's staff in 1964, "reported that Grant lost his temper only once while he was with him. One day Grant and his staff, riding along a Virginia road, came upon a teamster who was beating his horse over the head. Grant was furious; he jumped out of the saddle, seized the man by the throat and shook him fiercely. And before he rode away he ordered him to be tied to a post for six hours."[171]

People who consistently become angry are merely noise-makers, doing nothing to improve a situation and everything to worsen it. Familiar with such people, Mark Twain observed, "Noise proves nothing. Often a hen who has merely laid an egg cackles as if she had laid an asteroid."[172]

Further commenting on noisemakers is Morris Mandel, who recalls, "When I was growing up, there was a teakettle in our house with a lid that did not fit tightly. When steam began to rise, that lid would shake and rattle and make a terrible noise. Of course the lid was doing no good. In fact, it was allowing the steam to escape, but it made quite a racket and impressed you as being very busy and very important.

"I've always remembered that teakettle, and whenever I see a person who makes a lot of noise without really accomplishing much, I say to myself, 'That one has a loose lid.'"[173]

One moral of this story is "Don't be a teakettle with a loose lid." Another moral, especially for those who have to endure the noise of "loose lids," is "If you run across a teakettle with a loose lid, just give it wide berth and don't help create more steam."

Giving advice for those who do have loose lids is Jacqueline Schiff, who observes, "The best remedy for a short temper is a long walk."[174] Having had such experience, Donald Culross Peattie agrees: "I have often started off on a walk in the state called mad—mad in the sense of sore-headed, or mad with tedium or confusion. I have set forth dull, null and even thoroughly discouraged. But I never came back in such a frame of mind, and I never met a human being whose humor was not the better for a walk. It is the sovereign remedy for the hot-tempered and the low-spirited."[175]

The Chinese add their own bent, emphasizing that temper control is a enviable character trait worth attaining. Illustrating this attitude toward emotional intactness is a Chinese proverb conveying, "The man who strikes first admits that his ideas have given out."[176] Even the man who verbally strikes first may be a man whose "ideas have given out." And such ill-advised responses may have similar ill-fated consequences. As Ambrose Bierce advises, "Speak when you are angry and you will make the best speech you will ever regret."[177]

Probably wincing over Bierce's reflection is George Washington, who once did "make a speech he regretted." However, Washington, who was known for his terrible temper (and had, as well, a wish to overcome it), once masterfully recovered from a temper bout. As the story goes, in 1775—in the midst of an election campaign for seats in the Virginia assembly— Colonel Washingtonn insulted a hot-tempered man named Payne, who consequently whacked him with his hickory stick. As soldiers rushed in to avenge Washington, he requested they not intervene. The next day, Washington sent a message to Payne, asking for an interview at a nearby tavern.

When Payne arrived, he expected Washington to demand an apology and to challenge him to a duel. Instead, Washington apologized, acknowledging that his own insult had sparked the conflict, and he asked to mend feelings through a handshake—a request that was honored.[178]

Bierce's observation also applies to a father who now would probably agree with him. This father was inadvertently aided by his five-year-old son in curbing his temper while trying to impose a point upon his stepdaughter. In telling his story, this father relates, "My stepdaughter and I were embroiled in an argument and I was yelling when out of the corner of my eye, I could see my son in the doorway. I heard him say, 'Sticks and stones will break my bones but words will never hurt me'—a phrase I had taught him after he had been taunted by some bullies at school. The phrase really didn't fit the situation but it was his only reference point. I was struck by the acute pain he must be feeling because he didn't know how to stop the fighting."

Of his immediate reaction, the father reports, "I stopped midpoint and made an about face. I apologized for my behavior and began, for the first time ever, to problem-solve with my daughter. It worked. We were able to resolve the situation and to walk away feeling good."

In this instance, the father intuitively sensed something John Graham advises: "A good rule for going through life is to keep the heart a little softer than the head."[179]

Giving invaluable advice for overcoming anger is an unknown author, who tells a Quaker story: "Once a Quaker, calm and poised after a volley of bitter abuse, was asked how he conquered his patience. He replied: 'Friend, I will tell thee. I was naturally as hot and violent as thou art. Yet, when I observed that men in passion always speak loud, I thought if I could control my voice, I should repress my passion. I have therefore made it a rule never to let my voice rise above a certain key. By careful observance of this rule I have, by the blessing of God, mastered my tongue.'"[180]

In another instance, Sister Elizabeth Kenny, the famed Irish-Australian nurse, was asked how she stayed so constantly cheerful no matter what the provocation. Was she just born calm and smiling? "Oh, no," related Kenny. "As a girl my temper often got out of bounds. But one day when I became angry at a friend over some trivial matter, my mother told me, 'Elizabeth, anyone who angers you conquers you.'"[181]

Former President Ronald Reagan, who was usually good-natured, has some advice for anger control. Although he occasionally lost his temper and threw pencils or his reading glasses across the room, he always recovered quickly. He once remarked, "I learned a long time ago that if you're going to throw a club in anger, throw it in front of you so you won't have to go back and pick it up."[182]

These people, probably intuitively knowing that anger bouts decimate people and relationships, admirably took steps to control or eliminate their tempers. Jean Paul Richter, an eighteenth-century novelist and humorist, gives persuasive reason for such action: "A man takes contradiction and advice much more easily than people think, only he will not bear it when violently given, even if it is well founded. Hearts are flowers; they remain open to the softly falling dew, but shut up in the violent downpour of rain."

Thus, to substitute anger with tenderness, gentleness, and soft words is to open others' hearts "to the softly falling dew" of our own hearts, thus enlarging the world's goodness.[183]

♥ ♥ ♥ ♥ ♥ ♥ ♥ ♥

CARING FORGIVES

Caring knows that love and wrath cannot exist in the same heart. Only when anger is absent can a heart experience caring or the deep abiding love it has for another person. Therefore, caring forgives for the sake of everyone involved. "Everyone must be given a chance, and another, and another, as many as the heart can endure," declares John D. MacDonald.[184] And, in this respect,

Ruth Graham advises, "Just pray for a tough hide and a tender heart."[185]

To forgive is to permanently shed hurt feelings and to put something away, observes Edward Crowther. "It means drawing a line under something and saying, 'Finished.' Whatever the horror, whatever the nightmare, it's over because it's forgiven. The courage to forgive is gigantic, and the courage to acknowledge the need to forgive or to be forgiven is perhaps even greater."[186]

Holding grudges is a bit like carrying cannonballs around with you, notes James Alexander Thom: "Once armies carried cannonballs with them, afraid they would meet the enemy somewhere and have nothing to shoot at it. In terms of specific gravity, grudges are about as heavy as cannonballs. But it makes little sense to carry them. Most likely, the 'enemy' is unaware of your enmity, and surely would be surprised to learn that you've been stalking him with a cannonball in your pocket.

"So examine your grudges," Thom urges. "Do what armies do when hostilities are over; unload the cannonballs and stack them on the courthouse lawn. Then marvel at how much easier it is to get around."[187]

One man who forgave was an Austrian Jew who, during World War II, was attached to a hospital receiving German wounded. Previously, he had been in the concentration camps of Dachau and Buchenwald, one time being hung by the wrists, and another, nearly dying of gangrene. For the gangrene, he received no medical attention because such attention was forbidden in the concentration camps. He also believed that the Germans had taken his elderly mother to Poland two years previously.

The following is an excerpt from a letter this Austrian Jew wrote in November 1944, as he tells, "in the solitude of a ward in which I was guarding wrecked members of the Herrenvolk. It is so strange a situation that I can hardly describe what I am feeling. Loneliness is perhaps the only word for it. These are men who set out to conquer the world, and they and their kind have done unspeakable things to me and my kind, and I am supposed to hate them with all my strength, and would be right to do so according to recognized standards of human behavior.

"But I cannot hate, or is it that in the face of suffering hatred is silent? So it happens that the guard is turned into a nurse, and if a man, from losing too much blood, goes out of his mind and stammers incoherently, I have to talk him to sleep again. And it sometimes happens that men try to hold my hand when I have helped them. That makes me feel lonely.

"Only a few lines. It is midnight, and I am going off duty after having had a busy time with that man who lost so much blood that he went crackers. He had an operation and blood transfusion, and I was the only one able to talk to him. In the end he obeyed my orders instantly with 'Jowahl, Herr Doktor!' Once he said, 'Sie sind so ein feiner Mensch' and then 'Sie sind zu mir wie ein Vater. ('You are a good man' and 'You are like a father to me'). What shall I make of that? I can only draw one conclusion, which is that I am a terribly bad soldier and I am somehow glad about it."

Later, the man wrote, "The man I wrote about has died. The doctors fought for his life as if he were a celebrity."[188]

Speaking of her own long-ago difficult and challenging trek to forgive, Madam Chiang Kai-shek—wife of Generalissimo Chiang Kai-shek of China—describes the religious training she received at home. Her mother, who lived very close to God, spent hours "praying and communing with Him," she relates. "Whenever we had problems we would go to her and ask her to pray for us. What is more, she would not be hurried with God. By experience we learned that she could pray us through any-thing.

"To mother," says Madam Chiang Kai-shek, "praying to God was not merely asking Him to bless her children. It meant waiting on Him. With her, religion was not a one-way street. She lived according to His precepts to do justly, to love mercy, and to walk in spirit humbly with Him. She often emphasized to me that we should not ask God to do something if it would hurt someone else."

During the Sino-Japanese War, Madam Chiang Kai-shek and her family lived in a deadly nightmare for seven years while bombers came in seemingly never-ending waves of death. Forced by communists to leave their homes, multitudes of Chinese retreated, by every conveyance imaginable, to "the remote, rock, cavernous region of Szechuan province." There they lived in underground shelters almost as much as they lived above ground. The dugouts were very damp, with stones sweating and water dripping from the cave sides, and the dead air was vile.

The planes bombed almost nightly, but moonlit nights were the worst—then marauding planes came in successive waves. Relates Madam Chiang Kai-shek, "Whole sections of the city were turned into shambles by a few bombs, as the houses were so closely grouped together than one incendiary bomb set a whole block afire. We knew days when it was impossible to obtain coffins, as the toll of death mounted."

Knowing the enemy was trying to break their morale through sheer physical exhaustion, the people were determined to persevere though terrible tiredness permeated every nerve and bone. And Madam Chiang Kai-shek continues, "No greater tribute could be paid to our sorely tried people than this: that in all their sufferings never did they complain against their leaders."

Through prayer, Madam Chiang Kai-shek had been on a spiritual trek for years, feeling progressively closer to God. However, under such horrific circumstances, she describes herself as losing faith. During the third year of desolation, she remembers saying her prayers and they meant nothing. She realized then she was slowly poisoning herself through her own resentment, hate, and bitterness.

"Have you ever tried to pray for an enemy?" she asks. "Have you ever tried to love someone who is ruining your life? I knew what the teaching of Christ was, but I could not follow it. I could not ask blessings for the aggressors no matter how I tried. Surely even God could not ask that of me."

Then one morning, during a period when the bombing was most intense, Madam Chiang Kai-shek recalled an experience that ultimately restored her spiritual insight. Weeks before, she and her husband had visited an orphanage for blind children. Only out of duty had she gone; although she hated the instinctive tendency in herself, she had always been repulsed by any abnormality, mental or physical. As she looked at the children's expressions, they "seemed unnervingly dull and apathetic," and she instinctively shrank from them. Much later, the morning she recalled the incident, a thought flashed through her mind that "just as suddenly made [her now] want to embrace these children: If I am so repulsed by physical blindness, how much more repulsed must God be by my spiritual blindness?"

Soon after Madam Chiang Kai-shek was able to spiritually "see" again: At morning devotionals, she recalls, "I asked myself whether I was not being spiritually blind deliberately when I hated. Then my ears seemed to echo my mother's voice, saying: *'Vengeance is mine, saith the Lord.'* . . . Thus I was enabled to unload my hate at the foot of the Cross. Now when I pray I can turn the enemy over to God, His mercy and His justice."

Never again, reports Madam Chiang Kai-shek, was she ever consumed with hate.[189]

In the preceding instances, those who refused to hate, even

under the most heinous of circumstances, avoided wasting their lives. To hate is to be consumed by an insidious and toxic energy that might well be converted to a protective resolution of the circumstances arousing our wrath. Or for our sakes, that same energy might be channeled to resolve and release overwhelming bitterness and hatred.

It is impossible to hold the two powerful emotions of love and hate at the same time. We must choose. "Whatever our reason, bitterness is never worth it," advises Ardis Whitman. "Much that is lovely in life is destroyed by the insults we cherish, the old wounds we keep open, the humiliations we hug to ourselves. . . . Shackled to our own woes, we cannot rejoice in someone else's good fortune. . . . Indeed bitterness can affect our lives as though it had poisoned the blood stream, the cells, the tissues."

Conversely, teaches Whitman, as surely as hatred and resentment destroy, love and compassion invigorate. They allow us to refill the pool of our lives with new dreams and new enthusiasms. And to extend ourselves to help others, in itself a healing process, is an action not possible when we are consumed by bitterness.[190] Expanding on this point, Harry Emerson Fosdick, in fact, observes that "good will, even toward the ungrateful and hostile, is an indispensable element of emotional health."[191]

Forgiving also is to follow Christ's commandment: "Love your enemies, bless them that curse you, and pray for them which despitefully use you and persecute you" (Matthew 5:44). To most of us, such triumph doesn't come easily. Forgiving is an acquired grace made habitual by practice. Our quest is to meet the ultimate challenge: Asked how many times an enemy should be forgiven, Jesus replied, "Until seventy times seven" (Matthew 18:22).

♥ ♥ ♥ ♥ ♥ ♥ ♥ ♥ ♥

CARING SEEKS FORGIVENESS

Caring does not ignore what it has done wrong. Instead, caring takes responsibility for its failures and weaknesses, not transmuting them into resentment or blame of others. Nor does caring ignore circumstances, perpetuated by itself, that have unintentionally hurt someone. An extreme example of the latter is the story of Reverend John Plummer, as told by Anne Gearan, a newspaper writer.

Plummer, in June 1972, ordered bombers to rain fire on the village of Trang Bang during the Vietnam War. The mission was a success and "South Vietnamese bombers smoothly dropped heavy explosives and napalm canisters on the village twenty-five miles west of Saigon."

After, by radio, the American adviser thanked Plummer and, pleased the mission had been a success, Plummer turned his mind to other matters. Plummer was pleased, that is, until he saw the newspaper picture of an anguished nine-year-old Vietnamese girl screaming and running naked toward the lens of a camera as she fled an American-led assault on her village that killed her two brothers. The picture of Kim, taken by Nick Ut, was to become a Pulitzer Prize winner and one the world would come to know. The picture itself, one of the most indelible images of the Vietnam War, ultimately helped turn American public opinion against the war. Says Gearan of the picture, "A brutal image from a brutal war, it is imprinted on the American psyche."

The young girl's name was Pham Thi Kim Phuc. And Plummer will never forget the moment he saw the picture, "the anguished face of a little boy about his son's age, and, behind him, Kim." The nalpam had incinerated Kim's clothes. Her eyes were "screwed shut, her mouth spread wide in terror and uncomprehending pain." And "her arms flap[ped] awkwardly, as though she [did] not recognize them as her own."

For Plummer, the shock was profound. He had been told there were no civilians in the village. He could hardly comprehend the picture, which "knocked [him] to his knees." After that, Plummer struggled for the next twenty-five years with his conscience, never able to disengage from unanticipated flashes of the famous picture. Now it was Plummer who was in agony. He drank. He divorced several times. He searched for, and finally found, God. But he rarely talked about his experience. And he never preached about it—until he experienced the following event.

It was in June 1997, while Plummer was absently watching television, that a photo of Kim flashed across the screen and an announcement "promised a story about the girl in the photo, grown now and with a child of her own." Again, Plummer was in shock. He had never known whether or not the young girl had lived. Watching the special, he "saw for the first time the thick white scars the splashing napalm left on Kim's neck, arm and back. He learned how she had seventeen operations but still lives with pain."

Later, learning a week before Veterans Day that Kim was making a rare appearance in Washington, D.C., ninety minutes from his home, Plummer knew he had to see her. "It took a long time, but I came to realize I would never have any peace unless I could talk to [Kim]," he said. "I had to look her in the eyes and say how sorry I am."

So that autumn, "Plummer went to Washington, to hear Kim address the Veterans Day observance at the black granite monument that bears the name of each American who never came home from war a generation ago. And, sitting in the audience, he heard something he never expected to hear: 'If I could talk face-to-face with the pilot who dropped the bombs,' Kim said, 'I would tell him we cannot change history but we should try to do good things for the present and for the future to promote peace.'

"Plummer gasped. It was as though she was talking directly to him."

He scribbled a note—"Kim, I am that man"—and asked a police officer to carry the note to her; thereafter he began pushing his way through the crowd toward Kim. Informed that Plummer was behind her, Kim took a few steps away, and then she stopped. "I couldn't move anymore. I stop and I turn, and he looked at me," she said.

"No news photographer took this picture," notes Gearan. "But in the lee of the Vietnam War Memorial, the soldier, now forty-nine, and the child, now thirty-three, embraced."

Says Plummer of the experience, "She just opened her arms to me. I fell into her arms sobbing. All I could say is, 'I'm so sorry. I'm just so sorry.'"

Kim "patted Plummer's back. 'It's all right,' she told him. 'I forgive, I forgive.'"[192]

❧ ❧ ❧ ❧ ❧ ❧ ❧ ❧

CARING TAKES COURAGE

At times, to care is to risk our own lives or limbs. When tragedy looms—and if, because of our own ethics, we truly care—then we are compelled to rise to the occasion, to focus our entire faculties on the trouble at hand, and to collect ourselves to respond. Realizing, perhaps, that only we can avert tragedy or an otherwise shattering experience, we act to prevent pain, injury, or death, with little thought of consequences.

Says Harry Emerson Fosdick of the heroics of such moments,

"In those who thus rise to the occasion in serious trouble and marshal their forces to deal with it, one factor commonly is present—they are thinking about someone else besides themselves. They are not egocentric. They meet disaster with courage and fortitude for someone else's sake. If they break down, someone else will break down; if they go to pieces, someone else will collapse; if they can 'take it,' someone else will stand the gaff too. In this view, one young American officer in the First World War wrote home: 'You can truly think of me as being cheerful all the time. Why otherwise? I have thirty-eight men, that if I duck when a shell comes, all thirty-eight duck, and if I smile, the smile goes down the line.'"[193]

Smiling under fire is a form of bravery that one author, Ovidio Michel Magri, particularly reveres, observing, "When cheerfulness is kept up on principle, against all odds, it is the finest form of courage."[194]

To experience courage is to experience fear. If bravery is a quality that knows no fear, General George S. Patton observes, "I have never seen a brave man. All men are frightened. The more intelligent they are, the more they are frightened. The courageous man is the man who forces himself, in spite of his fear, to carry on."[195]

In face of peril, fear is often the healthy or the wise reaction to a situation. And, reflects Arthur Gordon, "If we behave with courage, even when we are inwardly afraid; we often feel braver for having acted that way."

As the media reflects, people sometimes do not mobilize to protect others, whether because of fear, because of not valuing human life enough to intervene, or because they feel incapable of neutralizing the threatening circumstances. People may also feel overwhelmed or immobilized by the enormity of the impending situation, and thus cannot act.

Gordon describes witnessing, as a small boy, a near-tragedy at a beach when a woman panicked when she stepped off a sand-bar into the deep surf. "At least twenty adults in bathing suits watched, apparently paralyzed, until suddenly a young man ran up, plunged in fully clothed, and brought the woman out.

"As I described the episode later to my parents," recalls Gordon, "my admiration for the young man was matched by the contempt I felt for those who failed to act. 'She was drowning,' I cried, 'and they didn't even care.'

"My father looked at me thoughtfully. 'The world often seems divided between those who care and those who don't care enough,' he said. 'But don't judge too harshly. It takes courage to care greatly.'

"That phrase has stayed with me through the years, because it is profoundly true," relates Gordon. "It does take courage to care, to fling open your heart and react with sympathy or compassion or indignation or enthusiasm when it is easier—and sometimes safer—not to get involved. But people who take the risk, who deliberately discard the armor of indifference, make a tremendous discovery: the more things you care about, and the more intensely you care, the more alive you become."[196]

Joseph Brisson is a courageous man who cared enough about the life of a stranger that he willingly jeopardized his own. A boat captain, Brisson jumped into the Elizabeth River in Chesapeake, Vermont, and spent almost a half-hour in freezing water to rescue Carnell Taylor, a member of a paving crew. While working on an interstate bridge, Taylor was hit by a pickup trick that slid on the ice. Knocked over the railing, he fell seventy feet to the water below.

Brisson, who was on a barge below the bridge, jumped into the forty- to fifty-degree water after Taylor. Helping Taylor to get his face above water, he managed to slide a piece of wood under him to keep him afloat. But the current made it impossible for them to get to safety.

When the cold made him lose his grip, Brisson resorted to locking his legs around Taylor's waist. "I just held onto him with a good death lock," Brisson said. "I told him I was not going to let him go, that if he went, I was going with him. We were a unit."

Brisson and Taylor were finally rescued by crew members, who used a small boat to reach the men and pull them from the water.[197]

Brisson's actions went beyond a reflexive action to protect life. During the few minutes he spent with a stranger, he consciously committed his own fate to that of Taylor's—together they would survive, or, as he assured Taylor, they would go down together. In that respect, Brisson's caring was larger than his own life or the danger in which he placed himself. His caring reflected a broader commitment to all mankind and an inextricable understanding of the preciousness of human life.

In many instances it is people like Brisson, spontaneously rising to the moment's crisis, who are this world's heroes. In fact, says Admiral "Bull" Halsey, in a famous quote on heroes, "There are no great men, only great challenges that ordinary men are forced by circumstances to meet."[198] Heroes are thus not born, but made; and they are often drawn from among the common man. Often it is the challenge of circumstances that brings out man's inherent determination to succeed and to contribute to the good of mankind.

"When a man is determined, what can stop him?" points out Ted W. Engstrom. "Cripple him, and you have a Sir Walter Scott. Lock him in a prison cell, and you have a John Bunyan. Bury him in the snows of Valley Forge, and you have a George Washington. Raise him in abject poverty, and you have an Abraham Lincoln.

. . . Make him second fiddle in an obscure South African orchestra and you have a Toscanini. The hardships of life are sent not
by an unkind destiny to crush, but to challenge."[199]

♥ ♥ ♥ ♥ ♥ ♥ ♥ ♥ ♥

CARING PERSEVERES

Caring is solid and trustworthy and keeps the faith, even over
decades of generations and difficult circumstances. Illustrating is
a story newspaper columnist Karen McCowan tells of University
of Oregon law professor Mary Wood, who helped her family
transform her beloved grandfather's most bittersweet memory
into healing action.

Wood recounts, as a child, sitting with her late grandfather
in his study, listening as he told stories of the Nez Perce and sang
songs he learned during two boyhood summers in the teepee of
Chief Joseph. Then, often tearful, C. E. S. "Erskine" Wood Jr.
would share his relentless grief, a bitterness that soured the sweet
and blighted those treasured moments.

Wood's great-grandfather, Lt. C. E. S. Wood, was the official
diarist for the Nez Perce campaign, and he and Chief Joseph
were close friends. During this period, "the U.S. Army seized the
tribal homeland in the Wallowa Valley, then pursued Joseph and
his band for more than one thousand miles as they attempted to
flee to freedom.

"It was he who took down Joseph's heartbroken and heartbreaking words at Bear Claw: 'Hear me, my chiefs. I am tired.
My heart is sick and sad. From where the sun now stands, I will
fight no more forever.'

"It was he, assigned the care and custody of Joseph, who
became captivated by the courage and character of his prisoner.
He left the Army, became a lawyer and worked for the return of

the Wallowa homeland to Joseph and his people, exiled to Oklahoma. The effort failed, but Congress agreed to let the Nez Perce return to the Northwest. Joseph and his remaining family (he lost four sons in the war) settled on the Colville Reservation at Nespelem, Washington.

"There Joseph, who had remained friends with Lt. Wood, took his son, Erskine Wood—into his own family to experience Nez Perce life. The boy kept a diary of his two summers-into-fall at Nespelem, eventually to be published at age eighty. 'Chief Joseph took me into his teepee and into his heart and treated me as a son,' he wrote. 'Truthfully, knowing him was the high spot of my entire life.'

"Sadly, it also occasioned the lowest point of his one hundred four years. At what would be their final parting, the fourteen-year-old Erskine and Joseph sat on their horses on a bluff over-looking the Columbia River. The boy conveyed a message from Lt. Wood, asking 'if there was anything my father could do for (Joseph)' as a show of gratitude. Joseph replied he would like 'a good stallion to improve the breed of his pony herd.'"

An anguished Erskine Wood later wrote, "I looked on Joseph as such a great man, a noble chief driven out of his ancestral home. I revered him so, that I thought his request for a stallion was too puny—was beneath him. I shook my head and said, 'No, that was not what my father meant.'"

Thus, Wood never informed his father of Chief Joseph's request and both died without Wood's father bestowing the wished-for gift. Speaking of her grandfather's inaction, Mary Wood defines it "as a tragic error of omission by a boy too young to grasp the significance of a seemingly simple gift."

"The weight of Erskine Wood's regret fell on the shoulders of his descendants," relates McCowan. "When the story of the ungiven gift became the capstone story in 'The West' (on the

PBS Series), five branches of Lt. Wood's family were moved to act."

Leading the group to raise money for a stallion, Mary Wood and Katherine Livingston of Camp Sherman considered over one hundred horses before selecting Zip's Wild Man, a black Appaloosa with white markings.

The group also raised twenty-six thousand dollars to fund a program focused on enabling Nez Perce youth to acquire skills in horsemanship and interest in cultural traditions. And "in a ceremony July 27, 1997, descendants of Lt. Wood gathered with descendants of Chief Joseph near Wallowa Lake and presented the spirited young stallion to Soy Redthunder, Joseph's oldest living descendant at Nespelem, a man who still practices the Seven Drums religion of his great-grandfather."

In bestowing the gift, the Wood family felt bound to honor Chief Joseph's exact request, not wishing to again err in underestimating a horse's value in native culture. From Mary Wood's perspective, the stallion not only fulfills words from the past, but "begins a line of horses which carry the words, their symbolism and the power of the gift into the future."

In a ceremony including representatives of all branches of the Nez Perce people, the stallion was graciously received. "'If a man's word is good after one hundred four years, surely you have to have hope,' Redthunder said as he accepted the gift."

Finishes McCowan, "And now the regret that had lain so heavily on Wood's shoulders had been replaced by her own gift from the Nez Perce: a Chief Joseph blanket, inscribed with the eloquent words that would have been lost to history, had not her great-grandfather taken them down. Consummating his gift, she said, 'has turned into the greatest joy of my life.'"[200]

Thus, caring kept the faith, prevailing in the form of dedicated people who fulfilled an ancestor's consuming desire to grant a friend's century-old wish. Apropos to the unique circumstances of bestowing such a long-belated gift are the words of Gurdjieff: "If you help others, you will be helped, perhaps tomorrow, perhaps in one hundred years, but you will be helped. Nature must pay off the debt. . . . It is a mathematical law and all life is mathematics."[201]

❤ ❤ ❤ ❤ ❤ ❤ ❤ ❤

CARING MENTORS

"The great use of life is to spend it for something that will outlast it," tells William James.[202] And there is nothing of greater consequence than mentoring this world's youth, for the positive influences on youth will impact generations to come, perhaps into perpetuity. Says Jacob M. Braude of the work to be done, "Whoever you are, there is some younger person who thinks you are perfect. There is some work that will never be done if you don't do it. There is someone who would miss you if you were gone. There is a place that you alone can fill."[203]

Actor Sidney Poitier knows what James means, for in his youth, someone invested in him in a manner that had lifelong effect. Fresh from the Bahamas, Sidney Poitier was employed as a dishwasher in a New York restaurant and his last chore of the day was to wash the dishes of the waiters, who had dinner at eleven o'clock. Waiting for the waiters to finishing eating, Poitier would laboriously read the day's newspaper, trying to improve his elementary reading skill. One night, Poitier asked a waiter— an elderly Jewish man—to interpret the meaning of a word, and when the man perceived Poitier's effort to improve his reading, he nightly committed himself to coaching him.

In his autobiography, *This Life*, Poitier comments, "This soft-spoken, natural teacher, with thick bifocals, bushy eyebrows and

silver-white hair, sat with me night after night in the twilight of
his years and gave me a little piece of himself. . . . I don't know if
he's alive or dead now . . . but a bit of him is in everything I
do."[204]

Mentoring Poitier was an elder who realized—by virtue of
his own maturity—he had a gift to offer Poitier. "No matter how
old you get you should still have something to offer the universe," advises Edward Fischer, author of *Life in the Afternoon*.
Fischer views the elderly as sharing a common vocation—"*All
need to give courage to those who are still on the way* . . . a model to those
who will some day face the inconveniences of accumulated
years."[205]

Also speaking of mentoring is naturalist Ronald Rood, who
credits Thornton Burgess with influencing his choice of career.
Rood recalls that as a child he took a walk with his father while
they were waiting for Thanksgiving dinner. The weather had
been warm the day before but had cooled during the night.

He writes, "As we kicked our way through the leaves at the
edge of the road, I uncovered . . . a baby wood turtle—stiff and
cold, but still alive." At this, he slipped the turtle in his pocket to
show his mother. Rood's father subsequently suggested he write
naturalist Thornton Burgess to ask "what faulty time schedule
had brought a little turtle out to freeze."

Rood was surprised several weeks later to get a reply from
Burgess. And, in the letter, he says, "the biographer of Peter
Cottontail assured me that the turtle had probably been wandering on the warm road the previous afternoon and had stayed
too long before trying to find shelter. 'If you hadn't come along
to rescue him,' Burgess wrote, 'the turtle surely would have perished.'"

Further, writes Rood, "the two-page letter, typed single-
spaced, was signed: 'Your friend, Thornton Burgess.' There and

then I decided that if one of the attributes of a naturalist was to take such pains with the query of a seven-year-old boy, I'd be a naturalist, too. I've never faltered in that resolve—although the turtle, alas, died from exposure a few days later."[206]

In the mid-1800s, an unsung Indiana schoolmaster patiently helped a young man develop talents ultimately enabling him to become a favorite American poet. Writes W. G. Montgomery of his story, "This educator took a young backwoods ruffian, leader of what today would be considered a gang of juvenile delinquents, and helped him develop the flickering spark of poetry that burned within him." James Whitcomb Riley—the fortunate boy—ultimate became well-known for his poems about children, including "Little Orfant Annie."

Years afterward, by then a celebrated poet, Riley assumed his own mentorship when a young black elevator man—the son of escaped slaves—sought him out. Although speaking to Riley about poems he had written, he had no samples to show because his mother burned every poem he wrote. Encouraged to bring his next poem to Riley, the boy did—and Riley mentored Paul Laurence Dunbar, another eminent American poet.[207]

Pablo Casals, acting as a mentor, was partially responsible in 1962 for violinist Pinchas Zukerman's coming to the United States to study music at the Juilliard School. Of as defining moment with Casals, Zukerman tells:

"To me he was a god. I'll never forget one time when Eugène Istomin took me to see 'the old man'—to play for him two years after I'd first done so. I was going through one of those periods when I was more interested in pool balls than in practicing. I played terribly, and I could sense Casals hated it. When I finished, all he said was, 'Come with me.' He took me by the hand to his room, alone, got out his cello and gave me a two-hour lesson on the G-major scale. Then he played the . . . *Sarabande*, with his pipe in his mouth. I'll never forget that. It was one of the greatest things I've ever experienced—and a turning point in my becoming serious about music."[208]

Of the teaching inherent in the mentoring role, Casals observes, "To be a teacher is to have a great responsibility. The teacher helps shape and give direction to the lives of other human beings. What is more important, graver, than that? Children and young people are our greatest treasure; when we think of them we think of the future of the world."[209]

❤ ❤ ❤ ❤ ❤ ❤ ❤ ❤

CARING VALIDATES

Caring takes advantage of many life opportunities to validate the worth of other human beings, knowing of the unalterable thirst of all others to know they are valued beyond measure—despite their frailties. A powerful and heartrending example of such validation is contained in *Les Miserables*, a 1892 novel written by the French novelist Victor Hugo. Hugo's story opens just as Jean Valjean, the novel's main character, has been released from the galleys—a fate to which he had been sentenced nineteen years earlier for trying to steal a loaf of bread to feed his sister and her starving children. In the first days of his release, Valjean's yellow passport, identifying him as an ex-convict, closes all doors to him, and, cold and hungry, he is rejected by all.

That is, until he is advised to knock on the door of the bishop. For the first time since his release, a desperate Jean Valjean honestly reveals his past, announcing to the bishop he is a convict and telling his story in a tone and demeanor revealing he is steadily braced for another rejection. However, that rejection is not forthcoming. Instead, the bishop treats Valjean as a special guest and immediately gives him food, offers him lodging without fee, and serves him with a silver place setting, even adding silver candlesticks to the table for better lighting. Furthermore, the bishop keeps calling Valjean "monsieur."

An incredulous Valjean is absolutely overcome by the welcome and his entitlement, for, as says Hugo, "Monsieur to a convict is a glass of water to a man dying of thirst at sea. Ignominy thirsts for respect." "Monsieur Cure," says Valjean with amazement, "you are good; you don't despise me. You take me into your house; you light your candles for me, and I hav'n't hid from you where I come from, and how miserable I am."

Gently touching Valjean's hand, the bishop responds, "You need not tell me who you are. This is not my house; it is the house of Christ. It does not ask any comer whether he has a name, but whether he has an affliction. You are suffering; you are hungry and thirsty; be welcome. And do not thank me; do not tell me that I take you into my house. This is the home of no man, except him who needs an asylum. I tell you, who are a traveler, that you are more at home than I; whatever is here is yours. What need have I to know your name? Besides, before you told me, I knew it."

"Really? You knew my name?" questions an astonished Valjean.

"Yes," answers the bishop, "your name is my brother."

Manifesting absolute trust for Valjean, the bishop shows him to his room, which is next to his own, and he leaves the door to his own bedroom unlocked. And for the first time in nineteen years, Valjean sleeps on a bed. But his peace is not to linger, for Valjean wakes in the middle of the night, uncomfortable in his comfortable surroundings; and, after much agonizing and wavering, he justifies in his mind, and acts upon, the taking of a basket of silver from a cupboard in the bishop's bedroom. Although his eyes are closed, the bishop is not asleep; nevertheless, he makes no move to intercede.

In the morning, informed by Madame Magloire, his sister, that the silver basket has been stolen, the bishop does not react. Instead, after a moment's silence, he asks mildly, "Now first, did this silver belong to us?" When his sister does not answer immediately, the bishop continues, "Madame Magloire, I have for a long time wrongfully withheld this silver; it belonged to the poor. Who was this man? A poor man evidently."

Then comes a knock at the door and thereafter enters a brigadier of gendarmes with three other men, as well as a sullen and downcast Jean Valjean. Before the brigadier can say anything, the bishop approaches Valjean and welcomes him. Then, addressing Valjean, the bishop questions, "I gave you the candlesticks also, which are silver like the rest, and would bring two hundred francs. Why did you not take them with your plates?"

At that, "Jean Valjean opened his eyes and looked at the bishop with an expression which no human tongue could describe," for he was being fairly accused by the brigadier of stealing the silver. It was simply a mistake, declared the bishop, for he had given the silver to Valjean; and, at that, he dismissed the gendarmes. Then approaching Valjean, who was close to fainting, the bishop said in a low voice, "Forget not, never forget that you have promised me to use this silver to become an honest man."

Having no recollection of this promise, Jean Valjean "stood confounded." The bishop, who had stressed these words as he uttered them, continued solemnly, "Jean Valjean, my brother: you belong no longer to evil, but to good. It is your soul that I am buying for you. I withdraw it from dark thoughts and from the spirit of perdition, and I give it to God!"[210]

And thus it was, through the bishop's actions, that Valjean

experienced—for the first time in his sad, miserable life—complete and unerring validation of body and soul.

❤ ❤ ❤ ❤ ❤ ❤ ❤ ❤

CARING EMANATES RESPECT

In 1962, Alexander Tvardovsky, the editor-in-chief of the Russian literary magazine *Novy Mir*, took some manuscripts home to read in bed. Unimpressed with what he was reading, one by one he tossed the manuscripts aside, until he came to the manuscript of Alexander Solzhenitsyn's now-classic novel, *One Day in the Life of Ivan Denisovich*, and read ten lines.

Describing his profound experience in interconnecting at that moment with the overwhelming message of the novel, and the impassioned writing and keen insight of its author, Tvardovsky later told a friend, "Suddenly I felt that I couldn't read it like this. I had to do something appropriate to the occasion. So I got up. I put on my best black suit, a white shirt with a starched collar, a tie and my good shoes. Then I sat at my desk and read a new classic."[211]

In his private but momentous gesture, Tvardovsky granted Solzhenitsyn consummate respect for the invaluable work and insight he gifted the world.

Respect is manifested in myriad ways, embodied especially in disregard of such socioeconomic factors as age, gender, or social status. Ralph Nader, for example, showed utter respect for women in an age in which "sexual discrimination" or "sexual harassment" were unknown cultural terms and women were demeaned in multitudinous ways simply because of gender. Says Charles McCarry, who wrote of Nader in the early 1970s, "Nader treats women, even beautiful women, exactly as he treats men—without condescension, and in a language directed exclusively to the mind. . . . Nothing in his manner draws attention to the fact of sexual difference." Of his inattention to such sexual differentiation, a young woman relates, "He'd never call you 'dear' or 'honey' or even 'Miss.' I always thought he was silently calling me 'Citizen.'"[212]

Respect also occurs as one person affirms another's intrinsic value. Frederick Collins sorts people into two categories—those who affirm and those who don't—observing, "There are two types of people—those who come into a room and say, 'Well, here I am!,' and those who come in and say, 'Ah, there you are.'"[213]

With respect to the latter category, Ralph Waldo Emerson possessed the ability to affirm—a propensity recognized by a scrubwoman who always attended his lectures. When asked if she understood Emerson's presentations, she replied she did not. But, she added, "I like to go and see him stand up there and look as though he thought everyone was as good as he."[214]

As well, respect is revealed in the dignity and reverence with which one imbues the human spirit. Nadia Boulanger, for example, speaks of Madame Duval, an eighty-year-old woman who cleaned the floor in her workplace. Boulanger—who regarded this cleaning woman with profound respect and reverence—tells of a day Madame Duval knocked at her door. When greeted by Boulanger, Madame Duval said to her, "Mademoiselle, I know you don't like to be disturbed, but the floor, come and see it; it shines!"

"In my mind Stravinsky and Madame Duval will appear before the Lord for the same reason," observes Boulanger. "Each has done what he does with all his consciousness." When Boulanger told the same to Stravinsky, who knew Madame Duval, Stravinsky said, "How you flatter me, for when I do something, I have something to gain. . . . But *she*, she has only the work to be done well."[215]

Respect is also conveyed through the dimension of choices. Because of another engagement, for example, author James Michener declined an invitation to attend a White House ceremony and to dine with a United States president. The conflicting engagement was an invitation to speak briefly at a dinner honoring a high school teacher he credited with teaching him vital writing skills. In a note to the White House, Michener explained the reason for his decline: "I know you will not miss me at your dinner, but she might at hers."

In his gracious reply to Michener, President Eisenhower, incidentally, joined Michener in according the teacher supreme respect, writing, "In a lifetime a man can live under fifteen or sixteen presidents, but a really fine teacher comes into his life but rarely."[216]

Respect may also be extended to animals, as in an instance involving George Schaller, one of America's most distinguished naturalists. Interviewing Schaller, journalist Michael Ryan tells of how, even after forty-five years in the field, Schaller "retains his sense of wonder at the animals he studies. His eyes lit up in almost childlike awe when he told me about an encounter with one of the world's most beautiful and most endangered animals. 'I was studying pandas one day,' he said. 'I was sitting on the ground and one female panda came walking through the bamboo. All you could see was her big white head, shining like a moon through the dusky bamboo. She just plopped down right next to me and fell asleep.

"'That kind of acceptance by an animal is a wonderful feeling,' Schaller added. 'If we treated all animals with respect, they would react to us like that, instead of instantly fleeing.'"[217]

Finally, respect is manifested by persons who view themselves as equals—and as only equals—to every other human being on earth and thus act accordingly. Carl Sandburg decries, in fact, people who assess themselves as being of more value than others. In his lifetime, Sandburg abhorred the word "exclusive," as the word applied to membership in exclusive clubs or living in elite communities. Exclusivity suggested superiority, Sandburg judged, which implied, in turn, that others were deemed unworthy of association and friendship.[218]

Among those whose lives reflected the concept of "absolute equality" was Abraham Lincoln. During Lincoln's visit to Richmond after the city had been evacuated by Confederate troops, an elderly black man approached him and, removing his hat, bowed and said, "May de good Lord bless you, President Linkum." Expressing ultimate respect, the President took off his own hat and bowed silently in return.[219]

Also illustrating President Lincoln's unequivocal sentiments regarding equality is his address to an Indiana regiment on March 17, 1865, in which he stated, "I have always thought that all men should be free; but if any should be slaves, it should be first those who desire it for themselves, and secondly those who desire it for others. Whenever I hear anyone arguing for slavery, I feel a strong impulse to see it tried on him personally."[220]

As with Lincoln, Great Britain's General William Booth, the founder of the Salvation Army, was a man who emanated ultimate respect toward all. Never losing the common touch, just before his death General Booth said of those less fortunate than himself, "While women weep as they do now, I'll fight; while little children go hungry as they do now, I'll fight; while men go to prison, in and out, in and out, I'll fight; while there yet remains one dark soul without the light of God, I'll fight—I'll fight to the very end."

Richard Collier writes of Booth that in his quest to address the ills of man, "during a sixty-year ministry Booth traveled five million miles, delivered almost sixty thousand sermons, drew sixteen thousand officers to follow his flag in fifty-eight countries, and preached the gospel in thirty-four languages." In his passing, he was mourned everywhere. At a three-day lying-in-state, one hundred fifty thousand persons filed past his casket, and on the day of his funeral, city offices were closed and the flags of all nations dipped to salute him. Around his grave lay wreaths from the king and queen and from titled heads of state throughout the world.

During the viewing, among those mingling with the elite who knelt beside Booth's casket to rededicate themselves to God and to the Army were others he had served—"thieves, tramps, harlots, the lost and outcast, [all] to whom Booth had given his heart."

Of Booth's funeral service, which forty thousand people attended, Collier writes, "Unknown to most, royalty was there, too. Far to the rear of the hall, almost unrecognized, sat Britain's Queen Mary, a staunch admirer of Booth. . . . She had elected to come at the last moment without warning.

"Beside the Queen on the aisle seat was a shabby, but neatly-dressed woman. Shyly, she confided her secret to the Queen: once she had been a prostitute and only the Salvationists had saved her from death. Years later, at a meeting, General Booth heard her story and told her gently: 'My girl, when you get to heaven, you'll have a place of honour because Mary Magdalene will give you one of the best places.'"

Continuing to confide, the woman told the Queen she had placed flowers on Booth's casket. She had thus "come early to claim an aisle seat, guessing that the casket would pass within feet of her—and as it did she unobtrusively placed the flowers on the glass lid." As the Queen was to later note, all through the service these flowers—three faded red carnations—were the only ones on the casket.

"During the service, the woman turned and, simply but eloquently, spoke to the Queen. The Queen, deeply moved by her words, heard what could easily stand as William Booth's epitaph: 'He cared for the likes of us.'"[221]

♥ ♥ ♥ ♥ ♥ ♥ ♥ ♥ ♥

CARING ENDOWS THE GIFT OF LIFE

It was in 1991, on a day when he went fishing, that Frank Rembert will never forget. Suffering from chronic renal failure, and having waited two years for a kidney transplant, Rembert—an airport sky cap—had little hope of living. Responding to his wife's urgings, a depressed Rembert went fishing at the Hermosa Beach pier near Los Angeles.

While fishing, Rembert met Rick Wilson, a machinist and apartment-building administrator, who often walked and fished the pier. The two connected when Wilson offered an adhesive bandage to Rembert when he cut his finger baiting a hook. The men spent the afternoon talking, and in the midst of sharing stories about their families, careers, and dreams, Rembert told of his need of a transplant. After that, the two men packed their tackle boxes, traded phone numbers, and left the pier.

Two days later, Rembert received a call from Wilson—Wilson wanted to give him one of his own kidneys. Remembers Wilson: "I couldn't imagine him dying when all it took was to get a kidney in him. And I had one to give." As it happened, both blood and tissue type matched, and the transplant was performed.

Michael Quintanilla—a newspaper reporter who five years later wrote of these two men—tells that they often fish together

and speak to church groups about the importance of organ donations. Of his gift, Rembert says gratefully, "I not only got a kidney. I got a friend for life."[222]

In the case of Wilson and Rembert, a living person gave the
gift of life to another living person. To give a kidney while
alive—to a near stranger—is an exception, but a wonderful
exception. Also a wonderful exception is the Associated Press
story of an Arab toddler who received the heart of a Jewish child
killed by a car. As the two mothers wept in each other's arms,
Braha Kaveh, whose eight-year-old son Yuval was killed while
riding his bike, said, "Do you know what heart she received? she
received an angel's heart—you don't know what a heart this boy
had."

Embracing Kaveh was Aani Aljaroushi, whose three-year-old
daughter Rim was listed in good condition three days after the
transplant. "'I know that it's very hard, but I thank you,' she said
through her own tears.

"The story struck a powerful cord in a country where Arabs
and Jews are most often depicted in bitter strife. It was a medical
milestone as well," notes the Associated Press. Assuming Rim sur-
vives, and doctors give her an excellent prognosis, this endeavor
will represent Israel's first successful pediatric heart transplant.

"Organ transplantation is a complicated subject in Israel," the
Associated Press continues. "Both Orthodox Jews and tradition-
alist Muslims believe that bodies should be preserved intact after
death and transplants are thus taboo for many." Thus, the
Kavehs, who also donated Yuval's organs to two other people,
had made a very difficult decision.

Sizan Aljaroushi, Rim's father, said he hoped the Kavehs
would become a part of Rim's life: "I want the Kaveh family to
visit Rim, and I want her to visit them because they gave part of
their son—a very, very precious part, the heart."[223]

In recent years, numerous courageous family members have given kidneys to others of their family or extended family—parents to children, siblings to siblings, an aunt or uncle to a relative, and the like. Often, too, persons have stated their wishes to relatives, signed donor cards, made living wills, or have requested special tags put on their driver's licenses to ensure that at death their own organs will perpetuate the life—or the quality of life—of another person.

Many times, family members of deceased loved ones have also faced an excruciating decision relative to donation. To some, to have one's body, or the body of a deceased loved one, disturbed to remove any tissue or organ may seem revolting or almost sacrilegious. And such was the case of Linda Rivers, who describes her own struggle with this issue.

Rivers will never forget the warm summer day in 1965 when her mother—at age thirty-six—suddenly died of an unexplained illness. Nor will she forget the police officer stopping at the home to ask her father's permission to use her mother's aorta valve and the corneas from her eyes. Says Rivers, "I was absolutely stunned. The doctors want to dissect Mom and give her away to other people! I thought as I ran into the house in tears.

"At fourteen, I just could not understand why anyone would take apart a person I loved. To top it off, my father told him, 'Yes.'" To this, Rivers screamed at her father, "My mom came into this world in one piece and that is how she should go out." Her father put his arm around her, telling her that the greatest gift you can give to others is a part of yourself. He also said that he and Rivers's mother had long ago decided to become organ donors.

Although Rivers was not to know this for years, her father's lesson that day was to play a primary role in her future life. Years passed, and Linda Rivers herself married and had a family of her own. In 1980, her father became seriously ill with emphysema and moved in with Rivers's family. Six years later—after many talks between father and daughter about life and death—Linda's father died.

Her father had cheerfully told her that he wanted to be an organ donor, giving especially his eyes. "Sight is one of the greatest gifts a person can give," he said. Pointing to Wendy, his own granddaughter, who could so imaginatively draw horses, and who had won award after award for her talent, he asked, Wouldn't it be wonderful if another child—an unsighted child— could see and draw like Wendy? He pointed to the pride Rivers would feel in knowing her father's eyes had made that possible.

So when, on April 11, 1996, Linda's father died, she carried out his wishes to donate his eyes. At the time, Wendy told her, "Mom, I'm so proud of what you did for Grandpa." When questioned, Wendy went on to explain, "You bet! Have you ever thought what it would be like not to see? When I die, I want my eyes donated like Grandpa."

Says Rivers, "What I couldn't know that day, as I held Wendy in my arms, was that only two weeks later I would once again be signing papers for the donor program. . . . My lovely, talented Wendy was killed when a truck hit her and the horse she was riding along the roadside. As I signed the papers, her words echoed over and over: Have you ever thought what it would be like not to see?"

Three weeks later, Rivers received a letter sent to both her and her husband from the Oregon Lions Eye Bank, which read, "We want you to know that the corneal transplantation was successful, and now two people who were blind have regained their sight. They represent a living memorial to your daughter—a person who cared enough about life to share its beauties."

Says Rivers of her daughter's future, "If somewhere across these states, a recipient discovers a new love for horses and sits down to sketch one, I think I know who the donor was."[224]

❤ ❤ ❤ ❤ ❤ ❤ ❤ ❤ ❤

CARING EMBRACES DIFFERENCES

"We all live under the same sky, but we don't have the same horizon," Konrad Adenauer has said.[225]

Perhaps the core challenge we human beings face with regard to goodness is that of dealing effectively with our respective differences—of living under the same sky but understanding that none of us has the same horizon or sees the world through the same lenses.

John Steinbeck speaks to the pressing need to examine our perspectives in general, for we tend to perceive everything in our own peculiar way. "It occurs to me to wonder and to ask how much I see or am capable of seeing," Steinbeck says, addressing his own vulnerability as a human being—a vulnerability to default to the familiar and not to perceive a larger picture. And, in recognizing his own vulnerability, he warns that people often reject ideas without a hearing simply because their experience pattern can bring up no recognition parallel.[226]

Our difficulty in accurately perceiving the world also extends to people: "It is very difficult to know people," relates W. Somerset Maugham. "For men and women are not only themselves, they are also the region in which they were born, the city apartment or the farm in which they learned to walk, the games they played as children, the old wives' tales they overheard, the food they ate, the schools they attended, the sports they followed, the poets they read, and the God they believed in. . . . You can know them only if you are them."[227]

And yet, Shelby Steele takes an opposite view, wondering why, when people share so many things in common, they have so much trouble understanding each other: "We have all grown up on the same sitcoms, eaten the same fast food and laughed at the same jokes," he says. "We have practiced the same religions, lived under the same political system, read the same books and worked in the same marketplace. We have the same dreams and aspirations, as well as fears and doubts for ourselves and for our children.

"How, then" Steele questions, "can our differences be so overwhelming?"[228]

And what is the answer? Possibly that, as human beings, we encounter the barrier of differences because we view them from the perspective of a black-and-white, rather than gray, framework. Thus, to perceive a difference is often to disparage that difference, or to conclude that we possess the "true" or "right" view of the world. In imposing our view, we judge others harshly because they don't see our truth. Tom Knight muses on this point:

"Isn't it funny, when the other fellow takes a long time to do something, he's slow. When I take a long time to do something, I'm thorough. When the other fellow doesn't do it, he's lazy. When I don't do it, I'm busy. When the other fellow does it without being told, he's overstepping his bounds. When I go ahead and do it without being told, that's initiative. When the other fellow states his opinion strongly, he's bullheaded. When I state my opinion strongly, I'm firm. When the other fellow overlooks a few rules of etiquette, he's rude. When I skip a few rules of etiquette, I'm doing my own thing."[229]

Embracing differences involves leaving ourselves open— without judgment—to optimum information regarding other people. "Judge only a bee by the first impression," Arnold Glasow cautions, speaking to the possibility that our perceptions will change, as we glean more information, often for the better. Eighteenth-century writer Samuel Johnson also alludes to the folly of judging men as he reveals, "As I know more of mankind I expect less of them and am ready to call a man a good man upon easier terms than I was formerly."[230]

To embrace differences, we must regard our own perspective as simply that—a perspective we have a right to hold, but not to impose. To this point, Eric Hoffer reflects, "We usually see only the things we are looking for—so much so that we sometimes see them where they are not."[231]

Ultimately, our challenge is to respect diversity yet affirm commonality, accepting all people as invaluable and thus worthy of total investment. The popular "Peanuts" comic strip, created by Charles M. Schulz and known worldwide, has served as a significant medium in building bridges between peoples. This was brought to Schulz's attention as he was traveling in Austria. Schulz had with him some little pins—representing characters in the strip—to give as mementos. And, while visiting the cemetery in Vienna where Beethoven is buried, he recalls placing a Snoopy at his grave site.

As Schulz did so, a small Austrian girl watching him inquired in words he didn't understand: *"Vas der Schroeder?"* Realizing Schulz didn't speak German, the girl's mother interpreted for her daughter: "She is asking why you place Snoopy there rather than Schroeder."

"'Peanuts' fans know of Schroeder's deep affection for Beethoven," tells Schulz. So Schulz excused himself, returning from his car with a Schroeder pin. As he placed the pin on Beethoven's grave, both mother and daughter smiled. At this, Schulz was overcome by emotion, suddenly recognizing, as he writes, "the power and universality of these characters" and that—in a peculiar way—"Schroeder was finally paying his respects to his hero."[232]

In another instance, writer David Holmstrom interviewed Schulz regarding his "Peanuts" cartoon, subsequently affirming that the cartoon strip acts as a leveler and organizer in human relationships. And he underscores, "The Charlie Brown, Snoopy, Lucy and Schroeder we know and love are real. . . . They are relatives and we are their family."[233]

Illustrating the acceptance of differences is a story Anne Cole writes. Called "The Wedge of Love," the story describes Anne's struggle for years with a back injury requiring a spinal fusion and of her relationship with her nurse, Helen, who had a "love for every single one of God's children, a love of almost tangible intensity."

Anne can't remember the first time she saw Helen—she was enveloped in her problems—and she had resisted every earlier attempt Helen had made to win her over. But she does remember Helen's hands preparing her for her third surgery, and at five that evening the same hands gently brushing damp hair from her eyes. Beside her husband, she saw Helen—whose name she didn't know—but she did know the name for the expression in her eyes. "The name was love."

When Anne's surgeon required she obtain a special nurse during her hospital recovery, Anne and her husband's first thought was "Money." They could not afford a nurse. "I'll stay," said Helen, who volunteered to alternate her job supporting her mother and a four-year-old son with unpaid special duty. During this time, Helen and Anne endured Anne's moments of emotional and physical pain, together sharing and conquering them. Relates Anne, "Her presence and understanding robbed the pain-filled nights of their horror. She was always there. . . . I gave her nothing. She gave me back a desire to live."

But one morning Anne comprehended the terrible reality: as it had twice before, her back was failing to heal. When Helen, entering the room, heard Anne's choking sobs and saw the despair in her eyes, she dropped the coffee cup she was holding. "The corners of her mouth tightened and she stood absolutely still." At this, Anne wondered how Helen could care so much. In the following days, Helen tried in many ways to coax a deeply depressed Anne out of her shell, but Anne ignored her and her efforts.

Then one day, while on rounds, the doctor suggested they try a fusion with live bone—not hers and not from a bone bank as had been used before. Anne adamantly refused his suggestion until Helen said, "Anne, you can have my bone." Tears welling up in her eyes, Anne could find neither the words or voice to express her gratitude. And then Helen, her eyes filled with tears, spoke again: "Anne, my bone is as white as yours."

Anne gasped. Of course, she had noticed, but only at this moment did she realize she and Helen belonged to different races. Anne tells that she is now walking and tomorrow she will walk some more. The operation was a success and she will be forever thankful for Helen's "wedge of love," a wedge that literally and figuratively supports her.[234]

❤ ❤ ❤ ❤ ❤ ❤ ❤ ❤ ❤

CARING OPTS FOR BROTHERHOOD

Caring opts for brotherhood, knowing an immeasurable truth conveyed by Sue Monk Kidd: "We are each a thread woven into the vast web of the universe, linked and connected so that our lives are irrevocably bound up with one another."[235]

Of such brotherhood, Willie Morris tells of an incident, long ago, that ever since he first heard it as a boy has stayed with him.

This incident involved Jackie Robinson, the first black man to play major league baseball. In his first seasons, says Morris, Robinson "faced venom nearly wherever he traveled—fastballs at his head, spikings on the bases, brutal epithets from the opposing dugouts and from the crowds. During one game in Boston, the taunts and racial slurs seemed to reach a crescendo."

In the midst of this, another Dodger, a Southern white named Pee Wee Reese, called time-out. Walking from his position at shortstop toward Robinson at second base, he put his arm around Robinson's shoulder and silently stood there for several minutes. "The gesture spoke more eloquently than the words: this man is my friend."[236]

In another instance, it was General Robert E. Lee, the South's great Civil War Leader, who made—as did Reese—a visible statement regarding brotherhood. An accounting of Lee's compassionate action is cited by Billy Graham: "Shortly after the close of the war," relates Graham, a black "entered a Richmond church one Sunday morning at the beginning of a communion service. When the time came, the black man walked down the aisle and knelt at the altar. A rustle of shock and anger swept through the congregation, whereupon a distinguished layman arose, stepped forward to the altar and knelt beside his [black] brother. Captured by his spirit, the whole congregation followed. The layman who set the example: Robert E. Lee."[237]

In visibly aligning themselves with persons who were undervalued and persecuted, Reese and Lee both modeled before the world a keen sense of brotherhood. James Michener unequivocally opts for such brotherhood, highlighting that all human beings are his brothers, having souls and minds just like his own. He has met brothers in every continent of the world, he relates: "In the most savage jungles of New Guinea I have met my brother and in Tokyo I have seen him clearly walking before me."[238]

Consistent with goodness, caring protects brotherhood, knowing that men need each other to survive, a point illustrated by Rod Dyer who, many years ago, found himself in desperate circumstances on Christmas Eve during the Great Depression. Homeless and penniless, Dyer was wandering the country searching for a job.

"This night—a cold one—I was in the railroad yards of a Midwest town I can no longer recall," Dyer relates. "To escape the penetrating cold, four other men and I climbed into a boxcar. Soon the train began to move and, as it picked up speed, the wind pushed through the cracks in the doors. The cold inside soon became as fierce as it had been outside. The car had been used for hauling flour and had some sheets of paper in it. We wrapped the sheets around our shivering bodies but we were still cold.

"Then one young man with a Spanish accent said, 'We make a star for warm. We sit on the floor back to back.'

"He tucked the paper all around us and took a place for himself. We sat huddled there with knees drawn and toes pointed out. Gradually heat from our bodies spread from one man to another, warming us. The young man began to sing, 'Noche de amor, noche de paz . . . ' The rest of us joined in with the familiar words, 'Silent night, holy night . . . ' We sang for a long time, cozy and warm, until I dozed off, dreaming of other—happier—Christmases. When dawn came, and the train stopped, we went our separate, lonely ways.

"That was long ago and my Christmases are comfortable and happy ones now. But I've never forgotten those fellows who shared the boxcar with me and I give thanks for them often. Especially to the young Spanish man who showed us that no matter how bleak and difficult circumstances may be, it is always possible to be warmed by the light of the Christmas star."[239]

Regarding brotherhood, Elie Weisel, writing in his Pulitzer-prize-winning *Night*, a chronicle of his terrible suffering in a Nazi concentration camp, writes of an incident in which the prisoners acted in a spirit of community. The Nazi soldiers had herded the Jews out of their barracks before dawn into a thickly falling snow to wait for a train transporting them deeper into Germany. Having already been denied food and water for three days, the Jews stood in the snow until evening, forbidden to sit or even bend over. When one prisoner spontaneously began eating the accumulated snow off the shoulder of the person ahead of him, the act spread through the line. At once, all the deeply suffering individuals standing in a row became a collective group who shared together their intense pain.[240]

Reflecting on men's critical need to join together for their common good, Daniel D. Mich stresses, "I look to a time when brotherhood needs no publicity, at a time when a brotherhood award would be as ridiculous as an award for getting up each morning."[241]

Albert Schweitzer also adds, "It is not enough merely to exist. It's not enough to say, 'I'm earning enough to support my family. I do my work well. I'm a good father, husband, churchgoer.' That's all very well. But you must do something more. Seek always to do some good, somewhere. Every man has to seek in his own way to realize his true worth. You must give some time to your fellow man. Even if it's a little thing, do something for those who need help, something for which you get no pay but the privilege of doing it. For remember, you don't live in a world all your own. Your brothers are here too."[242]

Shortly before his death, in addressing the topic of brotherhood, Harry Emerson Fosdick was asked about the future of civilization. Speaking in the form of a parable, he responded, "Once upon a time an ox and a colt went to a spring for a drink together but they quarreled about who should drink first. They were about to fight it out when they saw vultures wheeling over them, waiting for the battle. So they decided to drink together."[243]

People who refuse to "drink together"—that is, to get involved in the problems of others—are like the two shipwrecked men in a lifeboat, observes Rabbi Arthur Hertzberg. From one end of the boat, the pair watched as those at the other end frantically fought a losing battle to keep the boat afloat. One said to the other, "Thank heaven, the hole is not on our end of the boat."[244]

There is great folly in not recognizing we need to assist those "at the other end of the boat." As men and women taking the same perilous journey through life, we owe it to ourselves and others to buoy up those around us who are taking our common sojourn. G. K. Chesterton makes the dramatic observation that "we are all in the same boat in a stormy sea, and we owe each other a terrible loyalty."

Norman Cousins appends, "What is required today is not a catalog of reasons for turning away from people who are in desperate need but a full release of intelligence and ingenuity in facing up to the common interest. The question is not whether our lifeboat can accommodate more survivors but whether, since we are all in the same lifeboat, we make it safely to shore."[245]

To opt for brotherhood is also to opt to be a good neighbor. Lady Bird Johnson reflects on this vital linkage: "Americans have always attached particular value to the word 'neighbor,'" she says. "While the spirit of neighborliness was important on the frontier because neighbors were so few, it is even more important now because our neighbors are so many."[246]

In a spirit of brotherhood, it was in Newtown, Pennsylvania, that neighbors joined together, in their words, "to call a show of force against hate." The group effort began shortly after an act of vandalism against a Jewish home inspired Christians to take a stand.

Early on a Sunday morning in December, after the third night of Hanukkah, someone threw a rock through the front window of a Jewish home. Tearing from its place the electric menorah blazing in the window, this person and perhaps others mashed the menorah to the ground, breaking all nine bulbs.

Shocked at the fear and devastation experienced by the Jewish family—a woman and two children—a Christian neighbor took action. And so did her neighbors. And their neighbors. On Thursday, the seventh of the eight-day Jewish Festival of Lights, twenty-five Christian homes in the well-to-do neighborhood had menorahs burning in their windows.

After that, there was no more vandalism.

The Christian woman took action, deeming it likely that visible support from another person for the Jewish family would protect the family from further threat. The group effort soared after word of the incident and as neighbors saw the menorah in the Christian woman's window. And so it was that, as momentum grew, the woman raced from store to store in search of scarce menorahs for neighbors to display before candlelighting time arrived at sundown.

The targeted Jewish woman was a forty-two-year-old mother of two, who, to escape persecution, emigrated as a child with her parents from the Ukraine to the United States. Returning home after an absence, the woman saw the orange bulbs burning in the windows of her neighbor's homes. Their actions spurred her on to courageously replace the broken bulbs in her own menorah and put it back up in the window.

Seeing her Jewish neighbor's overwhelmed and unbelieving reaction to the menorahs, and the hope this sight restored, brought tears to the eyes of the Christian woman. The experience was so profound, she says, that she will put a menorah up again next year and for years to come.[247]

• • • • • • • • •

CARING OFFERS THE QUALITY OF MERCY

Says Shakespeare in *The Merchant of Venice*, "The quality of mercy is not strained, it droppeth as the gentle rain from heaven upon the place beneath: it is twice blessed; it blesseth him that gives and him that takes."[248]

The concept of caring exists across a continuum from absolute apathy to absolute caring. Theoretically, to embrace absolute caring, one must be willing to offer the quality of mercy, even under morally reprehensible circumstances. To address such situations, a person must operate firmly from an intrinsically-rooted conviction that his fellow men are invaluable. This includes the range of those who, in the eyes of the world, are regarded as the most noble or noteworthy to those who are the most despicable. Within such illumination, then, any man is worthy of the expenditure of goodness.

However, most people cannot embrace the concept of "absolute caring" when diabolic acts are involved. Some men are truly evil, having murdered, abused, raped, butchered, tortured, or otherwise brutalized others. In such instances, in the eyes of victims or others, perpetrators of such horrific crimes may find themselves—by virtue of the abominable nature of their actions—humanly ineligible for the condition of "quality of mercy." Mercy, in fact, for such people may not be forthcoming from any earthly quarter; and the grim task of exacting due penalty from such people for their evil becomes that of society, of the court system, and, ultimately, of God.

Kassie Neou, of Phnom Penh, Cambodia provides, to some

extent, an exception. Neou was able, in a ironical twist of circumstances, to offer the quality of mercy to a guard who several years earlier had brutally tortured Neou and others in a Khmer Rouge torture chamber. Neou saved his own life because "every night, sometimes exhausted and bloody from a day of beatings and interrogation," he told Aesop fables to the guards. "I told the stories all night long, with my ankles in leg irons like everyone else," Neou says. "And because of that, I became someone who was needed by the guards."

On an ill-fated night when Neou and the other prisoners were roped together and were being marched from the building to be killed, the commanding voice of a thirteen-year-old guard in charge was heard over the loudspeaker. Of Neou, the voice said, "I need him. Quick! Pull him out." Hidden by another guard, Neou survived the massacre.

Neou's painful story, written by news reporter Seth Mydans, is set within the context of "a radical Maoist philosophy" that—starting in 1975—"quickly slid into madness," utterly ravaging Cambodia for the next four years. The resulting holocaust occurred when "the Khmer Rouge government turned on its own people, ripping society apart and killing perhaps more than one million Cambodians." Today, nearly two decades later, like Neou, "virtually everyone of a certain age in Cambodia today is a survivor of the Khmer Rouge years—either a victim or a killer," both living side by side, the perpetrators unpunished.

When Neou was being tortured, he says, "he memorized the faces of his torturers, sustaining himself with thoughts of retribution. 'I told myself that when my time comes, I will take revenge five times worse than what they are doing to me. As a human being, you have that kind of anger.'"

Three years later, after the collapse of the Khmer Rouge government, Neou had his opportunity to take revenge. Having joined hundreds of thousands of people who fled across the border into Thailand, Neou had settled in a refugee camp. And, as one of the few educated people to survive the holocaust, he had been appointed administrator of an aid program in that refugee camp. It was at this camp he recognized one of his torturers.

Seeing Neou, the man turned completely pale and began to shake. Neou recalls, "I asked him, 'Oh, when did you arrive?' He could not talk because of his fear, and he only said, 'My wife is sick and my baby is dying.'

"Because of his fear, and because his baby was dying, I completely changed my mind about taking revenge through anger," Neou said. Instead, Neou accompanied the man to a feeding center, where he arranged for care for the man's wife and child.

In response to Neou's utterly unanticipated and magnanimous gesture, the man—trembling and with tears in his eyes—thanked Neou. "At this point," says Neou, "I realized that I had made my revenge."[249]

Perhaps Neou sensed instinctively what Proverbs 11:17 bespeaks: "The merciful man doeth good to his own soul: but he that is cruel troubleth his own flesh."

Germane to the possible offering of the quality of mercy is a remark made by Mary McCarthy: "Understanding is often a prelude to forgiveness," she observes, "but they are not the same, and we often forgive what we cannot understand (seeing nothing else to do) and understand what we cannot pardon."[250]

Despite even the most terrible adversity and suffering perpetuated on them in the most heinous of crimes, some people do valiantly keep their faith in greater humanity. Nowhere is this more poignantly expressed than in the words of Anne Frank, a Jewish teenager who, in the Netherlands in World War II, kept a diary while she and her family were in hiding from the Nazis. Anne, who later died in a concentration camp, wrote, "In spite of everything, I still believe people are really good at heart."[251]

Throughout her writings, Anne's belief in the inherent goodness of mankind was evident, as manifested in the reply of Justice Felix Frankfurter to a question posed to him: "And how do you know that the human race is worth saving?"

Replied the Justice, "I have read Anne Frank's diary."[252]

Writing in a much earlier era—and speaking of negative acts of a much lesser order than the profoundly abhorrent and hellish ones Anne Frank and her family experienced—Rabbi Schmelke speaks of ill will one person may harbor toward another: "It may sometimes happen that thine own hand inadvertently strikes thee," he admonishes. "Wouldst thou take a stick and chastise thy hand for its heedlessness, and thus add to thy pain? It is the same when thy neighbour, whose soul is one with thine, because of insufficient understanding does thee harm: shouldst thou retaliate, it would be thou who wouldst suffer."[253]

Illustrating is a fictional account of a thief, who in his old age, was unable to ply his "trade" and thus was starving. A wealthy man, hearing of the thief's distress, sent the man some food. Both the rich man and the thief died the same day and each in turn came before the Heavenly Court. The trial of the magnate occurred first, and found wanting, the Court sentenced the magnate to Purgatory. At the entrance, however, an angel came hurrying to recall the magnate and he was returned to the Court. There he learned that his sentence had been reversed: the thief whom he had aided on earth had stolen the list of his iniquities.[254]

Although himself apparently a man with serious flaws, the magnate did respond with caring to the needs of a fellow being—a person whom others might have felt was undeserving. As a result, the thief returned the magnate's gesture of caring in a manner that neither he nor the magnate could ever have anticipated.

In another instance, a rabbi ordered his warden to assemble ten men for a minyan—or quorum for prayer—to chant Psalms for the recovery of a sick man. When the quorum entered, a friend of the rabbi exclaimed, "I see among them notorious thieves."

"Excellent," replied the rabbi. "When all the Heavenly Gates of Mercy are closed it requires experts to open them."[255]

In the preceding instance, the rabbi—probably knowing himself not to be entirely perfect and thus himself in need of divine mercy—extended the quality of mercy to others. And so might we, if we should take into account an observation of Henry Wadsworth Longfellow: "If we could read the secret history of our enemies, we should find in each man's life sorrow and suffering enough to disarm all hostility."[256]

W. Somerset Maugham also appends, "It is curious that our own offenses should seem so less much heinous than the offenses of others. I suppose the reason is that we know all the circumstances that have attended them and so manage to excuse in ourselves what we cannot in others."[257]

Augmenting is Rabbi Samuel Kariver, who admonishes, "Cherish no hate for thy brother who offends, because you have not offended like him. If your fellow-man possessed your nature, he might not have sinned. If you possessed his nature, you might have offended as he has done. A man's transgressions depend not entirely upon his free choice, but often upon many other circumstances."[258]

Marcus Aurelius also observes, "It is a man's especial privilege to love even those who stumble. And this love follows as soon as thou reflectest that they are of kin to thee and that they do wrong involuntarily and through ignorance, and that within a little while both they and thou will be dead."[259]

Ironically, sometimes the caring extended, and the quality of mercy offered, come not from those who are "good," but from those who, in the sight of others, are deemed deficient or lower in status. Oscar Wilde, for example, speaks of caring behaviors he once experienced while in prison, and particularly of a kindness extended by a fellow inmate. Says Wilde, in pondering his experience, "I think of every single person who has been kind to me in my prison life . . . down to the poor thief who, recognizing me as we tramped round the yard at Wandsworth, whispered to me in the hoarse prison voice men get from long and compulsory silence: 'I am sorry for you; it is harder for the likes of you than it is for the likes of us.'"[260]

♥ ♥ ♥ ♥ ♥ ♥ ♥ ♥ ♥

CARING STANDS FOR THE RIGHT

Caring stands for the right, even when such a stand is potentially death-threatening. To take a courageous stand, however, demands that men view each other not as objects, but as living, often suffering, human beings:

"The true opposite of love is not hate but indifference," Joseph Fletcher reflects. "Hate, bad as it is, at least treats the neighbor as a thou, whereas indifference turns the neighbor into an it, a thing. This is why we may say that there is actually one thing worse than evil itself, and that is indifference to evil. In human relations the nadir of morality, the lowest point as far as Christian ethics is concerned, is manifest in the phrase, 'I couldn't care less.'"[261]

The true test of a man's character, Martin Luther King, Jr., declared, comes in hard times when he is called to the fore: "The ultimate measure of a man is not where he stands in moments of comfort and convenience, but where he stands at times of challenge and controversy. The true neighbor will risk his position, his prestige, and even his life for the welfare of others. In dangerous valleys and hazardous pathways, he will lift some bruised and beaten brother to a higher and more noble life."[262]

At one time, a stunned Loudon Wainwright realized that sometime, somewhere, someone did not, or could not, come to protect his neighbor: "Shortly after I saw *Shoah* [a documentary film about the Nazi death camps], I got into an elevator in my building with a man who lives a few floors below," he relates. "We'd had an elevator acquaintance for years—friendly, but limited to brief risings and fallings. In his slight European accent he asked me how I was. 'Not too good,' I said. . . . 'How about you?'

"He looked at me sympathetically. 'I decided long ago,' he said, 'that only I had the power to make myself happy. . . . You have to do this,' he went on. 'Otherwise life is too much.' The elevator stopped and the door opened. 'After a war, after a concentration camp,' he said as he stepped off with a modest wave, 'I find it's not too difficult to be happy.'

"Alone with my surprise as the door closed, I realized that in some other town, on some really bad day half a long lifetime ago, they must have come and taken my neighbor away."[263]

Of the urgency in protecting our neighbors, Susan Thorne says, "If we don't protect the most vulnerable in our society, from the very youngest to the very oldest, then which segment of our society will next be considered expendable."[264]

Throughout history, the instances of men standing for the right—often becoming martyrs themselves for righteous causes and for their neighbors or brothers—must truly number in the millions. Many such instances occurred during World War II. Speaking of one, Victor Gollancz tells of the grand Rabbin of

Lyons, who was a Jewish chaplain to the French forces in the 1914–18 war. "One day," relates Gollancz, "a wounded man staggered into a trench and told the Rabbi that a Roman Catholic was on the point of death in no-man's land, and was begging that his padre should come to him with a crucifix. The padre could not quickly be found. The Jew rapidly improvised a cross, ran out with it into no-man's land, and was seen to hold it before the dying man's eyes. He was almost immediately shot by a sniper; the bodies of the Catholic and the Jew were found together."[265]

A Christian newsletter dated April 17, 1946, also describes the fate of another martyr—Elizabeth Pilenko—to the righteous cause of protecting brotherhood. Pilenko, from a wealthy landowning family in south Russia, became a keen socialist revolutionary, and after the October Revolution, worked with extraordinary skill and audacity in rescuing victims from terror. Later, in Paris, she beseeched authorities of the Russian Church to allow her to become a nun and to found a monastery. To this request the authorities agreed, and, although accused by some of neglecting tradition, Pilenko took a stand: "I must go my way," she said. "I am for the suffering people." She was a familiar figure in the slum, feeding the poor in her faded black habit and her worn-out shoes.

Mother Maria, as she became known, worked among the poorest of Russian refugees in France. Discovering that many suffered with tuberculosis, with ten francs in her pocket she bought a chateau and opened a sanitarium. Then, discovering that hundreds of Russians had "disappeared"—no questions asked—in "lunatic asylums" all over Europe, she raised a public outcry. As a result, many were released.

When the German occupation took place, Mother Maria knew that her particular duty was to render all possible assistance to persecuted Jews. She knew that her actions would mean imprisonment and probably death, and she thus gave her chaplain the option of leaving, which he refused. For a month the convent was a haven for Jews, and, as a result, many were able to escape from the Germans, but soon the Gestapo came. Mother Maria was arrested and sent to the concentration camp at Ravensbruck. Her chaplain was sent to Buchenwald, where he died of starvation and overwork.

"The story of her life in the camp is only now being pieced together," reads the letter. "She was known even to the guards as 'that wonderful Russian nun,' and it is doubtful whether they had any intention of killing her. She had been there two and a half years when a new block of buildings was erected in the camp, and the prisoners were told that these were to be hot baths. A day came when a few dozen prisoners from the women's quarters were lined up outside the buildings. One girl became hysterical. Mother Maria, who had not been selected, came up to her. 'Don't be frightened,' she said. 'Look, I shall take your turn,' and in line with the rest, she passed through the doors. It was Good Friday, 1945."[266]

Finally, standing for the right was Irene Gut Opdyke, a Polish teenager, whose story of courage and heroism news reporter Karen Boren writes. Seventeen years old and away from home, Irene was studying nursing when Hitler and Stalin made a pact and divided up Poland. Stranded near the German border when the Russians invaded from the east and the Germans invaded from the west, Opdyke was sent to work in Germany.

One day the streets were barricaded with barbed wire and Opdyke witnessed for the first time Jews being murdered. Profoundly stunned by the massacre, she made a vow: "'If the opportunity arises, I will help.' In war, you don't make decisions, they are made for you."

Assigned to work in a munitions factory, one day Opdyke, ill from the chemicals, fainted in front of a German major. Her life in jeopardy, Opdyke explained in her best high school German that having just come from the Russian front, she *wanted* to work. Subsequently, she was assigned to serve lunch in an officers' barracks. There, she became the eyes and ears of the Jewish people.

While serving the officers one day, Opdyke overheard discussion of an unexpected raid. On another, she overheard plans to liquidate the entire ghetto. Both times, her information alerted the Jewish underground, saving hundreds of people. Responding to the impending ghetto liquidation, Opdyke's friends begged for her help. Without house or family, she could only pray. Then, unexpectedly, the major conscripted her to become his housekeeper.

Overjoyed, Opdyke took her friends to the major's villa, and in the dark of night, one by one they spilled through a window and down the coal chute into the cellar, where they hid. Hearing that a Jewish architect who had built the villa had constructed a hiding place, the group searched the villa. Miraculously, they found a tunnel from the cellar to a hiding place underneath the gazebo.

Opdyke was to face many terrifying trials before the eight-month ordeal ended. Of one, Boren writes, "The major had many parties, and one day Opdyke was terrified to see the head Gestapo officer walking outside for a tryst in the gazebo with his fraulein. The twelve Jews hiding in the room beneath the gazebo werre talking and laughing, unaware of the impending danger. Opdyke grabbed a bottle of wine and some hors d'oeuvres and called loudly 'Herr Sturmanfuhrer, Herr Sturmanfuhrer!' as she approached with the food. Intent on romance, the officer was immediately distracted by her intrusion. As he raged at her for disturbing him, the Jews became deathly still and Opdyke quietly slipped away having again saved her friends."

Another ordeal involved an unexpected visit by the Gestapo. Seeing them at the door, Opdyke warned the Jews in the kitchen by steadily pressing down the bell in the servants' quarters. Then racing through the kitchen camouflaging their presence, she wet her hair, wrapping a towel around her head. Answering the door, she explained her delay due to washing her hair. The Gestapo demanded to see the major, then accused him of hiding Jews, which the major laughingly denied. After partially searching the villa, the exasperated Gestapo left.

On another occasion, a couple in hiding came to Opdyke with a tragic request. The wife, Ida Haller, was pregnant and wanted medication to abort the baby, afraid its cries would expose the group. "But, I witnessed the little children going to death," relates Opdyke. "I told them 'no!' In the last minute there was a villa, in the last minute there was a gazebo." Moved by Opdyke's unshakable faith, Haller remained pregnant.

One day, while Opdyke was preparing food for the Jews who were with her in the kitchen, the major walked in and "stared in disbelief—looking from one Jew to the other, shaking in anger." As the Jews retreated to the gazebo, the major stormed into the library, where Opdyke followed him, crying as he screamed obscenities at her. Thereafter, he left, later returning drunk. To her reminder that Germany might soon lose the war, the major responded he had seen enough of murder. He kept his silence.

Shortly afterward, in March 1944, the major was ordered to evacuate the villa and Opdyke arranged for the safe transfer of her friends. Eventually ending up in a Jewish displaced persons camp, she immigrated to America in 1949. Six years later, marrying a U.N. representative who had interviewed her at the camp, she and her husband settled in California, where they raised a daughter. A few years ago, she "received a letter from a man living in Munich, Germany, who is alive because she had the faith and courage to oppose his abortion. Roman Haller, now a father of two little children of his own, began his letter, 'Dear Mother . . .'"[267]

• • • • • • • • •

CARING UNITES HUMANITY

"I can think of no more stirring symbol of man's humanity to man than a fire engine," observes Kurt Vonnegut.[268]

Yet, says Sydney J. Harris, for most people it is difficult to conceptualize the concept of "humanity" because it is an abstraction and "it is hard to feel passion or loyalty for words and abstractions. Hard, but necessary," he asserts.

And he further points out, "Everyone gives his loyalty to something larger than himself—the father to his family, the communicant to his church, the citizen to his country, even the juvenile delinquent to his gang.

"But who is loyal to humanity? Humanity has no flag, no song, no colors, no troops, no salutes, no rituals, no face nor body. It is a word, like justice or peace—cold, perfect, and dead."

The answer is that we must all be loyal to humanity—for the sake of humanity's—and our own very personal—survival, Harris emphasizes. Funny, he says, that "almost every other species of animal is loyal to its own kind, and not merely to its own pack or flock or den. Only man and the shark regularly attack their own kind and represent their own enemy."

Thus, Harris urges, while "other species are loyal by instinct . . . we must learn to be loyal by intellect." And, when the choice comes between a conflict of interest between loyalty to humanity and loyalty to a lesser cause, we must choose loyalty to humanity, and "the lesser loyalties must be curtailed or surrendered. If no one speaks for humanity alive, what is there to prevent humanity's death?"[269]

On another, more encouraging, note, Thurgood Marshall draws conclusions regarding the inherent goodness of men in instances where humanity is alive and well: "In recognizing the humanity of our fellow beings," he stresses, "we pay ourselves the highest tribute."[270]

During World War II, on a bitter cold Christmas Eve in 1944, loyalty to humanity on both sides won over a lesser and profoundly heinous cause of Hitler who aspired to control the fate and lives of the world's masses. It was at the war's near ending, during the Battle of the Bulge, that such humanity prevailed. Fritz Vincken, who witnessed this event, tells the story.

The battle itself raged all around a cabin deep in the forest near the German-Belgian border where twelve-year-old Fritz Vincken and his mother waited for the Allied front to pass. They could hear the incessant sounds of bombing, of field guns, of planes soaring overhead, and knew that around them were thousands of Allied and German soldiers fighting and dying.

Fritz and his mother had occupied the cabin for months, their provisions nearly diminised and the deep snow compounding their isolation. It was now Christmas Eve, and with cleared weather, "countless stars reclaimed the heavens." Fritz's thoughts were with his father, whom they sorely missed. Because of the deep snow, Fritz's father, having been conscripted as a baker in a town twenty miles away, could no longer contact them, and his fate was unknown.

Thus alone, Fritz and his mother were startled when they heard noise outside and quiet voices. Fritz's mother hastily blew out the candle and the two waited in fearful silence. Then came a knock, careful and full of anxiety, and then another. Responding, Fritz's mother slowly opened the door to find two steel-helmeted men standing there "like phantoms against the endless white background."

Standing motionless in the doorway, Fritz's mother recognized these men as Americans—strong men who could have forcefully entered—but who stood there, pleading silently with their eyes for help. One soldier pointed to another lying in the frozen snow who appeared more dead than alive. Finally, very deliberately, Fritz's mother moved aside, letting the soldiers enter, knowing full well that the penalty for harboring Americans was death.

"We relit the candle," relates Fritz. "It was warm in the cabin and now, after I had helped the soldiers take off their heavy coats, they looked like big friendly boys. And that was the way Mother treated them. We learned that the stocky, dark-haired fellow was Jim; his comrade, tall and slender, was Ralph. Herby was the wounded one now sleeping on my bed." As Fritz's mother extended the family meal with more potatoes and soup, she conversed with one American in French and learned that, separated from their battalion, the Americans had wandered for days through the snowy Ardennes Forest carrying their wounded friend.

Before long a tempting aroma filled the cabin and dinner was ready. As the group sat down to eat, suddenly there was another knock at the door. Expecting to find more straggling Americans outside, Fritz rushed to open the door. There stood four German soldiers.

Stepping outside, with a calmness that hid intense panic, Fritz's mother warmly greeted the soldiers. They were separated from their regiment, the soldiers explained. Could they come in and wait until daylight in the cabin? Of course, she responded— the night was freezing and the men could obviously use a hot meal. Her friendly, motherly reception obviously impressed the weary soldiers. But now she matched the corporal's eyes. Inside, she relayed, were three newly arrived half-frozen guests the Germans would not consider friends.

Who was inside, the corporal, the oldest of the three, demanded: "*Amerikaner?*" Yes, nodded Fritz's mother. But then she added, her voice confident as she took charge, "There will be no killing this Christmas eve." Any one man could have been her own son, she appealed, and all were in the same exhausted state, with one soldier seriously wounded.

Relates Fritz, "The corporal was speechless. Two or three endless seconds of silence followed. No inkling of support came from his little group, who seemed more than ready to accept this unexpected invitation. Mother broke the stalemate. 'Enough talking,' she commanded with convincing authority. 'Place your weapons here in the woodshed and hurry up. Dinner is ready.'" Slowly—dazedly—the corporal undid his own weapons, laying them just ouside the door, and the other soldiers quickly followed suit.

Turning, she led the Germans inside the house where she ordered the stunned Americans to give her their own weapons and, despite the strained atmosphere, she made effort to accommodate added guests to the meal. While waiting, the corporal, who until recently had studied medicine at a university, moved to examine the wounded soldier. After, he told the other Americans that because of the cold, their friend's wound was not infected and that he would recover with rest and nourishment.

Now ready to feed the men, Fritz's mother sat them down, with Germans and Americans touching shoulder to shoulder around the small table. Two of the Germans found a loaf of bread and a bottle of wine in their food packs which they added to the meal. Suspicion waning, and all beginning to relax, the soldiers intently watched Fritz's mother at the table.

Of what happened next, Fritz tells, "The mood had become somewhat festive, almost solemn, and even though they were very hungry, no one would start eating. Ralph took the hands of those sitting next to him, Jim did the same, and suddenly we were all holding each other's hands as Mother said a prayer, thanking God for the meal and this night of peaceful togetherness. And she added, 'please bring an end to this terrible war so we all can go home, where we belong. Amen.'"

After the meal, Fritz's mother led the men outdoors, inviting them all to look at Sirius, which, she said, was like the star of Bethlehem. To the men, in the still, cold silence of the quiet night—the night of Christ's birth—the war seemed far away, an almost forgotten event.

In the morning, the private armistice continued as a stretcher for the now-improved American soldier was fashioned out of two strong sticks and canvas from a German tent square. The Germans gave the Americans directions to find their own lines and a German compass changed hands. Giving the soldiers back their weapons, Fritz's mother wished God's blessing upon them as they left, and, as did the wise men of so long ago on the first Christmas day, the men "departed into their own country another way" (Matthew 2:12).[271]

❤ ❤ ❤ ❤ ❤ ❤ ❤ ❤

CARING WATCHES OVER GOD'S CHILDREN

"If you can't hold children in your arms, please hold them in your heart," Mother Clara Hale has said.[272]

To care is to be concerned about this world's children—even when they are not your own. To invest in a child who needs a home and parents, or to sponsor a child who needs mentorship through international programs is to add substantial goodness to the world's accumulation. To invest in children is also to invest in mankind, for each child truly nurtured and cared for creates a potential legacy. This legacy increases the probability that the perpetual offspring of such children will also receive the opportunity of being treated as they should—as one of God's precious children.

Some years ago, at a social gathering, a woman was surprised to learn that a second woman—a stranger—had eight children. The first woman, further taken aback when the second woman pointed out two of her daughters who seemed about the same age, remarked that having had two children so close together must have been difficult.

No, answered the second woman. She and her husband had adopted Wendy, one of the girls, several years ago. This answer again surprised the first woman, who asked if she didn't have enough children of her own. Of course she did, replied the second woman. "But Wendy didn't have anyone."

Many of the world's children, desperately in need of hearts and homes, also don't have anyone. Wendy's parents are among the people taking care of such children, but in some instances, saving this world's children is not nearly so easy, and, in fact, bodes danger. During World War II, a spectacular story of saving this world's children involved a Dutch woman, a member of a Dutch committee given the assignment of assembling Jewish children whom England was willing to accept. Going to Vienna, she secured an interview with Adolf Eichmann, explaining her mission. Referring to his papers, Eichmann told her that on Saturday she could have six hundred children. She was to arrange the transportation and if the children arrived in England and England accepted them, she could have more Jewish children.

With Saturday only five days away, Eichmann had made the

proposal purposely diabolic, and assembling and making arrangements for the children in that short time seemed impossible; but the Dutchwoman was equal to the challenge. On Saturday the train was ready and six hundred children began their journey, an antecedent to a series of train journeys that took more than ten thousand children out of Germany, Austria, and Czechoslovakia to England.[273]

Another man who felt responsibility for the world's children, was Sergeant Werner Krenzer. The story of Sergeant Krenzer played out in Korea, after the war in a country where homeless, hungry children, aged and wizened beyond their years, cowered in rags in corners and under stairways, and huddled against walls. Within this context, it was in a train station that Krenzer approached a child, holding out his last chocolate bar, only to see a strange expression on the child's face—a mixture of fear, yearning, and then something utterly savage. The child's lips suddenly curled in a fierce snarl and he ran, crying piteously.

With no more time left, the sergeant gave the candy bar to another child and hurried to rejoin his outfit. But, though he had been in the Army for eight years and known frontline warfare in the Pacific and one year with occupation forces in Japan, it was in Korea that he saw the destruction through the eyes of a child of war. The experience hit him hard and he wanted to go back to find the terrified child who had run from him.

And so it was to his great amazement that Sergeant Krenzer was soon assigned to a United Nations civil assistance unit that provided aid for homeless Korean civilians. One of his "first acts was to search among the children who haunted the railroad station for the boy who had snarled and fled. Krenzer found him at last, under a heap of filthy burlap bags where the boy had crawled away to die.

"He picked the lad up. There was no weight there. The

wasted legs and arms, covered with sores, hung limply, like those of a puppet. The child stirred, and the sergeant looked down into wide, terrified eyes.

"Instantly the boy bit him. The matchstick arms and legs clawed, kicked and hit in a frenzy that was gone almost as fast as it came. There was no strength left. Other children came to stare and one, an alert bright-eyed youngster of about eleven, said, 'Me Kim. Me speak Engliss.'

"'Good,' said Sergeant Krenzer. 'Tell this kid I'm trying to help him.'"

"And so began a partnership that was to save countless lives."

After finding the child, Krenzer took him to a United Nations orphanage, where Korean nuns nursed him and, by miracle, the child lived. The child, who was four years old, did not remember much of his previous life. But he did remember that communist soldiers had told him that if any American offered him food or candy, he was to run for his life, for the food would be poisoned.

Time and again, Krenzer was to run into this lie and until his rescue teams managed to spread the truth, starving children fled at the sight of an American soldier, and many of them perished. Facilitating was Kim, who became Krenzer's interpreter and, as Krenzer was to say of him, "He could charm a bird." Krenzer and Kim became a team and each night they wandered the streets, approaching the children one at a time, winning their confidence.

At the time Sergeant Krenzer began his work, there were only bleak barracks for shelter and rice and a meager amount of Army rations for food. Through intense solicitation, Krenzer enlisted the aid of organized charities and persuaded his friends, civilian and military alike, to turn the barracks into homelike orphanages. Then he had another idea: More than food and shelter, these children needed love, and the thousands of homeless women refugees wandering around looking for their own children and families were natural resources for his orphans.

Krenzer wasn't able to find each mother's own child, but he could ask each mother to care for an orphan. "And so—the childless mothers took the motherless children and cared for them. And these desperate mothers were given hope that their own children might find the same kind of refuge."

As the summer receded and winter began, Sergeant Krenzer faced a problem—his term of enlistment would soon be up. Each time he started to arrange passage home, he was stopped by the sight of another near-dying child who needed him. How could he desert these children in this war-wrecked land for his own comfort? His answer was that he could not. And so Sergeant Krenzer did not leave Korea and his beloved orphans but stayed on there to take care of God's children.[274]

♥ ♥ ♥ ♥ ♥ ♥ ♥ ♥ ♥

CARING PROTECTS GOD'S CREATURES

"You can tell all you need to about a society from how it treats animals and beaches," reflects Frank Deford.[275]

Inherent in the unfettered soul of men is a kinship with animals, connecting creature to creature, as man recognizes that all life emanates from same source. Thus, caring, as a condition, encompasses respect for all creatures, big and small, and reacts to protect all life when possible.

"The loneliness of man is the loneliness of the animal," notes Robert Ardrey. "We must have one another. The baboon seeks his troop, the bookkeeper his busy office, the buffalo his herd . . . the weary bricklayer his fellows at the corner pub, . . . the herring his school in the cold North Sea, all for quite the same reason: because we cannot survive without one another."[276]

The instances of men intervening to protect or to save creatures are innumerable. Such efforts, for example, are epitomized
in an instance in which twenty South Korean marines risked
their lives to save a bull caught in the mine-infested demilitarized
zone that divides North and South Korea. No one was sure
where the bull came from, but it was obvious that the animal had
drifted downstream in flood waters the summer before. It had
then subsequently washed up on a sandy islet at the mouth of
the Imjin River where it empties into the Yellow Sea. Writes the
story's author: When the bull washed up on the islet, "it stepped
onto a patch of no man's land jealously guarded by both South
and North Korea since their bloody 1950–53 war."

The bull managed to survive six months on the islet, but
when national TV footage showed the emaciated bull hobbling
because of an injury, "its fate gripped national attention."
Ordered to retrieve the bull, South Korean Marines trained for
two weeks for the mission, and, when the mission commenced,
half of the Marine division was put on alert. Describing what
happened next, the author says, "The twenty marines, including
a military vet, sailed to the forty-four acre islet in five rubber
boats. Five solders surrounded the bull and administered anes-
thesia, while others secured the islet.

The marines had to move inch by inch with mine sweepers
as they approached the bull, at the same time preparing for any
potential encounters with North Korean enemies. The mission
was a success, and, commented the vet upon return, "The bull
looked surprised when he saw us. But he didn't run away."[277]

In a second instance, a cow made first efforts to save herself,
and then compassionate others further ushered her on to safety.
In a slaughterhouse in Hopkinton, Massachusetts, Emily,
the cow, was in an unfamiliar and danger place, and she apparently sensed it. Growing increasingly nervous watching her

companion cows, in turn, disappear permanently through swing-
ing doors, Emily escaped while workers were at lunch.

Says Michael Ryan, who wrote Emily's story, "When Emily
made her move, jaws dropped and workers stared in amazement.
Suddenly, Emily, all fourteen hundred pounds of her, was air-
borne, sailing over the gate."

"Cows just can't do that," one resident told Ryan, but as Ryan
points out, "as residents of this rural area west of Boston were to
discover, Emily, a three-year-old Holstein, can do many things
cows aren't supposed to do."

After Emily's jump and run, slaughterhouse workers scoured
the nearby woods all day, but Emily eluded them, and when
tempted with hay, she didn't take the bait. At first, dozens of
sightings were reported, often published in the local newspaper,
but they suddenly dried up. Emily had captured the hearts and
imagination of the small community and local farmers even
started leaving out hay for her.

Attempting to rescue Emily, Lewis and Meg Randa, a Quaker
couple, approached the slaughterhouse's owner, offering to buy
Emily for their school for special needs children. Himself touched
by the plucky cow, the owner would sell. His first asking price was
three hundred fifty dollars, but at the urging of his granddaughter,
who had first named Emily, he reduced his price to one dollar.

The Randas eventually captured Emily and secured a veterinarian to examine her. In her adventure, Emily had lost five hundred pounds and—after her forty-day ordeal—needed medical
treatment. Quickly regaining her health and weight, Emily soon
had the company of Gabriel, the calf—donated to the school
rather than taken to the slaughterhouse. There she was soon
joined by a pair of turkeys; a mother goat and her two kids; and
three rabbits—all rescued from inhumane conditions and looked
after by school students.[278]

A final animal rescue occurred in spring, 1998, when three Salt Lake City, Utah, men skied six miles into the Tushar Mountains. As they traversed down from the top of 12,000-foot Mount Delano, skier Robb Welch spotted an animal in a rock outcrop at about eleven thousand feet. Hiking back up the mountain for a closer look, fellow skier Jim Paul found a seriously injured yellow Labrador retriever. "It was a very, very odd place to find a dog," says Marshall Denton, the third skier in the group.

The men carried the fifty-five-pound Labrador down to the mountain base where they fed her two bagels and a Power Bar and gave her a drink. Then, loading her into Denton's pack, they made the long trip back to the Elk Meadows ski resort, where ski patrol members helped stabilize her.

When discovered, the dog, who wore no collar, hadn't eaten or had anything to drink for over a week and couldn't stand or walk. Jim Woolf, a news reporter who wrote about Tushar (the dog's temporary nickname), describes her initial condition: "The Labrador's front right leg was broken in two places, her right canine tooth was cracked off, she had pneumonia, and there were wounds on her face from animals—possibly hawks or eagles."

In writing of Tushar, Woolf—noting her medical bills would well exceed a thousand dollars—indicated donations could be made to a Tushar's Surgery Fund.[279] Inasmuch as donations exceeded the veterinarian bill, the excess was given equally to two pet institutions and a Pet Assistance Fund, newly established to treat other injured homeless animals.

A month after Tushar's recovery, Marshall Denton, who temporarily adopted her, wrote a letter to donors containing the following excerpt:

"Dear Friends of Tushar: Tushar . . . would like to thank everyone so much for their generous donations. The funds have enabled her to pay off her medical bills and start living a happy life again. Although her right front leg has been amputated, she has adapted well and has no trouble going up and down stairs and has already gone on several hikes in the foothills! She is one of the happiest dogs I have known. Her tail is always wagging, she loves to be petted and she is just plain glad to be comfortable and alive. Her pneumonia is gone and she has just completed all her antibiotics.

"Her previous owner, Joy Caddell of Beaver, Utah, came forward on March 27th and clearly identified Tushar as her eleven-year-old lost dog whose real name was Snickers. I was prepared to give Snickers up to Joy Caddell as I believe she truly loved and cared for her, and she was undoubtedly the real owner. . . . In a very emotional meeting, Joy Caddell decided it would be best for Snickers to go home with me. For me, this was a very happy ending to this story, and a very happy beginning for Snickers' new life."

In an Associated Press article, Joy Caddell noted Snickers had been found five weeks after her disappearance and thirty-five miles from home. In coming to claim Snickers, she had every intention to do so, she also noted: "Then I saw her head lift up over her bowl and she looked at him—the gentleman that found her, well it seemed like he was in love with her."[280]

❤ ❤ ❤ ❤ ❤ ❤ ❤ ❤ ❤

CARING PROTECTS THE EARTH

"In one respect every natural area has a common uniqueness—it takes everyone forever to preserve it, but one person and one time can destroy it," reflects E. J. Koestner.[281]

No more poignant case for protecting the earth has been made than in a letter attributed to Chief Seattle, and reportedly sent to President Franklin Pierce, relative to an Indian land purchase. Regarding the letter, Timothy Egan notes that several versions of the letter exist and that once the letter may have been revised and rewritten in 1971 by a playwright for a film on ecology. However, he also notes, "By most accounts, Chief Seattle was a great speaker and skilled diplomat and . . . his [1854] speech was stirring, carried by the chief's strong voice."[282]

Despite debate regarding authenticity, authorship, or correct version, the Chief Seattle letter appears to have become classic—its message taking on a symbolic form and spirit larger than the letter itself. The letter—essentially embodying the North American Indian spiritual philosophy—has underpinned ecological movements around the world. As well, its compelling message continues to convey a strong environmental message relative to humanity's survival on earth.

In the letter that follows, of keen appeal is content that obviously reveres the earth and views it as God's greatest gift—a reverence that all peoples need to embrace:

"The Great Chief in Washington sends word that he wishes to buy our land. But how can you buy or sell the sky, the warmth of the land? The idea is strange to us. If we do not own the freshness of the air and the sparkle of the water, how can you buy them?

"Every part of the earth is sacred to my people. Every shining pine needle, every sandy shore, every mist in the dark woods, every meadow, and every humming insect is holy in the memory and experience of my people.

"We know the sap which courses through the trees as we know the blood that courses through our veins. We are part of the earth and it is part of us. The perfumed flowers are our sisters. The bear, the deer, the great eagle, these are our brothers. The rocky crests, the dew in the meadow, the body heat of the pony, and man all belong to the same family.

". . . If we sell you our land, you must remember that it is sacred. Each glossy reflection in the clear waters of the lakes tells of events and memories in the life of my people. The water's murmur is the voice of my father's father.

"The rivers are our brothers. They quench our thirst. They carry our canoes and feed our children. So you must give the rivers the kindness that you would give any brother.

"If we sell you our land, remember that the air is precious to us, that the air shares its spirit with all the life that it supports. The wind that gave our grandfather his first breath also received his last sigh. The wind also give our children the spirit of life. So if we sell our land, you must keep it apart and sacred, as a place where man can go to taste the wind that is sweetened by the meadow flowers.

"Will you teach your children what we have taught our children? That the earth is our mother? Whatever befalls the earth befalls the sons of the earth. Man did not weave the web of life, he is merely a strand in it. Whatever he does to the web, he does to himself.

"This we know: the earth does not belong to man, man belongs to the earth. All things are connected like the blood that unites us all.

"One thing we know: our God is also your God. The earth is precious to him and to harm the earth is to heap contempt on its creator.

"Your destiny is a mystery to us. What will happen when the buffalo are all slaughtered? The wild horses tamed? What will happen when the secret corners of the forest are heavy with the scent of many men and the view of the ripe hills is blotted with talking wires? Where will the thicket be? Gone! Where will the eagle be? Gone! And what is it to say goodbye to the swift pony and the hunt? The end of living and the beginning of survival.

"When the last red man has vanished from this earth, and his memory is only the shadow of a cloud moving across the prairie, these shores and forests will still hold the spirits of my people. For they love this earth as a newborn loves its mother's heartbeat. So, if we sell you our land, love it as we have loved it. Care for it as we have cared for it. Hold in your mind the memory of the land as it is when you receive it. And with all your strength, with all your mind, with all your heart, preserve the land for all children, and love it, as God loves us all.

"As we are a part of the land, you too are part of the land. This earth is precious to us. It is also precious to you.

"One thing we know—there is only one God. No man, be he Red or White man, can be apart. We are all brothers."[283]

♥ ♥ ♥ ♥ ♥ ♥ ♥ ♥

CARING INVESTS IN MANKIND

The actions of a young lawyer who lived in the 1800s illustrate how one person can make a difference in the lives of many people, including those of his or her own progeny. Edward W. Bok, former president of Harvard, tells of his grandfather in his autobiography published in 1924:

"Along an island in the North Sea, five miles from the Dutch Coast, stretches a dangerous ledge of rocks that has proved the graveyard of many a vessel sailing that turbulent sea. On this island once lived a group of men who, as each vessel was wrecked, looted the vessel and murdered those of the crew who reached shore. The government of the Netherlands decided to exterminate the island pirates, and for the job King William selected a young lawyer at The Hague."

By royal proclamation this young lawyer was made mayor of the island, and within a year was appointed judge.

The young man now decided to settle on the island and began to look for a home. The island was a grim place, barren of tree or living green of any kind.

"One day the young major judge called together his council. 'We must have trees!' he said; 'we can make this island a spot of beauty if we will!' But the practical seafaring men demurred; the little money they had was needed for matters far more urgent than trees.

" 'Very well,' was the major's decision—'I will do it myself.' And that year he planted one hundred trees, the first the island had ever seen.

" 'Too cold,' said the islanders, 'the severe north winds and storms will kill them all.'"

" 'Then I will plant more,' said the unperturbed mayor. And, every year for the fifty years that he lived on the island he did so.

"Moistened by the salt mist the trees did not wither, but grew prodigiously. In all that expanse of turbulent sea . . . there [had not been] a foot of ground on which the birds, storm-driven across the water-waste, could rest in their flight. Hundreds of dead birds often covered the surface of the sea.

"Then one day the trees had grown tall enough to look over the sea, [and] the first birds came and rested in their leafy shelter. And others came and found protection, and gave their gratitude vent in song. Within a few years so many birds had discovered the trees in this new island that . . . the island became famous as the home of the rarest and most beautiful birds." And throughout the years, artists flocked to paint the beautiful lanes and wooden spots. One great artist who took his students to the island annually declared to them, "There is no more beautiful place."

Many years have passed since these events occurred, but the

legacy of this young man perseveres. Describing the island in 1924, Edward Bok wrote of his grandfather's bequest to mankind, "The trees are now majestic in their height of forty or more feet, for it is nearly a hundred years since the young attorney went to the island and planted the first tree; today the churchyard where he lies is a bower of cool green, with the trees that he planted dropping their moisture on the lichen-covered stone on his grave.

"This much did one man do. But he did more.

"After he had been on the barren island two years he went to the mainland one day, and brought back with him a bride. It was a bleak place for a bridal home, but the young wife had the qualities of the husband. 'While you raise your trees,' she said, 'I will raise our children.' And within a score of years the young bride sent thirteen happy-faced, well-brought-up children over that island, and there was reared a home such as is given to few.

"One day when the children had grown . . . the mother called them all together and said to them, 'I want to tell you the story of your father and of this island.'" And after doing so, she admonished her children, "As you go out into the world I want each of you to take with you the spirit of your father's work, and each in your own way and place to do as he has done: make you the world a bit more beautiful and better because you have been in it."

So, from that island home, each child went into the world, each carrying their father's simple but beautiful work and their mother's elegant message. Each accomplished—some greater, some smaller—but each left behind the traces of a life well spent.

"As all good work is immortal, so today all over the world goes on the influence of this one man and woman, whose life on the little Dutch island changed its barren rocks to a bower of verdure, a home for the birds, and the song of the nightingale."[284]

And thus, through replete acts of goodness, as did this couple did, we each may create our own enduring legacy for mankind by following this mother's simple but resplendent admonishment: "Make you the world a bit more beautiful and better because you have been in it."

INTRODUCTION

1. Van Wyck Brooks, *A Chilmark Miscellany* (New York: Dutton, 1948), 6.

2. Albert Schweitzer, as quoted in Max Merritt Morrison, *Never Lose Heart* (Garden City, N.Y.: Doubleday, 1964), 28.

3. Cathy Morancy, as quoted in *Reader's Digest Quotable Quotes* (Pleasantville, N.Y.: The Reader's Digest Association, 1997), 47.

4. Rabindranath Tagore, as quoted in Ardis Whitman, "This, Too, Is Worship," *Reader's Digest*, May 1982, 20.

5. Powell Davies, as quoted in Ardis Whitman, "The Case for Sentiment," *Guideposts*, July 1955, 9.

6. Lewis Timberlake, *Timberlake Monthly*, as quoted in *Reader's Digest*, May 1989, 48.

7. Vii Putman, *Hard Hearts Are for Cabbages* (New York: Crown, 1959), 186.

8. Neil Millar, in *The Christian Science Monitor*, as quoted in *Reader's Digest*, March 1985, 179–80.

9. Henry David Thoreau, as quoted in Clyde Francis Lytle, ed., *Leaves of Gold* (Williamsport, Pa.: The Coslett Publishing Co., 1948), 149.

10. Phillips Brooks, as quoted in Audrey Stone Morris, comp., *1000 Inspirational Things* (Chicago: Spencer Press, 1948), 186.

11. Daphne Rose Kingma, as quoted in editors of Conari Press, *Random Acts of Kindness* (Berkeley: Conari Press, 1993), 3. Used by permission.

12. Pablo Casals, as quoted in Norman Cousins, *Present Tense* (Hightown, N.Y.: McGraw-Hill, 1967), 318.

13. Leo Buscaglia, *Born for Love* (Thorofare, N.J.: Slack, 1992), 232.

14. Harry Emerson Fosdick, *Dear Mr. Brown* (New York: Harper, 1961), 139.

15. M. Scott Peck, *People of the Lie* (New York: Simon & Schuster, 1997), 252.

16. John Steinbeck, *East of Eden* (New York: Penguin, 1992), 541.

17. Albert Schweitzer, as quoted in *Reader's Digest Quotable Quotes*, 41.

18. Paul Lowney, in *The Lifetime Reader*, as quoted in *Reader's Digest*, May 1983, 240.

❖ ❖ ❖ ❖ ❖ ❖ ❖ ❖ ❖

CHAPTER 1: ON LOVE

1. Vicki Lucas, in *Catholic Digest*, as quoted in *Reader's Digest*, March 1978, 176.

2. Maxim Gorky, "The Zykovs," in *Seven Plays of Maxim Gorky* (New Haven, Conn.: Yale University Press, 1945), 346.

3. Ardis Whitman, "This, Too, Is Worship," *Reader's Digest*, May 1982, 22.

4. Alain, as quoted in Andre Maurois, *To an Unknown Lady* (New York: Dutton, 1957), 124.

5. David Viscott, *How to Live with Another Person* (New York: Arbor House, 1974), 25.

6. Phil Cousineau, ed., *Soul: An Archaeology* (San Francisco: HarperSanFrancisco, 1994), 66.

7. Ardis Whitman, "How To Make Love Last," *Woman's Day*, 10 June 1983, 77.

8. Jack Benny and Joan Benny, *Sunday Nights at Seven* (New York: Warner, 1990), 4.

9. Stephanie Mallarme, as quoted in Sefra Kobrinn Pitzele, *One More Day* (New York: Harper/Hazelden, 1988), 255.

10. Howie Schneider, as quoted in *Reader's Digest*, May 1978, 58.

11. See C. S. Lewis, *The Four Loves* (New York: Harcourt Brace, 1960), 169.

12. Erich Fromm, *The Art of Loving* (New York: Harper & Row, 1956), 8–9.

13. St. Bernard of Clairvaux, as quoted in Sydney J. Harris, *Pieces of Eight* (Boston: Houghton Mifflin, 1982), 158.

14. Erich Fromm, *The Art of Loving*, 8–9.

15. Anne Morrow Lindbergh, *Locked Rooms and Open Doors* (New York: Harcourt Brace Jovanovich, 1974), 231.

16. Robert Conklin, *How to Get People to Do Things* (New York: Ballantine, 1985), 28–29.

17. Charles Morgan, *The Fountain* (New York: Knopf, 1932), 220.

18. Denise Gamino, "Friendship overcomes age, geography," *Austin Statesman*, 14 December 1993, A7.

19. Pearl Bailey, as quoted in *Reader's Digest Quotable Quotes* (Pleasantville, N.Y.: The Reader's Digest Association, 1997), 48.

20. Ardis Whitman, "How To Make Love Last," *Woman's Day*, 10 June 1983, 164.

21. Steven Covey, *First Things First* (New York: Simon & Schuster, 1994), 18–19, 35–36, 51.

22. Edward R. Murrow in *This Week,* as quoted in *Reader's Digest,* April 1956, 48.

23. Gary Burghoff, as quoted in David Reiss, *M*A*S*H: The Exclusive Inside Story of TV's Most Popular Show* (Indianapolis: Bobbs-Merrill, 1983), 17.

24. Anais Nin, *The Four-Chambered Heart* (Denver: Swallow Press, 1959), 48.

25. Shanti Niliya, "Thou Shalt Not Kill: What Does It Mean?," as quoted in Brent Barlow, "Many ways to kill loved ones and even silence love itself," *Deseret News,* date unknown.

26. Paul Johannes Oskar Tillich, as quoted in Edythe Draper, ed., *Draper's Book of Quotations for the Christian World* (Wheaton, Ill.: Tyndale House Publishers, 1992), 522.

27. Personal records of author.

28. Story contributed by Brent West, Salt Lake City, Utah.

29. Elizabeth Byrd, "Rewards of a Gracious Heart," *Together Magazine,* December 1959, 48.

30. See Douglas and Jewel Beardall, eds., *The Qualities of Love* (Salt Lake City: Hawkes Publishing, 1978), 10–12.

31. Victor Hugo, as quoted in Ted Goodman, ed., *The Forbes Book of Business Quotations* (New York: Black Dog & Leventhal, 1997), 383.

32. Walker Percy, as quoted in *Reader's Digest Quotable Quotes,* 40.

33. Erich Hoffer, as quoted in Alan Loy McGinnis, *The Friendship Factor* (Indianapolis: Augsburg, 1979), 105.

34. Eda LeShan, *It's Better to Be over the Hill Than Under It* (New York: Newmarket Press, 1990), 110–11.

35. Ruth Ryan, *Covering Home* (Dallas: Word, 1995), 226.

36. G. K. Chesterton, as quoted in Edythe Draper, ed., *Draper's Book of Quotations for the Christian World,* 399.

37. Christopher Morley, as quoted in editors of *Reader's Digest, The Reader's Digest Treasury of Modern Quotations* (New York: Thomas Y. Crowell Co., 1975), 143.

38. Faith Baldwin, "Make Special Moments Every Day," *Woman's Day,* May 1961.

39. Harold S. Kushner, as quoted in Eileen Herbert Jordan, "A Thanksgiving Message," *Woman's Day,* 11 November 1986, 84.

40. Ursula K. LeGuin, *The Lathe of Heaven* (New York: Scribner's, 1971), 153.

41. Ardis Whitman, "The Case for Sentiment," *Guideposts,* July 1955, 6.

42. Jamie Buckingham, *Where Eagles Soar* (Lincoln, Va.: Chosen Books, 1980), 204–5.

43. W. Stanley Mooneyham, *Come Walk the World* (Waco, Tex.: Word Books, 1978), 21.

44. Ralph Fiennes, as quoted in Dotson Radar, "Success? What About Happiness?," *Parade Magazine,* 9 March 1997, 6.

45. Eleanor Roosevelt, as quoted in Ardis Whitman, "The Case for Sentiment," *Guideposts,* July 1955, 8.

46. Jo Ann Larsen, "Season's Greeting: An Open Letter To All My Loved Ones At Christmas," *Deseret News,* 25 December 1988, S3.

47. J. Masai, as quoted in *Reader's Digest Quotable Quotes,* 79.

48. Edward L. Flom, "Leadership: Attributes and Attitudes," *Executive Speeches,* February/March 1994, 49.

49. P. L. Travers, as quoted in Alex Witchel, "Where Starlings Greet the Stars," New York *Times,* 22 September 1994, C1.

50. Nancy Sheehan, "A Sister's Helping Hand," *Worcester Telegram & Gazette,* 18 November 1995, A1.

51. Smiley Blanton, "The Magic of Being in Touch," *Guideposts,* August 1965, 22–23.

52. Ibid., 24.

53. Helen Keller, *The World I Live In* (New York: Century, 1910), 4.

54. David Smoot, "The Human Touch," *Guideposts,* date unknown.

55. Eleanor Roosevelt, as quoted in "Words to Love By," *Orange County Register,* 13 February 1998, E01.

56. David Grayson, *The Countryman's Year* (New York: Doubleday, 1936), 180.

57. Zelda Fitzgerald, as quoted in Nancy Milford, *Zelda* (New York: Harper and Row, 1970), 367.

58. Story contributed by Jo Ann Able, American Fork, Utah.

59. *Deseret News,* "Cat Rushes into Fire for Kittens—5 Times," 1 April 1996, A1.

60. "Brave Hearts," *People,* 14 July 1997, 106–8.

61. Jeffrey Moussaieff Masson and Susan McCarthy, *When Elephants Weep: The Emotional Lives of Animals* (New York: Delacorte Press, 1995), 64–65.

62. Jack Canfield et al., eds., *Chicken Soup for the Pet Lover's Soul* (Dearfield Beach, Fla.: Health Communications, 1998), 34.

63. Loren Eiseley, *The Immense Journey* (New York: Random House, 1957), 185–92.

64. Sigrid Undset, as quoted in "Thoughts on the Business of Life," *Forbes,* 25 December 1978, 76.

65. Howard Thurman, *The Mood of Christmas* (New York: Harper & Row, 1973), 23. Used by permission of Friends United Press.

66. Herb Caen in *San Francisco Chronicle,* as quoted in *Reader's Digest,* March 1969, 185.

67. Jo Coudert, "Love," *Woman's Day,* 23 February 1993, 140.

68. Goodman Ace, "Like Is a Many-Splendored Thing," *The Saturday Review Sampler of Wit and Wisdom* (New York: Simon and Schuster, 1966), 169–70.

69. Nathaniel Branden, as quoted in Richard Carlson and Benjamin Shield, eds., *Handbook for the Heart* (New York: Little, Brown and Co., 1996), 19–20.

70. Holman F. Day, *Up in Maine* (Boston: Small, Maynard & Co., 1901), 201.

71. Juddu Krishnamuri, *Think on These Things*, ed. D. Rajayopal (New York: HarperPerennial, 1964), 191.

72. Marjorie Holmes in *The Marjorie Holmes Calendar of Love and Inspiration* (Doubleday), as quoted in James B. Simpson, comp., *Simpson's Contemporary Quotations* (Boston: Houghton Mifflin, 1988), 172.

73. C. S. Lewis, *The Four Loves*, 54–63.

74. Iris Origo, *Images and Shadows* (New York: Harcourt Brace Jovanovich, 1971), x.

75. Bernard J. Westbrock, as quoted in *Reader's Digest*, April 1958, 16.

76. William Golding, as quoted in Clifton Fadiman, ed., *Party of Twenty* (New York: Simon and Schuster, 1963), 141–43.

77. Story contributed by Jo Ann Able, American Fork, Utah.

78. Clint Weyand, as quoted in Jordan and Margaret Paul, *Do I Have To Give Up Me To Be Loved By You?* (Minneapolis: Comp/Care Publications, 1983), 115.

79. M. Scott Peck, as quoted in Karen Casey and Martha Vanceburg, *The Promise of a New Day* (New York: HarperCollins, 1983), 52.

80. Anne Morrow Lindbergh, as quoted in Karen Casey, *The Love Book* (New York: Harper/Hazelden, 1985), 38.

81. Rainer Maria Rilke, as quoted in Alan Loy McGinnis, *The Friendship Factor*, 76.

82. Kahlil Gibran, *The Prophet* (New York: Alfred A. Knopf, 1973), 15–18.

83. Ann Oakley in *Taking It Like a Woman*, as quoted in Robert Andrews, ed., *The Columbia Dictionary of Quotations* (New York: Columbia University Press, 1993), 544.

84. Karl Stern, as quoted in Karen Casey, *The Love Book*, 12.

85. Smiley Blanton, "When Love Is a Sickness," *Woman's Day*, October 1966, 50, 106.

86. Ralph Waldo Emerson, as quoted by K. L. Rawling, "Two of a Kind," *The Times*, 28 February 1997, Features.

87. Karen Casey, *The Love Book*, 3.

88. Jess Lair, *I Ain't Much, Baby—But I'm All I've Got* (New York: Doubleday, 1972), 203.

89. Paul B. Lowney, *The Lifetime Reader*, as quoted in *Reader's Digest*, May 1983, 240.

90. Thomas Merton, as quoted in Michael Mott, *The Seven Mountains of Thomas Merton* (Boston: Houghton Mifflin, 1984), 392.

91. Jeffrey Moussaieff Masson and Susan McCarthy, *When Elephants Weep*, 120–23.

92. James Thurber, "An Old Hand at Humor with Two Hits on Hand: Thurber," *Life*, 14 March 1960, 108.

93. Ardis Whitman, "How to Make Love Last," *Woman's Day*, 10 June 1983, 77.

94. Mary-Lou Weisman, "The Falling-in-Love-Trap," *Woman's Day*, 12 June 1984, 190.

95. Thomas S. Szasz, *Heresies* (Garden City, N.Y.: Anchor Press, 1976), 20.

96. Ardis Whitman, "How to Make Love Last," *Woman's Day*, 10 June 1983, 77.

97. Eda LeShan, *It's Better to Be Over the Hill Than Under It*, 94.

98. Story contributed by Pamela Johnson.

99. Story contributed by Brent West, Salt Lake City, Utah.

100. June Callwood, *Love, Hate, Fear, Anger and the Other Lively Emotions* (New York: Doubleday, 1964), 46–47.

101. Glenn Cunningham with George X. Sand, *Never Quit* (Lincoln, Va.: Chosen Books, 1981), 1–143.

102. Nina Fischer, as quoted in *Reader's Digest*, June 1979, 87. Used by permission.

103. Norman M. Lobsenz, as quoted in Alan Loy McGinnis, *The Friendship Factor*, 57–58.

104. Leslie D. Weatherhead, *Prescription for Anxiety* (New York: Abingdon Press, 1979), 123–24.

105. William Manchester, *Goodbye, Darkness* (Boston: Little, Brown & Co., 1980), 391.

106. Story contributed by Mickey Jackson, Kimberly, Idaho.

107. Afton Grant Affleck, *Love Is the Gift* (Salt Lake City: Bookcraft, 1977), 13–14. Used by permission.

108. Sir Hugh Walpole, as quoted in Lillian Eichler Watson, ed., *Light from Many Lamps* (New York: Simon & Schuster, 1979), 243.

109. William Lyon Phelps, as quoted in Lillian Eichler Watson, ed., *Light from Many Lamps*, 243.

110. Brahman adage, as quoted in Lillian Eichler Watson, ed., *Light from Many Lamps*, 243.

111. Nathaniel Branden, "Did You Hug Your Husband Today?," *Redbook*, August 1985, 79.

112. Queen Elizabeth, as quoted in Martha Dunagin Saunders, *Vital Speeches of the Day*, 15 January 1994, 201.

113. Eileen Egan and Kathleen Egan, *Suffering into Joy* (Ann Arbor, Mich.: Servant Publications, 1994), 32.

114. Rabindranath Tagore, as quoted in Ted Goodman, ed., *The Forbes Book of Business Quotations*, 147.

115. Dana Reeve, as quoted by Melina Gerosa in "Who Fascinates Barbara Most," *Ladies Home Journal*, April 1996, 130.

116. Ivan Turgenev, as quoted in Ralph L. Woods, comp., *Wellsprings of Wisdom* (Norwalk, Conn.: The C. R. Gibson Co., 1969), 388–39.

117. Robert B. Powers, as quoted in Raymond Swing, ed., *This I Believe*, vol. 2 (New York: Simon and Schuster, 1954), 119.

118. "The Hands of a Friend," Stan and Sharon Miller, eds., *Especially for Mormons*, 4 vols. (Provo, Ut.: Kellirae Arts, 1976), 3:128–29.

119. Frances Farmer, *Will There Really Be a Morning?* (New York: G. P. Putnam's Sons, 1972), 309.

120. Marguerite Yourcenar, *With Open Eyes* (Boston: Beacon Press, 1984), 262.

121. Joseph Fort Newton, *Living Every Day* (New York: Harper, 1937), 126–27.

122. Jane Howard, *Families* (New York: Simon and Schuster, 1978), 236–37.

123. Isabel Norton, as quoted in *Touchstones: A Book of Daily Meditations for Men* (Center City, Minn.: Hazelden Foundation, 1991), 142.

124. Fulton J. Sheen, as quoted in Frederick Gushurst, comp. and ed., *The Quotable Fulton J. Sheen* (Anderson, S.C.: Droke House, 1967), 96.

125. Henri J. Nouwen, *Out of Solitude* (Notre Dame, Ind.: Ave Maria Press, 1984), 34.

126. Ralph Waldo Emerson, as quoted in Edythe Draper, ed., *Draper's Book of Quotations for the Christian World*, 228.

127. Ed Cunningham, as quoted in *Reader's Digest Quotable Quotes*, 40.

128. Merle Shain, *When Lovers Are Friends* (Philadelphia: Lippincott, 1978), 106.

129. Joe Senser, as quoted in Robert L. Veninga, *A Gift of Hope* (Boston: Little, Brown and Co., 1985), 112.

130. Margaret Mead, as quoted in Niela Eliason, "The Things That We Really Need," *St. Petersburg Times*, 30 November 1993, 30.

131. Joyce Brothers, as quoted in Dennis Wholey, ed., *Are You Happy?* (Boston: Houghton Mifflin, 1986), 200.

132. Robert Nathan, *So Love Returns* (New York: Knopf, 1958), 138.

133. Sharon Whitley, "The critical key: just one of Dad's thoughtful deeds," *San Diego Union*, 15 June 1991, B13.

134. Kendall Hailey, *The Day I Became an Autodidact* (New York: Ballantine, 1976), 4.

135. William Raspberry, "Strong Bonds, Created by Marriage," *The Record*, 25 April 1994, A14.

136. Jane W. Lund, *Evidence of Hope* (Salt Lake City: Lundcraft Heritage Arts, 1994), 2–3. Used by permission.

137. Anthony Brandt, as quoted in Karen Kile, "Keeping the Family in a Family Business," *Pennsylvania CPA Journal*, December 1996, 15.

138. Linda Ronstadt, in Divina Infusino, *Vis-à-Vis*, as quoted in *Reader's Digest*, October 1992, 97.

139. Og Mandino, *The Choice* (New York: Bantam, 1986), 103.

140. James Stewart, as quoted in Larry Rohter, "James Stewart Nods at Lady Luck for His Golden Age Film Career," *New York Times*, 23 April 1990, C11.

141. Harold Kushner, "Make More Family Time," *Redbook*, January 1990, 93.

142. Richard E. Byrd, as quoted in Lillian Eichler Watson, ed., *Light From Many Lamps*, 248–50.

143. Erich Fromm, *The Art of Loving*, 54.

144. Anne Morrow Lindbergh, *Gift from the Sea* (New York: Pantheon, 1955), 44.

145. Erich Fromm, *Glad to Be Me* (Englewood Cliffs, N.J.: Prentice-Hall, 1976), 24.

146. Bernie S. Siegel, "Follow Your Bliss," *New Woman*, September 1989, 52.

147. Bruce Barton, as quoted in John P. Bradley et al., comps., *The International Dictionary of Thoughts* (Chicago: J. G. Ferguson Publishing Co., 1969), 553.

148. George Herbert Palmer, as quoted in Rufus M. Jones, *New Eyes for Invisibles* (New York: Macmillan, 1943), 77.

149. Rufus M. Jones, *New Eyes for Invisibles*, 77.

150. Harry Emerson Fosdick, *Living Under Tension* (New York: Harper, 1941), 206.

151. Frank Norris, *Complete Works* (New York: Doubleday, 1903), 352.

152. Alan Loy McGinnis, *The Friendship Factor*, 13.

153. Martha Grimes, as quoted in Randi Feigenbaum, "Big Computer Is Watching The Office," Long Island *Newsday*, 14 July 1997, C02.

154. Clifton Fadiman, *Any Number Can Play* (Cleveland: World, 1957), 160.

155. Winston Churchill, as quoted in "Why Churchill Was a Glow-Worm," *The Daily Telegraph*, 14 March 1998, Books, 3.

156. Golda Meir, as quoted in Charlotte Chandler, *The Ultimate Seduction* (New York: Doubleday, 1984), 98.

157. Helen Hayes, with Sandford Dody, *On Reflection* (New York: Evans, 1968), 129.

158. Dennis Larsen, "Soul Touching Soul," unpublished manuscript.

159. Ardis Whitman, "Overtaken by Joy," *Reader's Digest*, 4 April 1965, 109.

160. Ardis Whitman, "Those Magic Moments at the Core of Life," *Reader's Digest*, September 1983, 95.

161. J. Allen Boone, *Kinship with All Life*, as quoted in Susan Haward, ed., *A Guide for the Advanced Soul* (Australia: Crows News, 1990), 112.

162. Paul Davies, *The Soul of the Universe*, as quoted in Tian Dayton, *The Quiet Voice of Soul* (Deerfield Beach, Fla.: Health Communications, 1995), 23.

163. Brian Swimm, as quoted in Tian Dayton, *The Quiet Voice of Soul*, 53.

164. Tian Dayton, *The Quiet Voice of Soul*, xii–xiv.

165. Zelda Sayre, as quoted in Antonia Fraser, ed., *Love Letters* (New York: Alfred A. Knopf, 1977), 41.

166. Contributed by author's daughter, Erin Larsen, Salt Lake City, Utah.

167. Baal Shem Tov, as quoted in Phil Cousineau, ed., *Soul: An Archaeology*, 65.

168. Thomas Moore, *Soulmates* (New York: HarperCollins, Publishers, 1994), 28, 49–50, 55, 57, 59, 61, 67, 68.

169. Tony Snow, "The Pain of Losing a Child to Be," *USA Today*, 20 May 1993, 11A.

170. Natan Sharansky, *Fear No Evil* (New York: Random House, 1988), 415.

171. Victor Frankl, *Man's Search For Meaning*, trans. Ilse Lasch (New York: Beacon Press, 1992), 47–50.

172. "Through Prison Walls," *Time*, 10 June 1957, 32.

173. Neil Millar, "The Wide Embrace," *The Christian Science Monitor*, 18 January 1982, 20.

174. Maryjane Hooper Tonn, *I Found God* (Milwaukee, Wis.: Ideals Publishing Corp., 1977), 27.

175. Mother Teresa, as quoted in Russ Hauck, "Saint and Sinner," *The Orlando Sentinel*, 12 September 1997, A14.

176. Daphne Rose Kingma, as quoted in editors of Conari Press, *Random Acts of Kindness* (Berkeley: Conari Press, 1993), 4. Used by permission.

177. Erich Fromm, *The Art of Loving*, 42.

178. Martin Luther King Jr., as quoted in editors of Conari Press, *Random Acts of Kindness*, 17.

179. Pierre Teilhard de Chardin, as quoted in Edythe Draper, ed., *Draper's Book of Quotations for the Christian World*, 394.

180. Corrie Ten Boom, *The Hiding Place* (New York: Bantam Books, 1971), 98–99, 170–71, 202, 217, 219, back cover.

181. Sarah F. Jensen, comp., *Ye Old Time Philosophy* (n.p.: Sarah F. Jensen, 1974), 27.

182. Mary Livingstone Benny and Hilliard Marks with Marcia Borie, *Jack Benny* (Garden City, N.Y.: Doubleday, 1978), 393.

183. Marjorie Holmes, *To Help You Through the Hurting* (New York: Doubleday, 1983), 66–74.

184. Stewart Powell, "A Sacred Place on the Potomac," *U.S. News & World Report,* 10 November 1986, 17. Copyright, November 10, 1986, *U.S. News & World Report.* Used by permission.

185. William Broyles Jr., "A Ritual for Saying Goodbye," *U.S. News & World Report,* 10 November 1986, 19. Copyright, November 10, 1986, *U.S. News & World Report.* Used by permission.

186. Helen Hayes, as quoted in Anvar Khan, "Morality," *The Herald,* 15 May 1998, 25.

187. Jill Furse, as quoted in Antonia Fraser, ed., *Love Letters,* 142.

188. Ralph Waldo Emerson, as quoted in Doron K. Antrim, comp., "Why I Believe in Immortality," *Reader's Digest,* March 1960, 135.

189. Norman Vincent Peale, *The Power of Positive Thinking* (New York: Prentice-Hall, 1956), 210.

190. Victor Hugo, as quoted in Sterling W. Sill, *Meditations on Death and Life* (Bountiful, Ut.: Horizon, 1983), 27.

191. Author unknown, as quoted in Sterling W. Sill, *Meditations on Death and Life,* 29–30.

192. Catherine Marshall, *To Live Again* (New York: McGraw-Hill, 1957), 54, 113.

193. Attributed to Strickland Gillilan, source unknown.

194. D. H. Martin, as quoted in Oscar Vance Armstrong, comp., *Comfort for Those Who Mourn* (Nashville: Cokesbury Press, 1930), 13.

195. Norman Vincent Peale, *The Power of Positive Thinking,* 210.

196. Ralph W. Sockman, as quoted in Doron K. Antrim, comp., "Why I Believe in Immortality," *Reader's Digest,* March 1960, 138.

197. Sri Chinmay, *Garden of the Soul* (Deerfield Beach, Fla.: Health Communications, 1994), 101.

198. Mohandas Gandhi, as quoted in Sefra Kobrin Pitzele, *One More Day,* 157.

199. Alexis Carrel, as quoted in Ardis Whitman, "Choose Life," *Reader's Digest,* November 1984, 209.

200. Abraham Lincoln, as quoted in Fulton Oursler, "What Prayer Can Do," *Reader's Digest,* January 1951, 9–10.

201. Abraham Lincoln, as quoted in Stanley and Sharon Miller, eds., *Especially for Mormons,* 1:287.

202. Eddie Rickenbacker, as quoted in *Paul Harvey's The Rest of the Story* (New York: Doubleday, 1977), 172.

203. Margaret Lee Runbeck, "We Were on That Raft—A Hundred Million of Us," in Audrey Stone Morris, comp., *1000 Inspirational Things* (Chicago: Spencer Press, 1948), 68–72.

204. "The Actor," in Stanley and Sharon Miller, eds., *Especially for Mormons,* 3:26.

205. "No Hands But Ours," in Stanley and Sharon Miller, eds., *Especially for Mormons,* 2:32.

206. Annie Johnson Flint, as quoted in Dale Turner, "Evangelism Needed: Christ Has No Hands—Except Our Own," *The Seattle Times,* 17 August 1996, D4.

207. Jerry Johnston, "Miracles can stem from one soul's caring acts," *Deseret News,* 21 February 1997, C-1.

208. General Booth, as quoted in Harry Emerson Fosdick, *On Being a Real Person* (New York: Harper & Brothers, 1943), 106–7.

209. Subir Bhaunik, Meenakshi, and Tim McGirk, "Mother Teresa, 1910–1997: Seeker of Souls," *Time,* 15 September 1997, 78–94.

210. Mother Teresa, as quoted in "In Our Opinion," *Deseret News,* 8 September 1997, A8.

211. Gordon B. Hinckley, "To Single Adults," *Ensign,* June 1989, 73.

212. Lilian Katz, *ECCE Newsletter,* as quoted in *Reader's Digest,* August 1982, 167–68.

❤ ❤ ❤ ❤ ❤ ❤ ❤ ❤

CHAPTER 2: ON COMPASSION

1. Henry David Thoreau, *Walden* (New York: Penguin, 1980), 12.

2. Philip Johnston, "Compassion," *Self,* April 1992, 196.

3. Jean-Jacques Rousseau, as quoted in Mortimer J. Adler and Charles Van Doren, eds., *Great Treasury of Western Thought* (New York: R. R. Bowker Co., 1977), 556.

4. Mother Teresa, as quoted in Kenneth L. Woodward, *Newsweek,* 29 October 1979, 60.

5. A. J. Cronin, "Why I Believe in God," *Woman's Home Companion,* July 1950, 35.

6. Elder Jared Turner to Terry and Kim Sandberg Turner, Salt Lake City, Utah.

7. *Yorkshire Evening Post,* 13 June 1944, as quoted in Victor Gollancz, *Man and God* (Boston: Houghton Mifflin, 1951), 206.

8. *Leicester Evening Mail,* 19 May 1944, as quoted in Victor Gollancz, *Man and God,* 205.

9. Pythagoras, as quoted in Clifton Fadiman, ed., *The Little, Brown Book of Anecdotes* (Boston: Little, Brown and Co., 1985), 459.

10. Jeremy Taylor, as quoted in Edythe Draper, ed., *Draper's Book of Quotations for the Christian World* (Wheaton, Ill.: Tyndale House, 1992), 583.

11. George Macdonald, in *Unspoken Sermon*, second series [1885], as quoted in John Bartlett, ed., *Bartlett's Familiar Quotations* (Boston: Little, Brown and Co., 1992), 504.

12. Henry J. M. Nouwen, as quoted in Edythe Draper, ed., *Draper's Book of Quotations for the Christian World*, 90.

13. Ibid.

14. Sue Monk Kidd, "Birthing Compassion," in John S. Mogabgab, *Communion, Community, Commonweal* (Nashville: Upper Room Books, 1995), 148.

15. Octavus Roy Cohen, "Richard Kirkland: American," *Together Magazine*, May 1956, 30–33.

16. Unknown author, as quoted in James B. Simpson, comp., *Simpson's Contemporary Quotations* (Boston: Houghton Mifflin Co., 1988), 185.

17. Stan and Sharon Miller, eds., *Especially for Mormons*, 4 vols. (Provo, Ut.: Kellirae Arts, n.d.), 3:284.

18. Pablo Casals, as quoted in *Reader's Digest Quotable Quotes* (Pleasantville, N.Y.: The Reader's Digest Association, 1997), 202.

19. George Matthew Adams, as quoted in L. M. Boyd, in *The Houston Post*, 20 January 1994, A16.

20. John D. McDonald, as quoted in Stephen King, *Night Shift* (New York: Doubleday, 1978), introduction.

21. Albert Schweitzer, *Memoirs of Childhood and Youth*, trans. Kurt Bergel and Alice R. Bergel (Syracuse: Syracuse University Press, 1997), 81–82.

22. Jerry Johnston, "All creation is patchwork quilt of diversity," *Deseret News*, 30 May 1998, E1. Used by permission.

23. Jane W. Lund, *Patchwork: Pieces of My Heart* (Salt Lake City: Lundcraft Heritage Arts, 1998), 3. Used by permission.

24. Ardis Whitman, "If I Should Die Before I Wake," *Reader's Digest*, December 1977, 220.

25. Thomas Savage, *Her Side of It* (Boston: Little, Brown, 1981), 276.

26. Arthur Gordon, "How Much Do You Care?" *Guideposts*, October, 1963. Used by permission.

27. Story contributed by Pamela Johnson.

28. W. MacNeil Dixon, *The Human Situation* (New York: St. Martin's Press, 1954), 365.

29. Leslie Laurence, "Empathy," *Self*, June 1991, 110.

30. Jess Lair, *I Ain't Much, Baby—But I'm All I've Got* (Garden City, N.Y.: Doubleday, 1972), 211.

31. Sue Monk Kidd, in *Communion, Community, Commonweal,* as quoted in Frederic and Mary Ann Brussat, eds., *Spiritual Literacy: Reading the Sacred in Everyday Life* (New York: Scribner, 1996), 436.

32. Jeff Wheelwright, "The Homeless, at Suppertime," *New York Times,* 16 December 1987, A35.

33. Helen Hudson, *Tell the Time to None* (New York: Dutton, 1966), 187.

34. Neil Millar, in *The Christian Science Monitor,* as quoted in *Reader's Digest,* June 1981, 112.

35. Sam Levenson, *In One Era and Out the Other* (New York: Simon & Schuster, 1973), 178.

36. Friedrich Nietzche, as quoted in Dennis Pollock, "From the Desk of Dennis Pollock," *Fresno Bee,* 15 September 1995, F2.

37. Woody Harrelson, as quoted by Philip Wuntch, "On a Decent Roll as Father and Star," *The Chicago Tribune,* 16 April 1993, C2.

38. Franz Kafka, as quoted in Gustav Janouch, *Conversations With Kafka* (London: Quartet, 1985), 179.

39. Karl A. Menninger, *The Human Mind* (New York: Knopf, 1930), 3.

40. Cy Fey, "Points to Ponder," *Reader's Digest,* June 1990, 52. Used by permission.

41. Nicholas Berdyaev, *The Fate of Man and the Modern World,* trans. Donald A. Lowrie (London: Student Christian Movement Press, 1935), 12.

42. Sam Levenson, *Everything but Money* (New York: Simon & Schuster, 1966), 201.

43. Leon Bloy, as quoted in Victor Gollancz, *Man and God,* 272.

44. Malcolm Muggeridge, *Something Beautiful for God* (New York: Harper & Row, 1971), 16–18, 21, 23, 28, 29, 52.

45. Anonymous work submitted to Minnesota Literary Council, as quoted in Amy E. Dean, *Night Light* (Center City, Minn.: Hazelden Foundation, 1992), 131.

46. Victor Gollancz, *Man and God,* 518, 526–27.

47. St. Isaak of Syria, as quoted in Victor Gollancz, *Man and God,* 171.

48. Meister Eckhart, as quoted in Frederic and Mary Ann Brussat, eds., *Spiritual Literacy: Reading the Sacred in Everyday Life,* 167.

49. Writings in The Kabbalah, as quoted in Frederic and Mary Ann Brussat, *Spiritual Literacy: Reading the Sacred in Everyday Life,* 167.

50. Scott Russell Sanders, *Writing from the Center* (Indianapolis: Indiana University Press, 1995), 104.

51. Albert Schweitzer, as quoted in Norman Cousins, ed., *The Words of Albert Schweitzer* (New York: Newmarket Press, 1984), 41.

52. Albert Schweitzer, *Memoirs of Childhood and Youth,* 38.

53. Albert Schweitzer, as quoted in Norman Cousins, ed., *The Words of Albert Schweitzer,* 38.

54. Jeffrey Moussaieff Masson, *Dogs Never Lie about Love* (New York: Crows Publishers, 1997), 94.

55. Debbie Sorenson, as quoted in Susan Chernak McElroy, *Animals as Teachers and Healers* (New York: Ballantine Books, 1996), 191–92.

56. "Mother Gorilla Rescues Tot Who Fell into Exhibit at Zoo," *Deseret News,* 17 August 1996, A3.

57. Jack Denton Scott, "That Remarkable Animal, the Porpoise," *Audubon Magazine,* January–February, 1962, 10.

58. Mary Devoe, ed., "Wild Wisdom," *Reader's Digest,* October 1964, 25C.

59. Jeffrey Moussaieff Masson and Susan McCarthy, *When Elephants Weep: The Emotional Lives of Animals* (New York: Delacorte, 1995), 156.

60. Mary Devoe, ed., "Wild Wisdom," *Reader's Digest,* February 1958, 106.

61. Personal observation of author.

62. Sharon Meininger, as quoted in Susan Chernak McElroy, *Animals as Teachers and Healers,* 70.

63. Alan Devoe, "How Animals Help Each Other," *Reader's Digest,* May 1955, 141.

64. Associated Press, "That 'quack' sound is duck's 911 call," *Deseret News,* 7 May 1977, A6.

65. Rajendra K. Saboo, as quoted in Ralph L. Woods, comp., *Wellsprings of Wisdom* (Norwalk, Conn.: The C. R. Gibson Company, 1969), 60.

66. John Cowper Powys, as quoted in *The Meaning of Culture* (New York: W. W. Norton, 1939), 242.

67. Itzhak Perlman, as quoted in Dan Chiszar, United Press International, "Domestic News," 28 January 1981, AM cycle.

68. Beverly Sills, as quoted in Margaret Carroll, "Parents of handicapped children, says Beverly Sills, must work as hard at their marriage as at helping the kids," *Chicago Tribune,* 1 July 1987, 9 SD.

69. Hubert Humphrey, as quoted in Edwin Warner, "Death of an American Original," *Time,* 23 January 1978, 25.

70. Charles Osgood, *CBS Morning News,* as quoted in *Reader's Digest,* November 1990, 185.

71. Ardis Whitman, "The Case for Sentiment," *Guideposts,* July 1955, 6.

72. C. S. Lewis, as quoted in Tian Dayton, *The Quiet Voice of Soul* (Deerfield Beach, Fla.: Health Communications, 1995), 5.

73. Jane W. Lund, *Evidence of Hope* (Salt Lake City: Lundcraft, 1994), 18–19. Used by permission.

74. Sarah F. Jensen, ed. and comp., *Ye Old Time Philosophy* (n.p.: Sarah F. Jensen , 1974), 27.

75. Karen Boren, "Tender WWII Love Story Brings the Audience to Its Feet at BYU," *Deseret News*, 15 February 1997, C-10. Used by permission.

76. Marcel Marceau, as quoted in Ted Goodman, ed., *The Forbes Book of Business Quotations* (New York: Black Dog & Leventhal, 1997), 767.

77. Story contributed by Pamela Johnson.

78. *Tales of the Hasidim*, as quoted in *Peacemaking: Day by Day* (Erie, Penn.: Pax Christi USA, 1985), 1:102.

79. Erma Bombeck, "Please, Listen," *Chicago Sun-Times*, 26 February 1977.

80. Ashleigh Brilliant, as quoted in John Cook, comp., *The Rubicon Dictionary of Positive Motivational, Life-Affirming and Inspirational Quotations* (Newington, Conn.: Rubicon Press, 1994), 90.

81. Ram Dass and Paul Gorman, *How Can I Help?* (New York: Alfred A. Knopf, 1985), 239.

82. Robert W. Youngs, as quoted in Jacob M. Braude, ed., *Braude's Source Book for Speakers and Writers* (Englewood Cliffs, N.J.: Prentice-Hall, 1968), 116.

83. B. A. Botkin, ed., *A Civil War Treasury of Tales, Legends and Folklore* (New York: Random House, 1960), 38–40.

84. Pope John XXIII, as quoted in Norman Cousins, *Human Options* (New York: Norton, 1981), 24.

85. Albert Schweitzer, "Your Second Job—Do Unto Others," *Reader's Digest*, October 1961, 71.

86. Wilfred Grenfell, as quoted in Laurence J. Peter, ed., *Peter's Quotations* (New York: William Morrow, 1977), 386.

87. Excerpt from "Epilogue: Letter to a Young Doctor," in Agnes W. Dooley, *Promises to Keep* (New York: Farrar, Straus & Giroux, 1961), 266–71. Used by permission.

88. Daphne Rose Kingma, as quoted in editors of Conari Press, *Random Acts of Kindness* (Berkeley: Conari Press, 1993), 66. Used by permission.

89. Roy Popkin, "Night Watch," *National Observer*, 21 December 1964, 12. Used by permission.

90. Peter De Vries, *Let Me Count the Ways* (Boston: Little, Brown, 1965), 292.

91. Helen Keller, *Teacher* (Garden City, N.Y.: Doubleday, 1955), 236.

92. Sue Monk Kidd, "Compassion," as quoted in Phyllis Hobe, ed., *Dawnings* (Carmel, N.Y.: Guideposts, 1981), 88.

93. Phillip Keller, *Lessons from a Sheepdog* (Waco, Tex.: Word Books, 1983), 15–28, 40–41.

94. Antoine de Saint Exupéry, *The Little Prince* (New York: Harcourt Brace, 1943), 70.

95. Arthur Gordon, "The Rewards of Caring," *Guideposts*, October 1963, 15. Used by permission.

96. Hermann Hegedorn, *The Roosevelt Family of Sagamore Hill* (New York: Macmillan, 1954), 262.

97. B. A. Botkin, ed., *A Civil War Treasury of Tales, Legends and Folklore*, 225–26.

98. James Michener, as quoted in *Reader's Digest*, August 1989, 37.

99. Mary McGovern, "Lost and Found," *Reader's Digest*, June 1979, 102. Used by permission.

100. D. B Hardeman, "Unseen Side of the Man They Called Mr. Speaker," *Life*, 1 December 1961, 21.

101. H. G. Wells, as quoted by Fanny Butcher, in *Chicago Tribune*, as quoted in *Reader's Digest*, April 1963, 181–82.

102. Catherine Marshall, as quoted in Phyllis Hobe, ed., *Dawnings*, 164.

103. In Clifton Fadiman, ed., *The Little, Brown Book of Anecdotes*, 468.

104. Henry Melville, as quoted in Ted Goodman, ed., *The Forbes Book of Business Quotations*, 554.

105. Henry David Thoreau, as quoted in Angela Partington, ed., *The Oxford Dictionary of Quotations* (New York: Oxford Univesity Press, 1992), 697.

106. Susan Chernak McElroy, *Animals as Teachers and Healers*, xvii, 9.

107. DeAnne George, 1982, in Human Condition Legends Collection, Brigham Young University, Provo, Utah.

108. Sharon Salzberg, *Lovingkindness* (Boston: Shambhala, 1995), 109–10.

109. Clarence W. Hall, "The Bad Habit of Judging Others," *Christian Herald*, May 1956, 30.

110. Sarah Brown, in H. Jackson Brown Jr., comp., *P. S., I Love You* (Nashville: Rutledge Hill, 1990), 102.

111. Anne McCaffrey, *Dragonquest* (New York: Ballantine, 1980), 71.

112. William Arthur Ward, as quoted in *Reader's Digest*, August 1977, 37.

113. Peter Ustinov, in Samuel Justine, [Paris] *International Herald Tribune*, as quoted in *Reader's Digest*, July 1982, 40.

114. Tom Brokaw, in *New York Times*, as quoted in *Reader's Digest*, June 1980, 69.

115. Author unknown.

116. Clarence W. Hall, "The Bad Habit of Judging Others," *Christian Herald*, May 1956, 50.

117. Phoenix Central Christian Church *Newsletter*, date unknown.

118. St. John of the Cross, as quoted in Victor Gollancz, *Man and God*, 175.

119. Bishop Fulton J. Sheen, as quoted in *The Quotable Fulton J. Sheen*, comp. and ed. Frederick Gushurst (Anderson, S.C.: Droke House, 1967), 130.

120. Bernard Grun, *Private Lives of the Great Composers, Conductors and Artists of the World* (New York: Rider, 1954), 31.

121. Max Ehrlich, "'Secret-keeping,' the art of helping fellow man," *Family Weekly*, 22 December 1968, 15.

122. Pamela Hennell, "The Mystery of the Blank Newspaper Columns," *Reader's Digest*, March 1952, 74–76.

123. *The Collected Later Poems of William Carlos Williams* (New York: New Directions, 1963), 24.

124. Paul G. Hewitt, *Conceptual Physics* (New York: HarperCollins, 1993), 27, 30.

125. Max G. Bunyan, as quoted in *Reader's Digest*, August 1972, 98. Used by permission.

126. L. M. Boyd, as quoted in *Reader's Digest*, July 1971, 138.

127. Pablo Casals, as told to Albert E. Kahn, *Joys and Sorrows* (New York: Simon and Schuster, 1970), 124–25.

128. Ardis Whitman, "The Awesome Power to Be Ourselves," *Reader's Digest*, January 1983, 81.

129. Ibid., 80.

130. Alexandra Stoddard, "Reaching Out to Others," *McCalls*, June 1991, 142.

131. Cliff Richard with Bill Latham, *Which One's Cliff?* (London: Hodder & Stoughton, 1977), 145.

132. C. Everett Koop and Allen V. Koop, *Koop: The Memoirs of a Former Surgeon General* (New York: Random House, 1991), 109.

♥ ♥ ♥ ♥ ♥ ♥ ♥ ♥ ♥

CHAPTER 3: ON KINDNESS

1. Van Wyck Brooks, *An Autobiography* (New York: Dutton, 1965), 563.

2. Humphrey Davy, as quoted in Edythe Draper, ed., *Draper's Book of Quotation for the Christian World* (Wheaton, Ill.: Tyndale House Publishers, 1992), 366.

3. Persian proverb, as quoted in *Reader's Digest*, October 1983, 151.

4. Charles Kuralt, *On the Road with Charles Kuralt* (New York: Ballantine Books, 1986), 17.

5. Mark Twain, as quoted in Michael Joseph, ed., *Man Is The Only Animal That Blushes . . . Or Needs To: The Wisdom of Mark Twain* (New York: Random House, 1970), 2.

6. Frederick William Faber, as quoted in Edythe Draper, ed., *Draper's Book of Quotations for the Christian World*, 365–66.

7. Sir Kenneth Clark, *Civilisation* (New York: Harper & Row, 1969), 279.

8. Ian Maclaren, as quoted in Edythe Draper, ed., *Draper's Book of Quotations for the Christian World*, 365.

9. Adam Lindsay Gordon, as quoted in Edythe Draper, ed., *Draper's Book of Quotations for the Christian World*, 366.

10. Eleanor Roosevelt, *You Learn by Living* (New York: Harper, 1960), 156.

11. Daphne Rose Kingma, as quoted in editors of Conari Press, *Random Acts of Kindness* (Berkeley: Conari Press, 1993), 61. Used by permission.

12. Jane W. Lund, "On discovering the joy of diversity," *Evidence of Hope* (Salt Lake City: Lundcraft Heritage Arts, 1994), 13–15. Used by permission.

13. Unknown author, as quoted in Sarah F. Jensen, ed. and comp., *Ye Old Time Philosophy* (n.p.: Sarah F. Jensen, 1974), 80.

14. Dan Rather with Mickey Hershkowitz, *The Camera Never Blinks Twice* (New York: W. W. Morrow, 1994), 115–16.

15. Ralph Waldo Emerson, *Letters and Social Aims*, as quoted in Justin Kaplan, ed., *Bartlett's Familiar Quotations* (Boston: Little, Brown and Co., 1992), 433.

16. Brad Darrach in *Life*, 11 August 1972, 43.

17. Anonymous author, as quoted in S. H. Simmons, *New Speakers Handbook* (New York: Dial,1972), 282.

18. As quoted in Herbert V. Prochnow and Herbert V. Prochnow Jr., *A Treasure Chest of Quotations for All Occasions* (New York: Harper & Row, 1983), 352.

19. O. A. Battista, *Quotoons* (New York: G. P. Putnam's Sons, 1977), 392.

20. Elizabeth Rich on "Mike Douglas Show," Westinghouse Broadcasting Co., as quoted in *Reader's Digest*, January 1971, 105.

21. Jed Carver story collected by Patricia B. Robbins, 1984, Human Conditions Legends Collection #3.10.2.49.1, Brigham Young University Folklore Archive, Provo, Utah. Names have been changed.

22. John Prutting with Patricia Curtis, "How to Conquer Stress," *Family Circle*, December 1972, 102.

23. Joyce Brothers, as quoted in "Thoughts on the Business of Life," *Forbes*, 22 September 1997, 288.

24. Sam Moses in "Yankee from Louisiana," *Sports Illustrated*, 22 January 1979, 62.

25. Dennis Gray, as quoted by Tom Zucco in "One of Life's Little Lessons," St. Petersburg *Times*, 8 September 1993, 1D.

26. Story contributed by Kim Sandberg Turner, Salt Lake City, Utah.

27. Abraham Lincoln, as quoted in Paul F. Boller Jr., ed., *Presidential Anecdotes* (New York: Oxford University Press, 1981), 135.

28. Blaise Pascal, as quoted in Clyde Francis Lytle, ed., *Leaves of Gold* (Williamsport, Penn.: The Coslett Publishing Co., 1948), 157.

29. Henry Van Dyke, as quoted in Jacob M. Graude, *Complete Speaker's and Toastmaster's Library* (Englewood Cliffs, N.J.: Prentice-Hall, 1965), 41.

30. N. Adams, as quoted in Clyde Francis Lytle, ed., *Leaves of Gold*, 160.

31. The Talmud, as quoted in Audrey Stone Morris, comp., *1000 Inspirational Things* (Chicago: Spencer Press, Inc., 1948), 161.

32. Unknown author, as quoted in Louis A. Bergman, ed., *Proverb, Wit & Wisdom* (New York: Berkley Publishing Group, 1997), 372.

33. Bob Monkhouse, *Just Say a Few Words* (New York: Evans, 1991), 175.

34. James Alexander Thom, in *Nuggets,* as quoted in *Reader's Digest,* November 1977, 229–30.

35. Robert Fulghum, *All I Really Need to Know I Learned in Kindergarten* (New York: Villard Books, 1990), 20.

36. Eknath Easwaran, *The Mantam Handbook* (Berkeley: Nilgiri Press, 1977), 87.

37. Dale E. Turner, "Regrettable Silences," *Let's Think About It* (Seattle: Seattle Times, 1996), 43.

38. As quoted in W. Francis Gates, ed., *Anecdotes of Great Musicians* (Philadelphia: Theodore Presser, 1895), 154.

39. Richard E. Merrifield, *Monadnock Journal* (Taftsville, Vt.: Countryman Press, 1975), 26.

40. Louis Nizer, as quoted in *Reader's Digest,* June 1975, 179.

41. Abraham Lincoln, as quoted in Edmund Fuller, ed., *2500 Anecdotes for All Occasions* (New York: Avenel Books, 1942), 54.

42. Herbert V. Prochnow and Herbert V. Prochnow Jr., *A Treasure Chest of Quotations for All Occasions,* 361.

43. Robert Browning, as quoted in Justin Kaplan, ed., *Bartlett's Familiar Quotations,* 467.

44. Blaise Pascal, as quoted in Ted Goodman, ed., *The Forbes Book of Business Quotations* (New York: Black Dog & Leventhal, 1997), 469.

45. Mother Teresa, as quoted by Andy Zubko, comp., *Treasury of Spritual Wisdom* (San Diego: Blue Dove Press, 1996),

46. Harriet Beecher Stowe, *Uncle Tom's Cabin,* ed. Kenneth S. Lynn (Cambridge, Mass.: The Belknap Press of Harvard University Press, 1962), 251.

47. Seneca, as quoted in Ted Goodman, ed., *The Forbes Book of Business Quotations,* 470.

48. Jeremy Bentham, as quoted in Richard L. Evans, ed., *Richard Evans' Quote Book* (Salt Lake City: Publishers Press, 1971), 173.

49. Jim Abbott, as quoted by Gregg Mazzola, "Personal Glimpses," *Reader's Digest,* September 1993, 16.

50. Katherine Hepburn, as quoted in Ellen Peck and William Ganzig, *The Parent Test* (New York: G. P. Putnam's Sons, 1978), 121.

51. Jane Lindstrom, "How Will You Know Unless I Tell You?," *These Times,* October 1976.

52. Jim Murray, in Los Angeles *Times*, as quoted in *Reader's Digest*, March 1968, 142.

53. Baruch Spinoza, as quoted in Robert L. Veninga, *A Gift of Hope* (Boston: Little, Brown and Co., 1985), 43.

54. Theodore Roosevelt, as quoted in Herbert V. Prochnow and Herbert V. Prochnow Jr., *A Treasure Chest of Quotations for All Occasions*, 320.

55. As quoted by E. E. Edgar, in *Reader's Digest*, November 1957, 141.

56. As quoted by Maurine P. McCarthy, in *Reader's Digest*, April 1969, 130.

57. Terry Dobson, "The Soft Answer," *The Graduate Review*, March/April 1981.

58. Story of Abraham Lincoln, as quoted in Paul F. Boller Jr., ed., *Presidential Anecdotes*, 135–36.

59. Story of Abraham Lincoln, as quoted in James C. Humes, ed., *Speaker's Treasury of Anecdotes About the Famous* (New York: Harper & Row, 1978), 188.

60. Arthur Wellesley Wellington, as quoted in Clifton Fadiman, ed., *The Little, Brown Book of Anecdotes* (Boston: Little, Brown and Co., 1985), 578.

61. Pat Frank, "I am happy with my time," in Edward P. Morgan, ed., *This I Believe* (New York: Simon and Schuster, 1952), 53.

62. Karen McCowan, "Caring Cop Was a Saint," *The Register-Guard*, 18 April 1995, B1. Used by permission.

63. Bob Greene, "A Moment's Effort Means the World," *Chicago Tribune*, 6 July 1987, 1C.

64. Randolph Ray, as quoted in James B. Simpson, comp., *Simpson's Contemporary Quotations* (Boston: Houghton Mifflin Co., 1988), 175.

65. Mother Teresa, as quoted in Malcolm Muggeridge, *Something Beautiful for God* (New York: Harper & Row, 1971), 69.

66. Freya Stark, *The Journey's Echo* (New York: Harcourt, Brace & World, 1963), 54.

67. John Lumpkin, "Remembering 25th Anniversary of Rayburn's Death," *The Associated Press*, 16 November 1986, Section: Domestic News.

68. William Moseley as told to Frances Spatz Leighton, *Fishbait: The Memoirs of the Congressional Doorkeeper* (Englewood Cliffs, N. J.: Prentice-Hall, 1977), 227.

69. Frederic and Mary Ann Brussat, *Spiritual Literacy: Reading the Sacred in Everyday Life* (New York: Scribner, 1996), 260.

70. Maeanna Chesterton-Mongle, "The Chaplain," *Sunshine Magazine*, as quoted in Herbert V. Prochnow and Herbert V. Prochnow Jr., *A Treasure Chest of Quotations for All Occasions*, 324.

71. Marjorie Terry Chanler, *Roman Spring: Memoirs, 1934*, as quoted in Donald Hall, ed., *The Oxford Book of American Literary Anecdotes* (New York: Oxford University Press, 1981), 123.

72. Jane Goodall, *In The Shadow Of Man* (Boston: Houghton Mifflin Co., 1988), 268.

73. Donald Hall, ed., *The Oxford Book of American Literary Anecdotes*, 82–84.

74. W. Francis Gates, ed., *Anecdotes of Great Musicians*, 185.

75. Max Zimmerman, as quoted in *The Reader's Digest 40th Anniversary Treasury* (Pleasantville, N.Y.: The Reader's Digest Association, 1961), 239–40.

76. Frederick W. Farrar, as quoted in Ted Goodman, ed., *The Forbes Book of Business Quotations*, 467.

77. Cort R. Flint, in *Quote Magazine*, date unknown.

78. Eric Hoffer, *The Passionate State of Mind and Other Aphorisms* (New York: Harper, 1955), 77.

79. Edmund Fuller, ed., *2500 Anecdotes for All Occasions*, 29–30.

80. Ralph Waldo Emerson, as quoted in Lillian Eichler Watson, ed., *Light from Many Lamps* (New York: Simon & Schuster, 1951), 198.

81. Charles G. Dawes, as quoted in Bascom Nolly Timmons, *Portrait of an American: Charles G. Dawes* (New York: Holt, 1953), 80.

82. Sarah F. Jensen, comp., *Ye Old Time Philosophy*, 122.

83. Pablo Casals, as told to Albert E. Kahn, *Joys and Sorrows: Reflections by Pablo Casals* (New York: Simon and Schuster, 1970), 162–65.

84. W. Francis Gates, ed., *Anecdotes of Great Musicians*, 13–14.

85. Paul F. Boller Jr., ed., *Presidential Anecdotes*, 138.

86. Frances J. Roberts, as quoted in Edythe Draper, ed., *Draper's Book of Quotation for the Christian World*, 366.

87. G. Young in *The Irish Digest*, February 1967, 62.

88. Gerda Weissmann Klein, as quoted in Kristin Helmore, "A Story of Courage, Tenacity, and Hope That Has a Happy Ending," *The Christian Science Monitor*, 7 May 1985, 1.

89. Victor Frankl, *Man's Search for Meaning* (Boston: Beacon Press, 1992), 104.

90. William Zinsser, *American Places* (New York: HarperCollins, 1992), 79–89.

91. Abraham Lincoln, as quoted by Carl Sandberg, "What Would Lincoln Do Today?," *Woman's Day*, February 1948; reprinted in *Woman's Day*, September 1967, 45.

92. Emily Dickinson, as quoted in Thomas H. Johnson, ed., *The Complete Poems of Emily Dickinson* (Boston: Little, Brown and Co., 1960), 254.

93. Rabbi Harold S. Kushner, "How to Have Hope When Things Seem So Bad," *McCalls*, April 1994, 115–16.

94. Helen Hayes, "In My Darkest Hour—Hope," *True Experience*, January 1952.

95. Clare Boothe Luce, as quoted in *People*, 25 July 1977, 32.

96. Richard Rhodes, *A Hole in the World: An American Boyhood* (New York: Simon & Schuster, 1990), 15–180.

97. Richard Rhodes, "Don't Be a Bystander," *Parade Magazine,* 14 October 1990, 4–7.

❤ ❤ ❤ ❤ ❤ ❤ ❤ ❤ ❤

CHAPTER 4: ON GIVING

1. Beulah Collins, ed., *For Benefit of Clergy* (New York: Grosset & Dunlap, 1966), 13.

2. Sri Chinmoy, *Lessons on Living in Peace, Happiness and Harmony* (Deerfield Beach, Fla.: Health Communications, 1994), 47–48.

3. John Gunther, *Taken at the Flood* (New York: Harper & Row, 1960), 264.

4. George Gissing, *The Private Papers of Henry Ryecroft* (New York: E. P. Dutton & Company, 1927), 48.

5. The editors of Conari Press, *More Random Acts of Kindness* (Berkeley: Conari Press, 1994), 6.

6. Stephanie Salter, "Why 'Seinfeld' lost a potential fan," *San Francisco Examiner,* 14 May 1998, A-23.

7. John C. Cornelius, "The Joy of Giving," *Reader's Digest,* January 1964, 66.

8. Ralph L. Woods, ed., *Wellsprings of Wisdom* (Norwalk, Conn.: C. R. Gibson, 1969), 11.

9. Rachel Peden, *Speak to the Earth* (New York: Knopf, 1974), 179.

10. Martin E. Marty, "Make Yourself Available!," *Reader's Digest,* October 1987, 179–80.

11. Louis Ginsburg, *The Everlasting Minute and Other Lyrics* (New York: Liveright, 1937).

12. Leonard Nimoy, as quoted in editors of *Reader's Digest,* eds., *Reader's Digest Quotable Quotes* (Pleasantville, N.Y.: The Reader's Digest Association, 1977), 42.

13. Story contributed by Boyd Ware, Salt Lake City, Utah.

14. Helen Keller, "Quotes," *The Gazette,* 28 April 1997, C3.

15. Myles Connolly, "The Greatest Art," *This Week Magazine,* 10 December1950.

16. Anne Morrow Lindbergh, *The Flower and the Nettle* (New York: Harcourt Brace Jovanovich, 1976), 77–78.

17. R. Lee Sharpe, as quoted in Sarah F. Jensen, comp., *Ye Old Time Philosophy* (n.p.: Sarah F. Jensen, 1974), 141.

18. Roy H. Barnacle, "The Home Forum," *The Christian Science Monitor,* 19 May 1983, 21.

19. Arthur Gordon, "My Words to Grow On," *Guideposts*, October 1986, 42–43.

20. Walt Whitman, as quoted in Donald Hall, ed., *The Oxford Book of American Literary Anecdotes* (New York: Oxford University Press, 1981), 100–101.

21. Aristotle, as quoted in Edmund Fuller, ed., *Thesaurus of Anecdotes* (New York: Crown Publishers, 1942), 41.

22. Johannes Brahm, as quoted in Edmund Fuller, ed., *Thesaurus of Anecdotes*, 43.

23. Alexander Pope, as quoted in Edmund Fuller, ed., *Thesaurus of Anecdotes*, 42–43.

24. Edmund Fuller, ed., *2500 Anecdotes for All Occasions* (New York: Avenel Books, 1978), 43.

25. Donald Hall, ed., *The Oxford Book of American Literary Anecdotes*, 306.

26. Edmund Fuller, ed., *Thesaurus of Anecdotes*, 104.

27. Edmund Fuller, ed., *2500 Anecdotes for All Occasions*, 104.

28. Francis Bacon, as quoted in Ted Goodman, ed., *The Forbes Book of Business Quotations* (New York: Black Dog & Leventhal, 1997), 466.

29. Clifton Fadiman, ed., *The Little, Brown Book of Anecdotes* (Boston: Little, Brown and Co., 1985), 8.

30. Harleigh M. Rosenberger, "Lessons from Life," *Sunshine Magazine*, November 1959, 8A.

31. A. N. Mechel, as quoted in staff of *Quote Magazine*, eds., *The Speaker's Special Occasion Book* (Anderson, S. C.: Droke House, 1954), 487.

32. E. H. Chapin, as quoted in editors of *Reader's Digest*, eds., *Reader's Digest Quotable Quotes*, 79.

33. Edmund Fuller, ed., *Thesaurus of Anecdotes*, 42.

34. Coronet, as quoted in staff of *Quote Magazine*, eds., *The Speaker's Special Occasion Book*, 267–68.

35. Ralph Kinney Bennett, "The Greatest Gift I Ever Received," *Reader's Digest*, July 1990, 9–12. Used by permission.

36. Judith Newman and Giovanna Breu, "Twenty-five years after Vietnam, an Army nurse and a terribly wounded soldier reunite," *Time*, 22 November 1993, 50.

37. Suzanne Chazin, "Love Beyond All Understanding," *Reader's Digest*, February 1996, 151.

38. Eric Hoffer, *The Passionate State of Mind and Other Aphorisms* (New York: Harper & Row, 1955), 136.

39. Machiavelli, as quoted in Christopher Mathews, "The Other National Pastime," *The New York Times*, 24 February 1991, 15.

40. Contributed by Jo Ann Able, American Fork, Utah. Used with permission.

41. Andrew Simmons, as quoted by Associated Press, date unknown.

42. Richard M. Siddoway, "There is still room in the inn and plenty to spare this night," *Deseret News,* 21 December 1997, A1. Used by permission.

43. Emma Lou Thayne, "The Gift," *Exponent II,* Fall 1986, 6. Used by permission.

44. Thomas Carlyle, as quoted in Jacob Braude, ed., *Braude's Source Book for Speakers and Writers* (Englewood Cliffs, N.J.: Prentice-Hall, 1968), 122.

45. Keith Miller and Bruce Larson, *The Edge of Adventure* (Waco, Tex.: Word Books, 1974), 29.

46. Albert P. Hout, "A Little Human Happiness," *The Lion* (Oak Brook, Ill.: International Association of Lions Clubs, 1918), 34.

47. Ralph Waldo Emerson, as quoted in Robert Andrews, ed., *The Columbia Dictionary of Quotations* (New York: Columbia University Press, 1993), 370.

48. Richard Jefferies, as quoted in Samuel J. Looker, ed., *Richard Jefferies: The Story of My Heart* (London: Constable Publishers, 1947), 103–4.

50. Michael David Harris, *Always on Sunday* (New York: Meredith Press, 1968), 70–71.

50. Henry Fogel, as quoted by Peter Goodman in Long Island, New York, *Newsday,* as quoted in *Reader's Digest,* December 1987, 158.

51. "Jack O'Brian's Critics Circle," WOR, New York, as quoted in *Reader's Digest,* May 1981, 142.

52. Edmund Fuller, ed., *Thesaurus of Anecdotes,* 164.

53. Henry Wadsworth Longfellow, as quoted in Patricia Dreier, ed., *A Pocketful of Joys* (Norwalk, Conn.: C. R. Gibson Co., 1985), 77.

54. Eileen Egan and Kathleen Egan, *Suffering into Joy* (Ann Arbor, Mich.: Servant Publications, 1994), 105, 120.

55. Story contributed by anonymous author.

56. As quoted in editors of Conari Press, *More Random Acts of Kindness,* 15.

57. Eulalie Leavitt Taggart. Original document in possession of Grant Taggart. Used by permission.

58. Jane W. Lund, "Ministering Angels," *Once More With Feeling . . .* (Salt Lake City: Lundcraft Heritage Arts, 1989), 19.

59. Karen Goldman, *The Angel Book* (New York: Simon & Schuster, 1992), 45–46.

60. Ram Dass and Paul Gorman, *How Can I Help?* (New York: Alfred A. Knopf, 1995), 5.

61. Susan Chernak McElroy, *Animals as Teachers and Healers* (New York: Ballantine Books, 1967), 115.

62. *Indianapolis Star Magazine,* as quoted in staff of *Quote Magazine,* eds., *The Speaker's Special Occasion Book,* 141.

63. Dale Fife, "The Fruit of the Seed," *Together Magazine,* June 1960, 17–18.

64. Fulton J. Sheen, *From the Angel's Blackboard* (Chicago: Triumph Books, 1977), 234–35.

65. Billy Graham, *Angels: God's Secret Agents* (Dallas: Word Publishing, 1975), 21.

66. Dawn Raffel, "Angels All around Us," *Redbook*, December 1992, 84.

67. Nancy Gibbs, "Angels among Us," *Time*, 17 December 1993, 56.

68. Sophy Burnham, *A Book of Angels* (New York: Ballantine Books, 1990), xiii.

69. Dawn Raffel, "Angels All around Us," *Redbook*, December 1992, 84.

70. Ibid.

71. David Johnson, Associated Press, in *Deseret News*, 26 December 1996, B1.

72. Story contributed by Pamela Johnson, Forest Grove, Oregon.

73. Joan Wester Anderson, *Where Angels Walk* (New York: Ballantine Books, 1992), 160.

74. Clifton Fadiman, ed., *The Little, Brown Book of Anecdotes*, 508.

75. A. J. Cronin, "Why I Believe in God," *Women's Home Companion*, September 1950, 103.

76. Ewart A. Autry, "The Old Hitching Tree," *Together Magazine*, April 1968, 25.

77. Halford Luccock, in *Living without Gloves* (New York: Oxford University Press, 1957), 161–62.

78. Story contributed by anonymous author.

79. Abraham Lincoln, as quoted in Lucy Gertsch, comp., *Minute Masterpieces* (Salt Lake City: Bookcraft, 1953), 35.

80. Leo Rosten, in *Christian Science Monitor*, date unknown.

81. Story contributed by Lidia Rawska, Salt Lake City, Utah.

82. Herbert V. Prochnow and Herbert V. Prochnow Jr., eds., *A Treasure Chest of Quotations for All Occasions* (New York: Harper & Row, 1983), 373–74.

83. Lillian Eichler Watson, ed., *Light from Many Lamps* (New York: Simon & Schuster, 1979), 37–38.

84. William F. McDermott, "Here's How Sallman Painted It," *Together Magazine*, October 1956, 47–48.

85. "Clinton urges firms to invest more in Germany," *Deseret News*, 14 May 1998, A4.

86. Gail S. Halvorsen, *The Berlin Candy Bomber* (Bountiful, Ut.: Horizon Publishers, 1990), 96–150.

87. W. Somerset Maugham, *The Painted Veil* (London: Heinermann, 1923), 233.

88. Margaret Lee Runbeck, *Hope of Earth* (New York: Houghton Mifflin Co., 1947), 280.

89. Harold Kushner, as quoted in Sefra Kobrin Pitzelle, *One More Day* (New York: Harper/Hazelden, 1988), 262.

90. George Macdonald, as quoted in Clyde Francis Lytle, ed., *Leaves of Gold* (Williamsport, Penn.: The Coslett Publishing Co., 1948), 33.

91. Emily Dickinson, *Favorite Poems of Emily Dickinson* (New York: Avenel Books, 1978), 24.

92. Ishbel Ross, *Journey into Light* (New York: Appleton-Century-Croft, Inc., 1951), 332–60.

93. Helen Keller, *Teacher* (Garden City, N.Y.: Doubleday & Co., 1955), 41, 62, 125, 217, 247.

94. Julia Ward Howe, as quoted in Richard L. Evans, ed., *Richard Evans' Quote Book* (Salt Lake City: Publishers Press, 1971), 165.

95. Soren Kierkegaard, as quoted in editors of Conari Press, *Random Acts of Kindness* (Berkeley: Conari Press, 1994), 49.

96. Gandhi, as quoted by Dale E. Turner, "A Tragedy," in *Let's Think About It* (Seattle: *The Seattle Times*, 1996), 5.

97. John Ruskin, as quoted in Audrey Stone Morris, ed., *1000 Inspirational Things* (Chicago: Spencer Press, 1948), 312.

98. Dale E. Turner, "Belief Isn't Enough," in *Let's Think About It*, 4.

99. Archibald T. Davison, "Ten Black Seconds," in Raymond Swing, ed., *This I Believe* (New York: Simon and Schuster, 1954), 44–45.

100. Clyde Francis Lytle, ed., *Leaves of Gold*, 130.

101. Cicero, as quoted in Ted Goodman, ed., *The Forbes Book of Business Quotations*, 349.

102. Cicero, as quoted in editors of Conari Press, *More Random Acts of Kindness*, 82.

103. Clifton Fadiman, ed., *The Little, Brown Book of Anecdotes*, 339.

104. Clifton Fadiman, ed., *The Little, Brown Book of Anecdotes*, 339.

105. Ralph L. Woods, comp., *Wellsprings of Wisdom*, 47.

106. Clifton Fadiman, ed., *The Little, Brown Book of Anecdotes*, 231.

107. Ram Dass and Paul Gorman, *How Can I Help?*, 10.

108. Dale E. Turner, "Belief Isn't Enough," in *Let's Think About It*, 4.

♥ ♥ ♥ ♥ ♥ ♥ ♥ ♥ ♥

CHAPTER 5: ON CARING

1. Arthur Gordon, "How Much Do You Care?" *Guideposts*, October 1963, 15–16. Used by permission.

2. Mstislav Rostropovich, as quoted by Kathleen Hinton-Braaten in *Accent*, in *Reader's Digest*, June 1983, 170.

3. Joann C. Jones, as quoted in *Guideposts*, January 1996, 8.

4. Ardis Whitman, "Let Us Speak to One Another," *Woman's Day*, October 1964, 38.

5. Ruth Stafford Peale, "Long Walk," in editors of *Guideposts*, eds., *The New Guideposts Christmas Treasury* (Carmel, N.Y.: Guideposts, 1988), 167–68.

6. Faye Field, "Gardenias for Mama," *Guideposts*, May 1982, 43–44.

7. Alice Duer Miller, as quoted by Henry Wise Miller, *All Our Lives* (New York: Coward-McCann, 1945), 124–25.

8. Sue Atchley Ebaugh, *Each Day a New Beginning* (New York: Hazelden, 1982), 7.

9. William Stringfellow, *A Keeper of the Word* (Grand Rapids, Mich.: William B. Eerdmans Publishing Co., 1994), 169.

10. William Butler Yeats, "The Lake Isle of Innisfree," as quoted in the Glasgow *Herald*, 4 October 1997, 4.

11. Catherine de Hueck Doherty, *Poustinia: Christian Spirituality of the East for Western Man* (Notre Dame, Ind.: Ave Maria Press, 1975), 161.

12. Douglas Steere, as quoted in Frederic and Mary Ann Brussat, *Spiritual Literacy* (New York: Scribner, 1996), 283.

13. Donald E. Smith, "The Healing Touch of Attention," *Guideposts*, April 1969, 22–25.

14. Henry Miller, as quoted in Margaret Petter, ed., *The Harper Religious and Inspirational Quotation Companion* (New York: Harper & Row, 1989), 401.

15. Jean Shinoda Bolen, as quoted in Richard Carlson and Benjamin Shield, eds., *Handbook for the Soul* (New York: Little, Brown and Co., 1995), 4.

16. Andrew V. Mason, as quoted in editors of *Reader's Digest*, eds., *Reader's Digest Quotable Quotes* (Pleasantville, N.Y.: The Reader's Digest Association, 1997), 125.

17. Roy H. Barnacle, "Doing the old soft shoe routine," *The Christian Science Monitor*, October 1988, 31.

18. Albin Krebs and Carey Winfrey, in *The* [London] *Sunday Times*, 12 November 1978, 1.

19. James Reston, in *The Quill*, as quoted in *Reader's Digest*, February 1975, 182.

20. Leo Aikman, in Atlanta *Constitution*, as quoted in *Reader's Digest*, November 1976, 83.

21. J. Wallace Hamilton, as quoted in *Quote Magazine*, 6 September 1964, 7.

22. John Masefield, as quoted in editors of *Reader's Digest*, eds., *Reader's Digest Quotable Quotes*, 17.

23. Jack Denton Scott, in *Viewpoints*, as quoted in "Count Your Compliments," *Reader's Digest*, December 1976, 87.

24. Arthur Gordon, "Don't Wear Your Raincoat in the Shower," *Christian Herald*, August 1969, 46.

25. Alan Loy McGinnis, *The Friendship Factor* (Indianapolis, Ind.: Augsburg, 1979), 116.

26. Sean Maxwell, "Getting Things Done," *Irish Digest*, November 1965, 11.

27. Timothy Tung, as quoted by Ron Alexander in New York *Times*, 15 August 1984, 2C.

28. James C. Humes, ed., *Speaker's Treasury of Anecdotes about the Famous* (New York: Harper & Row, 1978), 36.

29. Arthur Gordon, "The Search," *Woman's Day*, January 1963, 27, 60.

30. Robert Orben, as quoted in Edythe Draper, ed., *Draper's Book of Quotations for the Christian World* (Wheaton, Ill.: Tyndale House, 1992), 91.

31. Phyllis Theroux, "In Praise of Praise," *Parents*, August 1997, 60.

32. Doris Ann Krupinski, in Greendale [Wisconsin] *Village Life*, as quoted in *Reader's Digest*, April 1986, 188.

33. Phyllis McGinley, "Flattery can get you somewhere," *Saturday Evening Post*, April 21, 1962, 68–69.

34. Edith Wharton, as quoted in Karen Casey and Martha Vanceburg, *The Promise of a New Day* (New York: Harper Collins Publishers, 1983), 311.

35. Margaret Cousins, "Words That Warm the Heart," *Woman's Day*, August 1971, 32.

36. William L. Stridger, *Sunshine Magazine*, November 1959, 9–10.

37. William James, *The Letters of William James*, ed. Henry James (Boston: The Atlantic Monthly Press, 1920), 2:33.

38. Hilaire Belloc, *The Silence of the Sea*, as quoted in Edward F. Murphy, *The Crown Treasury of Relevant Quotations* (New York: Crown Publishers, 1978), 488.

39. Story contributed by Pamela Johnson.

40. Samuel Johnson, as quoted in Justin Kaplan, ed., *Bartlett's Familiar Quotations* (Boston: Little, Brown and Co., 1992), 317.

41. Donald Hall, ed., *The Oxford Book of American Literary Anecdotes* (New York: Oxford University Press, 1981), 97.

42. Story of Pacchierotti, as quoted in W. Francis Gates, ed., *Anecdotes of Great Musicians* (Philadelphia: Theodore Presser, 1895), 43.

43. Joe J. Mickle, as quoted in Edward P. Morgan, ed., *This I Believe* (New York: Simon and Schuster, 1952), 120.

44. Jeffrey Moussaieff Masson, *Dogs Never Lie about Love* (New York: Crown Publishers, 1997), 43–44.

45. James A. Farley, "The Two Magic Words," *Guideposts*, January 1964, 2–3. Used by permission.

46. Bonnie Binschus, as quoted in "Laughter, the Best Medicine," *Reader's Digest*, April 1987. Used by permission.

47. Ken Stuart, "Unforgettable Norman Rockwell," *Reader's Digest*, July 1979, 109.

48. Robert W. Youngs, in *Quote Magzine*, 16 August 1964, 7.

49. Celeste Holm, "Reporter's Notebook," *The Buffalo News*, 19 February 1998, 5C.

50. Douglas Woodruff, as quoted in editors of *Quote Magazine*, eds., *The Speaker's Special Occasion Book* (Anderson, S. C.: Droke House, Publishers, 1954), 152.

51. Mary Ann Bird, "A Genius for Loving," *Guideposts*, January 1985, 29. Used by permission.

52. Benjamin Disraeli, as quoted in John Cook, comp., *The Rubicon Dictionary of Positive, Motivational, and Life-Affirming and Inspirational Quotations* (Newington, Conn.: Rubicon Press, 1994), 85.

53. Jacob M. Braude, *Complete Speaker's and Toastmaster's Library: Remarks of Famous People* (Englewood Cliffs, N.J.: Prentice-Hall, Inc., 1965), 13.

54. Duke Ellington, as quoted in Nat Hentoff, *Boston Boy* (New York: Knopf, 1986), 123.

55. John M. Drescher, *If I Were Starting My Family Again* (Intercourse, Penn.: Good Books, 1994), 36.

56. W. Francis Gates, ed., *Anecdotes of Great Musicians*, 39.

57. Schuyler Chapin, *Musical Chairs* (New York: G. P. Putnam's Sons, 1977), 162–63.

58. Margaret Cousins, "Words That Warm the Heart," *Woman's Day*, August 1971, 32.

59. John L. Elliott, as quoted in *Quote Magazine*, 6 September 1964, 10.

60. Herbert V. Prochnow and Herbert V. Prochnow Jr., eds., *A Treasure Chest of Quotations for All Occasions* (New York: Harper & Row, 1983), 313.

61. "Lincoln, the Underprivileged," *Sunshine Magazine*, February 1959, 6A.

62. Paul F. Boller Jr., ed., *Presidential Anecdotes* (New York: Oxford University Press, 1981), 236.

63. Tony Parker, *Studs Terkel* (New York: Henry Holt, 1996), 127.

64. Ralph Waldo Emerson, in *Letters and Social Aims*, as quoted in *Bartlett's Familiar Quotations*, 433.

65. Janik Press Service, as quoted in *Reader's Digest*, January 1980, 107–8.

66. Willy Ley and the editors of Time-Life Books, *The Poles* (New York: Time, 1962), 55.

67. E. E. Edgar, as quoted in *Reader's Digest*, February 1965, 23.

68. Emily Post, as quoted by Jeanne Perkins Harman in *Such Is Life* (New York: Thomas Y. Crowell Co., 1956), 129.

69. Freya Stark, *The Journey's Echo* (New York: Harcourt, Brace & World, 1964), 128.

70. Phyllis McGinley, *Sixpence in Her Shoe* (New York: Dell, 1964), 212.

71. Michael Korda, "The Hidden Message of Manners," *Success,* 18 December 1984, 40.

72. Jo Coudert, "Excuse Me, Your Manners Are Missing," *Woman's Day,* 21 May 1995, 150.

73. Owen Edwards, "End of the Rude," *Town & Country,* June 1992, 47.

74. Mark Twain, as quoted in Donald O. Bolander, comp., *Instant Quotation Dictionary* (Mundelein, Ill.: Career Institute, 1969), 176.

75. Charlie Jones, as quoted by Neil Morgan in *San Diego Union-Tribune,* 25 July 1989, B1.

76. Elizabeth Post, *Please Say Please* (Boston: Little, Brown and Co., 1972), 139.

77. Eda LeShan in *Woman's Day,* as quoted in *Reader's Digest,* September 1983, 204.

78. Norman Vincent Peale, "When To Say 'I'm Sorry,'" *Reader's Digest,* December 1973, 135.

79. Mstislav Rostropovich, as quoted by Irina Bogat in *Literary Gazette International,* in *Reader's Digest,* March 1991, 161.

80. Robert Conklin, *How To Get People To Do Things* (New York: Ballantine, 1985), 51–53.

81. Unknown author, as quoted in *Reader's Digest,* January 1964, 23.

82. Joseph Addison, as quoted in Audrey Stoney Morris, comp., *1000 Inspirational Things* (Chicago: Spencer Press, 1948), 363.

83. Jean Schwartzstein, as quoted by Lawrence Van Gelder in *New York Times,* in *Reader's Digest,* September 1980, 133.

84. Peg Bracken, *A Window over the Sink* (New York: Harcourt Brace Jovanovich, 1981), 30.

85. Author unknown, as quoted by Gene Bluhm in *Salesman's Opportunity Magazine,* in *Reader's Digest,* April 1982, 189.

86. Bob Elliott, as quoted in Glenn Collins, "Metropolitan Diary," *New York Times,* 5 January 1983, 2.

87. Harold Helfer, "The Iron Fence," *Sunshine Magazine,* November 1959, 3–7.

88. Will Rogers, as quoted in Laurence J. Peter, ed., *Peter's Quotations* (New York: William Morrow and Co., 1977), 285.

89. Langston Hughes, as quoted in Laurence J. Peter, ed., *Peter's Quotations: Ideas for Our Time,* 498.

90. Erma Bombeck, as quoted in Maria Braden, *She Said What? Interviews with Women Newspaper Columnists* (Lexington, Ky.: University Press of Kentucky, 1993), 40.

91. Romain Gary, *Promise at Dawn* (New York: HarperCollins, 1961), 136.

92. Leo Rosten, *The Return of Hyman Kaplan* (New York: Harper & Row, 1966), 14.

93. Will Rogers, as quoted in Robert Hendrickson, *American Literary Anecdotes* (New York: Facts on File, 1990), 196.

94. Jay Hammond, as quoted in Jeff Wheelwright, "Portrait: Jay Hammond, Governing Alaska Is Like Flying a Bush Plane with a Grizzly Bear," *Life*, September 1980, 19.

95. Cab Calloway, as quoted by Irving Hoffman in *The Hollywood Reporter*, in *Reader's Digest*, March 1968, 141.

96. Jacob M. Braude, ed., *Braude's Source Book for Speakers and Writers* (Englewood Cliffs, N.J.: Prentice-Hall, 1968), 11.

97. Tim Conway, on NBC *Tonight show*, as quoted in *Reader's Digest*, July 1981, 113.

98. Peggy Noonan, *What I Saw at the Revolution* (New York: Random House, 1990), 179.

99. Story collected by Peggy Wiseman, "'Well, We've Been Through Hell and High Water Now': A Look at Some Early Rexburg Flood Lore," 1976, Item 23, Focused MS #451, Folklore Archive, Brigham Young University, Provo, Utah.

100. Marty Adelstein, as quoted by Jon Hilkevitch in *Chicago Tribune*, 30 January 1991, 14C.

101. James Thurber, as quoted in Justin Kaplan, ed., *Bartlett's Familiar Quotations*, 697.

102. Langston Hughes, as quoted in editors of *Reader's Digest*, eds., *Reader's Digest Quotable Quotes*, 498.

103. James M. Barrie, *Peter Pan*, act 1, as quoted in Angela Partington, ed., *The Oxford Dictionary of Quotations* (New York: Oxford University Press, 1992), 54.

104. Arnold Glasow, as quoted in Laurence J. Peter, ed., *Peter's Quotations*, 286.

105. Victor Hugo, as quoted in *Instant Quotation Dictionary*, 166.

106. Mort Walker, as quoted in Andy Zubko, comp., *Treasury of Spiritual Wisdom* (San Diego: Blue Dove Press, 1996), 286.

107. Peter Ustinov, *Dear Me* (Boston: Little, Brown, 1977), 49.

108. Chinese proverb, as quoted in Donald O. Bolander, comp., *Instant Quotation Dictionary*, 197.

109. Elaine Jarvik and Susan Whitney, "Falling in Love," *Deseret News*, 29 June 1997, L2. Used by permission.

110. Paul Sweeney, as quoted in editors of *Reader's Digest*, eds., *Reader's Digest Quotable Quotes*, 76.

111. Vaughn Monroe, as quoted in Jacob M. Braude, ed., *Braude's Source Book for Speakers and Writers*, 201.

112. Author unknown, in *Anglican Digest*, as quoted in *Reader's Digest*, November 1977, 229.

113. Joseph Fort Newton, in *The Atlantic*, as quoted in *Reader's Digest*, April 1989, 21.

114. Thomas á Kempis, as quoted in Clyde Francis Lytle, ed., *Leaves of Gold* (Williamsport, Penn.: The Coslett Publishing Co., 1948), 73.

115. Robert Whatley, as quoted in Andy Zubko, comp., *Treasury of Spiritual Wisdom*, 161.

116. Goethe's mother, as quoted in Audrey Stone Morris, comp., *1000 Inspirational Things*, 51.

117. Clifton Fadiman, ed., *The Little, Brown Book of Anecdotes* (Boston: Little, Brown and Co., 1985), 426.

118. Louis S. B. Leakey, as quoted by Michael T. Kaufman in *New York Times*, in *Reader's Digest*, October 1976, 61.

119. Charlie W. Shedd, as quoted in Karen Casey and Martha Vanceburg, *The Promise of a New Day*, 60.

120. Arnold Glasow, as quoted in Laurence J. Peter, ed., *Peter's Quotations*, 375.

121. Elspeth Huxley, *The Flame Trees of Thika* (London: Chatto & Windus, 1959), 264.

122. George Washington Carver, as quoted in Ted Goodman, ed., *The Forbes Book of Business Quotations* (New York: Black Dog & Leventhal Publishers, 1997), 539.

123. Louise Erdrich, "What my mother taught me," *Ladies Home Journal*, May 1993, 85.

124. Mother Teresa, as quoted in Joseph Gerth, "Nun's work for 'poorest of the poor' reached all the way to Kentucky," *The [Louisville, Kentucky] Courier-Journal*, 6 September 1997, 4A.

125. Charles F. Kettering, as quoted in T. A. Boyd, ed., *Prophet of Progress* (New York: Dutton, 1961), 44.

126. Abraham Lincoln, as quoted in Ted Goodman, ed., *The Forbes Book of Business Quotations*, 672.

127. Peter Drucker, as quoted in editors of *Reader's Digest*, eds., *Reader's Digest Quotable Quotes*, 101.

128. Dwight D. Eisenhower, as quoted in Edythe Draper, ed., *Draper's Book of Quotations for the Christian World,* 495.

129. Dwight D. Eisenhower, as quoted in Moses P. Saldana Sr., Editorial, *Austin American-Statesman,* 2 February 1997, J2.

130. Dwight D. Eisenhower, as quoted by Elliot L. Richardson in Gordon Hoxie, *Command Decision and the Presidency* (New York: Reader's Digest Press, 1977), foreword.

131. Peter Guber, as quoted in Diane K. Shah, in "The Producers," *New York Times Magazine,* 22 October 1989, 27.

132. George G. Jackson, as quoted in *My Job and Why I Like It* (Detroit: General Motors, 1947), 101.

133. Henry David Thoreau, as quoted in Ted Goodman, ed., *The Forbes Book of Business Quotations,* 71.

134. Emily Ann Smith, as quoted by Shirley Williams in *Louisville Courier-Journal & Times Magazine,* in *Reader's Digest,* April 1979, 55.

135. Robert Jacobson, as quoted in *Reader's Digest,* August 1972, 112.

136. Albin Krebs, "Lillian Carter addresses students at Univ Coll in Dublin," *New York Times,* 16 November 1977, 2.

137. "Peterborough," in [London] *Daily Telegraph,* as quoted in *Reader's Digest,* February 1979, 64.

138. Andrew H. Malcom, "Canadians Learn About 'Flora Power,'" *New York Times,* 26 August 1979, 52.

139. Francis Gay, in Glasgow *Sunday Post,* as quoted in *Reader's Digest,* October 1984, 50.

140. D. L. in *Spokane Spokesman-Review,* as quoted in *Reader's Digest,* December 1977, 122.

141. James D. Newton, *Uncommon Friends* (San Diego: Hartcourt Brace Jovanovich, 1987), 19.

142. William D. Brown, *Welcome Stress!* (Minneapolis, Minn.: CompCare, 1983), 156.

143. Buckminster Fuller, as quoted by Phyllis Theroux, "Bucky Fuller's global game," *The Washington Post,* 19 July 1982, C1.

144. Charles F. Kettering, as quoted in *Reader's Digest,* May 1989, 47.

145. Julia Child, as quoted in John DeMers, "Julia Child Grande Dame of the kitchen and TV's quirkiest star: Julia Child has changed America's food attitudes," United Press International, 3 June 1986, Lifestyle Section.

146. Alice Duer Miller, as quoted by Henry Wise Miller, *All Our Lives,* 9.

147. Robert Townsend, *Up the Organization* (New York: Knopf, 1970), 115.

148. Mark Twain, *More Maxims of Mark* (New York: n.p., 1927), 5.

149. Mohandas Gandhi, as quoted by Dale Turner, "Our Beliefs Bring Purpose to Our Lives," in *The Seattle Times,* 13 November 1993, A12.

150. Tug McGraw, as quoted in Ron Luciano and David Fisher, *The Umpire Strikes Back* (New York: Bantam, 1983), 126.

151. Leo Aikman in *Atlanta Constitution*, as quoted in *Reader's Digest*, August 1980, 125.

152. Mignon McLaughlin, quoted in editors of *Reader's Digest*, eds., *Reader's Digest Quotable Quotes*, 42.

153. Hal Chadwick, as quoted in *Reader's Digest*, September 1976, 158.

154. Judith Martin, *Common Courtesy* (New York: Atheneum, 1985), 27.

155. Roger Rosenblatt, in *Washington Post*, as quoted in *Reader's Digest*, September 1980, 11.

156. J. B. Priestley, as quoted in *Reader's Digest*, September 1977, 102.

157. Kenneth Tynan, as quoted in Alison Jones, ed., *Chambers Dictionary of Quotations* (New York: Chambers, 1997), 1035.

158. Charlie Brower, ed., *Me and Other Advertising Geniuses* (New York: Doubleday, 1974), 107.

159. Bern Williams, as quoted in editors of *Reader's Digest*, eds., *Reader's Digest Quotable Quotes*, 78.

160. Jocco Grand, as quoted in *Reader's Digest*, March 1980, 16.

161. Norman Vincent Peale, as quoted in *Peter's Quotations*, 400.

162. Abraham Lincoln, as quoted in Edythe Draper, ed., *Draper's Book of Quotations for the Christian World*, 235.

163. James Dobson, *What Wives Wish Their Husbands Knew about Women* (Wheaton, Ill.: Living Books, 1975), 40–41.

164. Golda Meir, *As Good as Golda*, ed. Israel and Mary Shenker (New York: McCall, 1970), 7.

165. Will Rogers, as quoted in Jane Ely, "Will Rogers' velvet-tipped harpoons," *The Houston Chronicle*, 13 August 1995, Outlook 2.

166. Henry Ford, as quoted in "Thoughts on Business Life," *Forbes*, 20 May 1985, 284.

167. John Morley, as quoted in Louis A. Berman, *Wit and Wisdom* (New York: Berkley Publishing Group, 1997), 67.

168. Edmund Fuller, ed., *Thesaurus of Anecdotes* (New York: Crown Publishers, 1942), 167.

169. Cort Flint, as quoted in *Quote Magazine*, 9 August 1964, 8.

170. Lane A. Concha, as quoted in *Reader's Digest*, April 1963, 229.

171. Paul F. Boller Jr., ed., *Presidential Anecdotes*, 160.

172. Mark Twain, as quoted in Michael Joseph, ed., *Man Is the Only Animal That Blushes . . . Or Needs To: The Wisdom of Mark Twain* (New York: Random House, 1970), 20.

173. Morris Mandel, in *Jewish Press*, as quoted in *Reader's Digest*, August 1979, 20.

174. Jacqueline Schiff, as quoted in editors of *Reader's Digest*, eds., *Reader's Digest Quotable Quotes*, 88.

175. Donald Culross Peattie, in *New York Times Magazine*, as quoted in *Reader's Digest*, January 1994, 108.

176. Chinese proverb, as quoted in *Peter's Quotations*, 55.

177. Ambrose Bierce in *Devil's Dictionary*, as quoted in Margaret Petter, ed., *The Harper Religious and Inspirational Quotation Companion*, 33.

178. Alan Loy McGinnis, *The Friendship Factor*, 148–49.

179. John Graham in Alma, Georgia *Times*, as quoted by Leo Aikman in *Atlanta Constitution*, in *Reader's Digest*, September 1979, 26.

180. Jacob M. Braude, ed., *Braude's Source Book for Speakers and Writers*, 267.

181. Sister Elizabeth Kenny, as quoted in Jacob M. Braude, ed., *Braude's Source Book for Speakers and Writers*, 8.

182. Paul F. Boller Jr., ed., *Presidential Anecdotes*, 355.

183. Jean Paul Richter, as quoted in *Reader's Digest*, March 1981, 76.

184. John D. MacDonald, *On the Run* (Greenwich, Conn.: Fawcett, 1963), 7.

185. Ruth Graham, as quoted in Sefra Kobrin Pitzele, *One More Day* (New York: Harper/Hazelden, 1988), 255.

186. E. Edward Crowther, *Intimacy: Strategies for Successful Relationships* (New York: Dell, 1986), 146–47.

187. James Alexander Thom, in *Nuggets*, as quoted in *Reader's Digest*, June 1990, 52.

188. Unknown author, as quoted in Victor Gollancz, *Man and God* (Boston: Houghton Mifflin Co., 1951), 206–7.

189. Madam Chiang Kai-shek, *The Sure Victory* (Westwood, N.J.: Fleming H. Revell Co., 1955), 7–20.

190. Ardis Whitman, "How to cope with bitterness," *Family Herald*, 16 January 1958, 25.

191. Harry Emerson Fosdick, as quoted in Ardis Whitman, "How to cope with bitterness," *Family Herald*, 16 January 1958, 25.

192. Anne Gearan, "Meeting with napalm victim gives Vietnam veteran solace at last," *Deseret News*, 13 April 1997, A9.

193. Harry Emerson Fosdick, *On Being a Real Person* (New York: Harper & Brothers, 1943), 106.

194. Ovidio Michel Magri, *Reflexions sur la Femme, l'Amour, La Vie* (Paris: la Pensee Universelle, 1974), 58.

195. George S. Patton Jr., *War As I Knew It* (Boston: Houghton Mifflin, 1947), 340.

196. Arthur Gordon, "The Rewards of Caring," *Guideposts*, October 1963, 141. Used by permission.

197. "Barge captain leaps into river to save fallen man," *Deseret News*, 24 December 1996, A4.

198. William Frederick Halsey, as quoted in June Callwood, *Love, Hate, Fear, Anger and the Other Lively Emotions* (New York: Doubleday, 1964), 57.

199. Ted W. Engstrom, as quoted in Edythe Draper, ed., *Draper's Book of Quotations for the Christian World*, 8.

200. Karen McCowan, "Family Takes Gift to Hearth," *The Register-Guard*, 1 June 1997, B1. Used by permission.

201. Gurdjieff, as quoted in editors of Conari Press, *Random Acts of Kindness* (Berkeley: Conari Press, 1993), 51.

202. William James, as quoted in Ted Goodman, ed., *The Forbes Book of Business Quotations*, 523.

203. Jacob M. Braude, *Braude's Source Book for Speakers and Writers*, 5.

204. Sidney Poitier, *This Life* (New York: Knopf, 1980), 88–89.

205. Edward Fischer, *Life in the Afternoon* (New York: Paulist Press, 1987), 3, 5–6.

206. Ronald Rood, *Who Wakes the Groundhog?* (New York: Norton, 1973), 154–55.

207. W. G. Montgomery, "Your Biggest Gift," *Together Magazine*, December 1960, 20.

208. Roy Hemming in *Ovation*, as quoted in *Reader's Digest*, April 1981, 207.

209. Pablo Casals, as told to Albert E. Kahn, *Joys and Sorrows* (New York: Simon and Schuster, 1970), 54.

210. Victor Hugo, *Les Miserables* (New York: Fawcett Premier, 1961), 1–37.

211. Alexander Tvardovsky, as quoted in *Time*, date unknown.

212. Charles McCarry, *Citizen Nader* (New York: Saturday Review Press, 1972), 129–30.

213. Frederick L. Collins, as quoted in *Reader's Digest*, June 1994, 19.

214. Clifton Fadiman, ed., *The Little, Brown Book of Anecdotes*, 195.

215. Nadia Boulanger, as quoted in James Nelson, ed., *Wisdom for Our Time* (New York: Norton, 1961), 263.

216. James Michener, as quoted in Herbert V. Prochnow and Herbert V. Prochnow Jr., eds., *A Treasure Chest of Quotations for All Occasions*, 347.

217. George Schaller, as quoted in Michael Ryan, "We Have to Protect What We Have," *Parade Magazine*, 2 February 1997, 19.

218. Carl Sandburg, as quoted by Gloria L. Charnes in Chicago *Tribune*, in *Reader's Digest*, May 1978, 218.

219. Clifton Fadiman, ed., *The Little, Brown Book of Anecdotes*, 360.

220. Abraham Lincoln, as quoted in Justin Kaplan, ed., *Bartlett's Familiar Quotations*, 451.

221. Richard Collier, *The General Next to God* (New York: E. P. Dutton & Co., 1965), 246–47.

222. Michael Quintanilla, "Body and Soul," *Los Angeles Times*, 4 March 1996, E-1.

223. Associated Press, "Jewish 'angel's heart' keeps Arab girl alive," *Deseret News*, 14 October 1997, A4.

224. Linda Rivers, "Through her eyes," *The Oregonian*, 24 April 1988, D1. Used by permission.

225. Konrad Adenauer, "Quotation," *The Charleston Gazette*, 1 February 1996, P2D.

226. John Steinbeck, as quoted in Garden City, N.Y., *Newsday*, in *Reader's Digest*, December 1967, 159–60.

227. W. Somerset Maugham, *The Razor's Edge* (New York: Penguin Books, 1992), 8–9.

228. Shelby Steele, in *Imprimis*, as quoted in *Reader's Digest*, January 1993, 155.

229. Tom Knight, as quoted by Charles McHarry in *New York Daily News*, in *Reader's Digest*, March 1977, 24.

230. Samuel Johnson, as quoted in Ted Goodman, ed., *The Forbes Book of Business Quotations*, 351.

231. Eric Hoffer, *The Passionate State of Mind and Other Aphorisms* (New York: Harper & Row, 1955), 137.

232. Charles M. Schulz, with Lee Mendelson, *Happy Birthday, Charlie Brown* (New York: Random House, 1979), 120–21.

233. Charles M. Schulz, as quoted by David Holstrom in *The Christian Science Monitor*, 2 October 1985, 1.

234. Anne Cole, "The Wedge of Love," *Together Magazine*, February 1961, 33–34.

235. Sue Monk Kidd, as quoted in John S. Mogabgab, *Communion, Community, Commonweal* (Nashville: Upper Room Books, 1995), 155.

236. Willie Morris, "Good friends: dogs, sons, and others," *Parade Magazine*, 7 September 1980, 22.

237. Billy Graham, as quoted in Clarence W. Hall, "The Noblest of Human Graces," *Reader's Digest*, May 1975, 138.

238. James Michener, "This I Believe," in Raymond Swing, ed., *This I Believe*, 2:96.

239. Rod Dyer, "A different kind of star," in "Christmas Stories," unpublished manuscript.

240. Elie Wiesel, *Night* (New York: Avon Books, 1958), 109.

241. Daniel D. Mich, source unknown.

242. Albert Schweitzer, as quoted in William Nichols, ed., *The Best of Words to Live By* (New York: Pocket Books, 1945), 15.

243. Harry Emerson Fosdick, as quoted in Nardi Reeder Campion, "Unforgettable Harry Emerson Fosdick," *Reader's Digest*, January 1971, 73.

244. Rabbi Arthur Hertzberg, as quoted in *Peacemaking: Day by Day* (Erie, Penn.: Benet Press, 1989), 2:55–58.

245. Norman Cousins, *Human Options* (New York: W. W. Norton & Co., 1981), 64.

246. Lady Bird Johnson, as quoted in Marie Smith, *The President's Lady* (New York: Random House, 1964), 185.

247. "Windows fill with menorahs in town's rejection of hate," *Deseret News*, 13 December 1996, A4.

248. William Shakespeare, *The Merchant of Venice* 4.1.184–87.

249. Seth Mydans, "Captive retold fables and saved his life in the 'killing fields,'" *Deseret News*, 28 June 1997, A1.

250. Mary McCarthy, as quoted in *The Writing on the Wall and Other Literary Essays* (New York: Harcourt Brace Jovanovich, 1970), 62.

251. Anne Frank, *The Diary of a Young Girl* (Garden City, N.Y.: Doubleday, 1967), 262.

252. Louis de Jong, "The Girl Who Was Anne Frank," *Reader's Digest*, October 1957, 393.

253. Rabbi Schelke of Nikolsburg, as quoted in Louis I. Newman, comp. and ed., *The Hasidic Anthology* (New York: Bloch Publishing Co., 1944), 221.

254. The Yehudi, as quoted in Louis I. Newman, comp. and ed., *The Hasidic Anthology*, 473–74.

255. Hasidic story, as quoted in Louis I. Newman, comp. and ed., *The Hasidic Anthology*, 474.

256. Henry Wadsworth Longfellow, as quoted in Catharine Reeve, "The Face of War," *Chicago Tribune*, 7 May 1995, 3.

257. W. Somerset Maugham, *The Summing Up* (New York: The New American Library of World Literature, 1938), 36.

258. Rabbi Samuel Kariver, as quoted in Louis I. Newman, comp. and ed., *The Hasidic Anthology*, 129.

259. Marcus Aurelius, *Marcus Aurelius*, ed. and trans. C. R. Haines (Cambridge: Harvard University Press, 1916), 173–74.

260. Oscar Wilde, *De Profundis* (New York: Philosophical Library, 1950), 122.

261. Joseph Fletcher, *Situation Ethics: The New Morality* (Philadelphia: Westminster, 1966), 63–64.

262. Martin Luther King Jr., *Strength to Love* (New York: Fortress Press, 1963), 31.

263. Loudon Wainwright, in "A Movie Made for Remembrance," *Life,* December 1985, 7.

264. Susan Thorne, as quoted in Elaine Cannon, ed., *Notable Quotables from Women to Women* (Salt Lake City: Bookcraft, 1992), 196.

265. Victor Gollancz, *Man and God,* 205.

266. Victor Gollancz, *Man and God,* 207–9.

267. Karen Boren, "Remembering the Holocaust: Portrait of a Heroine," *Deseret News,* 27 April 1989, C1–C2.

268. Kurt Vonnegut, as quoted in editors of *Reader's Digest,* eds., *Reader's Digest Quotable Quotes,* 203.

269. Sydney J. Harris, *Pieces of Eight* (Boston: Houghton Mifflin Co., 1982), 151–52.

270. Thurgood Marshall, as quoted in *Reader's Digest,* June 1993, 157.

271. Fritz Vincken, "Let There be Peace Tonight! Boyhood memories of Christmas 1944." Unpublished manuscript. Used by permission.

272. Mother Clara Hale, as quoted in editors of *Reader's Digest,* eds., *Reader's Digest Quotable Quotes,* 60.

273. George Kent, "Antidote to Eichmann," *Together,* February 1962, 23–24.

274. George Scullin, "The Sergeant Didn't Go Home," *True Confessions,* May 1953.

275. Frank Deford, as quoted in editors of *Reader's Digest,* eds., *Reader's Digest Quotable Quotes,* 179.

276. Robert Ardrey, *The Social Contract* (New York: Atheneum, 1970), 66.

277. "Soldiers march into the horns of a dilemma . . . ," *Deseret News,* 17 January 1997, A4.

278. Michael Ryan, "The Cow Who Saved Herself," *Parade* Magazine, 4 May 1997, 30.

279. Jim Woolf, "Skiers rescue injured dog in remote cliffs," *Salt Lake Tribune,* 23 March 1998, B1–3.

280. Associated Press, "Dog's owner lets rescuer keep pooch," *Deseret News,* 30 March 1998, B2.

281. E. J. Koestner, as quoted in editors of *Reader's Digest,* eds., *The Reader's Digest Treasury of Modern Quotations* (New York: Reader's Digest Press/Thomas Y. Crowell Co., 1975), 742.

282. Timothy Egan, "Chief's Speech of 1854 given new meaning (and Words)," The New York *Times,* 20 April 1992, A1.

283. Chief Seattle to Franklin Pierce.

284. Edward W. Bok, *The Americanization of Edward Bok* (New York: Charles Scribner's Sons, 1924), preface.

A c k n o w l e d g m e n t s

Grateful acknowledgment is hereby expressed to all those who have contributed to this book.

AFTON GRANT AFFLECK for excerpts from *Love Is the Gift.*

CONARI PRESS for excerpts from Daphne Rose Kingma quotations in *Random Acts of Kindness* by the editors of Conari Press. Copyright © 1993 by The Editors of Conari Press. Used by permission of Conari Press.

DOW JONES & COMPANY, INC., for excerpts from "Night Watch" by Roy Popkin. Reprinted by permission of *National Observer,* 21 December 1964. Copyright © 1964 Dow Jones & Company, Inc. All Rights Reserved Worldwide.

ELAINE JARVIK AND SUSAN WHITNEY for "Falling in Love." Reprinted with permission from *Deseret News,* 29 June 1997.

EMMA LOU THAYNE for "The Gift," *Exponent II,* Fall 1986.

FARRAR, STRAUS & GIROUX, INC., for excerpts from "Epilogue: Letter to a Young Doctor" from *Promises to Keep* by Agnes W. Dooley. Copyright © 1961 by the Estate of Thomas A. Dooley. Copyright renewed © 1989 by Mrs. Malcolm Dooley. Reprinted by permission of Farrar, Straus & Giroux, Inc.

FRIENDS UNITED PRESS for excerpts from "The Work of Christmas" from *The Mood of Christmas* by Howard Thurman. Used by permission of Friends United Press.

GUIDEPOSTS for excerpts from Mary Ann Bird, "A Genius for Loving." Reprinted with permission from *Guideposts Magazine,* January 1985. Copyright © 1985 by Guideposts Associates, Inc.,

Carmel, New York 10512. Also for excerpts from "The Two Magic Words" by James A. Farley. Reprinted with permission from *Guideposts Magazine,* January 1964. Copyright © 1964 by Guideposts Associates, Inc., Carmel, New York 10512. Also for excerpts from Arthur Gordon, "The Rewards of Caring." Reprinted with permission from *Guideposts Magazine,* October 1963. Copyright © 1984 by Guideposts Associates, Inc., Carmel, New York 10512.

JANE W. LUND for "Ministering Angels" from *Once More with Feeling* . . . Copyright © 1989 by Lundcraft Heritage Arts. And for "On the Value of Appreciation," "On Discovering the Joy of Diversity," and 'The Evidence of Hope" from *The Evidence of Hope.* Copyright © 1994 by Lundcraft Heritage Arts. And for "Patchwork" from *Patchwork: Pieces of My Heart.* Copyright © 1998 by Lundcraft Heritage Arts.

JERRY JOHNSTON for "All creation is a patchwork quilt of diversity," *Deseret News,* 30 May 1998. And for "Miracles can stem from one soul's caring acts," *Deseret News,* 21 February 1997.

NEW DIRECTIONS PUBLISHING CORPORATION for poem by William Carlos Williams from *Collected Poems 1939–1962,* volume II. Copyright © 1953 by William Carlos Williams. Reprinted by permission of New Directions Publishing Corp.

READER'S DIGEST for excerpts by Nina Fischer. Reprinted with permission from the June 1979 *Reader's Digest.* Copyright © 1979 by The Reader's Digest Assn., Inc. And for excerpts from "Lost and Found" by Mary McGovern. Reprinted with permission from the June 1979 *Reader's Digest.* Copyright © 1979 by The Reader's Digest Assn., Inc. And for excerpts by Max G. Bunyan. Reprinted with permission from the August 1972 *Reader's Digest.* Copyright © 1972 by The Reader's Digest Assn., Inc. And for excerpts from "Points to Ponder" by Cy Fe. Reprinted with permission from the June 1990 *Reader's Digest.* Copyright © 1990 by

The Reader's Digest Assn., Inc. And for excerpts by Bonnie Binschus. Reprinted with permission from the April 1987 *Reader's Digest.* Copyright © 1987 by The Reader's Digest Assn., Inc.

READER'S DIGEST for Ralph Kinney Bennett, "The Greatest Gift I Ever Received." Reprinted with permission from the July 1990 *Reader's Digest.* Copyright © 1990 by The Reader's Digest Association, Inc.

REGISTER-GUARD for excerpts from "Caring Cop Was a Saint" by Karen McCowan. Reprinted with permission from the *Register-Guard,* 18 April 1995. Also for excerpts from "Family Takes Gift to Hearth" by Karen McCowan. Reprinted with permission from the *Register-Guard,* 1 June 1997. Copyright © the Eugene, Oregon, *Register-Guard.*

RICHARD M. SIDDOWAY for "There is still room in the inn and plenty to spare this night," *Deseret News,* 21 December 1997.

U.S. NEWS & WORLD REPORT for excerpts from "A Ritual for Saying Goodbye" by William Broyles Jr.; and excerpts from "A Sacred Place on the Potomac" by Stewart Powell. Copyright © November 10, 1986, U.S. News & World Report.

The author has made every effort to accurately cite quotations. If there are any inaccuracies or inadvertent omissions of credit, they will be gladly be corrected in future editions.

I n d e x

To my readers:

As the first of three books, *The Heart of Goodness* explores man's relationship to his fellowman. The second book in the trilogy will focus on man's development of character—that is, his relationship to himself—and the third book will explore man's relationship to God and the universe.

If you would be interested in contributing touching stories or heart-felt quotations relative to any of the three preceding subjects, I would be very appreciative. If possible, please include complete citation, including publication source (if any), date, and page number. Contributions may be sent to the following address:

Jo Ann Larsen, D.S.W.
Prowswood Plaza, Suite 250
4885 South 900 East
Salt Lake City, Utah 84117

To all of my readers, warm regards . . .

Jo Ann Larsen